WRESTLING WITH THE ANCIENTS

Wrestling

with the

Ancients

Modern Greek Identity
and the Olympics

Alexander Kitroeff

GREEKWORKS.COM · NEW YORK

2004

© 2004 Alexander Kitroeff

greekworks.com
info@greekworks.com
337 West 36 Street
New York, NY 10018–6401

Library of Congress Cataloging-in-Publication Data

Library of Congress Control Number: 2003116061.
  Kitroeff, Alexander.
  Wrestling with the Ancients: Modern Greek Identity and the Olympics.
    p. cm.
  Includes index / bibliographical references.
  1. Greece. 2. Olympics. 3. Sports. 4. Politics. 5. Culture.
  I. Title.
  ISBN 0–9747660–0–3 (cloth)

PRINTED IN THE UNITED STATES OF AMERICA
BY
ATHENS PRINTING COMPANY
337 West 36th Street
New York, NY 10018-6401

For Natalía

ACKNOWLEDGMENTS

THIS BOOK BENEFITED GREATLY from the help of many people in many places. Haverford College offered me a hospitable and supportive academic environment in which I could pursue this project. Greg Kannerstein, who co-teaches a course on sports and society with me, and all the students who took that course over the years, contributed greatly to my understanding of the connections between sport, society, and national identity. Haverford College's faculty-research and -support funds generously underwrote my travel to Greece for research; over three summers, it also provided me with energetic student assistants Stephen Jankiewicz, Mike Gordon, and Vasilikē Ariston (who also traveled to Athens, where she collected valuable material). Haverford's Magill Library staff—reference librarians James Gulick and Margaret Schaus, as well as interlibrary loans specialist Rob Haley—provided me with excellent support.

The Hellenic Olympic Committee generously allowed me access to its impressively preserved archives and collection of photographs in its building just across from the Olympic Stadium in Athens. In this connection, I am especially grateful to Mr. Nikos Filaretos, for enabling me to observe the opening session at the International Olympic Academy in ancient Olympia in the summer of 2000. This was an important experience in learning about the contemporary Olympic movement, and it gave me access to the academy's library. The academy's dean, Kōstas Geōrgiadēs, a scholar of Olympic history, was also very helpful during my visit, as was the academy's librarian, Themis Lainēs. In Athens, historian Christina Koulouri kindly shared with me her rich knowledge, both of the history of Greek sport and of the HOC archives, which were catalogued under her guidance. At the archive itself, Katerina Dede was extremely helpful in helping me obtain most of the photographs that appear in this book. A special thank-you is due to Vasilikē Tzachrēsta, who helped me navigate through the documents and was an invaluable resource throughout this project.

My efforts at synthesizing my research into a book-length manuscript benefited from the careful editorial work of Kaia R. Motter. The next step, transforming the manuscript into a book on relatively short notice, is due to the enthusiastic support of *greekworks*'s Peter Pappas and Stelios Vasilakis, who embraced this project in a spirit of intellectual partnership. Stelios's vision made this book a reality, while Peter's diligent editorial review coupled with his insightful recommendations helped sharpen its analytical focus immeasurably. Melanie Wallace also assisted in the editorial work and, just as important, came up with the idea for the book's title. My wife, Anita Isaacs, supported this project from its inception while writing her own book. Finally, our daughter Natalía's athletic interests have been an unfailing reminder of the daily social significance of sport.

—Alexander Kitroeff
Haverford, Pennsylvania
November 2003

Contents

Foreword   1

CHAPTER 1
Greece's Olympics   5

CHAPTER 2
The 1896 Olympic Games in Athens   25

CHAPTER 3
The Athens Interim Olympics of 1906   53

CHAPTER 4
Rediscovering the Classical Legacy   77

CHAPTER 5
Greece and the Berlin Olympiad   101

CHAPTER 6
Olympia and the Cold War   121

CHAPTER 7
Greece as the Permanent Olympic Venue?   141

CHAPTER 8
Atlanta 1996 and How Greece Lost the Centenary Games   161

CHAPTER 9
Winning and Almost Losing the 2004 Athens Olympiad   185

CHAPTER 10
Countdown to Athens 2004   209

Afterword   235

Appendixes   241

Sources Cited   257

Index   267

FOREWORD

I WAS FIRST MADE AWARE OF Greece's connection to the Olympic Games while in middle school in Athens. My teacher had announced to her class that, as it was April 6, this was "Olympic Games Day." She then proceeded to instruct us on the ancient and modern Olympics. She explained how the games had originated in 776 BCE in ancient Greece and had been revived in the nineteenth century. She mentioned the name of the founder of the modern games, Baron Pierre de Coubertin, in reverent tones, emphasizing that he was a great philhellene. We listened proudly as we learned of yet another major contribution by our ancestors to world civilization, and we were awed to learn that modern Greece held pride of place in the modern Olympic movement. It was not just that the first contemporary games had taken place in Athens, but that the protocol developed for the subsequent games stipulated that the Greek flag and Greek team lead the parade of nations that opened each Olympiad.

My teacher's comments acquired a new context for me many years later when I was researching the history of Greece's relationship to the Olympic Games. I discovered that in 1966, in a tactical move designed to rally public opinion behind its efforts to strengthen Greece's role in the Olympic movement, the Greek government had proclaimed April 6 as "Olympic Games Day." This was the date on which the first modern Olympics had opened in Athens in 1896—although because Greece observed the Julian calendar at the time, the date actually corresponded to March 25, which had been chosen by the organizers because it was Greece's Independence Day. An athletic meet was held in the Panathenaic Stadium in Athens on April 6, 1966, and, as part of the events marking the occasion, teachers throughout the country had talked about the Olympics to their classes earlier that day.

* * *

This is a book about how Greece experienced its dual identity, as the heir to classical traditions and as a modernized, European state, through its role in the international Olympic movement. The idea that the modern Greeks are directly descended from the ancient Greeks is one of the pillars of modern Greek identity. It is a concept that was first proposed by Enlightenment-era thinkers such as Adamantios Koraēs, who created the visionary context for imagining a modern, independent Greek state liberated from the Ottoman empire. Nineteenth-century historian Kōnstantinos Paparrēgopoulos was the first to suggest that Greek identity unfolded in a continuum, from the classical era through Byzantium and on to the present. Throughout the nineteenth century and beyond, the definition and redefinition of Greek identity relied heavily on establishing continuity with the past. The choice of Athens as the capital of the modern Greek state, the proliferation of neoclassical architecture in the city, and a heavy bias on classics and ancient history in education were all examples of that self-formative process.

Nineteenth-century Greece also wished to be considered part of Europe, however. Gaining acceptance by the advanced European states—the model for the type of state that Greek leaders sought to build—was a permanent concern of the Greeks (one that arguably remains to this day, more than two decades after Greece's full accession in 1981 to the European Economic Community, the predecessor of the European Union). Indeed, the theory of Greek continuity was as much about Greek self-definition as it was about the ways Greeks sought recognition and validation in the eyes of the "more advanced" Europeans. The Enlightenment's rediscovery and veneration of modern Greece had a profound effect on Koraēs and the other architects of Greek identity in the eighteenth century. Clearly, by suggesting continuity between ancient Greece and the modern Greeks, the early advocates of Greek nationalism sought to legitimize and validate Greek claims to nationhood and gain acceptance as a European state. This idea of continuity served the Greeks well in the 1820s, when important figures of European romanticism saw the Greek struggle for independence as the yearning for liberation of the descendants of the ancient Greeks. A strong current of philhellenism in Europe and North America bolstered the cause of Greek independence and the subsequent emergence of modern Greece.

The revival of the Olympic Games by Baron de Coubertin in the 1890s, and the emergence of an Olympic movement that traced its origins to the ancient games, offered Greece a domain in which to gain international recognition. It could do so not only by virtue of its status as modern heir to its ancient culture but because it was also the heir to, and custodian of, the *physical space* in which ancient Greek civilization had achieved its great distinction. Greece was an insignificant factor on the world scene, but—the thinking among many Greeks went—if it combined its heritage with the ability to respond to the challenges of modernity that faced the Olympic movement, it could conceivably become a significant element of this international sporting institution. This was easier said than done, however, as this book hopes to show. The invented tradition of the continuity with antiquity that Greece and the Olympic movement shared was not enough to guarantee Greece's relevance to the Olympics, especially when the movement began to struggle to reconcile its sense of heritage with the need to confront the problems spawned by politics, economics, and technology.

It is the argument of this book that Greece managed to maintain its privileged place in the international Olympic movement because it regarded its role both as an affirmation of its ancient heritage and as a means through which to gain international recognition. This dual role enabled Greece to modify its tactics (not always successfully) according to the fluctuations in the value of ancient tradition in the eyes of the Olympic movement's leaders, in an attempt to present itself both as the heir to classical Greece but also as a nation that could consistently respond to the needs imposed on the Olympics by modernity and development.

* * *

This short monograph cannot satisfactorily recount the rich and complex tale of Greece's role in the international Olympic movement. Its purpose, in any case, is different: to provide an overview of this story, primarily by tracing its unfolding in a narrative and chronological form. Yet I have also tried to identify and discuss the key factors that shaped the narrative: Greece's ongoing dialogue with its classical past, the country's relationship to the international community, and the decisive evolution of its sporting culture and interaction with the international Olympic movement. I argue, simply, that Greece's relationship to the Olympic movement meant that the modernizing impulse eventually had to overshadow Greece's umbilical connection to its ancient past, but that the invented tradition of continuity was preserved nevertheless precisely because it was—and remains—as much a part of the Olympic movement's identity as of the identity of modern Greeks.

This book itself can be considered a product of the importance that Greece attaches to the Olympic Games. The backbone of the study consists of material collected and classified recently, a project undertaken by the Hellenic Olympic Committee in the context of launching its bid for the 1996 and 2004 Olympic Games. The primary sources used are located in the committee's archives, currently being processed after years of neglect, which are housed in its newly built headquarters across from the Olympic Stadium in Athens. Unfortunately, the bulk of the material on the first Olympics has not survived, while the data available do not reach beyond the early 1970s. The bulk of the secondary material, books, and pamphlets has been made available recently to researchers at the newly constructed library of the International Olympic Academy, a mere stone's throw away from the site of the quadrennial games in ancient Olympia.

The range of materials absorbed in this study includes a distillation of numerous works by Greek authors on Greek sports history and the Greek Olympic movement, along with the considerable body of books and monographs produced by historians and other scholars, based mainly in Great Britain and the United States, who are engaged in the study of modern sport. There are several major studies on the revival of the modern Olympics in 1896 that account, *inter alia*, for Greece's role. While studies on the subsequent evolution of the games in the twentieth century do not examine Greece's place, they have provided a very valuable framework that illustrates the devastating effects of ideology, Cold War politics, and commercialization on the Olympics. These works made my task of understanding and analyzing Greece's role much easier. The core material upon which this study relies, however, is made up of unpublished and published Greek sources synthesized so as to provide an introduction to Greece's relationship to its ancient past and European future as expressed through its intimate ties to the modern Olympics.

CHAPTER 1

GREECE'S OLYMPICS

G REECE'S RELATIONSHIP TO SPORT in the nineteenth century
reflected the overarching importance of the ancient past in the formation of the modern nation-state. A decade-long uprising that began in
1821 led to the formation of an independent Greece carved out of the multiethnic Ottoman empire. The following decades witnessed the dual process of
nation- and state-building in which the construction of national identity was
as important as the creation of a modern state infrastructure. The politics of
identity formation reflected the need for a clean break from the Ottoman
past and a sense of thorough cultural independence that placed Greece and
its people squarely within so-called civilized Europe. The Ottomans had
ruled over the Greek lands for several centuries, during which religion was
the primary form of identification. The creation of a modern Greek identity,
whose aim was to turn Greeks from Christian subjects of the Ottomans into
members of a free nation, relied on an awareness of a language and history
that went back to ancient Greece. For the modern Greeks, their ancient heritage was the cornerstone of self-definition: it was the font of their identity,
the source of their cultural legitimacy.[1]

The enormous tasks of nation-building served to accentuate the importance of identity formation, as well as this formation's reliance on a sense of
continuity with a glorious classical heritage. Greece emerged from its decade-
long struggle against the Ottomans as a fragile entity with little more than
formal political independence. The war had ravaged the country and
depleted its resources and finances. The state's territory was only a third of its
present size, its frontiers disputed, and its provinces plagued by brigands.
Nation-building would be a long and painful process, dependent on the great

---

[1]For English-language summaries of Greek history in the nineteenth and twentieth cen-
turies, including the evolution of Greek identity, see Richard Clogg, *A Concise History of
Greece*, Cambridge University Press, Cambridge, 1992, and Thomas W. Gallant, *Modern
Greece*, Arnold/Oxford University Press, New York, 2001.

powers and on the financial assistance of wealthy Greeks living in the Ottoman lands or in the diaspora. The decision by the great powers to designate the young Bavarian prince Otto as King Othōn of Greece, and Othōn's subsequent arrival, along with an entourage of Bavarian advisors, in the newly independent country in 1833, signaled the beginning of a socially wrenching struggle to establish a centralized state and gain acceptance in the eyes of Europe.

Inevitably, the country's political and intellectual elite responded to the harsh realities of post-independence Greece by producing mostly impractical but inspiring calls for a recovery of the brilliant ancient past, not only as a sense of identity but also as a model for the present. The choice of Athens as the new nation's capital was typical in that sense. The Peloponnesian town of Nauplion had served as the capital at the moment of liberation from Ottoman rule, but Athens—which at the time was not much more than a large village clustered around the Acropolis and other ancient ruins—obviously had much more symbolic potential. The other defining example of antiquity's sway over nation- and state-building was the insistence on creating a form of the Greek language, *kathareuousa*, which was artificially modified so as to evoke the language of Attic Greek; among other things, this rare example of language creation reinforced the study of ancient Greek in school and at the University of Athens. *Kathareuousa*'s existence would cause conflicts among linguists, writers, and educators well into the twentieth century. (In fact, the matter wasn't definitively settled until *kathareuousa* was finally abolished in official governmental and educational use in the mid-Seventies, following the fall of the military dictatorship.)

The revival of the Greek Olympic Games endowed the nascent sports culture of modern Greece with a strong sense of attachment to the ancient past. This would prove to be a false start, however, both in terms of the Olympic revival and as far as Greek sport was concerned. The Greek Olympics, known as the Zappas Olympics, were held four times between 1859 and 1889. Named after Euangelēs Zappas (1800–1865), a wealthy diaspora Greek who had funded them, they were an ersatz affair, modeled on assumptions of how sports were played in antiquity, and never approached the magnitude of the games that Coubertin would revive and launch in the 1890s. The story of these Greek games shows how the modern Greeks considered the ancient Olympics to be part of their heritage, but also how they lacked any developed sporting culture and understanding of competitive sport. The sense of continuity with antiquity overshadowed any sense of sporting culture or organizational knowledge of athletic competition. Although the Greeks considered the Olympics their heritage, they were in no position to translate that heritage into the kind of viable international competition that Coubertin created in the 1890s.

The underdeveloped nature of sport in Greece prior to 1890 was due to the country's general underdevelopment, as well as to the particular policies of its leaders. Unlike the situation in Greece, where economic development began slowly only during the last third of the nineteenth century, the more rapid pace of modernization in Europe had created more time for leisure; within that context, forms of play gradually became more structured and led to the emergence of organized sport. Schools and universities promoted physical exercise as a form of discipline and socialization, with the British favoring competitive forms of sport and the central Europeans preferring gymnastics. Exercise in educational institutions was associated in many countries with training young men for military service after graduation. By the late nineteenth century, organized sport, played by amateur or professional athletes, acquired wide popularity, signaling the emergence of spectator sports.

With the exception of the gradual introduction of physical exercise in schools, none of these developments were reflected in Greece to any great degree until the very end of the nineteenth century. King Othōn's Bavarian administrators, who effectively ruled until the constitution of 1844, and the Greek political elite that ruled under the king afterward, showed little interest in developing sports. Othōn's ouster in the early 1860s and the arrival of a Danish prince who became King George I of the Hellenes did not bring any immediate results, although the country edged more explicitly toward European models of development. The central European impulse, to train young men as soldiers through physical exercise, certainly seemed less urgent to the Greeks, whose conscript army obtained more direct experience through a series of border clashes with the Ottomans throughout the 1850s. King George and his son, Crown Prince Constantine, would eventually become enthusiastic supporters of the Olympic Games conceived by Coubertin, but, until that occurred in the 1890s, they did little to promote a domestic sporting culture.

By the latter part of the nineteenth century, one could discern three strands of thought regarding sport and physical exercise. One reflected the wish to emulate the practices of the ancient Greeks, who considered them very important; the second viewed physical exercise as a prerequisite for military training; and the third, also modeled on European practice, saw sport and physical exercise as leisurely pursuits that were healthy and socially fulfilling. Thus, after 1870, Greece witnessed the gradual emergence of athletic clubs, modeled on European ones, formed by middle-class Greeks as part of a broader trend that saw the mushrooming of civic associations. Nonetheless, sport would not really "take off" in Greece until the first Olympic Games in Athens in 1896.[2]

There is a surprisingly large body of literature on the Zappas Olympics that not only examines them in considerable detail but also takes sides in a debate concerning the question of who can rightly claim credit for reviving the modern Olympics. At issue is the conventional view that we owe the revival of the games to Coubertin—a view cultivated by the baron himself and echoed by the International Olympic Committee, the body he established in 1894 to oversee them. Next to a range of studies by Iōannēs Chrysafēs and several other Greek authors, an American-based scholar, David C. Young, has produced a remarkably well-researched study that points to the Zappas Olympics and also to the Olympics organized by William Penny Brookes in the village of Much Wenlock in Shropshire, England, and suggests that these were important and influential antecedents that Coubertin neglected to acknowledge fully.[3]

Nevertheless, while the Zappas Olympics were a genuine revival of the Olympic Games that preceded Coubertin's initiatives, nineteenth-century Greece was ill-equipped to launch the type of international revival that Coubertin envisioned. The success and broad appeal of the baron's vision were

[2]Christina Koulouri, *Athlētismos kai opseis tēs astikēs koinōnikotētas. Gymnastika kai athlētika sōmateia 1870–1922* [*Sports and Aspects of Bourgeois Socialization: Gymnastic and Athletic Clubs, 1870–1922*], IAEN, Athens, 1997; Geōrgios Kokkinos and Elenē Fournarakē, " . . . peri tēs sōmatikēs anagennēseōs tou ethnous ēmōn" [". . . on the physical regeneration of our nation"], *To Vēma*, March 17, 1996.

[3]The major English-language study is David C. Young, *The Modern Olympics: A Struggle for Revival*, The Johns Hopkins University Press, Baltimore, 1996; there are several Greek studies that discuss the Zappas Olympics, including Iōannēs E. Chrysafēs, *Oi synchronoi diethneis Olympiakoi Agōnes*, Athens, 1930; Paraskeuas Samaras, *Ē anaviōsē tōn Olympiakōn Agōnōn stēn Ellada 1797–1859* [*The Revival of the Olympic Games in Greece, 1797–1859*], Vogiatzēs, Athens, 1992; Thōmas V. Giannakēs, *Zappeies kai synchrones Olympiades* [*Zappeian and Modern Olympiads*], Athens, 1993; Eleutherios Skiadas, *100 chronia neoterē ellēnikē istoria*, Ta Nea, Athens, 1996. To these studies, one should add a doctoral dissertation by Kōstas Geōrgiadēs, currently being prepared for publication.

due to his effective linking of sports competition to the ancient past, investing athletics with the heritage of ancient Greece. Coubertin's Olympics were conceived as a celebration of sport colored by ancient traditions. In contrast, the Zappas Olympics were a celebration of ancient traditions colored by sport.

REVIVING THE ANCIENT PAST, RESTORING THE OLYMPICS

The notion of reviving the ancient Olympics came somewhat naturally to Panagiōtēs Soutsos (1806–1868), a poet, writer, and intellectual who would call upon Greece's leaders to realize his idea several times during his career. Soutsos stressed the ancient Olympics as part of a broader strategic invocation of ancient Greece by modern Greeks as they contemplated creating their new nation. In Soutsos's long, two-part poem, "Dialogue of the Dead and the Ruins of Ancient Sparta," published in 1833, Plato confronts the modern Greeks and, ruing their present condition, asks, "Where are your Olympic Games?" In "The Ruins of Ancient Sparta," which salutes the arrival of Prince Otto, the great Spartan warrior Leōnidas offers advice to the young monarch. He tells him to work toward bringing back the ancient glories: "[L]et the only contests that you have be those national games, the Olympics, to which the olive branch once summoned the sons of Greece in ancient times."[4]

Soutsos turned to a more pragmatic treatment of the Olympic past when he joined the ministry of the interior in 1834 and drafted a proposal the following year to introduce "modern Greek sports games that would imitate the older [ancient] ones." He envisioned the games taking place every four years, always in a different location, from the maritime island of Ydra to the town of Nauplion, from Athens to Corinth. Soutsos also proposed that the games always begin on March 25 in order to commemorate the anniversary of the outbreak of the revolution in 1821. Interior Minister Iōannēs Kōlettēs supported this proposal. That was not the case with Ignaz von Rudhard, a member of Othōn's Bavarian entourage who was serving as prime minister (because the king was still in his minority) and had the final decision on the matter. The only thing the Bavarian administrator thought useful was the commemoration of the revolution's anniversary.[5] Undeterred by Rudhard's rejection, Soutsos reiterated his proposal in the dedication to King Othōn of

---

[4]Young, *The Modern Olympics . . .* , pp. 2–4.
[5]Giannēs Lefas, *Panagiōtēs Soutsos*, Athens, 1991, pp. 73–74.

a lyric drama on the life of 1821 revolutionary Geōrgios Karaïskakēs, which was published in 1842.

Soutsos's vision of reviving the Olympics was just one of many contemporary proposals for modern Greece to restore the glory of its ancient ancestors. Soutsos's ideas belonged to an intellectual tradition that stressed the revival of antiquity, not the promotion of sport in the newly independent nation. Soutsos was a major figure of Greece's romantic school of literature. The romantic intellectuals who shaped the literary scene in the post-independence era called upon modern Greece to emulate the glories of its ancient forebears. Before independence, their intellectual predecessors, the Enlightenment-era thinkers, had concentrated on establishing the cultural ties between ancient and modern Greeks that would mobilize their compatriots in the struggle for nationhood.[6]

In another Olympics-related example of the prevalent sense of continuity between antiquity and modernity, the municipality of Letrinoi, located next to the as-yet-unexplored site of ancient Olympia, proposed its own version of a revival of the Olympic Games. Marking the anniversary of the Greek revolution of 1821, the municipality announced its intention in 1838 to recreate the Olympic Games every four years and to hold them in the nearby town of Pyrgos. The municipality established a committee, which it entrusted with planning and supervising the games. Nothing ever came of this initiative, although P. Emmanouēl Giannopoulos, one of the committee members, would become vice-president of the Zappas Olympics of 1875.[7]

Within the broader movement to revive the ancient past, Greeks understood the term, "Olympic Games," not as exclusively athletic competitions but as "supreme contests" in the way defined by the ancients. The events held in ancient Olympia included artistic and cultural competitions in addition to athletic ones, as did the Pythian Games in Delphi and the Nemean Games in Nemea. Significantly, although King Othōn did not use the term, "Olympic," his first piece of legislation involving athletic contests saw them as part of a larger event that would include other activities. The king ratified a law establishing a committee to work toward encouraging national industry in 1839. One of its clauses called for holding exhibitions of industrial affairs that

---

[6]The standard work on this subject is Kōnstantinos Th. Dēmaras, *Ellēnikos Romantismos* [*Greek Romanticism*], Ermēs, Athens, 1982; for an English-language summary, see Roderick Beaton, "Romanticism in Greece," in Roy Porter and Mikulas Teich, editors, *Romanticism in National Context*, Cambridge University Press, Cambridge, 1988, pp. 92–108.

[7]Chrysafēs, *Oi synchronoi diethneis Olympiakoi . . .* , p. 17.

would also provide "public games, including horse racing, wrestling, running, discus, the javelin throw, national dances, and other sports."[8] When nothing came of this, Soutsos, writing in 1851, again called for the revival of the games, reversing the order of the original plan for the exhibitions. Since Greece could not match countries such as England in organizing industrial exhibitions, he said, it could reestablish the Olympic Games as well as the Panathenaic Games, which were held in Athens in antiquity and also included athletic contests. At first, nothing came of this proposal either, but things soon changed.

THE ZAPPAS DONATION: CHOOSING BETWEEN HERITAGE AND MODERNIZATION

Soutsos's proposals to revive the Olympics caught the imagination of Euangelēs Zappas, who offered King Othōn a donation made up of shares in his shipping company and cash. An official announcement by the palace, published in the press,[9] estimated the gift's value at 600,000 drachmas.[10] The sum was designed to underwrite the reestablishment of the "Olympian" games in Athens. Zappas, born in the village of Lambovo (in present-day Albania), made a fortune in the Romanian principalities, where he became one of the largest landowners. His generous contribution to his (chosen) homeland was part of a much larger pattern of donations to Greece by merchants who made their fortunes in commercial centers throughout the Ottoman empire, the Mediterranean basin, or the Black Sea. Nonetheless, it is the only contribution among many that was specifically earmarked for athletic activities.

When Zappas made his donation, Greece was juggling the demands of forging its identity with the requirements of establishing a modern state. The

---

[8]Royal decree of January 25/ February 6, 1837, FEK 87/1836.

[9]Chrysafēs, *Oi synchronoi diethneis Olympiakoi . . .* , p. 24–25.

[10]Currency equivalencies are elusive for this period, but, as a rule of thumb, we can assume that one drachma was the equivalent of a French franc, with five francs to the US dollar and twenty-five to one English pound. Calculating drachma value in the nineteenth century is extraordinarily difficult because of fluctuating exchange rates that differed according to whether the sum consisted of gold or *trapezogrammatia* (notes issued by banks). Prior to 1882, for example, the gold drachma was valued at roughly twelve percent less than the gold franc, but the exchange rate was different for *trapezogrammatia*. Calculating Zappas's donation is even more complicated; it is unclear if the value of the shares remained roughly the same, while the cash donation's fluctuation in value is also difficult to estimate. (My thanks to Christos Hadziiosif for his expertise on this issue.)

late 1850s were a time of economic crisis, and many in government saw modernization as a much more urgent task compared to what had by then
become the almost routine invocation of ancient splendors. Greece had
backed Russia in the Crimean War, which ended with a victory for Britain
and France. As a result, British and French troops temporarily occupied
Athens and blockaded the country's major ports, which led to economic dis-
tress. There was a backlash against the pro-Russian politicians, and a more
pro-Western and pro-modernizing group of politicians gained influence.
Athletics were barely present in the educational curricula or in the army's
training, and sporting activities were virtually unknown. Thus, for many
government officials, the idea of reviving the Olympics had more to do with
heritage than with athletic development, but the question remained: Should
valuable resources go toward such a project at a time when modernization
acquired even more urgency?

Alexandros Rizos Rangavēs (1809–1892), the newly appointed minister
for foreign affairs to whom the king had passed on Zappas's proposal, supported modernization. As opposed to many of his contemporaries, however,
he did not see much value in sport. This was typical of the mindset of the
Greek elite, even during the push for Europeanization and modernization
that got underway in the late 1870s. In terms of education, the government
managed to promote both gymnastics and military training in the schools in
the 1880s, but that was it: no one seriously believed that leisure time should
be taken up by any form of sport, which was seen as deflecting from intellectual development. The Greek bourgeoisie embraced arts and culture but
remained disinterested in athletics. The reasons for this stance are complex
and still not fully understood. Many commentators have mentioned the tendency by many intellectuals to pursue knowledge for knowledge's sake, an
effete and snobbish phenomenon described in Greece as *logiotatismos*,
defined by a contemporary Greek dictionary as "the tendency to use archaizing language forms in a *kathareuousa* discourse."[11] Future researchers will
surely address the social basis of the denigration of sport; in the event, the
absence of a landowning elite prevented the development of such "traditional" activities as horse racing or hunting, while the lack of a domestic commercial bourgeoisie ensured that the spirit of competition was deficient
among the social elite.

[11]See entry for "logiotatismos," *Ellēniko Lexiko*, Ekdoseis Armonia, Athens, 1991, fifth edition, p. 427.

Rangavēs tried to undermine Soutsos's proposal by suggesting that, instead of underwriting games, Zappas's funds go toward organizing industrial exhibitions with prizes.[12] In his memoirs, Rangavēs explains quite candidly that he wrote to Zappas to explain that times had changed since antiquity, and that modern nations gained distinction by demonstrating their abilities not in athletics but in industry. Zappas agreed, and Rangavēs began plans for building a hall to be named the Zappeion, which would be located in the center of Athens. Zappas's agreement is fairly typical of the trust that diaspora benefactors showed toward the Greek state. Ultimately, the two men reached a compromise. Zappas augmented his financial contribution, and the program of the first Zappas Olympics devoted three Sundays in October 1859 to the selection of the best producers in the fields of industry, agriculture, and animal husbandry, while the fourth Sunday was given over to athletic games. The foundation stone for the Zappeion was laid in 1874 and the building, designed by architect Theofil Hansen (1813–1891), was completed in 1888. Rangavēs provided a detailed account of his activities in a newspaper article that year in which he spoke openly of his efforts to redirect Zappas's vision.[13] (To this day, by the way, the Zappeion remains Greece's most famous exhibition and reception hall, although it has been used more for EU summits during the last couple of decades than for exhibits of animal husbandry.)

A protest against Rangavēs's initiative by Mēnas Mēnōidēs (1790–1860), a Greek philologist based in Paris, serves to highlight the handful among the Greek elite in the mid-nineteenth century who valued sport. While the modernizers devalued athletics, the students of Greek antiquity naturally supported its development. Mēnōidēs was about to publish an edited version of a classical Greek treatise on physical exercise by Philostratus (170–249 CE). Minōidēs was hardly a sports fan, but having discovered this text in the library of a monastery on Mount Athos, he treated it with reverence as a record of Greece's classical past. At the conclusion of his study, Mēnōidēs added a commentary of his own on the subject of the revival of the Olympics in Greece. He praised Zappas's conception, but then proceeded to criticize the 1858 decree's inclusion of trade competitions, saying that he was sure Zappas had made his contribution in order to revive "the real Olympic Games, in order to

[12]Chrysafēs, *Oi synchronoi diethneis Olympiakoi . . .* , p. 24.

[13]Alexandros Rangavēs, *Apomnēmoneumata* [*Memoirs*], Volume 2, Athens, 1894, pp. 378–379; Chrysafēs, *Oi sygchronoi diethneis Olympiakoi . . .* , pp. 46–50.

crown athletes, runners, wrestlers, etc." Mēnōidēs went on to propose that the Zappas Olympics become exclusively athletic and that they be held in the Panathenaic Stadium after its renovation. To be sure, Mēnōidēs was a passionate classicist who became an advocate of sport by default, an instance that reflects the relationship to sport of most of the Greek elite.[14]

As mentioned, the first Zappas Olympics took place in the fall of 1859 and included the trade exhibition and an athletic component. The sports contests, bearing strong signs of the legacy of ancient Greece, were held on a very cold Sunday, November 15/27 (all dates separated by a virgule indicate Julian reckoning for the first date, and Gregorian for the second), 1859, in the presence of the royal family and members of the government. The schedule included several events, most of which were held in antiquity, with two or three innovations added by the organizers. There were three races: 200, 400, and 1,400 meters. There were also three kinds of jumps, including a long jump and a jump over a trench. There were two types of discus throw, one for distance and one for height, and two types of javelin throw, one for distance and the other for accuracy, with the target being an ox-head. With a little improvisation, the organizers added pole-climbing and an event that required competitors to balance on an inflated, greased sack.

The athletes wore sandals and short tunics, in the first of what would prove to be several unfortunate sartorial attempts to link modern athletes with their ancient counterparts.[15] The titles of the judges and officials (*alytarchai, ellanodikai*) were those used in antiquity. The prizes for the winners consisted of an olive branch and one hundred drachmas (a sum that was well over a month's pay for most laborers or employees at the time); athletes coming in second received an olive branch and fifty drachmas, and those in third place got an olive branch and commendation. The organizers also indicated that the winners would receive preferential treatment in filling the positions of trainers for the next Olympics. Interestingly, the industrial and agricultural contests held earlier during the month had no prize money: the winners simply received an olive wreath, the prize in the ancient Olympics.

In the aftermath of the games, their supporters discovered that reviving an ancient tradition did not always meet with universal approval. The games were marred by very poor organization, which was reported extensively in the Athenian press and which several writers saw as an affront not only to the

---

[14]Chrysafēs, *Oi synchronoi diethneis Olympiakoi . . .* , pp. 27–29.
[15]Young, *The Modern Olympics . . .* , pp. 13–23.

development of sport in Greece but also to the country's duty to its ancient past. At the end of a long diatribe on the glaring deficiencies of the 1859 Olympics, the writer in the Athens daily *Aiōn* was able to muster only a few words of praise. Along with the other newspapers reporting on the event, the *Aiōn* ridiculed the poor organization, the comic efforts of some competitors, and the lack of decorum that surrounded the games. Above all, the journalists registered horror at the way their fellow Athenians had turned an ancient institution into a caricature of itself. Nonetheless, concluded the report in the *Aiōn*, "one cannot deny the positive things about these games" because of their contribution to cultivating self-control, healthy bodies, good upbringing, and a measured way of living. Because of the need for these virtues, the newspaper counseled the games' organizers to ensure that they were performed properly and "the memory of our ancestors [was] not ridiculed."[16]

THE SECOND ZAPPAS OLYMPIAD, 1870

The second Zappas Olympics, unlike the first, were successful from an organizational perspective, but, like the previous games, bore the strong influence of classical Greek sporting practices. Yet this time, because the games were well-organized and well-attended, the ancient elements lent the event a sense of grandeur in the eyes of observers. The second series of games took place later than originally scheduled because Greece had experienced dynastic and constitutional changes in 1863 (the aforementioned King George I succeeding Othōn), but the institution survived because Zappas, who had died in 1865, left his fortune to be used to organize a quadrennial Olympiad. His cousin, Kōnstantinos Zappas (1812–1892), took over his affairs and played an important role in ensuring that Euangelēs's wishes were respected.

Upon receiving word of Zappas's bequest, the Greek government took steps to ensure that his vision was realized, but with the focus on organizing the actual games rather than on taking the opportunity to promote physical exercise or sport. The bequest was a large one, and, in this new political era, the Greek state was beginning to cultivate its diaspora in the hope that its donations and investments could help the homeland's economic development. The government instructed the Olympic committee to work toward constructing the Olympic building and excavating and renovating the Panathenaic Stadium. Because of Rangavēs's lack of enthusiasm, and because

[16]Chrysafēs, *Oi synchronoi diethneis Olympiakoi . . .*, pp. 24–50.

Zappas's original contribution was considered insufficient for all the work involved, neither project had progressed. The government also announced that the second Olympics would take place on the first three Sundays in October 1870 and would include athletic games. The Olympic committee took these games seriously and required the small number of persons involved in the competitions to train for three months under the supervision of professional trainers who themselves held trials just before the games. The committee also saw to it that work was done on the stadium, including clearing and flattening the surface of the field and landscaping the banked slopes so as to accommodate a dais for dignitaries and an area for spectators.

The athletic competition in 1870 was much broader and varied than the 1859 games, and it included several contests that reflected either the organizers' wish to mirror antiquity or their penchant for innovation. These included a race along the length of the stadium, the triple jump and long jump, the discus throw, the javelin throw using a target, the pole vault (over a trench), wrestling, pole-climbing, rope-climbing, and tug-of-war. Aside from athletic contests and a horse-and-chariot race, the second Olympics were also supposed to have included shooting, as well as swimming and boat-racing in the Bay of Faléron just south of Athens. The swimming competitions included a race along a straight line, a circular race around buoys, an underwater race, diving, and balancing on a greased wooden pole. Participants in the diving contest had to dive nine meters to retrieve a five-drachma coin from the seabed. The boating competitions included two rowing and two sailing races, and an event in which the crews of two boats tried to knock their opponents off each other's boats and into the sea. However, as the games, initially scheduled for October, had to be postponed to mid-November (probably because work at the stadium had lagged behind), only the athletic contests took place, as the weather was not conducive to the events in the bay. The shooting events were also canceled.

The second Zappas Olympics took place on November 15/27 in the presence of the royal family and a very large crowd of spectators estimated at 25,000–30,000. The athletic and the horse-racing events went smoothly, and the performances impressed everyone in attendance. King George sent a letter of congratulations to the committee that same day and bestowed a medal on its president. The very same newspapers that had criticized the 1859 games heaped praise on these games. "Never before has Athens witnessed such a festive, pleasant, and entertaining spectacle, and this situation contributed to making this national celebration more glorious," wrote the *Alētheia*. The *Aiōn* agreed, calling the occasion marvelous and unique, an "unbelievable success."[17]

The ancient Greek themes had been more pronounced in the second Olympics than in 1859. The official names of most events were in ancient Greek, much to the confusion of trainers and athletes, who were less educated than the honorary organizing committee composed of three professors from the University of Athens. The athletes wore sandals as they had in 1859. Although this time they did not have to wear tunics, their athletic clothes were of a light color meant to resemble that of human skin, in imitation of the nude athletes of antiquity. There was even an attempt to combine the games with a religious service, a memorial to Euangelēs Zappas, but the archbishop of Athens did not wish to officiate over the memorial outside the metropolitan cathedral.

The success of the athletic component of the second Olympics notwithstanding, the organizers shared Rangavēs's view that the athletic competitions were less significant than the exhibitions of and contests among industrial and agricultural products. Indeed, the opening ceremony of the athletic games included a speech by Philippos Iōannou, professor of classics at the University of Athens and an authority on Greek philology, who described the "progress" of the human race from exhibitions of physical strength to skill in the arts and sciences, which were the disciplines of manifest utility to society. Finance Minister Dēmētrios Chrēstidēs had also touched upon this theme when he had inaugurated the industrial exhibition a few weeks earlier, remarking that the "only" difference between modern and ancient Greeks was that the moderns had included industry in the Olympics because they valued the equal development of physical strength and the mind.[18] In a telling example of the arrogant anti-sport attitude of some members of the Greek elite at the time, Chrēstidēs had pointedly ignored (or forgotten) the ancient Greek dictum of a sound mind in a sound body.

SPORT AND SOCIETY IN LATE NINETEENTH-CENTURY GREECE

The predominance of classical Greek motifs in the Zappas games was all the

[17] *Ibid.*, pp. 79–82.
[18] *Ē engainiasis tēs B' periodou tōn Olympiōn* [*The Inauguration of the Second Period of the Olympics*], Athens, 1870; Chrysafēs, *Oi synchronoi diethneis Olympiakoi . . .*, pp. 51–88; Young, *The Modern Olympics . . .*, pp. 42–52.

more pronounced because sport and physical exercise were undervalued in Greece. The fact that the two first Zappas Olympiads took place and included a sport component is quite remarkable, given how underdeveloped sport was in Greece through the 1870s. The creation of an independent Greek state and society, beginning in the 1830s, gave little thought to sport. Although the rudimentary measures taken by Othōn and his Bavarian advisors consisted of introducing German-style exercises in the schools, even these remained largely on paper: only a handful of German and Greek gymnasts taught a few hours of physical exercise in a small number of private schools. The lack of training facilities was another sign of governmental indifference. The first to open was for the exclusive use of Queen Amalia's equerry in 1858, but began accepting the public in 1860. Athletic facilities appeared in the 1870s, one near the stadium and two belonging to two newly founded sports clubs in Athens, *Panellēnios* (Pan-Hellenic) and *Ethnikos* (National.)

The absence of regular sporting activities or physical exercise explains much of the resistance to Zappas's ideas, as well as the particular arrangements made in connection with the first and second Zappas Olympiads. Several observers associated the events included in these Olympiads with the types of shows put on by roving acrobats and strongmen. The ancient Greek veneer of the Zappas Olympics did not make a difference as far as some critics were concerned, as some traveling performers had engaged in their own appropriation of the past, dressing up with "lion skins" and brandishing wooden clubs so as to imitate Hercules. Indeed, in common parlance, these groups were called "the clubs." Given this background, we can appreciate the consternation caused by the appointment of a gymnast who was also a former acrobat, Daniēl Tziotēs, as a trainer for the 1870 Olympics.

The absence of regularly practiced sporting activities also explains the decision of the organizers of the 1859 and 1870 Olympiads to offer monetary prizes to the winners as a form of encouragement to participate. The lack of widespread participation in sporting activities further explains why the organizers of the 1870 games mandated a supervised training period for all competitors. Finally, the list of victors in 1859 and 1870 shows that they were mostly laborers and employees: only two victors in 1870 were students. The elite, in other words, was absent, yet another confirmation of its disdain for such activities, in sharp contrast to the situation in Europe and North America, where physical exercise was flourishing in the schools and organized sporting activities were gradually gaining popularity. Greece would have to wait for the growth of manufacturing and the emergence of a more modern society to create the mindset that would wrench sport away from its association with strongmen and physical exploits, and develop it as a competitive leisure activity organized by middle-class clubs.[19]

THE THIRD AND FOURTH ZAPPAS OLYMPIADS

Iōannēs Fōkianos (1845–1896), a revered figure in the history of Greek sport, was the epicenter of the post-1870 changes in athletics. Fōkianos abandoned his studies at the University of Athens to become a gymnastics trainer, working in schools and also becoming a personal trainer for the few who were interested in, and could afford, a regimen of physical exercise. He got a position as a trainer in the public gymnasium in Athens in 1868, but his breakthrough came in 1874, when the Olympic committee assigned him the responsibility for training the athletes of the third Zappas Olympiad scheduled for 1875. Fōkianos believed that the upper classes, and especially students, should practice sports. Having associated with German trainers in Greece, he was also an advocate of gymnastics performed on apparatuses such as the vault, rings, and parallel and horizontal bars. His ardor for these was not dampened even after a brother died when the parallel bars he was using gave way.

With sport gaining in popularity in the 1870s, members of the upper classes who had been drawn to it because of a certain snob appeal went from being classicists to social engineers. The first step toward a new era came with the judges' report by Iōannou on the 1870 games. His appointment as an Olympic judge was itself an indication of the importance attached by the government to the Zappas Olympics. Iōannou had been displeased by the predominance of lower-class athletes in previous games and therefore recommended that sport be cultivated in schools and the university. His proposal that only well-educated youth—and, by implication, amateurs—be involved in sport was an almost inevitable outcome of the steady growth of sport in Greece and of the ways Greek reformers looked to Europe for inspiration. Iōannou's elitism was a reflection of the conflicts over the relationship of amateurism to sport in Europe. In Greece, there was little debate: sport

[19]Koulouri, *Athlētismos kai opseis . . .*, pp. 47–59. For an English-language summary of Koulouri's views, see Christina Koulouri, "Voluntary Associations and New Forms of Sociability: Greek Sports Clubs at the Turn of the Nineteenth Century," in Philip Carabott, editor, *Greek Society in the Making, 1863–1913*, Ashgate/Variorum, Aldershot, 1977, pp. 145–160.

became a student monopoly, as lower-class athletes were simply pushed to the margins. Iōannou's move was an example of how Greece was catching up to European trends, at least faintly. For example, Britain was experiencing a clash at the time between gentlemen amateurs and manual workers who found themselves interacting awkwardly in sport. The elite wasted no time in excluding the lower classes from competition against them in the name of a contrived, purist attitude toward sport, although this tactic soon failed in the sphere of the more popular sports such as soccer and cricket.[20] Although the clash was not as intense in Greece, it signaled the bourgeoisie's commitment to embracing and promoting, as well as manipulating, the growth of sport.

The athletic segment of the third Zappas Olympiad took place at the Panathenaic Stadium on May 18/30, 1875, in the afternoon, and it turned out to be a less impressive affair compared with the Olympiad held five years earlier. There were some obvious changes in the program and in the number of participants that bore the stamp of Fōkianos's influence. The events included a race, wrestling, climbing a pole and a rope, the pole vault, the javelin throw, discus, exercises on a bar, and the parallel bars. There were only twenty-four competitors, all students. The number of spectators was about half of those attending in 1870. Worse still, the games were not well-organized, with long waits between events or delays in announcing results, prompting one writer to describe them as "pan-Hellenic patience games." The stadium had also not been properly prepared. Seating had not been cut into the earthen slopes, and spectators began rolling down the sides and crashing into those seated below. The expensive seats—wooden benches, actually—were no more comfortable, as they kept breaking, demanding the attention of a stadium employee who busied himself all afternoon sawing and nailing in an attempt to fix them.

The organizers of the 1875 games also toned down the historical Greek imagery of the previous Olympiad, another sign of the shift away from imitating antiquity and a tentative gesture toward European practices. The athletes wore white pants and sports shirts instead of tunics. The judges wore suits and tall hats, widely considered typical "European" attire in Greece. One reporter even complained that the music was inappropriate, as the band insisted on polkas and compositions by Offenbach. Ultimately, the press and the public deemed the 1875 games a failure. The Olympic committee

[20]Richard Holt, *Sport and the British: A Modern History*, Oxford University Press, Oxford, 1990, pp. 98–116.

dismissed Fōkianos, although it did not plan to return to the older format of the games. In 1879, however, the committee appointed Fōkianos as director of a new gymnasium built very close to the stadium and funded by the Zappas bequest.[21]

Nonetheless, the third Zappas Olympics were followed by a more serious engagement with sport on the part of the government and Greek officials. The 1880s, a period of modernization under Prime Minister Charilaos Trikoupēs, witnessed the first steps to harness sport to educational values. For example, the government made gymnastics compulsory in high school and appointed trainers to teach schoolchildren two hours per week. In 1882, the time devoted to these exercises was raised to three hours, and, in the same year, the government created a physical-education school to train coaches, co-directed by Fōkianos. The following year, high schools acquired the necessary apparatus for gymnastic exercises.

The committee charged with organizing the games announced that the fourth Zappas Olympics would take place in October 1888, along with the inauguration of the Zappeion Hall, as well as the celebration of the twenty-fifth anniversary of King George's ascension to the throne. It is unclear why there was such a long gap between the third and fourth Zappas Olympics; it may have had to do with the government's modernization priorities. In any case, the sports component of the Olympics, the committee decided, would be open to all participants and would include athletic games in the stadium, as well as a shooting competition with five contests for military men and two for civilians. Winners would receive monetary prizes and olive wreaths or branches. All this remained on paper, however, since the committee, concerned perhaps that its preparations were insufficient and fearing another fiasco, canceled the games. Fōkianos immediately volunteered to replace them with an event he would run on his own, and the committee gladly agreed.

Whether it was the committee or the government that was to blame for ignoring the athletic side of the fourth Olympics, we should note that the significance of the industrial and agricultural exhibition was, in the eyes of many, a matter of national importance. With modernization being at the core of Trikoupēs's policies, the economic side of the Olympic exhibition inevitably shunted aside the need to organize athletic games. The exhibition opened in the Zappeion Hall in the presence of Kōnstantinos Zappas, who

---

[21]Chrysafēs, *Oi synchronoi diethneis Olympiakoi . . .* , pp. 89–111.

made his one and only trip to Athens on this occasion. Stefanos Dragoumēs, the minister of the interior, opened the proceedings by calling upon the king to declare the exhibition open. George I made some brief remarks to the effect that he hoped the exhibition was a sign of Greece's wealth. Zappas spoke then, and recalled how his cousin Euangelēs had been inspired by patriotism and the example of classical Greece. The Athens daily *Paliggenesia* editorially sang the praises of the exhibition the next day, stating that it proved that Greece was on the path to progress and on course to take its place among the civilized countries of the world.[22]

The games organized by Fōkianos took place in May 1889 and included a range of athletic events by university and high-school athletes trained by him and preceded by a gymnastics exhibition by high-school students. They took place in the public gymnasium in the presence of government ministers, but, because of the crush of people, many of them students, the contests had to be interrupted and rescheduled. More careful organization enabled them to take place a few days later. They included a race, discus, pole-vault, high jump, running high jump, stone-throw, parallel bars, weightlifting with one and two hands, rope-climbing, and pole-climbing. The victors in at least two events were high-school students. At the end of the contests, Fōkianos received an award (from Stefanos Koumanoudēs, a distinguished professor of philology at the University of Athens) for his work in promoting physical exercise in the schools and among university students. Fōkianos had ensured that the athletic segment of the Olympics had been entirely co-opted by a small group of coaches who, like him, favored student athletes. Many of those athletes later became important public figures, such as the novelist Geōrgios Drosinēs. He and others contributed to lionizing Fōkianos in the years to come.[23]

The fourth Zappas Olympics were the last to be held, ostensibly because the Romanian government began blocking the transfer of funds from the Zappas estate to Greece. The Greek government challenged this impounding and the clash led to a serious deterioration in diplomatic relations between the two countries that lasted for several years. In the event, the committee in Athens had spent most of the money on the Zappeion Hall and the small park surrounding it, and therefore plans for any future Olympics were, as it turned out, permanently shelved.

[22]Editorial, *Paliggenesia*, October 21, 1888.
[23]Chrysafēs, *Oi synchronoi diethneis Olympiakoi . . .* , pp. 112–130.

Meanwhile, William Penny Brookes, the organizer of the Olympics in England, had been trying in vain to get someone in Athens to join him in organizing international games. Brookes had been following Greek efforts to revive the Olympics and was in contact with Iōannēs Gennadios, the Greek ambassador to London and a close associate of Trikoupēs. Brookes succeeded in persuading King George to donate a cup for the winner of the pentathlon in the 1877 Olympics in Wenlock. Three years later, Brookes began his campaign to persuade Gennadios to help him interest Greece in organizing international Olympic Games. In David Young's words, "for more than a decade, from 1880 to 1893, Brookes hounded Gennadius [*sic*] to help him found international Olympic Games."[24] It was to no avail, as Gennadios rebuffed Brookes politely and did nothing. There is only a brief mention in the Trikoupēs-Gennadios correspondence of the Greek community in London having any interest in the exhibitions of the fourth Olympics in 1888, and no mention of Brookes.[25]

The end of the Zappas Olympics is not at all surprising. Lacking funds, and without a strong domestic sports culture to promote their athletic component, they were doomed to failure. Ultimately, they remain a symbol of nineteenth-century's Greece's preoccupation with its ancient past rather than its sporting future. To be sure, they deserve pride of place in the genealogy that culminated in Coubertin's Olympics. But it is also true that a great deal about this attempt to repeat the history of the ancient Olympics was mired by mechanical imitation of symbols of the past, by piecemeal adoption of modern sporting events, and, finally, by the absence of an international dimension. The limited scope of the Zappas Olympics in Greece and the Brookes Olympics in England paved the way for Baron Pierre de Coubertin to step onto the world stage and create the modern Olympic Games.

---

[24]Young, *The Modern Olympics . . .* , p. 56.

[25]Lydia Tricha, *Diplomatia kai politikē. Charilaos Trikoupēs-Iōannēs Gennadios Allēlografia 1863–1894* [*Diplomacy and Politics: Charilaos Trikoupēs-Iōannēs Gennadios Correspondence, 1863–1894*], ELIA, Athens, 1991, p. 239.

CHAPTER 2

THE 1896 OLYMPIC GAMES IN ATHENS

S PYROS LOUĒS STOPPED BRIEFLY at an inn on the twenty-second kilometer of the marathon race. He chose a glass of *retsina* wine over the
other beverages available to runners, which included water, lemonade,
orange juice, and cognac. He declined any of the hardboiled eggs, bread, and
oranges that were also on offer, however. "I'll soon catch up with them," he
said upon hearing that seven runners were well ahead of him. Ten kilometers
later, he overtook Frenchman Albin Lermusiaux, moving into second place
behind Australian Edwin Flack.

A total of twenty-five runners had started the race on March 29/April 10,
1896, in the village of Marathon, close to the site of the battle between the
Greeks and the Persians in 480 BCE. Before he signaled the start of the race,
Major Geōrgios Papadiamantopoulos of the Greek army's engineering corps
gave a brief pep-talk of sorts to the Greek runners, telling them that Greece
expected a victory in the race. Sōkratēs Lagoudakēs, a Parisian Greek who
was running under the French colors, addressed the foreign competitors and
wished them luck. The major gave his signal at 1:56 pm, and the runners
charged ahead. On their heels came a procession of attendants, race officials,
and doctors, riding bicycles and driving horse-drawn carriages.

Almost three hours later, the spectators in the packed Panathenaic Stadium waited with bated breath for the marathon's finish. They heard all sorts
of rumors about who was in the lead. A cannon-shot announced that the
leader of the race was only a kilometer away from the finish-line. The crowd's
excitement mounted as it heard the cheers of people who had lined the street
leading to the stadium. The chief of the Athens police entered the stadium on
horseback, hastening toward the dais, crying out, "A Greek, a Greek!" Word
spread throughout the vast, horseshoe-shaped, marble stadium. Within

minutes, the officials at the stadium's entrance parted as a white-clad runner covered in dust, sweating profusely but running upright, made his way to the finish-line. A group of sailors in charge of raising the winner's national flag at the entrance quickly checked the runner's number. Seventeen. It belonged to Spyros Louēs. Quickly, they raised the Greek flag. The crowd let out a deafening roar and kept on cheering. Hundreds of white doves were released into the sky. As hats flew into the air and a celebrating crowd waved handkerchiefs and Greek flags, Crown Prince Constantine and his brother, Prince George, left their father's side and jumped on to the track to run next to Louēs as he covered the last few meters to victory. The winner was led to the king. Louēs bowed. The monarch responded with a military salute and the words, "I congratulate you; you have honored the nation."[1]

The story of Louēs's victory is spoken of in Greek schools in the same breath as such glorious victories as those of the Athenians over the Persians in the battles of Marathon or Salamis. And the longer Greece went without an Olympic medal in the twentieth century, the more Louēs's aura grew. It remains one of those moments in Greek history cited to prove how an underdog, driven by the Greek spirit, can succeed against all odds—and foreigners.

The eruption of national pride as a Greek won the marathon in the 1896 Olympiad in Athens is commonly cited as proof of Greece's nationalistic embrace of these games, as is King George's call, made a few days after the games ended, that Greece become the permanent host of the Olympics. Noting that the Greek organizers tried to ignore Baron Pierre de Coubertin during the ceremonies that took place during the games, scholars have suggested several reasons why Greek leaders sought to make their country the permanent venue. These include national pride, financial gain as well as the potential benefits accruing to the royal family, and the government's desire to rally the country behind its quest for a "Greater Greece."[2]

Obviously, Greece stood to gain if Athens became the permanent site of the Olympics, not least because of the boost it would deliver to national prestige. The Greek victory in the marathon was a source of national pride because, above all, it was achieved in an international context. Nineteenth-century Greece considered Europe to be the model for the socioeconomic

---

[1]Nikos Politēs, *Oi Olympiakoi Agōnes tou 1896 opōs tous ezēsan tote oi ellēnes kai oi xenoi* [*The Olympic Games of 1896 as they were Experienced by Greeks and Foreigners*], Achaïkes Ekdoseis, Patras, 1996, pp. 85–106.

[2]Richard Mandell, *The First Modern Olympics*, University of California Press, Berkeley, 1976, pp. 152–156.

modernization that would allow the country to realize its national and terri-torial goals. The revival of Athens-based Olympics would offer Greece unique prestige in the international arena at a time when it was beholden to the great powers in the spheres of diplomacy, politics, economics, and even culture. "We have joined the club of Europe," the Greek representative attend-ing the congress that decided to revive the Olympics told a gathering of Greek students in Paris.[3]

It is important, however, to contextualize the nationalism ignited by Louēs and expressed by the royal family when it claimed that Greece deserved to become the permanent venue of the Olympics. These sentiments emerged only toward the end of the games, and they did not overshadow Greece's pride over its heritage or the international recognition it was gaining. In claiming the games, Greece was seeking to *internationalize itself* rather than Hellenize the Olympics. Greece was a very small power at the time, beholden to greater powers; a permanent association with the games would have entailed permanent international prestige. This fusion of nationalism with internationalism was evident from the first moment that Baron de Coubertin called for the revival of the Olympics until the very conclusion of the Athens games in 1896.

Several studies have analyzed the Olympic games' entanglement with politics, and with nationalism in particular.[4] The case of Greece is no excep-tion. The point has to be made, however, that Greek nationalism was defined by a sense of continuity with the past and a struggle for international accept-ance, culturally as well as diplomatically. Thus, Greek nationalist interaction with the Olympics was not xenophobic; quite the opposite, it was interna-tionally oriented—and has remained so to the present.

COUBERTIN AND THE REVIVAL OF THE OLYMPICS

Pierre de Coubertin was born in Paris on January 1, 1863, to Baron Charles Louis Fredy de Coubertin and his wife, Agathe Marie Marcelle Gigault de

[3]Petros N. Linardos, *D. Vikelas. Apo to orama stēn praxē* [*D. Vikelas: From the Vision to the Act*], EOA, Athens, 1996, p. 116.

[4]Richard Espy, *The Politics of the Olympic Games*, University of California Press, Berke-ley, 1981; John Hargreaves, *Freedom for Catalonia? Catalan Nationalism, Spanish Identity and the Barcelona Olympic Games*, Cambridge University Press, Cambridge, 2000; Christo-pher R. Hill, *Olympic Politics*, second edition, Manchester University Press, Manchester, 1996, Chapter 5.

Crisenoy. Young Pierre initially considered a career in the military, an appropriate choice for someone belonging to the old French aristocracy, but he soon realized that he was better equipped to become an educator. France's defeat in the Franco-Prussian War of 1870–1871 cast a long shadow over his generation, and Coubertin identified the lack of physical training in French schools as a major cause of his country's setback. He devoted the early part of his career to rectifying this situation, but rather than draw inspiration from the physical education practiced by Germans in their schools, he looked to England, where competitive sport rather than exercise prevailed; indeed, it virtually dominated the curricula of Eton and Harrow and the other elite schools. Coubertin believed that Thomas Arnold, the legendary head of the Rugby School, was responsible for the significance acquired by competitive sport in English schools.

In fact, Arnold had been misrepresented in Thomas Hughes's *Tom Brown's Schooldays*, the author's idealized memoir, which appeared in 1856 and was read by Coubertin in a French translation twenty years later. While Arnold was actually not enthusiastic about sport, however, it is true that the senior staff he appointed at Rugby in the 1830s believed that organized athletics would instill badly needed discipline and organization. It set in motion major innovations by which organized and codified forms of play, the predecessors of several sports such as soccer, replaced the brutal rough-and-tumble of earlier forms of games played by the students. In a context in which students gained entry to the school precisely because of their privileged social class rather than academic abilities, sport inevitably became more and more important. In the words of a historian of British sport, "gradually sport ceased to be a means to a disciplinary end and became an end in itself. The culture of athleticism steadily came to dominate the whole system of elite education."[5]

By the time Coubertin encountered Britain's burgeoning sporting culture, the late Victorian era had transformed it into the repository of a combination of principles that defined the British ruling classes. Sport, it was thought, offered a balance between the exercise of individual initiative, on the one hand, and that social cohesion and obedience (masquerading as "team spirit"), on the other, which were the essential ingredients of Britain's domestic and imperial power structure. Thus, "the idea of a healthy mind and body merged into a garbled Darwinism that was itself often intermingled with

[5]Richard Holt, *Sport and the British*, p. 81.

notions of Christian and imperial duty."[6] The French baron saw this British amalgam as a panacea, both for France's backwardness in physical training and for its domestic tensions between his own class, the old aristocracy, and the increasingly assertive urban bourgeoisie. In 1899, a visit to the United States, where the British way had found its own dynamic expression, impressed Coubertin immensely.

Inspired by English sport, Coubertin embarked on a mission that began with an exhortation to his fellow French educators to imitate their neighbors and resulted in his vision to revive the ancient Olympic Games. By doing so, the baron became a leader in the rise of French sport and the emergence of a French sporting culture that favored internationalism and universalism. According to Wolfgang Schivelbusch's cultural history of defeat in war, embracing these impulses, rather than a more straightforward and immediate *revanche* against Germany—which few French considered realistic—was an indirect but effective form of French national compensation in the wake of the Franco-Prussian War. France's post-1871 "culture of defeat" (to use Schivelbusch's term) spawned many strategies of national revival; in the sphere of sport, these were tempered by a sense of pragmatism. Thus, in Schivelbusch's words, "France appropriated the English idea of competitive sports, refashioning it as a celebration of humanity and brotherhood. The revival of the Olympic Games . . . cast the *grande nation* not only as the true heir to the original cultural nation, Hellas, but also as the director of the entire international sports movement."[7]

The revival of the Olympics represented the culmination of Coubertin's intellectual formation, which began under the shadow of post-1871 French *angst* and proceeded through his encounter with Victorian education, and the latter's obsession with competitive sport. It included his visit to the village of Much Wenlock in Shropshire, where another visionary, William Penny Brookes, had combined the English mania for sport with the Victorian reverence for Greek antiquity by holding locally based athletic games modeled on the Olympics. Among the many myths the Greeks believe about the modern Olympics, the idea that Coubertin was primarily a philhellene takes pride of place. To be sure, Coubertin's intellectual formation and motivations were complex, and they have been captured with considerable detail and

---

[6] *Ibid.*, p. 87.

[7] Wolfgang Schivelbusch, *The Culture of Defeat: On National Trauma, Mourning and Recovery*, Henry Holt, New York, 2003, p. 174.

nuance in John MacAloon's study of the baron's role in the revival of the Games.[8] In general, however, one can say that Coubertin was first an anglophile and only then a philhellene, literally: he came to embrace Greece only after he had absorbed England's appropriation of the Greek spirit. It is not surprising that he conceived of the revival of the Olympics only after having encountered the English version of that revival in Shropshire.

Yet, in a sense, Coubertin's old-fashioned philhellenism made it easier for him to include Greece in his plan to revive the ancient Olympics. Unlike many other philhellenes of the late nineteenth and early twentieth centuries who grew restless with the idea of modern Greece's evocation of its classical past, Coubertin attached himself to an older, romantic notion that held that the spirit of classical Greece was embodied in the physical spaces once inhabited by the ancients. Thus, when he imagined the revival of the ancient Olympics, he also imagined they could involve present-day Greece—indeed, that they might even be held there.

Romantic philhellenes considered Greece's physical space integral to their relationship to classical Greece. As Fani-Maria Tsigakou has explained in her study of travelers and painters to Greece in the romantic era, "it was generally thought that the visitor's physical presence at an actual site would stimulate almost miraculously a revival of its ancient ethos. . . . [T]he concept of the 'spirit of place' which Greece seemed to offer was attractive, to say the least, and Europeans were eager to experience it."[9]

The power of the "spirit of place," however, had waned by the late nineteenth century, weakened by new realist cultural trends and the frustration of many philhellenes with the prosaic reality of modern Greece. But this left Coubertin unaffected, for two reasons. The first was that his philhellenism passed through what Ian Buruma has described as his "Anglomania," namely an admiration for Thomas Arnold, English education, and an English sporting culture already constructed on the foundations of romantic philhellenism.[10] The second was that, upon arriving in Athens in the fall of 1894, he found the Greek capital "traditional" but also "alive," not at all the backwater described by other European travelers. Coubertin actually saw the potential for Greece to develop if it could recover its classical heritage. MacAloon

[8]John J. MacAloon, *This Great Symbol: Pierre de Coubertin and the Origins of the Modern Olympic Games*, University of Chicago Press, Chicago, 1981.

[9]Fani-Maria Tsigakou, *The Rediscovery of Greece: Travelers and Painters of the Romantic Era*, Caratzas Publishers, New Rochelle, 1981, p. 27.

[10]Ian Buruma, *Anglomania*, Random House, New York, 1998, pp. 151–156.

explains that the baron shared the Durkheimian belief that society is defined by the idea it forms of itself; in the event, Coubertin thought that the modern Greek embrace of its ancient heritage, evident all around, was bound to bring material and social progress.[11]

Coubertin's strong belief in the "spirit of place" would, in due course, shape the Olympic movement's relationship to modern Greece. Since the movement evolved under the shadow of its founder's beliefs, it took with it, well into the twentieth century, an attachment to the physical spaces of Greece that many philhellenes, a disappearing breed, were abandoning in the era of modernism. This apparently outmoded way of conceiving Greece meant that the modern descendants of the ancients would always enjoy a privileged place in the movement's value system. Indeed, the sense that modern Greece evoked the spirit of ancient Greece would resurface after the Second World War, as we will see, shorn of its more idealist and romantic connotations. In an era of growing tourism and the "discovery" of the Mediterranean, the natural beauties of ancient sites regained significance in the eyes of many international visitors as untouched physical spaces that once hosted an ancient civilization.

All this meant that Greece would figure in the revival of the Olympics that Coubertin launched in 1894 at a congress he organized at the Sorbonne. The baron had ostensibly convened this international meeting of seventy-eight sports administrators from nine countries to discuss the problems posed to amateurism in sport, as well as the possible revival of the Olympics; he used the congress almost exclusively for the latter purpose, however. Before it was over, not only had the delegates approved his proposal, but they had also agreed that the games would be held in Athens in 1896 and in Paris four years later. The baron's tactic of frequent allusions to antiquity was aimed at making his idea of reviving the Olympics palatable to everyone present. He had already made his wish to revive the games public in 1892; this time, his proposal was designed to produce concrete results. The baron arranged for the opening ceremonies, held in a room adorned with neoclassical paintings, to include a performance of the ancient *Hymn to Apollo*, discovered the previous year during the French Archaeological School's excavations at Delphi. Choosing the right moment, Coubertin formally proposed that the congress approve the revival of the Olympics, while also suggesting that the first games be held in Athens. On the same day (June 23) that

[11]MacAloon, *This Great Symbol . . .* , pp. 184–185.

the delegates approved the revival of the Olympics, they also empowered Coubertin to select a fourteen-person committee to organize the games; it was this committee that soon came to be known as the International Olympic Committee (IOC), the governing body of the Olympic movement. Dēmētrios Vikelas, the Greek delegate to the congress, was chosen as the committee's first president, but Coubertin replaced him in 1896 and served as president through 1927.

Thus, the 1894 congress at the Sorbonne gave birth to the modern Olympic movement and its governing body. As was the case at the inaugural congress, the IOC's members do not represent their countries; rather, the committee chooses them in the same way Coubertin chose the participants in 1894, and they are supposed to represent the IOC *in* their respective countries. Coubertin insisted that the IOC appoint its own membership, in order to maintain its independence, rather than accept government nominations. Gradually, each country acquired its own national Olympic committee to promote the Olympic movement within its borders.

GREEK REACTIONS TO THE 1894 CONGRESS

Coubertin could not have picked a worse moment to solicit Greece's help in what promised to be a risky and costly project: the country had just declared bankruptcy. On January 1, 1894, an editorial in the Athens daily *Paliggenesia* looked back on the events of the previous year. Who would have thought, the commentary noted, that Greece would have suffered insolvency under Charilaos Trikoupēs. He was the leader, the editorial continued, who from 1882 to 1892 had said he would take us to the promised land, despite heavy indebtedness and high taxes; he was a politician we considered an "Olympian." A few weeks later, an editorial marking the anniversary of the Greek revolution of 1821 called upon Greece to continue its struggle for progress: in light of the previous year's bankruptcy, however, it recommended small and realistic steps in that direction. The celebrations of independence that year were muted since, according to an unnamed German foreign correspondent, the Greeks were shouldering a triple burden: higher taxes, unfulfilled national dreams, and political dissolution.[12]

Greece had suffered the consequences of an ambitious, decade-long drive toward modernization that had begun slowly in the second half of the

[12]Editorial, *Paliggenesia*, January 1; editorial, March 25; unsigned article, April 28, 1894.

nineteenth century and picked up momentum in the 1880s. Extensive public works, underwritten by foreign loans and increased taxes, had been at the core of this bid for economic development. It was a finely balanced project that went awry when, beginning in 1890, Greece's agricultural exports dropped in value along with its currency. The economic crisis peaked in 1893, and Trikoupēs effectively declared national insolvency by reducing by seventy percent the interest paid by Greece on foreign loans. In what was subsequently to become a famous expression of shattered Greek dreams, Trikoupēs pithily summed up the situation by announcing to parliament, "Gentlemen, we are bankrupt."

This was the situation that Baron Pierre de Coubertin stepped into with his proposal that Greece host the first modern Olympic Games. If he had been aware of the atmosphere in Greece at the time, he would probably have thought twice about his idea. As it turned out, however, Coubertin's move was not quite so ill-timed, since it gained the support of Trikoupēs's political opponents, including, most importantly, the royal family. The modernization program launched by Trikoupēs in the 1880s, which had been the culmination of a trend that for two decades saw Greece choosing domestic development over the pursuit of nationalist-minded territorial claims, was not universally admired in the country. Trikoupēs's main rival, Theodōros Delēgiannēs, espoused a different policy, which made territorial claims a priority. While both leaders supported modernization and Europeanization, Delēgiannēs, a populist, tended to harp on the more nationalistic theme of pursuing the idea of a Greater Greece: one, in other words, in which all the "unredeemed" areas of the Balkans and Asia Minor, with their significant ethnic Greek populations, would be incorporated into the Greek state. Trikoupēs saw that goal as something to be achieved only after modernization. Under the circumstances, the Olympics were precisely the type of populist item that appealed to Delēgiannēs. As it turned out, the royal family also believed they were an opportunity to enhance its own standing.

Yet the Olympic revival attracted a segment of the Greek leadership for reasons beyond the obvious possibility of political gain immediately identified by the royal family and Delēgiannēs. The revival allowed Greece to join a project that proclaimed its commitment to humanity and internationalism, while leading to national regeneration, as in France's case following the defeat of 1871. Although Greece had not suffered a comparably devastating setback, it was reeling from its failed modernization program and craved

compensation for its flagging morale. One can argue that Greece was permanently invested in gaining European recognition for both its ancient heritage
and modern identity, but the circumstances that obtained in this small country in the 1890s certainly contributed to its attitude toward the Olympic
revival.

There had been great interest in Greece at the announcement of the Sorbonne congress. Fōkianos quickly drafted a memorandum for the assembly
when the Greek sports club, *Panellēnios Gymnastikos Syllogos*, received Coubertin's invitation to attend. Fōkianos's memorandum mentioned the Zappas Olympics, but made sure to express approval of Coubertin's vision of the
Olympic revival because these new games "would extend their influence well
beyond Greece's ethnographic boundaries," since "all civilized nations that
had been enlightened by [ancient] Greece would take part." The rest of the
memorandum consisted of an account of the ancient Olympics, indicating
that Fōkianos, one of the most important figures of the Greek sports world,
saw the games primarily in terms of reviving and disseminating the glory of
ancient Greece rather than as an athletic contest.[13]

The choice of Dēmētrios Vikelas (1835–1908), an intellectual who was
not associated with sport but conveniently located in Paris, to be *Panellēnios's*
representative to the congress was in tune with Greek views that this was an
event honoring the legacy of antiquity. Vikelas was born in Ermoupolis, on
the island of Syros, one of the important commercial ports of the eastern
Mediterranean, and had moved to London at the age of seventeen to work
for Melas Brothers, a merchant company owned by relatives. Vikelas combined his commercial activities with a great deal of reading and writing.
Translated into several languages, his best-known work was *Loukēs Laras*, a
fictional account of the fortunes of a boy who escapes the destruction of the
island of Chios during the Greek revolution.[14] Vikelas was a man of broad
interests, but sport was not one of them, and most accounts indicate that he
was happy to follow Coubertin's lead. A recently published biography of
Vikelas, written by veteran Greek sportswriter Petros Linardos, attempts an
across-the-board rebuttal of the view that Vikelas played second fiddle to

---

[13]Chrysafēs, *Oi synchronoi diethneis Olympiakoi . . .* , p. 183.

[14]For a biography of Vikelas, see Alexandros A. Oikonomou, *Treis anthropoi, tomos
deuteros, Dēmētrios M. Vikelas (1835–1908)* [*Three Persons, Volume Two, Dēmētrios M. Vikelas
(1835–1908)*], Ellēnikē Ekdotikē Etaireia, Athens, 1953; for the "literary" Vikelas, see Dēmētrēs
Tziovas, "Dimitrios Vikelas in the Diaspora: Memory, Character Formation and Language,"
Kambos, No. 6, 1988, pp. 111–133.

Coubertin and attributes the idea of holding the 1896 Olympiad in Athens to the Greek writer. Linardos, who even cites research showing that Vikelas did some rowing and fencing in his youth, suggests that the Greek intellectual had a more active and dynamic role in the revival of the Olympics than even that credited to him by David Young, who has gone a long way in establishing the Greek contribution to Coubertin's revival of the Olympics.[15]

Upon learning that, in addition to reviving the Olympics, the Sorbonne congress had proposed that Greece host them, the Trikoupēs administration promptly rejected the idea. Trikoupēs was still in power, desperately trying to strike a deal with Greece's foreign creditors and also trying to stave off a political offensive by an opposition that saw the opportunity to regain power. Young, who has examined the papers of Stefanos Dragoumēs, one of Trikoupēs's right-hand men, sees evidence of what he considers to be the "anti-athletic clique" of the Greek elite at work. According to Young, Dragoumēs was against sport in the same way Rangavēs had been earlier. To be sure, economics must have played a primary role in this decision, as Trikoupēs was unlikely to approve a project involving more public expenditure; but one should also acknowledge Young's important findings about Dragoumēs's attitude toward athletics.[16]

There was, however, a formidable alliance emerging, headed by the royal family, in favor of holding the games in Greece. Coubertin had asked the director of the American Archaeological School in Athens, Charles Waldstein, to lobby on behalf of the revival of the Olympics. King George telegraphed his support during the Sorbonne congress; at its conclusion, he also stated that he would place the Athens games under his patronage. Opposition leader Delēgiannēs, who had an unfailing eye for popular causes, also backed the games—indeed, with even greater gusto when Trikoupēs's objections became known. The prospect of holding the games in Athens was popular not only for reasons of international prestige and national pride but also because of the financial gains that would accrue to the capital's large number of shopkeepers, who just happened to be part of the opposition leader's electoral base—a very early sign of the role that commercial interests would play in the Olympic movement.

[15]Linardos, *Apo to orama . . .*, pp. 79–91 and 107–112.
[16]Young, *The Modern Olympics . . .*, pp. 110–114.

THE BATTLE OF ATHENS

The struggle over whether or not Greece would host the 1896 Olympics lasted just under three months, beginning with Coubertin's arrival in the Greek capital in November 1894. Coubertin made the trip because Vikelas's early contacts with the government had been unproductive; moreover, the Greek writer's wife had fallen fatally ill in Paris, leaving the baron effectively in charge of the Olympic committee's efforts. Coubertin tried to assuage the government's concerns about economic costs by producing as small a budget for the games as possible, roughly 125,000 drachmas.[17] He also stoked the fires of support with skillful private and public interventions. Although he was preaching to the converted, his presence helped the cause by galvanizing the pro-Olympics side.

Although Coubertin's mission started badly, it gained ground steadily. Upon his arrival, he was handed a long letter from Dragoumēs, which had already been sent to him, telling him not to come to Athens because Greece could not hold the games, and that, in any case, the country had no modern athletics. Two days later, Coubertin met with Trikoupēs, who reiterated his objections on economic grounds. Coubertin responded by pointing out that a great deal of the necessary infrastructure was already in place and that, in fact, he was impressed by how Athens looked like a modern capital city. Trikoupēs gave him a set of budgetary facts and invited him to study them so as to realize the impossibility of the project. Crown Prince Constantine, however, also met with Coubertin and expressed his confidence that Greece could hold the games. The prince's attitude appears to have been based on political rather than financial or organizational considerations, and on his confidence that the royal family's patronage of the games would somehow mobilize the necessary willpower and resources.

Coubertin's supporters also organized a public lecture for him at the philological society *Parnassos*. Being an accomplished public speaker, the baron made the most of it. Most of the Athens intellectual elite was naturally able to follow a lecture given in French. It was an ideal venue because *Parnassos*, formed in 1865, was the most prestigious intellectual society in Greece and the host of important speeches by the country's major intellectual figures. In his address, Coubertin made the requisite allusions to ancient Greece and carefully stroked as well as challenged Greek national pride. Crucially, all

[17] *Ibid.*, p. 114.

the newspapers, including the pro-Trikoupēs *Asty*, gave the event extensive and positive coverage.[18]

With the tide turning in favor of Coubertin, and Trikoupēs pledging neutrality, the former tried to mobilize the Zappas Olympic committee to assume the organization of the games. But Coubertin was out of his depth. The committee was headed by Dragoumēs, who was succeeded a little later by another Trikoupist politician, Stefanos Skouloudēs, who was also opposed to holding the games in Athens. They listened respectfully to Coubertin and appeared to go along with him when they met, but, within days of Coubertin's departure from Athens, Skouloudēs informed the crown prince that there were no funds and that the Zappas committee had decided that the games could not be held in Athens.

The opposition immediately challenged the government's claim of financial difficulties and declared that it was Greece's responsibility to uphold its heritage and not be humiliated internationally. Parliament discussed the Olympics on the very day the Zappas committee had tried to wash its hands of the project. There was a long and acrimonious debate between two political parties whose rivalry was exacerbated by Greece's bankruptcy. Both Dragoumēs and Skouloudēs tried to explain the lack of funds, but the opposition would have none of it. Two former ministers of education, Andreas Zygomalas and Athanasios Eutaxias, ripped into the government and accused it of undermining Greece's stature and helping its enemies. Delēgiannēs rose toward the end of the debate and accused the government of making unverified statements. The next day, an anti-Trikoupēs newspaper, eagerly looking forward to his demise, predicted that Greece would soon find the funds for and lose a government opposed to the Olympics.[19]

At this juncture, the crown prince decided to take matters into his own hands by establishing a new Olympic committee while also moving to engineer the fall of its pro-Trikoupēs administration. Constantine gave old members a chance to affirm or rescind their resignations, and thus got rid of Trikoupēs's supporters; he then proceeded to appoint a committee made up of his collaborators and politicians from the Delēgiannēs camp. By that time, there was already a rift between Trikoupēs and the royal family concerning the prime minister's refusal to provide stipends for the princes

---

[18]Skiadas, *100 chronia neoterē . . .*, pp. 76–77; Geōrgios Sourēs, the renowned commentator-satirist, also remarked on the lecture.

[19]Young, *The Modern Olympics . . .*, pp. 116–118.

serving in the military. The rift widened after the crown prince took over the Olympic committee and, finally, intervened to prevent a pro-Trikoupēs demonstration in Athens, which had been called to counter a large anti-tax, anti-Trikoupēs gathering. This was the last straw for the beleaguered Trikoupēs, who submitted his resignation in early January 1895. Almost inevitably, his party would lose the elections held in April that year; worse still, Trikoupēs lost his own seat. Trikoupēs's resignation, meanwhile, had suggested to the crown prince that the road for the Athens Olympiad was clear. Constantine convened the new committee on January 13/25, 1895, and touched upon the themes of continuity and pride. "We render a tribute of gratitude to the founders of the renowned Panhellenic Games . . . held in Olympia [and] we extend their noble purpose toward a closer union of civilized peoples." He concluded by saying, "I place my trust in the . . . pride and in the pure and sincere worship of Greeks everywhere in the glorious Greek tradition of antiquity. . . ."[20]

Constantine had taken charge and, in so doing, inaugurated what would become seventy years of conservative control of Greece's national Olympic committee, bolstered by the continued presence and involvement of the Greek royal family. As with the international Olympic committee, the Greek committee members were not elected; in this instance, they were appointed by the head of state—which is to say the crown—in consultation with the government of the day. Hence, the royal family was able to determine the committee's make-up, and did so until 1967, when the royal family fled Greece, never to return. (There was one serious interruption of royal hegemony over the committee: while the short exile of the Greek monarch from 1917 to 1920, forced upon him by political circumstances during the First World War, did not affect control very much, a longer spell in exile for the royal family—from 1924 to 1935—enabled the antiroyalist government of Eleutherios Venizelos to make appointments of its own choice. As this was a period of considerable social unrest in Greece, however, and sport was not high on Venizelos's agenda, his government's involvement with Greece's Olympic committee was limited.)

---

[20]Pierre de Coubertin *et al.*, *Les Jeux Olympiques*, Charles Beck, Athens, 1896, pp. 112–114.

GREEK PREPARATIONS

The Greek authorities understood their task of preparing Athens for the 1896 Olympics as a duty to uphold the legacy of Greece's ancient past, as well as an opportunity to show the world that their country was modern and European. This task, imbued with a strong sense of patriotism and national pride, thus also epitomized the sense of Hellenism as an internationalism that underscored Greece's relationship to the Olympic Games from the moment of their revival to the present. Later, during the games, the Greeks would ratchet up national pride to a nationalistic level by celebrating, wherever possible, Greek victories over foreigners.

The press made sure that the fundraising campaign took on a patriotic tone by invoking the country's national interest in raising the required monies. One newspaper told its readers that *The Times* of London had written that a precondition for successful preparations was the Greeks' awareness that the eyes of Europe were upon them, and it exhorted them to respond appropriately. The press recorded a truly widespread response to the fundraising appeals from all over the country and the diaspora.[21]

The organizers also saw fundraising in a similar nationalist light and couched their appeals accordingly, a tactic that produced a crucial breakthrough. The Olympic committee contacted a man already considered a national benefactor. Geōrgios Averōf (1818–1899) was a wealthy merchant based in Alexandria, Egypt, a major commercial and cotton-exporting center with a flourishing Greek community. By the 1890s, Averōf was one of the richest foreign residents in Egypt and the leader and major benefactor of Alexandria's Greek community. Aside from donations to his hometown, Averōf had made several large contributions to the Greek state that had gone toward completing construction of the university's polytechnic school and building the army cadet school. The committee now requested assistance for the largest work-related expenditure on the Panathenaic Stadium: preparing the track and providing seating on the sides of the hills on either side of it. In a manner typical of his modesty and directness, Averōf responded immediately, saying he would do "all he could": in fact, he donated over half a million drachmas. Indeed, he continued to add to that sum as work progressed, finally giving 900,000 drachmas (900,000 gold francs), three times the total of all other donations.

[21]Skiadas, *100 chronia neoterē . . .* , pp. 76–78.

The decision to build a stadium on the site of a previous ancient one in Athens brought with it both the advantages and disadvantages of modern Greece's singleminded orientation toward antiquity. The project of restoring the ancient stadium, rather than building a modern one, carried with it undeniable cachet since it signaled the symbolic restoration of precisely the antiquity whose revival the modern Olympics were meant to celebrate. The Greeks also believed that such a move would serve them well in the eyes of international observers. "Since the foreigners wish to hold Olympic Games . . . these should take place in the Panathenaic Stadium, as they did in the fourth and fifth centuries BC," argued a member of the organizing committee. Averōf wrote that he hoped that the restored stadium would function as a starting-point for the renewal of Greece's "national forces" and the realization of "its national dreams." The great philanthropist also hoped it would satisfy the philhellenes, who by honoring ancient Greece were also honoring modern Greece.[22]

Unfortunately, the ancient stadium's restoration was done too faithfully, at the expense of its capacity to function as a modern sports arena. The architect, Anastasios Metaxas, relied on archeological excavations that had already taken place in 1873 by Ernst Ziller (1837–1923). Classicists also advised Metaxas. They tried to recreate the stadium's original shape when it was first built by Herod Atticus (101–178 CE) on the site of an older athletic field in 131 CE. The outcome was an impressive set of stands on either side but a very narrow, horseshoe-shaped, running track. The sharpness of the curve made it difficult for runners in any race longer than 100 meters. To be faithful to the original, Metaxas decided the stands should be made of marble, excavated from nearby Mount Pentelē. A more rational expenditure would have produced a swimming pool, which, as it turned out, was a glaring deficiency of the 1896 games. The organizers built a velodrome in Piraeus and a shooting range, but they decided that the swimming events would take place in what turned out to be the freezing waters of the Bay of Falēron. Despite its sharp horseshoe curve, the Panathenaic Stadium survived as a venue for track and field in the Athens area well into the twentieth century. Ultimately, Karaïskakēs Stadium, built on the site of the old velodrome, overshadowed the venerable Panathenaic Stadium, at least as a sports venue (possessing the shape and surface of a modern track, it hosted the European track and field championships in 1969).

[22] *Ibid.*, pp. 80–81.

The issue of commemorative stamps—which inaugurated a long tradition of commemoration and collection of Olympic memorabilia—was inevitably another exercise in harping on ancient Greek themes. The purpose of the issue was to raise money, and indeed it yielded 400,000 drachmas, the second highest overall sum after Averōf's contribution. It included twelve categories of stamps showing eight depictions of ancient Greek sporting motifs. The issue signaled the beginning of a long tradition of Greek stamps commemorating subsequent Olympic Games. Other countries soon joined in, beginning with Belgium on the occasion of the 1920 Antwerp Olympiad. (In 1982, the IOC formed the International Philately Federation in order to promote the Olympic Games. By the late twentieth century, the commemoration of the Olympics had spread to numismatics and lapel pins, both of which gained wide popularity.)

Concerns with antiquity, however, were accompanied by concerns with presenting a modern, European face to foreign visitors. The preparations made by the city of Athens were strongly influenced by the imperative of showing that the Greek capital was a European city. The municipality of Athens tried to make the city as presentable as possible. It sprayed the unpaved roads with water several times a day to control the dust (asphalt was not used in Athens until a later date), installed more lighting in public spaces, painted lampposts, and built public lavatories and obliged storeowners to provide bathroom facilities. Prices for horse-drawn carriages, restaurants, and hotel and rented rooms were fixed in order to prevent locals from charging excessive amounts. The Athens police were clothed in new uniforms, and they could rely on the help of fifty officers, reassigned from their posts in the provinces, whose knowledge of a foreign language earned them a temporary posting in the capital. Not known for their good manners, the Athens police also sat through a lecture on dealing with incidents involving foreigners and other out-of-towners, especially diaspora Greeks. Local businessmen did their part as well to ensure that the city had enough to eat; butchers ordered a total of two thousand lambs from the provinces. Athens's only brewery, Fix, imported machinery from abroad in order to raise its daily production.[23]

The preparations of the Greek athletes, finally, show a sporting culture caught between its ingrained respect for antiquity and the need to focus on modern realities. The major track-and-field event of 1895 took place not in

[23]Skiadas, *100 chronia neoterē* . . . , pp. 80–81 and 97–103; Politēs, *Olympiakoi Agōnes tou 1896* . . . , pp. 38–41; for the impressions of an American traveler, see Burton Holmes, *The Olympian Games in Athens, 1896*, Grove Press, New York, 1984.

Athens but, oddly enough, on the island of Tēnos. This was because the meet was held in conjunction with that island's famous annual celebration of the Dormition of the Virgin. This venue, of course, was deemed logical, despite the lack of facilities on the island, since the ancient Olympics were also part of a religious festival. Soon, however, with the Olympics approaching, and with rising concerns about how Greek athletes would do, preparations took on a distinctly more modern tone. Kōnstantinos Manos, a member of the organizing committee, traveled to Britain to learn the best training methods. He returned with a mix of useful as well as superficial ideas that led to mis-understandings with other officials, including Fōkianos, during the track-and-field trials that took place two weeks before the opening of the games. Manos had noted some innovations that proved helpful in terms of condi-tioning athletes for competition. But he also sought to imitate English meth-ods blindly. Deeming the diet of Greek athletes inappropriate, he decided that they should take their meals at one of Athens's leading restaurants, the Averōf, and be served red meat and beer. All of his methods grated with the elderly Fōkianos, who retained his preference for non-competitive physical training based on the German model. Undeterred, Manos, an appointee of the crown prince, tried to introduce another element into Greek practice that he had picked up from the English: a definition of "amateurism" so restric-tive that it excluded many athletes who were not from the upper classes and, therefore, had to work, albeit in jobs that were unrelated to the sports they pursued. In the face of much protest, the IOC intervened and obliged Manos to relax his criteria, which prevented unrest from boiling over.[24]

The painful birth pangs of modern sporting practices in no way over-shadowed the abiding fascination with ancient Greece. The marathon caught the public's imagination: this modern race exemplified the constructed nature of the Olympic revival. In antiquity, after the Athenians had defeated the Persians at Marathon, they sent a runner to Athens to report the victory. The inclusion of a competition based on that historic event caught the imag-ination of many Greek runners on the eve of the 1896 Olympics. After the trial marathon, more and more prospective runners made their intentions known through the press, which took up their cause, and persuaded the organizing committee to hold another trial on the eve of opening day. Eighty-five hopefuls registered for the race although only thirty-eight started in an

---

[24]Paulos N. Manitakēs, *100 chronia neoellēnikou athlētismou 1830–1930* [*100 Years of Mod-ern Greek Athletics, 1830–1930*], Athens, 1962, pp. 47–49.

attempt to surpass or equal the winning time of 3 hours, 18 minutes, run at the Pan-Hellenic trials by Charilaos Vasilakos, an unaffiliated athlete. Ultimately, four runners ran faster, while another was only 27 seconds behind and a sixth was a minute and 15 seconds behind; all six were allowed to compete in the games. The fifth runner was Spyros Louēs.[25]

THE ROLE OF ATHENS IN THE REVIVAL

The city of Athens, the actual physical space that evoked ancient glories, was an important factor in making the revival of the Olympics more realistic and contributed, ultimately, to the Greeks' desire to hold the games permanently in their capital. Athens itself had been "revived" when independent Greece emerged out of the Ottoman empire. Neoclassical architecture, a style that dominated the city's main public buildings, sought to associate modern Athens with its celebrated ancient past.[26] In their preparations for the Olympics, the authorities tried their best to echo that strategy in the ways they incorporated the city and its sites into the games. In this, they had the approval and support of many foreigners, who grew enchanted with Athens during their stay and, in a sense, helped legitimize the Greek concept of a revival of ancient Greece being possible only in Greece.

The spread of the modern city at the time of the Olympics had not obscured the ancient monuments, least of all the Acropolis high on its hill, and this meant that the classical past could not be missed. An early twentieth-century American travel writer, Philip Sanford Marden, wrote in 1907:

> Athens has been so fortunate as to retain many of her ancient structures in such shape that even today a very good idea is to be had of their magnificence in the golden age of Hellenic Empire. The Greek habit of building temples in high places, apart from the dwellings of men, has contributed very naturally to the preservation of much that might otherwise have been lost. The chief attractions of the classic city were set on high, and the degenerate modern town that succeeded the ancient capital did not entirely swallow them up, as was so largely the case at Rome.[27]

[25] *Ibid.*, pp. 55–56.
[26] See Eleni Bastéa, *The Creation of Modern Athens: Planning the Myth*, Cambridge University Press, Cambridge, 1999.
[27] Philip Sanford Marden, *Greece and the Aegean Islands*, Houghton Mifflin, Boston, 1907, p. 77.

After traveling to Athens in 1904 and visiting the Acropolis, Sigmund Freud produced a typically complex text analyzing his reactions, which were triggered by the sense of awe Freud felt when he found himself at the ancient site and realized that all he had read about really did exist. He explained the excitement in the following way: "When first one catches sight of the sea, crosses the ocean and experiences as realities cities and lands which for so long had been distant, unattainable things of desire—one feels oneself like a hero who has performed deeds of improbable greatness."[28]

The hosts did their best to accentuate the city's ancient heritage and highlight the connection between the modern and ancient Olympics. The main streets had flags and shields with "O.A. [*Olympiakoi Agōnes*/Olympic Games] 776 BC–1896 AD" inscribed on them. The Acropolis was lighted every evening; ancient Greek drama was performed in the main theaters. The ancient heritage was also present everywhere in the games themselves. The names of all officials were those used in antiquity, and the events, aside from the marathon, included the discus, with which only a few Europeans were familiar, and the stone throw, which only the Greeks practiced. There was a compromise between the ancient protocol of recognizing only the winner of each race and the contemporary practice of recording the sequence of all finalists. The winners were awarded a silver medal (gold was considered too ostentatious), while those in second place received bronze; both were crowned by an olive branch cut from trees in Olympia. The medals bore ancient Greek motifs, with the head of Zeus on one side and the Acropolis on the other. The diplomas received by the winners featured the Parthenon.

Most of the foreigners who visited Athens for the 1896 Olympiad describe a sense of awe and excitement, accentuated by the circumstances of the revival of the Olympics. For American athlete Ellery Clark, "the flavor of the Athenian soil—the feeling of helping to bridge the gap between the old and the new—the indefinable poetic charm of knowing one's self thus linked to the past, a successor to the great heroic figures of olden times . . . there is but one first time in everything, and that first time was gloriously, and in a manner ever to be remembered the privilege of the American team of 1896."[29]

Another American, Rufus Richardson, was caught up in the atmosphere exuded by ancient and modern Athens: "If it did not have the old setting at

[28]Sigmund Freud, "A Disturbance of Memory on the Acropolis," in *Collected Papers*, Volume V, The Hogarth Press, London, 1950, p. 311.
[29]Ellery H. Clark, *Reminiscences of an Athlete*, Houghton Mifflin, Boston, 1911, p. 140.

Olympia, which was the growth of ages, all that could be done to replace this was provided. The restored Panathenaic Stadion; the innumerable bands of music; concerts; illuminations at Athens and Piraeus; torchlight processions and fireworks; the presence of the royal family of Greece in the Stadion . . . gave something to replace Olympia, and almost persuaded one that the old times had come around again when there was nothing more serious to do than to outrun, out leap [*sic*] and outwrestle."[30]

The sense that Athens was the place where a revival of the past could occur had captivated many foreign athletes and spectators by the end of the games. At the closing ceremonies, Oxford athlete G. S. Robertson spontaneously recited an original ode in ancient Greek, in the style of Pindar, who had written famous odes to the ancient Olympics. More important, all the American athletes decided to submit a memorandum supporting the king's proposal that the games be held permanently in Greece. It contained a set of arguments that relied heavily on the idea that ancient Greek traditions were indigenous to modern Greece. The Americans justified their view on "the existence of the [Panathenaic] Stadion as a structure so uniquely adapted to its purpose; the proved ability of Greece to competently administer the games; and above all, the fact that Greece is the original home of the Olympic Games; all these considerations force upon us the conviction that these games should never be removed from their native soil."[31] Indeed, of all the international visitors, the American athletes, who were students, displayed the greatest awe and fascination with the ancient Greek dimension of the games.

PATRIOTISM AND INTERNATIONALISM

Greek national pride was much in evidence during the games, but so was a spirit of internationalism on the part of the hosts. In a sense, Greece becoming host to the rest of the world, or an important part of it at any rate, generated national pride. Two years earlier, Vikelas had told Greek students at the Sorbonne that by participating in the Olympic revival, Greece was becoming part of Europe. The population of Athens showed it shared this sentiment in 1896. More than a few foreign visitors noted the warm reception they received in Athens, both formally, through official welcoming events at

[30]Rufus Richardson, "The New Olympian Games," *Scribner's Magazine*, Volume 20, September 3, 1896, pp. 267–286.

[31]George S. Robertson, "The Olympic Games by a Competitor and Prize Winner," *Fortnightly Review*, 354, June 1, 1896, pp. 944–957.

the port of Piraeus and several banquets in Athens during the games, and informally, in the streets of the city and the stands of the Panathenaic Stadium. Clark described the welcome the Americans received in Piraeus as "magnificent."

Moreover, the display of Greek national pride during the opening ceremony contained elements of internationalism as well as images of ancient Greek heritage, although the opening day was chosen because it was Greek Independence Day. Before the games began, a service at the cathedral was attended by the royal family, the government, and the diplomatic corps. In the afternoon, a band saluted the king's arrival at the Panathenaic Stadium by playing the Greek national anthem. When the royal party took its places, Crown Prince Constantine, flanked by the organizing committee he had appointed fourteen months earlier, addressed his father, the head of state, asking him to formally open the games. Constantine spoke of how Greece had a duty to hold the games because they were born and flourished in Greece, and he also expressed his hope that the games would bring Greece closer to the civilized world and forge ties between its people and other peoples. When the king formally announced the games' opening, he added the words, "Long live the nation! Long live the Greek people!" This was followed by the playing of the *Olympic Hymn*, which was based on the words of a poem by a leading Greek poet, Kōstēs Palamas, which had been put to music by Greek composer Spyros Samaras. The hymn, which the IOC made a part of all opening ceremonies in 1958, opened with the lines, "Ancient immortal spirit, unsullied father of/that which is beautiful, great and true,/Descend, make thyself known and shine, hero, /on this earth and below these skies/witness of Thy Glory."[32]

Greek hopes for national triumph in some of the sporting events, especially in track and field, which was considered the most important competition, were initially muted but began to build as the games unfolded. Fourteen nations joined Greece at the first Olympics, although, as was also the case in subsequent Olympics, not all teams represented independent nations. Two national teams, Austria and Hungary, represented Austria-Hungary, and the organizers allowed Greek athletes from the British-ruled island of Cyprus and the Ottoman-ruled city of Smyrna (Izmir) to form their own national teams. A total of 245 men (and no women) participated in the events (some of them in more than one); over half of them (166) were Greeks. The novelty

[32]Skiadas, *100 chronia neoterē . . .* , pp. 90–91.

of the Olympics meant that several top performers in several sports chose not to participate, either because of uncertainties over the level of competition or lack of understanding of the competitive nature of this new institution. Whether or not the Greeks would take advantage of this situation remained to be seen.

The predominance of American athletes in the games would test the Greek crowd's attitude toward foreigners. On the first day, the student athletes from the United States quickly established their dominance. Harvard student James Connolly won the triple jump, with a Greek, Iōannēs Persakēs, coming in third. The next final was the discus throw, in which Princetonian Robert Garret overcame two Greek challengers, Panagiōtēs Paraskeuopoulos and Sōtērios Versēs. This was a disappointment for most of the spectators because the discus throw was a sport practiced by the Greeks, albeit in a style supposedly resembling that used in antiquity. It would be learned later that Garret had practiced with a much heavier discus made by history professor William Milligan Sloane, who had taken part in the Sorbonne conference and became the first US member of the International Olympic Committee.

On the second day, the Greeks had another close second-place, losing again to Garret, who was among the three Americans who won in track and field that day. Garret defeated Miltiadēs Gouskos in the shotput by the narrow margin of seventeen centimeters. Garret led from his first attempt, and Gouskos's best effort came in his last throw of 11 meters, 3 centimeters, longer than his record at the Pan-Hellenic games earlier that month (the crowd, thinking he had won, let out a big cheer). The 400-meter final followed, and Thomas Burke of the United States was the winner. Then came the 1,500-meter final, won by Australia's Edwin Flack. It was an eight-man race with four Greeks bringing up the rear.

By all accounts, the Greeks reacted to American victories warmly. Miss Maynard Butler was impressed by the Greek crowd's response to Garrett's narrow win over Paraskeuopoulos in the discus: "There is for a moment an uncomfortable silence, and then, with their accustomed politeness and never-failing kindliness, [the Greek crowd] joined the [American] cheers. Let every nation represented at this first international contest in 1896 remember this lesson in courtesy taught them by the Greeks."[33] Thomas Curtis, the winner of the 110-meter hurdle race, recounted how well the Greeks treated the

[33]Miss Maynard Butler, "The Olympic Games," *Outlook*, Volume 53, May 30, 1896, pp. 993–995.

American winners: "The Greek people, from high to low, treated us with great courtesy and friendliness. Sometimes their kindness was embarrassing. If we had won an event, our return to our quarters would be attended by admiring followers shouting '*Nike*—Victory!' Shopkeepers would herd us into their shops and invite us to help ourselves to their wares gratis."[34]

In one of the few accounts that downplay the Greek crowd's reactions, Richardson concedes that the applause was "generous."[35] And in a description of the games noted for its restraint in discussing the level of organization in Athens, the Oxford athlete Robertson noted nonetheless that "the Greek organizers dealt with foreign athletes throughout in the most sportsmanlike way."[36] Curtis also wrote about how fascinated the Greek crowd, including the royal family, was with the Boston Athletic Association's cheer— "B.A.A. Rah! Rah! Rah!"—shouted three times followed by the name of an athlete. The king asked the Boston athletes to repeat it in the stadium as well as at one of the banquets.

The first Greek victory in the Panathenaic Stadium came on the fourth day, in the ring event in gymnastics, held on the infield of the track.[37] After a split decision in which three judges placed Greece's Iōannēs Mētropoulos first and three judges scored Germany's Herman Weingartner first, Prince George of Greece cast the deciding vote in favor of Mētropoulos. This triggered cheers and applause that continued when the Greek flag was hoisted in honor of the victor. Weingartner did not leave Athens disappointed, however; he had already won two first-places with the German team in the parallel- and horizontal-bar events, came in third in the horse vault, and the next day won the horizontal-bar event. With the exception of Mētropoulos's win and Nikolaos Andriakopoulos's victory the following day in rope-climbing, the Germans dominated gymnastics.

The crowd's excitement was palpable on the fifth day because of the marathon, scheduled in the afternoon. Until that point, Greece had won a total of five first-places: Mētropoulos, Andriakopoulos, Iōannēs Geōrgiadēs in the saber competition, Leōnidas Pyrgos in foil for masters, and Pantelēs Karasevdas in the military-rifle competition. Greece would eventually win three

[34]Thomas P. Curtis, "High Hurdles and White Gloves," *The Sportsman*, Volume 12, July 1, 1931, pp. 60–61.

[35]Richardson, "The New Olympian Games," pp. 267–286.

[36]Robertson, "The Olympic Games," pp. 944–957.

[37]For all the results in the 1896 Olympics, see Bill Mallon and Ture Widlund, *The 1896 Olympic Games: Results for All Competitors in All Events, with Commentary*, McFarland & Company, Jefferson, 1998.

more events: Geōrgios Orfanidēs in freestyle rifle-shooting, Iōannēs Frangoudēs in pistol-shooting, and Iōannēs Malokinēs in 100-meter freestyle swimming (this latter event, by the way, was open only to members of the Greek navy and its listing as an official Olympic competition is a little odd). Nevertheless, there had been no victories in the most popular category of sport, track and field, which was closely associated with ancient Greece. There was a particularly large and expectant crowd on hand in the stadium. The crowd's size and excitement contributed to an especially enthusiastic welcome for the royal family and its guest, the king of Serbia, upon their arrival. The events began with the final of the 100-meter race won by Thomas Burke of the Boston Athletic Association; the Greek runner Alexandros Chalkokondylēs came in fifth and last. Ellery Clark, also of the BAA, who had won the long jump on the second day, won the high jump (there had been no Greek competitor either in this event or in the 110-meter hurdles won by Curtis). A little before the marathon leaders were due to finish in the stadium, the pole vaulting had begun with the participation of two Americans and three Greeks. The Americans, Welles Hoyt and Albert Tyler, came first and second, respectively; they were so superior that they began jumping at the height that the Greeks failed to clear. The event was interrupted, however, by the pandemonium caused by the marathon's finish, and was completed later that day.

The eruption of Greek national pride at Louēs's victory understandably overshadowed the internationalist spirit of the hosts. The crowd's anticipation a little before the end of the marathon is recorded in many sources. In his memoirs, Ellery Clark confirms the atmosphere of expectation in the stadium. "The Greeks," he wrote, "seemed to feel that the national honor was at stake; the excitement was so great as to be almost painful; and on all sides we heard the cry, 'The other events to the Americans; the Marathon [*sic*] to a Greek.'"[38]

The connection the Greeks felt to the marathon is just another example of how deeply emotions ran when there was an issue of continuity with the past, even though its "construction" was blatant. There was a battle of Marathon in 490 BCE, but no marathon race in antiquity, nor had such a race ever been held anywhere before 1896. It was the idea of another Frenchman, Michel Bréal, who had accompanied his friend Coubertin to Greece in 1895. Bréal, a true romantic admirer of ancient Greece, said he would be glad to offer a prize if the organizing committee revived the run made by the soldier

[38]Ellery H. Clark, *Reminiscences . . .* , p. 137.

from Marathon to Athens to announce the victory over the Persians. The Greeks loved the idea because it fused athletics with the revival of something that was part of a famous Greek victory. The first person to complete the 42-kilometer (26-mile) race was Geōrgios Grēgoriou, an athlete of the *Ethnikos* club, who did a practice run on February 11, 1896. It is thanks to him that the organizing committee realized how bad the road was and took measures to improve it. On March 10, a marathon was run as part of the Pan-Hellenic trials with twelve contestants. The winner, Spyros Belokas, would come third to Louēs in the Olympics although he would later be disqualified, apparently for taking a carriage for a short part of the race.

Louēs's victory set off days of celebrations. Several authors, including Coubertin, mention the spontaneous offers of gifts that Louēs received that day and for many days afterward. Coubertin wrote about a golden bracelet unfastened by a lady on the spot and given to Louēs, and other sources provide a list of the goods and services donated to him. The Greek who came second, Charilaos Vasilakos, also received many similar gifts. The crowd had a final opportunity to salute Louēs and the other victors during the award ceremonies that were held on the final day. (The awards were made on the final day because that was how it had been done in antiquity.) In addition to the medals and olive branches for first and second places, all participants received commemorative medals and diplomas. A large crowd generously applauded the athletes. It was then that Robertson spontaneously recited his Pindaric-style Olympic ode and received an award from King George.

Greece as the permanent site?

Two days after Louēs's victory, the king gave a speech at the palace at a reception for athletes and administrators. He concluded with a controversial suggestion: "Greece, the mother and nurturer of gymnastic games in antiquity, took on these Games and organized them courageously before the eyes of Europe and the New World. Now that their success has been acknowledged, Greece can hope that the foreigners who have honored it would designate the country as the peaceful meeting-place of nations and continuous and permanent venue of the Olympic Games."[39] Most of those present greeted the proposal positively, with one significant exception: Coubertin.

Coubertin opposed Greece's bid for the Olympics even though the king's

---

[39]Manitakēs, *100 chronia neoellēnikou athlētismou . . .*, p. 65.

announcement had not come as a total surprise. The Greeks had consistently ignored the baron and the IOC in preparing the Olympiad and proceeded to do likewise throughout the games. Coubertin's biographer claims that "nationalism and factional interest dictated that Coubertin would be eliminated from the picture"[40] and that the Greeks had misrepresented Coubertin's attitude toward the Germans as an excuse to sideline the IOC during the preparations. The Greek royal family was pro-German, and it might have reacted unreasonably to false claims that Coubertin did not wish to include the Germans in the games. It is, however, important to add that the organizers' sense that broad international participation was guaranteed meant that, in some way, Coubertin had become redundant. Displaying poor taste, the organizers continued to refuse to acknowledge Coubertin and his IOC colleagues whenever possible throughout the Athens Olympiad. As the baron put it, "the efforts that the Greeks made to 'suppress' me at every occasion hurt, though they came as no surprise. The changes that were occurring in their minds made their attitude understandable, sincere, even excusable. . . . [T]hey were preparing to lay claim to the exclusive possession of the Olympic Games." Indeed, Coubertin claims that his isolation enabled him to evaluate the Greek proposal more dispassionately: "Given the sort of mental solitude I had been left, I had plenty of opportunity to examine the basis of these aspirations. . . . [T]o me they seemed utterly unreasonable, from the point of view of the institution itself and of the goal that I sought in restoring the Games."[41]

Looking around him, Coubertin considered the attendance at the games insufficiently international. He noted that Greece was relatively isolated from the rest of Europe in terms of transport. He also reflected on the economic burdens that regularly held Olympics would place on Greece, as well as the possible political problems. It did not take him long to make up his mind: "I was quickly convinced that locating the seat of Olympism permanently and exclusively in Greece meant suicide for my work." Coubertin thus geared up for the struggle to defend his work, resolving "to fight with all my strength against the obstacles that had sprung up in [my] path, in the space of a few days."[42]

The Greek side backed down easier than Coubertin anticipated because it could not afford to alienate him or the international Olympic movement,

[40]MacAloon, *This Great Symbol . . .*, p. 203.

[41]Coubertin, *Olympism: Selected Writings*, edited by Norbert Muller, International Olympic Committee, Lausanne, 2000, p. 348.

[42]*Ibid.*, p. 348.

and thus lose the legitimacy conferred on it by "Europe." The organizers had probably overestimated the numbers of participants and spectators from abroad. We have already noted the absence of several leading European athletes. Most probably, in the cold light of the day after, the organizers realized that they still needed Coubertin to sustain the international scope of the Olympic revival. Their nationalism was tempered, after all, by the need to preserve the internationalist dimension of the Olympics. One should also not forget that, in political and diplomatic terms, Greece remained in conflict with the Ottoman empire over their mutual boundary in northern Greece, as well as the status of Crete, so that the continued goodwill of the Western powers remained a major consideration for the country.

Coubertin wrote that, before he left Athens, Crown Prince Constantine, upon the baron's suggestion, had "limited himself to the idea of Pan Hellenic Olympiads."[43] Whether this was a tactical move or a genuine retreat by the Greek royal family, the point is that the prince knew only too well that Greece could not ignore international opinion. Without international approval, the Greeks would not dare to take the initiative of organizing the Olympics on their own, since they were as dependent on international validation as the revival of the Olympics were on ancient Greece.

[43] *Ibid.*, p. 421.

CHAPTER 3

THE ATHENS INTERIM OLYMPICS OF 1906

THE INTERIM OLYMPIC GAMES, held in Athens in 1906, were the outcome of a compromise reached by Baron de Coubertin and Greece. Even though Crown Prince Constantine had told Coubertin at the end of the 1896 Olympiad that Greece would drop its claims to hosting the games on a permanent basis and organize, instead, a form of interim games in Athens, both sides hoped they could gain an advantage. Coubertin believed he could force the Greeks to desist from holding any type of games in Athens, while the Greeks still clung to the possibility of becoming the permanent hosts. What in fact happened, as both sides jockeyed for position after the 1896 games, was that both ran into serious difficulties. The Olympic movement faltered, burdened by the poor organization of both the second Olympiad in Paris in 1900 and the third Olympiad in St. Louis in 1904. For its part, Greece suffered a stinging defeat in a war against the Ottomans that it initiated in 1897, which resulted in its national finances being placed under international control. What did not change was Greece's continued, self-perceived need to acquire a positive international profile. This functioned as a guarantee of its ongoing commitment to the broadest possible international Olympics. The outcome was a compromise that returned things back to where they had been at the moment Coubertin and the Greek prince spoke at the end of the 1896 games: Greece would be permitted to hold intercalary or interim Olympics, the year for the first such games being fixed for 1906, chronologically between the St. Louis games of 1904 and the games scheduled in Rome in 1908, which in fact were held in London because of the disastrous eruption that year of Mt. Vesuvius, which caused great disruption in Italy.

The 1906 Olympics are a calendrical anomaly of twentieth-century sport, if for no other reason than they turned out to be the only intercalary Olympiad ever held. The second interim games should have taken place in

Athens in 1910, but the political turbulence in Greece at the time precluded such a possibility, as the country had just experienced a coup that ushered into power the liberal Venizelos, who immediately embarked upon a program of far-reaching social reform that did not allow much consideration for sport. There was not even any planning for interim Olympics in 1914 since Greece had just emerged from the Balkan Wars of 1912–1913, through which it had acquired considerable territories at the expense of the Ottoman empire, including the city of Thessalonikē, but had lost its ability to summon the resources required to plan and organize athletic competitions. After the First World War, the issue of the interim Olympics was quietly dropped.

Precisely because they were held only once, and went very well, several voices have been raised in favor of according them recognition as "official" rather than "intercalary" Olympics. Reflecting Coubertin's discontent with holding these games, the International Olympic Committee did not consider them "official." Yet, long after they ended, the status of the 1906 games was disputed. IOC members eventually came back to the debate in 1948 and rejected a motion to recognize the 1906 games as official Olympic Games. Thus, the games of 1906 remain known as the "intercalary" or interim Olympics. Nonetheless, contemporary observers, and others writing at a later date, have also acknowledged that the success of the 1906 Olympics made a crucial contribution to the fledgling Olympic movement, which had suffered in the wake of the badly organized Olympiads in Paris and St. Louis. Historians, meanwhile, differ widely in their assessments and treatment of the role of the interim games in the evolution of the Olympics. Olympics scholar Allen Guttmann, for example, devotes less than a page to them in his standard history of the Olympics.[1] In contrast, John Findling and Kimberly Pelle treat the 1906 games as equal to all the officially recognized games in their historical dictionary of the Olympics, and Mark Dyreson does the same in his study of American sports culture and the early Olympics.[2] Greek authors, inevitably, treat the 1906 games as official at least in spirit and devote considerable space to recounting not only the events but their successful organization and positive impact.[3]

[1]Allen Guttmann, *The Olympics: A History of the Modern Games*, University of Illinois Press, Urbana, 1992, p. 27.

[2]John E. Findling and Kimberly D. Pelle, *Historical Dictionary of the Modern Olympic Movement*, Greenwood Press, Westport, 1996; Mark Dyreson, *Making the American Team: Sport, Culture, and the Olympic Experience*, University of Illinois Press, Urbana, 1998.

[3]Manitakēs, *100 chronia neoellēnikou . . .* ; Skiadas, *100 chronia neoterē . . . .*

COUBERTIN'S MOVES, 1896–1905

When Coubertin bid adieu to the Greeks in 1896, he could never have suspected that, less than ten years later and despite his efforts to promote it, the Olympic movement would be, according to Guttmann, "on its last legs."[4] Moreover, he would have been incredulous—and perhaps even appalled—at the idea that the very Greeks who were threatening to take away his games would ultimately help the movement recover by organizing interim games. Coubertin left Athens determined to bolster the IOC and the institution of the Olympics, and he scored some early successes. He managed to strengthen the International Olympic Committee in a series of moves, while several major countries began establishing their own national committees. Whatever one thinks of the baron, one must concede that he displayed tremendous energies in pursuing his goals.

Coubertin and Vikelas began a correspondence aimed at reconciling the Greek view that Greece should hold the games permanently with the baron's rejection of that idea, with Vikelas pushing for the interim Olympics as the compromise. Vikelas agreed that Greece should not host the games permanently, but he rejected Coubertin's proposal that the interim games be called "Athenian Games." Vikelas stated that Greece had the right to the term "Olympic" since the Greeks had used it for the games funded by Zappas in Athens in 1859, 1870, and 1875; he assured Coubertin, however, that these games would not compete with Coubertin's Olympics.[5] Coubertin told a different story in his memoirs, depicting Vikelas as more confrontational and petitioning the IOC to approve "the creation of the Greek Olympiads, according them the same character and the same privileges as the international Olympiads."[6] The discrepancy in these accounts, more one of interpretation than difference of opinion, may well stem from Coubertin's opposition to the Greek plan whatever its status and content.

Following the exchanges between the two men, the issue was supposed to have been taken up at the Olympic congress in Le Havre in 1897. This second Olympic congress was not a decisionmaking body, but something akin to an academic conference, an occasion for the International Olympic Committee's members to meet formally. The congress was held to discuss issues of sport hygiene and pedagogy, and to legitimize the Olympic committee as

[4]Guttmann, *The Olympics* . . . , p. 27.
[5]Young, *The Modern Olympics* . . . , pp. 164–165.
[6]Coubertin, *Olympism* . . . , p. 365.

a major administrative factor in international sport. Vikelas, meanwhile, had stepped down, but the new Greek member of the IOC, Alexandros Merkatēs, did not come to Le Havre. Coubertin understandably did not raise the issue of the Greek proposal. He had envisioned this particular congress as a session devoted to the more abstract principles of the modern Olympics. In the event, as the baron himself noted, he was not prepared to permit the 1897 congress to overturn the decisions of the 1894 congress and weaken the IOC or, worse still, "to allow it to fall into something of a vassal relationship to the Greek organization." Any revision of Olympic regulations would be unwise at a time when "the political horizon in the east was growing dark, and who knew if Greece, a year later, would still be talking about holding games in the future at all?"[7]

The congress went according to Coubertin's plans, providing the baron with the opportunity to turn away from his philhellenism and embrace the other pillar of his original conception of the games, English sporting culture. The high point of the proceedings as far as he was concerned was a speech "in a French of the greatest purity" by an English delegate, the Reverend Courcy Laffan, on the moral value of sport. This new turn, coupled with the absence of the Greeks, led Coubertin to comment thirty-four years later that "the Hellenism that had permeated the atmosphere of this first Congress in 1894 started to fade before the influence of England."[8]

The successful congress at Le Havre, however, was followed by a series of organizational difficulties that plagued the Paris Olympiad of 1900. The French sports authority, the *Union des Sociétés Francaises des Sports Athlétiques* (USFSA), initially showed no interest in collaborating with the IOC in organizing the games, so Coubertin had to use his influence in his country's governing circles to secure an agreement that the games would be part of the *Exposition Universelle* to be held in Paris in 1900, an exhibition designed to showcase the achievements of French civilization. The problems continued, however. The organizers of the exhibition disliked the idea of including sports, while suddenly the USFSA decided it would take charge after all, and sidelined the IOC. Worse yet, the games, which included several distinctly unathletic contests such as a fireman's drill, were spread out over two months and were so marginal to the main event of the exposition that many people were unaware they were even taking place. The conclusion of this series of

[7] *Ibid.*, p. 365.
[8] *Ibid.*, p. 372.

fiascos left the IOC embarrassed and Coubertin vulnerable to attack. James Sullivan (1862–1914), an important and ambitious sports administrator in the United States, declared the IOC defunct and announced that the next Olympics would be organized by his organization, the American Athletic Union.[9]

Alexandros Merkatēs had not remained inactive, but had worked discreetly to persuade IOC members that Greece should hold interim Olympic Games; he ultimately extracted concessions from Coubertin, who reluctantly agreed. A childhood friend of Crown Prince Constantine, Merkatēs also had other advantages that suited him for the post of Greek member of the IOC. He hailed from a noble Florentine family (he held the title of count) that had settled on the Ionian island of Zante (Zakynthos), which was incorporated into Greece in 1862. A cosmopolitan aristocrat, he fit in well with the rest of the IOC, of which he was a member through 1927. (He was evidently less comfortable with his fellow Greeks. The Nobel Prize-winning poet Geōrgios Seferēs noted in his diary in 1938 that Merkatēs, an aide-de-camp to King George II at the time, was incredulous that the inhabitants of a village in Attica had requested that the king's train stop at their little station so that they could cheer him. "I'd prefer the train runs them down," he exclaimed.)[10]

Merkatēs's work bore fruit. Meeting in Paris in 1901, the IOC agreed on interim games to be held in Athens in 1906. The proposal had come from three German members, who suggested a second series of games organized in Athens to take place between the regular series of Olympic Games. This German initiative on Greece's behalf presaged German actions a generation later when, in the context of the 1936 Berlin Olympiad, Germany's tradition of classicism and philhellenism would again work in Greece's favor.

The St. Louis Olympiad of 1904 represented yet another setback for the Olympic movement and seemed to justify the return of the games to Athens. After a dispute over whether they should be held in Chicago or St. Louis, the games became a series of events that were on the periphery of another world's fair, this one to mark the centennial of the Louisiana Purchase. The Olympic events were stretched out for months, from May to November; even worse, they included two "anthropological days" during which the organizers persuaded exhibitors at the fair who were from Africa, Asia, and the Americas to

[9]Guttmann, *The Olympics . . .* , pp. 21–25.
[10]Geōrgios Seferēs, *Politiko ēmerologio A' 1935–1944* [*Political Diary, Volume 1, 1935–1944*], Ikaros, Athens, 1979. p. 15.

perform their "native" sports and then try their untrained hand at the sports that were part of the Olympics. This blatantly racist exercise represented the nadir of the early phase of the Olympic movement.

Yet, Coubertin was still fighting the demons of the concept of Greece as a permanent host. By the time of the next Olympic congress in 1905, held in Brussels and called to discuss sport and physical education, the founder of the games began to feel more and more confident. Coubertin viewed the newly created British Olympic Association and its already-existing German equivalent as important allies: "London and Berlin now possessed permanent Olympic centers working with us and under us to a certain extent," he noted. "This placed us in a much stronger position with regard to Athens." This was crucial, he added, because "Our colleague Mercati [*sic*] had taken immediate advantage of the fact to establish closer relations, which the Crown Prince moreover had continued to favor as much as he could." There was reason to rejoice, albeit cautiously, according to Coubertin. The IOC session held during the 1905 congress "had succeeded in achieving the maximum Olympic peace that we had ever had." Nonetheless, he added darkly, this did not mean that "we had heard the last of our enemies."[11] Coubertin must also have been encouraged by the growth of the IOC; it had acquired twenty-five members by 1900, and had grown to thirty members by 1904, representing a broad array of nations from Europe and the Americas, potentially a formidable international alliance against a Greek "plot." Nonetheless, determined to distance himself from the interim games of 1906, Coubertin organized yet another Olympic congress, this one in Paris and timed to coincide with the opening of the games in Athens. The congress was centered on the arts, literature, and sport, and "precluded" Coubertin from being able to attend the Athens games.

TURN-OF-THE-CENTURY GREECE

Greece was in no position to take advantage of the IOC's troubles; it had suffered its own setbacks after the 1896 Olympics. In 1897, it went to war with the Ottomans, in support of a Greek uprising in Ottoman-ruled Crete. It was a war initiated by a nationalist group, the *Ethnikē Etaireia* (National Society), which had recklessly sent irregular troops across the Greek-Ottoman border into Macedonia, which was then also an Ottoman province.

[11]Coubertin, *Olympism . . .*, p. 413.

The Greek army followed in support of the irregulars, but the Greek offensive soon turned into a rout. Within a few weeks, the Ottoman counterattack drove deep into Greek territory; had the great powers not intervened, the beleaguered Greeks might have soon had to think about defending Athens. As a result of the war, the great powers placed Greece's finances under their control in order to prevent further military spending that would lead to more military campaigns.

Greece's defeat in 1897 took the wind out of the sails of the militant nationalists and returned the country to the type of modernization espoused by Trikoupēs. Militant nationalism was still a danger, but the logic of going to war in the name of territorial claims was abandoned. When an uprising in Macedonia in 1903 sparked regional nationalist rivalries, Athens was careful to send in irregular troops only, leaving the army on the Greek side of the frontier. Officially, Greece focused its effort on the diplomatic front rather than on the battlefield, appealing to the great powers for help in securing what it considered to be the Greek part of Macedonia. The first decade of the twentieth century saw moderate governments in Greece, prudently eschewing militant policies that would alienate the country from the great powers and dedicated instead to continuing the task of domestic modernization. Geōrgios Theotokēs (1844–1916), who became prime minister in 1899 at the age of fifty-five and governed for most of the first decade of the twentieth century, was ideally suited to reconcile the warring parties at a particularly turbulent moment in Greek history. There was pressure for modernization, continued disillusionment with the defeat of 1897 and its aftermath, turmoil in Macedonia, and social tensions that led to a series of violent public demonstrations in the capital. Theotokēs, who had served as a minister under Trikoupēs, avoided confrontation by working out political problems through copious backstage negotiations, managing to keep most politicians satisfied most of the time. He was also felicitously predisposed to combine his support for modernization with loyalty to the royal family, which also served to calm political passions.

Theotokēs's program of modernization included upgrading the country's sporting infrastructure by incorporating physical education into schooling and establishing the Hellenic Olympic Committee (HOC) officially as the *Epitropē Olympiakōn Agōnōn*, literally the "Olympic Games Committee," an interesting choice of words considering that all other national Olympic committees formed at the time included each country's name in their title, e.g.,

British Olympic Committee, *Comité National Olympique et Sportif Français,* *Sveriges Olympiska Kommitté,* and United States Olympic Committee.[12] The committee that had organized the 1896 games had ceased to function, and the purpose of this move was to make the new committee a permanent body. The legislation that established the HOC was introduced by the minister of church affairs and public education, Athanasios Eutaxias, in 1899 and confirmed by royal decree in 1900. The first committee had Crown Prince Constantine as its president and Athens University professor Spyridōn Lambros as its general secretary. The other nine members, appointed by royal decree, were all political figures. The legislation charged the HOC with overseeing the development of Greek sport, holding the annual Pan-Hellenic Games, and organizing the Olympic Games every four years—this latter responsibility either optimistically anticipating IOC approval of the interim Olympics or revealing the lingering hope that the games might be moved permanently to Greece. In any case, one of the HOC's first tasks was to lead the preparations for the 1906 games.[13]

Lambros (1851–1919), a nationalist who was politically aligned with the royal family, was the first to state publicly in 1897 that the spread of physical training would invigorate Greece and help it overcome the consequences of its recent defeat in war.[14] He served as the HOC's general secretary through 1917, when King Constantine I was forced to abdicate by the Allies because of his attempt to keep Greece neutral in the First World War in a policy that favored the Central Powers. (Constantine had dismissed Prime Minister Venizelos in 1915 because of the latter's pro-Allied stance. Lambros, who had not held any government posts until then, served as prime minister of the royalist government of 1916–1917, retaining his position on the HOC. When the Venizelists returned to power, they confiscated his property and exiled him to the island of Ydra in 1918 and later to the island of Skopelos. He died the following year.)

---

[12]The Greek committee, nonetheless, described itself as the HOC in English and, in 2000, officially changed its name to *Ellēnikē Olympiakē Epitropē,* bringing its Greek self-description into line with that of the other national committees throughout the world.

[13]For a basic history of the HOC, see Giōrgos Liverēs, *1894–1994. Ē istoria tēs Epitropēs Olympiakōn Agōnōn tēs Ellados* [*1894–1994: The History of the Hellenic Olympic Committee*], HOC, Athens, 1995; for the HOC's history through its archives, see Christina Koulouri, editor, *Archeia kai istoria tēs Epitropēs Olympiakōn Agōnōn* [*Archives and History of the Hellenic Olympic Committee*], Athens, DOA, 2002.

[14]Spyridōn Lambros, *Logoi kai arthra 1878–1902* [*Speeches and Articles, 1878–1902*], Sakellariou, Athens, 1902, p. 637.

The games offered Greece another opportunity to stake its claim as an important factor in the international Olympic movement. As was the case a decade earlier, however, the hosts had to carefully balance their wish to promote Greece's status with the need to preserve international goodwill toward the country. This time, things were easier because there were no voices calling for Greece to become permanent host of the Olympics. Overall, the organizers managed the games very successfully and were also able to invest them with a spirit of Hellenism as well as internationalism. In considering Greece's role in the organization and hosting of the 1906 games, most scholars have agreed that it was fueled by a sense of patriotism and nationalism, the very sentiments that had generated the idea of Greece as the permanent Olympic site. John Lucas writes that the first Olympics and their success revived "a strong but latent Hellenic patriotism" that in turn led to calls for a permanent Olympics in Greece or Greek games between the quadrennial Olympiads.[15] Dyreson, based on the reports of the games published in *The Nation* by Dimitrios Karopothakis, writes, "Greece wanted to use the Olympics to display their national spirit."[16] One only has to remember that the defeat by the Ottomans combined with the international financial-control regime had produced a climate of pessimism among intellectuals and disillusionment in the public.

Nonetheless, it is important to understand that strengthening Greek national spirit during that particular era entailed preserving international goodwill rather than engaging in displays of national superiority. Greece wished to gain international status politically through organizing successful games. The 1906 games were primarily an opportunity to demonstrate to the world Greece's national virtues off the athletic field. Greece could proudly put itself on the map by organizing and hosting this important international athletic meet. Small countries can derive a great deal of national importance, if not international stature, by organizing such high-profile events. By organizing the games successfully, Greece stood a chance of convincing the international Olympic movement that it could hold intermediate games regularly or even become the permanent host of the Olympics. Whether or not Greeks celebrated athletic victories once the games got underway was a secondary consideration. What was far more important was that, first, the games take

---

[15]John Lucas, "American Involvement in the Athens Olympian Games of 1906," *Stadion*, Volume 6, 1908, p. 217.

[16]Dyreson, *Making the American Team . . .* , p 131.

place despite Coubertin's objections; second, that there be broad international participation; and, third, that foreign guests leave Athens with positive impressions from their stay.

Finally, one should note that there was actually no chance that Greece could use this occasion to bolster national pride through athletic dominance. That was a privilege of developed countries such as the United States. Dyreson has written that "The United States was in Athens to demonstrate its national superiority."[17] Greece was hardly able to match the Europeans and North Americans on the field, and thus its own sense of pride was contingent on its ability to ensure wide international participation in the games and to ensure that they ran smoothly. This was neither an exercise in affirming physical superiority or an inward-looking self-celebration of Greek national character.

Still, Greek pride was involved, but it did not spill over into any unrealistic expectations of Greek athletic predominance. An editorial writer of the Athens daily *Astrapē* reflected this pragmatism when he wrote that "this celebration has its origins in Ancient Greece, this proud source of civilization. . . . [T]his celebration is now being revived today in Athens, in the Panathenaic stadium. . . . [A]ncient Greece rises from the ashes of the past." The foreign competitors, wrote the editorialist, would sense the glories of the past more directly by their presence in Greece. "They are discovering the place in which Ancient glories flowered . . . they gaze on the Ancient gods face to face . . . everything around them is alive as it was in that era. . . ." But when he went on to consider the actual competition, the writer was more restrained. He warned his readers that because Greeks had lived under slavery and barbarism for many centuries between the glorious past and the present, they did not yet have the right to consider themselves equal to their foreign friends on the playing field. Consequently, he called upon Greeks to imitate the athletic examples set by foreigners.[18]

PLANNING THE 1906 OLYMPICS

Crown Prince Constantine gave the signal for the preparations for 1906 to start in earnest at a special meeting of the Hellenic Olympic Committee in

---

[17] *Ibid.*, pp. 131–32.

[18] Kōnstantinos Syrrakos, *Olympiakoi Agōnes* [*Olympic Games*], Eurotyp, Athens, 1984, p. 234.

October 1905 attended by the minister of education, the mayors of Athens and Piraeus, and the Greek Orthodox metropolitan (archbishop) of Athens. In his speech, the prince stressed the pure "Greekness" of athleticism and the institution of the Olympics, and he urged everyone present to work for the success of the games in Athens.[19] Yet, in rallying patriotism, the crown prince was calling upon the Greeks to work toward not only well-organized games but international ones as well.

A large part of the preparations for the games involved contacts with other countries in order to ensure and facilitate their participation. This was a time when national Olympic committees (NOCs) were only just being formed. Iōannēs Chrysafēs traveled through Europe in August 1905 to talk to government officials and sports administrators. The Hellenic Olympic Committee also contacted railroad and steamship companies, to request reduced fares for the athletes visiting Athens for the games, and the companies responded positively. As for the preparations themselves, they ranged from infrastructural work at the major athletic facilities to the more symbolic but important task of producing commemorative postage stamps.

The considerable work undertaken by the organizers to establish committees in several countries to ensure athletic participation from abroad is a good example of the efficiency of the preparations. With the help of Greek embassies and consulates around the world, the HOC established committees composed of local sports administrators in fourteen countries: Austria-Hungary, Belgium, Britain, Egypt, France, Germany, Italy, the Ottoman empire, Romania, Russia, Spain, Sweden, Switzerland, and the United States. In many cases, the leading members were also the leaders of their respective NOCs. They had to ensure each country's participation since the IOC could not be relied upon to ensure either widespread participation or funding. In April 1905, the Greek ambassador in London informed the Olympic committee in Athens that it was his impression that the IOC, albeit divided between supporters and opponents of Coubertin's view of the interim games, would not be offering any logistical assistance.[20]

The organizers were so eager to ensure the widest possible international participation that they were even willing to ignore contemporary conflicts in the Balkans. Five months before the interim Olympics were scheduled to open in Athens in April 1906, the HOC wrote to the Greek foreign ministry

[19]Manitakēs, *100 chronia neoellēnikou . . .* , p. 161.
[20]Skiadas, *100 chronia neoterē . . .* , pp. 159–161.

asking it to help in securing the widest participation of "all governments."
The organizers were so eager to achieve this goal that there was even discussion about inviting Bulgaria, a neighboring country with which Greece was
virtually at war over the future of Ottoman-controlled Macedonia.[21] Ultimately, the foreign ministry decided against inviting Bulgaria. Nevertheless,
the joint efforts of the HOC and the ministry ensured an impressive range of
foreign participants.

The correspondence between Lambros and James Sullivan, who became
the secretary of the American committee, illustrates the extraordinary
lengths to which the Greeks went in order to ensure the participation of
American athletes. The HOC's activities in the US got off to a bad start when
it asked the Greek consul in Chicago, Nicholas Salsopoulos, to establish a
committee there. After the consul managed to create a group headed by the
future mayor, William Hale Thompson, who was also president of the
Chicago Athletic Association, the HOC changed its mind and asked that the
committee be absorbed into one formed by Consul Dēmētrios Botasēs in
New York under Sullivan's leadership. Most of the Chicago committee members ultimately refused this indignity and the Hellenic Olympic Committee
went ahead with the New York group, with Sullivan as its secretary and
sportswriter Casper Whitney as president.

Sullivan, who was still secretary of the Amateur Athletic Union, was an
effective leader of the American Committee of the Olympian Games at
Athens. He managed to raise $10,000, which enabled twenty athletes to travel
to the city. Among those making large donations were J. Pierpont Morgan,
George J. Gould, S. R. Guggenheim, and August Belmont. The HOC donated
another $2,000, allowing ten more Americans to travel to Greece. The
American committee selected the team following trials in February. Sullivan
was pleased with the selections and wrote Lambros, "I feel very proud indeed
of this team. . . . I think this is one of the best teams sent by America to compete in any country . . . we are sending you the best men we can. . . ."[22] The
Greeks were even more impressed when Sullivan secured the support of President Theodore Roosevelt, who became the American committee's honorary
president.

While Sullivan was an enthusiastic proponent of US participation in the
Athens Olympics, he was also a demanding one. Soon after the American

[21]HOC Archives, k4/f11/1905; k4/f4/1905.
[22]Ibid., k14/f5/p. 22/1906.

committee was formed, he asked if the games could be postponed until later that year because March and April were inconvenient for most American student athletes.[23] This was not possible, but the HOC was happy to accommodate Sullivan's additional request that no event take place on opening day because it fell on a Sunday. Consul Botasēs, writing to Lambros in December 1905, noted that Whitney felt so strongly about this that he had threatened to resign from the committee if any events were scheduled on a Sunday. "You are aware, sir," Botasēs pointed out, "how strictly the Sunday holiday is observed in the Anglo-Saxon countries."[24] Lambros responded quickly, saying that no events would be scheduled on Sunday, and that the program that day would include only the ceremonial opening and certain gymnastic exhibitions.

In late March, Sullivan, already in London en route to Athens, wrote to Lambros to suggest ways in which the hosts could improve the facilities available to the press. American journalists told Sullivan that the existing arrangements made dispatches from the Panathenaic Stadium difficult and also that the Greek government charged "exorbitant" prices for cables. He suggested special rates for journalists. Sullivan knew how to play on Greek sensitivities. He added: "I realize fully that you will grasp the importance of this, because it would mean a great deal to the Greeks to have the Olympic games exploited in all of the American and English papers. . . . [I]n that way the games would become historical and if at any time in future you desire to repeat the games of 1906, and I understand it is your intention to have them at intervals of two years, you can readily understand that publicity in the papers before and after will mean a great deal."[25]

In the midst of all the preparations, Sullivan wrote Lambros that his wife and children, who were "enjoying a rest" in Nice in February, planned to travel to Athens to attend the games. Because they would arrive before him, he requested Lambros to "have some one look out for them and see they reach their destination in safety," offering to do the same should any of Lambros's friends ever visit New York.[26] Again, the hosts were happy to oblige, and they even went as far as to invite some of the American athletes who had distinguished themselves in the games of 1896 to come to Athens.

There were limits to how far the organizers could go in meeting Sullivan's

[23] *Ibid.*, k6/f3/p. 20/1905.
[24] *Ibid.*, k6/f4/p. 18/1905.
[25] *Ibid.*, k14/f5/p. 28/1906.
[26] *Ibid.*, k6/f4/p. 9/1906.

numerous wishes, however. The HOC had accommodated a British request for a five-mile run to be included in the program, but it was unable to accede to Sullivan's request to add a 220-yard run and a 220-yard race over hurdles that were 2½ feet in height, both of which Sullivan described as "standard events in America."[27] This request had been made only a month before the games, while the announcement of the five-mile run had come in December. Meanwhile, other preparations, designed to advertise the games internationally, were gaining momentum. In early 1906, the HOC produced several publications designed to remind foreigners of the upcoming games. It published three monthly bulletins in Greek and French, as well as 5,000 copies in French of the program of events that it sent abroad. It also produced 500,000 stickers to announce the Olympics, which were placed on airmail envelopes mailed abroad.

HELLENISM AND INTERNATIONALISM

The organizers of the 1906 Olympics gave the cultural events that took place in conjunction with the games both an ancient Greek coloring and an international dimension. The Hellenic Olympic Committee stressed the importance of the cultural events as a way of establishing a link between the modern and ancient Olympics, which were part of a religious festival. At the same time, the HOC was careful not to allow these events to overshadow the actual games in the way that the exhibitions of 1900 in Paris and 1904 in St. Louis had done during the previous two Olympiads.

A good example of the cultural fusion of ancient Greek and international themes occurred on the day in which there was a performance of Sophocles' *Oedipus Tyrannus* by the Greek Royal Theater at the Panathenaic Stadium in the afternoon, while a "Venetian festival" was held that evening near the port of Piraeus. The festival was modeled on the *Festa del Redentore* (Feast of the Redeemer) celebrations held in Venice every July and featured a regatta and fireworks display (fireworks specialists from Italy came to Athens in order to make the necessary arrangements). The Greek royal family attended both events. The accent placed by the organizers on Greece's ancient heritage relied a great deal on promoting the history of Athens. Athens obviously remained a powerful symbol of Greek antiquity and clearly reminded everyone of the first Olympics held there a decade earlier. Moreover, the city

[27] *Ibid.*, k14/f5/p. 16/1906.

itself—cleaned up for the occasion—and its antiquities displayed the obvious connection between present and past.

Special events were organized to highlight the city's ancient past. The Acropolis was illuminated every evening for the duration of the games, and the Panathenaic Stadium, with its impressive tiers of marble seats, was, naturally, symbolic of this ancient past. The organizers included several visits to ancient sites for foreign visitors, as well as guided tours of the Acropolis, the other major archeological sites of the city, and the national archeological museum. At the same time, modern plays and concerts were also performed along with *Oedipus Tyrannus*, and a lecture series included non-Greek sports themes such as, for example, a talk on Nordic sport by Colonel Viktor Balk, an important figure in the Olympic movement from Sweden.

Nonetheless, just in case anyone had missed the point, the Greek royal family harked on the ancient Greek connection in its speeches during the games, while also reminding its audience of Greece's intention to hold the Olympics in Athens every four years. Crown Prince Constantine addressed his father, King George, in his ceremonial call to the king to open the games at the Panathenaic Stadium. The crown prince asked that the winners not forget "that we have crowned their heads with laurels from Olympia, that have grown on the banks of the Alpheus. . . . [L]et them not forget they have been applauded and crowned as Olympic victors on the sacred ground of Athens by the descendants of Ancient Greece."[28] On the last day of the games, King George addressed the foreign representatives at a special luncheon. After thanking them for their contribution, he referred to the future, saying that Greece "will feel the same pleasure every four years, when according to the laws of the Greek kingdom, Greece will have an opportunity to renew the bonds of peace with all the nations with whom she is happy to co-operate for the good of civilization and progress."[29]

THE GAMES

The Panathenaic Stadium was packed with 60,000 spectators when the 1906 Olympics began with a splendid opening ceremony on April 22. In addition to the entry of King George and Queen Olga, the royal procession included King Edward VII and Queen Alexandra, George's sister, of Great

[28]English version in James E. Sullivan, *The Olympic Games at Athens, 1906*, Spalding's Athletic Library, no. 272, American Sports Publishing Company, New York, 1906, p. 9.
[29]*Ibid.*, p. 29.

Britain and other members of the Greek and British royal families, as well as representatives of other European courts. King Edward's presence was noted by the Athenian press in a way that illustrates the extent to which Greek observers saw the international dimension of the Olympics as important to national interests. The *Patris* commented that the most memorable moment of the proceedings was when the British king applauded the entrance of Greeks from Ottoman-controlled Macedonia. The *Embros*, meanwhile, called attention to the way the crowd welcomed the British king, commenting that on no other occasion had Edward been received so profoundly and enthusiastically.[30]

The distinguished guests included the prime minister of Greece and his cabinet, the archbishop of Athens, the diplomatic corps resident in the capital, and naval officers from visiting warships anchored in Piraeus. Also present were five members of the IOC, the entire HOC, and many foreign correspondents. A band played Samaras's *Olympic Hymn*, which was followed by the "march of nations." Now a standard part of the opening ceremony, the march stressed the event's international character. In his memoirs, Coubertin wrote that the first such parade had taken place in London in 1908. Apparently, he was unaware of the parade at the opening ceremony in Athens, or perhaps did not mention it because he did not recognize these games.[31] Each team marched behind its flag-bearer, with the Germans marching first and the Greek hosts coming at the end of the procession. As mentioned previously, according to the agreement between the HOC and Sullivan, there were no competitions on that day, as it was a Sunday, but there were gymnastics exhibitions that were applauded enthusiastically by the crowd, with an especially loud show of approval for the display put on by the Danish women's team.

Greece's overall concern with organizational matters did not preclude hopes for a good showing by its athletes. Ironically, however, Greece's success in attracting athletes to Athens from abroad, and its efforts to include a wide range of athletic events, limited its own athletes' chances. A total of 847 athletes from twenty nations took part, and they competed in seventy-four events. Over a quarter, or twenty-one, of these events were in track and field, twelve in fencing, eight in shooting, six each in cycling and rowing, four each in gymnastics, swimming, lawn tennis, and wrestling, and the rest in diving,

---

[30]Syrrakos, *Olympiakoi Agōnes*, pp. 230–231.
[31]Coubertin, *Olympism . . .* , p. 424.

soccer, tug-of-war, and weightlifting. Greece fielded 310 competitors, who were involved in all the events; only eighty-three Greeks competed in track and field, however, and the largest Greek contingent, 113 athletes, took part in the rowing events.

Greece's participation in the previous two Olympic Games in Paris and St. Louis had been minimal. In Paris, the only notable performance had been a fourth place in the discus by Panagiōtēs Paraskeuopoulos, who had won the silver medal in Athens in 1896. None of the other three members of the Greek team, another discus thrower and two fencers, did well. The Greek presence in St. Louis consisted of two athletes from Greece and thirteen Greek immigrants living in the United States. The two from Greece did very well. Weightlifter Periklēs Kakousēs won a gold medal and Nikolaos Geōrgantas won the bronze medal in the discus. By coming fifth in the marathon, Dēmētrios Veloulēs was the highest-placed Greek American.

Greeks living beyond Greece's boundaries were frequently included in Greek Olympic teams. Until 1922, there were tens of thousands of Greeks in the major Ottoman cities such as Istanbul and Izmir, where the foreign communities engaged in sporting activities, as was the case with Alexandria in Egypt, a cosmopolitan center with a large Greek element. By the time the Greek presence had diminished in those commercial cities of the eastern Mediterranean, almost 400,000 Greeks had settled in the United States, and a few of them, top athletes who had retained their Greek citizenship, would take part in the Olympics as members of the Greek team at least through the Second World War.

In 1906, there was much more pressure on the Greeks to do well, and training and preparations had begun a year earlier. The Hellenic Olympic Committee sought to attract the best athletes from the major Greek communities in the Mediterranean and scheduled trials in Alexandria, Constantinople (Istanbul), and Smyrna. In Greece itself, the HOC organized three trial marathons in the fall of 1905. As the year drew to a close, officials issued "urgent appeals to Greek athletes, calling upon them to increase their training rate unsparingly, notwithstanding the hardships and difficulties." The prospects for a successful Olympics were excellent, according to officials, but they were just as sure that the competition the Greeks would face would be very tough "and there were no guarantees they would gain distinctions, let alone victories."[32] In athletic terms, however, the preparations did not go

[32]Manitakēs, *100 chronia neoellēnikou . . .* , p. 163.

well. The winter was unusually cold and rainy; it even snowed through mid-March before the track-and-field trials. Training for almost all the athletes was thus held up by the bad weather conditions, and the results at the Pan-Hellenic Games were not very encouraging, with the exception of good showings in the high jump, pole vault, and marathon.

By the time the games opened, the enthusiasm and expectations of the Greek public had grown considerably. While the newspapers had warned Athenians that Greece faced a difficult challenge in track and field, there were legitimate hopes it could do well in fencing, soccer, gymnastics, rowing, shooting, tennis, tug-of-war, and weightlifting. Greeks were also competing in diving, cycling, and wrestling, but were not expected to do well in those sports. The more popular track-and-field events were scheduled to begin on the fifth day, after the less popular competitions, which only served to heighten interest. The Greeks scored several victories outside of track and field, but public enthusiasm was limited because most of these events were not spectator sports. The press hailed the victories, but it is clear that all eyes were turned toward track and field. In many cases, the largest number of competitors in an event was Greek, so positive results from the home side were more or less expected.

In women's lawn tennis, such distinctions were predetermined, as all the competitors were Greek. In soccer, aside from the Danish team, the eventual winners, and the Greek team, the other two participants were teams from the Ottoman empire, one made up of Greeks from the city of Thessalonikē (which won second place) and a multiethnic team from Smyrna. In rope-climbing, thirteen of the seventeen competitors were Greek, and they did very well overall, not surprisingly, with twenty-six-year-old Geōrgios Alimprantēs, a Greek from Constantinople, coming first and Kōnstantinos Kozanitas third. Other sports, such as fencing, were for the most part exclusive to the upper classes and failed to capture the imagination of the broader public. Nevertheless, the Greeks garnered a first-place, three second-places, and one third-place in that sport. Iōannēs Geōrgiadēs, who had won in 1896, won the individual saber competition again after a controversially judged "fence-off" with the German and Italian opponents with whom he had tied for first place. The Greek team came second to the German team in the team saber event that followed. Iōannēs Raïsēs, a fencing coach in the army, won second place in the saber for masters and third place in the épée for masters. Other sports, such as shooting, were largely the preserve of army men, or, as in the case of rowing, navy men. In the shooting events, Geōrgios Orfanidēs and Kōnstantinos Skarlatos won first place in two different pistol competitions, while three of their compatriots placed second in other shooting events, with three more coming in third. In rowing, rowers from Greek warships gained a first place, two second-places, and three third-places.

The Greek public showed great interest in the wrestling and weightlifting competitions, and were rewarded with a Greek victory in weightlifting, albeit a controversial one. The weightlifting events were held in conjunction with track and field in the Panathenaic Stadium, which made them more accessible to the public. Dēmētrios Tofalos, a future wrestling legend, won the two-hand barbell competition, beating the Austrian favorite, world champion Josef Steinbach. The culmination of the contest between the two came when each attempted to lift 142.4 kilograms. Steinbach wanted to use a particular style that was not allowed at the Olympics and was angry with the judges. As one reliable account puts it, "After he had lost . . . Steinbach returned to the lifting platform and picked up the winning weight in his own style, moving it to his shoulders in two movements and then jerked it overhead six times in succession. . . . [T]he Greek crowd, unaware of the rules, initially thought that Steinbach had been cheated of victory. . . ."[33] Officials roundly criticized Steinbach for his "unsportsmanlike" behavior. Fortunately for the Austrian, he won a different weightlifting event with relative ease two days later.

When the track-and-field events began, several Greek athletes did very well, but it soon became clear that, more than anything else, the crowd was anticipating the marathon that was to conclude this series of competitions. Nikolaos Geōrgantas, the twenty-six-year-old teacher who had won third place in the discus in St. Louis, came first in the stone throw, an event added to these games but which was never again to be part of the Olympics. Michaēl Dōrizas, competing in the first of three Olympic Games, came third in the stone throw. Geōrgantas came in second in the Greek-style discus throw, another event inserted by the organizers, and in the freestyle discus, won by the great Irish American athlete, Martin Sheridan. Two more Greeks won third places, Kōnstantinos Spetsiōtēs in the 1,500-meter walk and Themistoklēs Diakidēs in the high jump. All of these successes merely stoked the spectators' excitement over the marathon.

Ultimately, Greek hopes for patriot-boosting success rested on the

[33]Bill Mallon, *The 1906 Olympic Games*, McFarland, Jefferson, 1999, p. 145.

marathon. That event, as all Athenian commentators noted at the time, was the Greek event *par excellence* in terms of both its ancient heritage and the fact that a Greek had won the first such race at the Olympiad of 1896. Although no Greek competed in the marathon at the Paris Olympics in 1900, there had been nine entries in the event at St. Louis, with the best performance being Veloulēs's fifth place. The 1906 marathon was therefore the event in which the home crowd expected, indeed demanded, a Greek victory. The marathon became a test of Greek resolve and ability: resolve to do well in a "Greek" race and ability to show the virtues of Greek athleticism and character. Nonetheless, several observers warned that the Greeks should be prepared to cheer the winner irrespective of nationality.

The fifty-three runners (twenty-two foreigners and thirty-one Greeks) set off at 3:05 pm on May 1 from a point near the site of the battle of Marathon, northwest of Athens at a distance of 42.195 kilometers from the Panathenaic Stadium. Road transportation was so tricky along the route that the athletes had arrived a day earlier and spent the night in the small village. It was neither a very efficient arrangement nor a comfortable one, but it ensured that everyone was at the starting-line on the day of the race. This was the so-called classic marathon route, a punishing, and long, uphill climb for most of the way (it became an easier downhill run at the final stage, as the athletes entered Athens). At the tenth kilometer, where the route starts its slow uphill climb, the American William Frank was in the lead followed by a group of six runners. At the twentieth kilometer, almost halfway to the finish, Australia's George Blake led the race. By that time, several runners had fallen behind or abandoned the effort. One of them, an early leader, was Italy's Dorando Pietri, who was involved in the controversial finish of the 1908 marathon in London in which he was helped across the finish-line. At the twenty-fifth kilometer, Canada's William Sherring went ahead, followed by Frank, Blake, and a Swede, Johan Svanberg. It was at that point that one of the Greek favorites, Anastasios Koutoulakēs, made his move from further back in the field. Koutoulakēs, winner of the race over the same route back in March in the Pan-Hellenic Games, began threatening the leaders as he moved up into tenth position.

Meanwhile, the crowded stadium in Athens was growing restless. As the marathoners made their way toward the city, the spectators watched as the American athletes showed their superiority in the remaining track-and-field events. Robert Leavitt of Williams College won the 100-meter hurdles. In the

800 meters, defending champion James Lightbody of the University of Chicago came in second after Paul Pilgrim of New York, who had won the 400 meters the previous day. Ray Ewry of Purdue University won the standing high jump.

The afternoon events completed, the expectant crowd received unpleasant though unconfirmed news that Koutoulakēs had collapsed and abandoned the race and that the other Greek runners were lagging behind Sherring, who led the race with about ten kilometers left. The papers would report the next day that the Hamilton, Ontario, native had looked relaxed and had acknowledged the crowd as he pulled away from the rest of the field. When Sherring entered the stadium a few minutes before six o'clock, the crowd swallowed its disappointment and transformed itself from what could have been a frustrated nationalist mass into a sportingly cheering throng of sports-lovers. It was an easy transition, in a sense, because the dominant theme of the 1906 Olympiad all along had been Greece's ability to host the games effectively, not Greece's glorification through athletic superiority. As Paulos Manitakēs put it, the crowd gave a rousing welcome to Sherring by "suppressing the pain, and recalling our [Greek] obligations as hosts and our inherent and centuries-long gallantry and love of sport."[34] For good measure and in order to prompt the crowd, Crown Prince Constantine jumped on to the track and ran next to Sherring, as he and his brother had done when Spyros Louēs entered the stadium triumphantly to win the marathon in 1896.

The next day, the newspapers informed the public about the reasons for Koutoulakēs's sad failure. When the runners had gathered at Marathon the day before the race, the foreigners relaxed, ate lightly, and some even stopped speaking in order to rest their lungs. Unfortunately, the newspaper reports explained, "our runners" did the opposite. They spent their time in coffeeshops in the village of Marathon, playing cards and shouting at each other, and ate a heavy dinner washed down by *retsina*. Koutoulakēs reportedly ate a whole roasted chicken on the very day of the race. Inevitably, the contrast between the foreign and Greek preparations for the race became a metaphor for the deficiencies of the Greek character compared to that of Westerners. The papers reported how Sherring had arrived in Athens two months before the marathon and diligently trained, using the route of the race. This was in stark contrast to how the Greek runners had trained. The Athens papers rued the inability, or unwillingness, of the Greeks to train systematically, and

[34]Manitakēs, *100 chronia neoellēnikou* . . . , p. 184.

several writers noted humbly that the Canadian Sherring had taught the Greek nation a lesson.

ANCIENT HERITAGE AND POLITICAL REALITIES

If Greece's athletic weakness dampened local nationalism, the association that foreigners made between modern and ancient Greece threatened to revive the thorny issue of making Greece the permanent site of the Olympics. Several newspapers wrote that many foreign visitors had come round to believing that Greece was the only place where the Olympics could take place in the future. The *Astrapē* wrote that three-quarters of the IOC supported this view, but it also noted the absence of the "odd baron Coubertin," who had claimed he was too ill to attend the Athens games, according to the newspaper's reporter, who had disregarded Coubertin's more elaborate excuse about the IOC congress on arts, literature, and sport.[35] As soon as the games ended, the Greek parliament began a new session, and the king mentioned in his speech to the chamber that the Olympics would be held in Athens again in four years' time. A year later, the Peloponnesian sports club organized an athletic meet in Olympia dedicated to reviving the ancient games.[36]

International observers were extremely complimentary, both in their assessment of the games and of Greece's potential as either permanent or, at least, frequent host of the Olympics. E. B. Saint Hilaire, a well-known French journalist and commentator, hailed the successful return of the games to the land of their origin.[37] Sullivan was also caught up in the symbolism of Greece. In his account of the games, he wrote of how impressed he was by the marble stadium and the ancient ruins. Yet he thought there was something else that made the games special: "The people seemed enthused over something that meant more than sport; they had taken hold of the Olympic Games, and apparently, to them these Olympic Games were a sacred festival . . . ," and, he concluded, "the history of the Olympic Games is part of the history of the Greeks."[38] This was the same type of romantic nationalism that had inspired Coubertin, a sense that modern Greece was the same place in which ancient civilizations were rooted. This sentiment would gradually dissipate during the twentieth century, as we will see further on, but

[35]Syrrakos, *Olympiakoi Agōnes . . .* , p. 215.
[36]Skiadas, *100 chronia neoterē . . .* , pp. 181, 183.
[37]*Ibid.*, pp. 180–181.
[38]Sullivan, *The Olympic Games . . .* , pp. 21–23.

it remained strong around the turn of the century. A traveler could still see Athens through romantic lenses, writing, for example, that the city "strives to renew the glories of ancient Hellas."[39] Thus, in a sense, Greece had it both ways in 1906. It was able to show off its organizational skills and international spirit, while at the same time evoking the type of response that could support future claims on the Olympics. It was all to be lost, however, in the wake of the region's and the country's geopolitical turmoil.

The immediate aftermath of 1906 was deceptive. Athletic activities in Greece multiplied, as did the public's interest in the Olympics. A meeting was held in Olympia in the summer of 1907 to plan the best way for local inhabitants to work toward reviving the ancient Olympics. The following year, the organizers of the meeting tried to organize athletic games involving the entire Peloponnese, but the plans fell through. Greece was able to send a relatively large group of competitors to the London Olympiad that year, composed of twelve track-and-field athletes, seven sharpshooters, and one cyclist. Twenty-year-old Kōnstantinos Tsiklētēras won second place in the standing high jump and the standing long jump, and Dōrizas came in second in the javelin. Sharpshooter Anastasios Metaxas, the architect who had helped redesign the Panathenaic Stadium for the 1896 Olympics, also came in second in two shooting events.

When the time came to plan for the next interim Olympics in 1910, however, the furthest the Greek government got was to budget for the issue of a series of stamps. In 1909, Greece had experienced one of the most significant turning-points in its modern history. After a summer-long political crisis, a popularly supported coup by army officers sidelined the political leaders and called upon Eleutherios Venizelos, a young politician from Crete, to take power. Venizelos's entry into Greek politics meant the beginning of a new era, marked by a radical restructuring of the nineteenth-century *ancien régime* and a new drive toward modernization and territorial expansion. Ominously, Venizelos had clashed with Crown Prince Constantine over Greece's policies in Ottoman-ruled Crete, although it is unclear whether this affected Venizelos's attitude toward the Olympics. At any rate, the state budget for 1910 did not include any funds for the interim Olympics. After a struggle and several rounds of negotiations, the government earmarked only 80,000 drachmas, a third of the original sum requested by the HOC. Reluctantly, the committee had to quietly abandon the plan to hold the games in 1910.

---

[39]Mrs. R. C. Bosanquet, *Days in Attica*, Macmillan, New York, 1914, p. 255.

A combination of domestic and external political considerations put an end to the HOC's plans to organize interim Olympics in 1914. The upheavals relating to the political changes in 1909 were more or less over by January 1912, and the government was able to allocate funds at the last minute to finance the Greek team's participation in the Stockholm Olympiad. Greece sent a thirty-four-member team to Sweden, but only Tsikletēras returned with medals, a gold for his victory in the standing long jump and a bronze for the standing high jump. Several Greek athletes placed among the top six finalists in track and field and shooting, so Greece came in seventh overall in the point table. Almost immediately after the Olympics, Greece plunged into the Balkan Wars of 1912–1913. Thus, the HOC could not begin to plan in earnest for the interim Olympics of 1914 until November 1913. Lambros, as the HOC general secretary, met with Prime Minister Venizelos, who expressed grave doubts about the feasibility of successful games on such short notice and in an uncertain political climate. After further consideration, the government decided that it would be unwise to proceed with interim Olympics in 1914.[40]

The interim Olympics of 1906 showed that, under certain circumstances, Greece could play an important role in the Olympic movement, and did so in the movement's first years, although it was unable to sustain that role over time. The Greeks derived a great sense of national pride from organizing the Olympics in a manner that they believed worthy of their ancestors, and by ensuring that the games were international. The historic connection they felt to the institution of the games had nothing to do with athletic prowess or with a wish to dominate them athletically. In that sense, irrespective of the status of the 1906 games, they made a positive contribution to the fledgling Olympic movement. By the same token, its limited resources and the political conjunctures of the early twentieth century prevented Greece from sustaining its role as the host of interim games. Thus, the Olympics would remain an international event dominated, naturally, by the wealthiest and most powerful countries.

[40]Skiadas, *100 chronia neoterē . . .*, pp. 207–208.

CHAPTER 4

REDISCOVERING THE CLASSICAL LEGACY

F IVE WELL-BUILT YOUNG MEN STAND ABREAST, ready to start a race in
a stadium. They wear loincloths and carry shields. Three of them look
ahead, peering out from under ill-fitting helmets. The other two look to their
left expectantly, awaiting the orders of a starter. Behind them, a thin crowd of
young boys, wearing their Sunday best, stands, watching in anticipation. This
is one of the photographic images that remains from the Classical Games
held in the Panathenaic Stadium in Athens in 1934 (see inset). The games
were an attempt to recreate the type of athletic competition supposed to have
taken place in antiquity. The purpose was to unearth the roots of ancient
Greek sport in an attempt to restore its purity. This revival was supposed to
counteract the decline of the high moral purpose of the contemporary
Olympics.

The bizarre scenes that took place in the venerable stadium that hosted
the first Olympiad in 1896 were emblematic of the confusion suffered by
Greeks in the first half of the twentieth century in their attempts to celebrate
their ancient heritage. For the Greeks, this heritage was not, and still is not,
an abstract concept such as civilization or democracy. Rather, it is a vital
inheritance, born largely of the inescapable awareness of living on the very
same land where the ancients realized their great achievements. This relationship is also conditioned by the myths of cultural, and indeed racial, continuity taught in Greek schools. In the interwar years and later, Greeks
reenacted the ancient past with the same reverence and eye for historical
detail that other peoples bring to the recreation of their more recent history,
such as Americans reenacting events from the War of Independence or the
Civil War.

The interwar period in the West, however, was an era in which modernism eclipsed the earlier, romantic infatuation with antiquity. In light of

the prevailing sensibility, the recreation of the so-called Classical Games appeared quaint. This was not an era known for any romantic attachment among Europeans and North Americans to ancient Greece, although the classical tradition influenced important writers such as T. S. Eliot and Ezra Pound. More broadly, however, the old romanticism was eroding dramatically. Travelers' accounts of Greece are a very good example of how these notions were being transformed. For the nineteenth-century generation of philhellenes, the *land* of Greece was the site of a myth, and their visits there afforded them an opportunity to reflect on their own lost origins. The experience affirmed the lineage and roots of Western civilization. By the twentieth century, however, modernist thinkers had begun to reconsider previously unassailable ideas about the universality of ancient Greek heritage. Intellectuals reacted less enthusiastically when they visited Athens, and they questioned Western assumptions about Greece as the physical origin of Western civilization. By that time, it was indeed hard to ignore a contemporary Greek landscape in which, as the doyenne of modernism, Virginia Woolf, put it, evoking a modernist criticism of classicism, "the donkeys stumble so on the stones."[1]

The International Olympic Committee, however, remained attached to the earlier, romantic views on Greece. It was still in the grip of its leader, Coubertin, who was ever the typical romantic philhellene. He still believed strongly in the symbolic and moral value of venerating ancient Greece. The only transformation experienced by Coubertin in the interwar period was in his relationship to *modern* Greece. Before the First World War, he had opposed Greek attempts to take the games permanently to their land of origin. Angry over Greek persistence in this matter, he had not visited Greece since the first Olympics in 1896. Now, with the Olympic movement in need of some creative symbolism, and with the modern Greeks no longer petitioning to become permanent hosts, Coubertin would make the most of exploiting Greece as the *locus classicus* of the games.

The Greek establishment was only too happy to oblige by rallying to the task of presenting modern Greece as the heir of classical Greece. The interwar period witnessed a general nationalist trend in Greece that entailed several forms of a search for identity ranging from a return-to-the-roots movement to debates about the continuity of the Greek "race" from

---

[1] Artemis Leontis, *Topographies of Hellenism*, Cornell University Press, Ithaca, 1995, pp. 105–107.

antiquity through the present. An important dimension of the intellectual exchanges over definitions of Greekness was the gradual slide of the liberal authors of the so-called Generation of the Thirties over to more conservative positions, which involved notions of race and continuity with the classical past.[2] This continuity thesis eventually became part of state policy after 1936 when a dictatorship replaced the constitutional regime. But there were plenty of signs that confirmed that this definition of Greekness was increasingly popular. This has prompted one historian to suggest the evolution of a "royalist nationalism" that, among other things, venerated the classical past.[3] One example of a public celebration of the ancient past that was not explicitly political was the Delphic festival organized in 1927 by Angelos Sikelianos and his American wife, Eva Palmer-Sikelianou. This was an attempt to "revive" the "spirit" of ancient Delphi, as Sikelianos, a leading poet of the interwar era, believed that classical traditions could promote humanism and international understanding. Another example is the extensive restoration program between 1923 and 1933 on the Acropolis, in which engineer Nikolaos Balanos attempted to recover "the Parthenon's fallen grandeur, to make the building appear more like it had done in ancient times but at the same time to give it a stronger modern image for both Greeks and foreigners."[4] The opportunity to connect Greece with its ancient past via the Olympics was therefore gratefully taken in Athens. Indeed, after the First World War, Greece took on a role in the Olympic movement that gradually increased until the Classical Games were held in 1934.

THE OLYMPIC MOVEMENT AFTER THE FIRST WORLD WAR

The First World War eviscerated the idealist principles of the still-young institution of the Olympics. The VIth Olympic Games, scheduled for 1916 in Berlin, were canceled due to the conflict. Any idealist voices that argued that sport could displace armed conflict as a means of competition among nations were stifled by the remorseless reality of war. Sports administrators

[2]Takis Kayalis, "Logotechnia kai pneumatikē zōē" ["Literature and Intellectual Life"], in Christos Hadziiosif, editor, *Istoria tēs Elladas ston Eikosto Aiōna: Mesopolemos 1922–1940* [*History of Greece in the 20th Century: Interwar Period, 1922–1940*], Volume B2, Vivliorama, Athens, 2002, pp. 315–352.

[3]Kostas Vergopoulos, *Ethnismos kai oikonomikē anaptyxē* [*Nationalism and Economic Development*], Athens, Exantas, 1978, pp. 137- 141.

[4]William St. Clair, *Lord Elgin and the Marbles*, Oxford University Press, Oxford, 1998, p. 328.

appeared to have been caught up in the atmosphere. At war's end, the victors, in no mood for reconciliation, excluded Germany and its wartime allies from competing in the 1920 Olympiad. Germany and the other central powers were readmitted in 1924 for the VIIIth Olympiad in Paris, but the games lacked their prewar idealist luster. A climate of uncertainty still hovered around the games, calling into question their very future; there was even talk of the League of Nations taking over. At the dawn of an era enervated by war, it was not at all clear whether the Olympics would survive.

Coubertin was active in defending and promoting the institution he had created. He noted in his memoirs that he approached the Antwerp games of 1920 with the aim of creating a "religious ceremony." A central element of the new emphasis on ceremony was its appropriation of ancient Greek imagery. According to Coubertin, a reaffirmation of the classical roots of the games was in order. Such a move not only restored the moral high ground assumed by their founders in the late nineteenth century; it also functioned as a unifying element, bringing together the European powers that had gone to war in 1914 by stressing their common heritage. The return to classical roots entailed the use of Olympic and ancient Greek symbols designed to defuse the ideologically and nationalistically charged atmosphere of the immediate postwar era.

Coubertin pushed for a return to classical roots, confident that this would also probably prevent Greece from renewing its claims on the games. Any invocation of the ancient heritage of the Olympics would necessarily involve Greece as the site and inheritor of Olympic traditions. In the recent past, this had led Greece to demand that it become the permanent site of the games, a suggestion that Coubertin considered anathema. The games' universality, he believed, would be prejudiced if held in Greece rather than in different, and rotating, parts of the world. Indeed, the use of classical Greek symbolism in the Olympics had decreased after the inaugural games in Athens, possibly because Coubertin had made every effort to discourage demands by Greeks to become the permanent hosts. After the war, Coubertin saw that war-ravaged Greece was in no condition to renew these demands in any persuasive manner.

GREEK SPORT IN THE INTERWAR PERIOD

Coubertin was right to assume that Greece was in no position to revive its claims to the Olympics. The country had experienced a decade of war, beginning with the Balkan Wars, followed by the royalist-Venizelist clash over the country's attitude toward the First World War, belated entry into the conflict, and then the fateful military campaign deep into Ottoman territory from 1919 through 1922 that ended with a devastating defeat at the hands of the Turks, who forced the Greek troops and hundreds of thousands of indigenous Greeks to flee. The "Asia Minor Disaster" brought a million and a half Ottoman Greek refugees to Greece, plunging the country into a period of socioeconomic and political unrest. By the mid-Twenties, therefore, the expensive proposition of claiming the Olympics as their birthright, and making the necessary preparations to support that claim, was the last thing on the minds of Greek leaders struggling to restore order and settle destitute refugees.

Coubertin's wish to emphasize the Olympics' classical heritage also benefited from Greece's willingness and ability to contribute to the project. The religious, ceremonial trappings that Coubertin introduced in Antwerp were simple and easy to perform, but, as we will see, Greece would be drawn into this invention of tradition more and more as the interwar period unfolded. The Greeks were willing to go along with all of it because they themselves were weighing the significance of classical traditions at a time when sporting activities, and sport as mass spectacle, were getting underway in the 1920s. Moreover, the development of a fledgling Greek sporting culture brought wider public involvement in sport, both in terms of participants and spectators. The growing importance of sport in Greek society, along with an increase in international competition, ensured that it became a sphere of popular culture that could no longer be ignored by the government, educators, intellectuals, and others engaged in the definition and redefinition of modern Greek identity. As Spyros Louēs's victory in the marathon in 1896 had shown, public opinion would rally to the Olympic cause if the country gained some distinction on such an important international stage. Post-First World War Greece was far from producing any champion athletes, but sport was being taken more seriously and the debate grew on how modern athletics could be made to incorporate classical tradition—and thus enhance international exposure. The Olympics and Greece's sporting role in them began to capture the public's imagination. In 1918, the newly established "Didaskaleion," a two-year college for physical-education teachers, stated that one of its roles was "to participate in the Olympics."[5]

<hr>

[5]Koulouri, *Athlētismos kai opseis . . .*, p. 78.

The influx of one and a half million refugees from Turkey in the wake of the Asia Minor Disaster strengthened Greek sport and also provided a link between past and present. The Greeks in the Ottoman empire had created several athletic clubs that promoted track and field, soccer, and other sports. After they were uprooted and fled to Greece, they either transplanted their clubs to their new homeland or created new ones. Among the clubs that moved across the Aegean were two with classical Greek names, *Paniōnios* (Pan-Ionian) and *Apollōn* of Izmir. Each settled in refugee neighborhoods in Athens. Greek athletes belonging to the Pera Club of Istanbul formed AEK (*Athlētikē Enōsis Kōnstantinoupoleōs*, or Athletic Union of Constantinople), which chose the Byzantine colors of gold and black and the Byzantine two-headed eagle as its emblem. Refugees in Thessalonikē established the Pan-Thessalonikan Athletic Club of Constantinopolitans (*Panthessalonikeios Athlētikos Omilos Kōnstantinoupolitōn*, or PAOK), which also adopted the double-headed eagle as its symbol.

The presence of refugee-based sports clubs galvanized the indigenous sports scene, and the activities generated underscored the significance of antiquity for Greek athletes and administrators. Concerned by the presence of refugee clubs in its hometown, the Athens-based Pan-Hellenic Soccer Games Club decided in 1924 to adopt a name that reflected its claim on the city's loyalty—although, or perhaps because, it was identified with the Athens bourgeoisie. The name chosen was *Panathēnaikos* (Pan-Athenian) Athletic Club. Interestingly, while the name evoked a collective Athenian scope, it also invoked the name of the Panathenaic Games that were held in the city in classical times.[6] A year later, Athens's port, Piraeus, witnessed the establishment of *Olympiakos*, formed by local entrepreneurs. They wished to affirm their pride in Piraeus and a corresponding rivalry with Athens, but they wanted to choose a name that would give their club a wider significance. Hence "Olympiakos," meaning "of the Olympic Games," which was accompanied by a club emblem consisting of the head of a male athlete crowned by the olive branch awarded to victors in ancient Olympia.[7] The choice of the name "Olympiakos" was one of many examples of how the Greek sporting world

---

[6]Nikos Goumas *et al.*, editors, *Ē istoria tou Panathēnaikou 1908–1968* [*The History of Panathēnaikos, 1908–1968*], Alvin Redman Hellas, Athens, 1969, pp. 1108–1110.

[7]Vasias Tsokopoulos, "Ta stadia tēs topikēs syneidēsēs. O Peiraias, 1835–1935" ["The Stages of Local Identity: Piraeus, 1835–1935"], in *Neoellēnikē Polē* [*Modern Greek City*], EMNE, Athens, 1985, pp. 247–248; Vasilēs Kardasēs, *Katalogos istorikou archeiou Olympiakou Peiraiōs* [*Catalogue of the Historical Archives of Olympiakos Piraeus*], Dokimes, Athens, 1997, pp. 13–22.

looked toward antiquity. There were several other clubs with ancient names, among the most important being *Ēraklēs* (Hercules) and *Arēs* in Thessalonikē. There are several important sports clubs with classical names in Europe, among them Ajax Amsterdam, Olympique Marseille, and Olympia Ljubljana; not surprisingly, however, Greece is the only country in which such names abound.

The growth of sports activities in the 1920s brought a proliferation of international contests beyond the Olympics involving Greek teams; these were inevitably the occasions on which the Greeks compared themselves (mostly unfavorably) to other nations. While this was, admittedly, more of an exercise in fostering an underdog culture rather than in bemoaning the loss of national superiority, at least in the early stages, the important thing is that sport was becoming a sphere of popular culture in which national identity was being defined. Greece established a national soccer team whose first official game was played in April 1929 (a 4–1 defeat at home to Italy's "B" side). The same year, the Balkan nations inaugurated the annual Balkan track-and-field games in which Greece was scoring some important successes by the mid-1930s. Club teams also began playing exhibition games in the mid-1920s against visiting foreign teams, mostly from the Balkans or central Europe. An advertising leaflet for a tournament between Greek and foreign teams invited fans to attend the contests at which "Greek soccer would be judged."[8]

The final piece of the jigsaw puzzle was the government's growing involvement in sport, recognition that the laissez-faire amateurism of old was being replaced by an activity of growing mass appeal and of new relevance to the national discourse. Sport was no longer an upper-class diversion, and the growing numbers of people taking part as athletes or spectators demanded the government's attention. In a country like Greece, in which patron-client relationships between politicians and voters were strong, governments slipped effortlessly into the habit of doing favors for the sports world. While, for example, *Panathēnaikos*'s plans to build a stadium in Athens were momentarily frustrated because the open field they wished to develop had been taken over by a refugee camp, the government and the Athens municipality moved swiftly to relocate the squatters. Track-and-field athletes, meanwhile, no longer members of the social elite who could pay their own way, required support, and they formed an association that functioned like a labor union.

There was also more direct government involvement in the affairs of the

[8]Ēlias Lekkas, *Istoria tēs AEK* [*History of AEK*], Alexandrēs, Athens, 1996, p. 8.

Hellenic Olympic Committee. Improbably, political polarization during the events leading to the Asia Minor Disaster had had a benign effect on the government's relationship to domestic sport. The sharp rift between republicans and royalists that split the Greek political world had led to the dismissal of the monarchy in 1917. This meant that the HOC had lost its head, King Constantine. In his absence, the new republican-oriented committee managed to get legislation passed that approved government support for the Olympic team. The Greek royal family had always been an ardent supporter of the Olympics; in the name of preserving "amateurism," however, the king had blocked any government funding of Greek teams, which had to rely on donations. Once in power, the republicans did not shy from becoming involved in matters pertaining to sport. Not only did the government offer funding, but it also encouraged the Hellenic Olympic Committee to take certain initiatives to develop the country's sport infrastructure.

From Antwerp in 1920 to Los Angeles in 1932

In the twelve years between the Olympiads in Antwerp and Los Angeles, classical motifs surrounding the games increased, as did Greece's symbolic role. Coubertin was the motor force behind these developments, but, when he began to step aside in the mid-1920s, his successors in the leadership of the Olympic movement helped maintain the momentum. Meanwhile, despite its adverse economic condition, Greece managed a modestly respectable appearance at each Olympiad, which helped to sustain its contribution to the Olympic movement's attempt to consolidate the games as an institution.

The 1920 games in Antwerp signaled the beginning of Coubertin and the IOC's efforts to stress tradition through several rituals, some of which were meant to emphasize the games' classical Greek heritage. Coubertin introduced the oath of the athletes and the Olympic flag of five rings against a white background. The oath was a component of ancient Greek athletic competition. The five Olympic circles of the flag was Coubertin's idea (which did not prevent claims made later that the design was found on a stone in the sanctuary in Delphi during excavations in the late nineteenth century). In yet another reference to antiquity, one of the official posters of the 1920 games, designed by Walter Van der Ven, depicted a loinclad discus-thrower. Doves, a symbol of peace, were also set free for the first time during the opening ceremony at Antwerp.

On that occasion, Greece's role was minimal, as was its presence on the athletic field. Greek athletes were poorly prepared due to a decade of inter-mittent warfare. Many were in uniform, and some were already serving on the front in Asia Minor. Strenuous efforts were made to ensure their release in time for them to train before going to Belgium. As always, Greeks from abroad volunteered to join the team, some from the Ottoman empire and others from farther afield. Among them was Panagiōtēs "Peter" Trivoulidas, winner of the Boston marathon that year. Trivoulidas, whom the *Boston Globe* described as "a swarthy, heavy-legged native of Sparta, Greece," had moved to the United States in 1917 and worked as a busboy at Wanamaker's department store in New York City. Trivoulidas had done very well in marathons in Greece before the war, but his inability to make a satisfactory living prompted him to emigrate. In Antwerp, Trivoulidas abandoned the marathon toward the end of the race. His disappointing performance was typical of the rest of the team. After a strong showing, the track-and-field ath-lete and future president of the HOC, Apostolos Nikolaidēs, was forced to withdraw, suffering from a high fever. No Greek broke into the top six places in track and field. The only distinction gained by the Greeks was second place in one of the team pistol-shooting events. On a positive note, because of gov-ernment support, the Greek delegation to the games proved to be much bet-ter organized than had previously been the case.

Just before the Paris Olympiad of 1924, administrative changes within the Hellenic Olympic Committee served to invigorate Greek sport. The government appointed a former politician, Geōrgios Averōf (1867–1930), to head the HOC. Averōf's uncle and namesake had been the wealthy Alexandrian Greek who had funded the construction of the Panethenaic Stadium for the first Olympics in 1896. The younger Averōf also became a member of the IOC from 1926 until his death in 1930. Under Averōf, the com-mittee regularized the annual Pan-Hellenic track-and-field games and used the 1924 tournament as trials for the Olympics. Averōf also presided over efforts to promote the idea that athletics in Greece were an integral part of the country's classical heritage. These efforts included plans to build a mod-ern stadium near Olympia to hold athletic events that would adhere to the ancient Greek custom of having each local community send participants. The HOC also dealt with a short-lived athletes' "strike" and successfully pres-sured the government to increase funding for the Greek team that would travel to Paris. Acting on the advice of Alexandros Merkatēs, the Greek IOC member, Greece sent a relatively small delegation of 45 athletes to the 1924 Olympiad.

A new ceremonial element was introduced at the Paris Olympiad: raising the Greek flag in the closing ceremony. For the first time ever, three flags—Greek, French, and Dutch—were raised simultaneously in the stadium while a band played the respective national anthems. The purpose of this was to serve as a symbolic reminder of the history and continuity of the games. France had been the host of the games that had just taken place, the Netherlands would be the next host, and Greece was, of course, the "home" of the permanent Olympic restoration.[9]

The Greeks made no impact on the athletic field in Paris, but they did make a mark in several events that occurred in conjunction with the Olympics. The French organizers, guided by Coubertin, had decided to widen the scope of the games and imitate sporting contests held in antiquity by organizing musical, literary, and artistic events. Greek sculptor Kōstas Dēmētriadēs won first prize for his sculpture featuring a discus-thrower. In his honor, the Greek flag was raised and the Greek national anthem was played. There was a broader significance to the non-athletic events that took place in the Champs Elysées theater: they signified IOC approval of the emphasis on the classical past. Philhellenism was certainly in evidence. Paulos Manitakēs, who was a member of the Greek delegation to Paris, claims he proposed a toast to Baron de Coubertin and the leaders of the French sports association during an official dinner hosted by the latter. They responded by raising their glasses and crying out, in Greek, "Zētō ē Ellas" (Long Live Greece)!

Coubertin's expressions of philhellenism were consistent with his desire to stress the classical roots of the games; they were in no way meant as a concession to earlier Greek demands. Speaking at an Olympic congress in Prague in 1925, as he was stepping down as president of the IOC, Coubertin stressed the universality of the Olympics: "Is there any need to recall that the Games are not the property of any country or of any particular race, and that they cannot be monopolized by any group whatsoever? They belong to everyone."[10] And true to his classicism, in the same speech, the outgoing president called for the revival of the "municipal Gymnasium of antiquity."

[9]Montserrat Llines, "The History of Olympic Ceremonies," in Miquel de Moragas *et al.*, editors, *Olympic Ceremonies: Historical Continuity and Cultural Exchange*, IOC, Lausanne, 1996, pp. 63–81.

[10]Coubertin, *Olympism . . .*, p. 558.

As far as the HOC and Greek public opinion were concerned, Greece's relationship to ancient Greece meant that any reference to antiquity from within the Olympic movement was a positive sign. Within two years, Coubertin was returning to Greece as an honored guest. Coubertin had not been to the country since 1896, so this was an emotional return, both for him and his hosts. The highlight of his sojourn was the unveiling of a marble column in Olympia commemorating the restoration of the Olympic Games. Coubertin's trip was of great significance regarding Greece's place in the Olympic movement. Although he had stepped down from the position of IOC president, he remained the movement's revered figurehead. His return to Olympia, and the important speeches he made while on Greek soil, served to remind the movement that Greece remained the Olympics' *locus classicus*. This was conveyed in the message "to the young athletes of all nations" he issued on April 17, 1927, which began: "Today, amid the illustrious ruins of Olympia, the monument commemorating the restoration of the Olympic Games, proclaimed thirty-three years ago, was unveiled. Through this gesture of the Greek government, the initiative that it has sought to honor has taken its place in history. Now it is up to you to maintain it."[11]

Coubertin responded positively to the honors bestowed on him by the Greeks in 1927, but he was not fully aware that they saw his philhellenism primarily as a validation of modern Greece. It was clear from the warmth of their welcome that the Greeks had forgiven Coubertin for rejecting their bid to host the Olympics permanently. He wrote in his memoirs: "Various events had been organized in Athens mainly as a result of the efforts of J. E. Chrysafes, director of physical education [at the Greek ministry of education]. . . . [H]e and the new member of the IOC for Greece, Mr. George Averoff . . . seemed to me to be doing everything in their power to erase from my memory any recollection of the unfortunate episodes of the first Games. But in fact nothing remained. That my ideas should have met with objections at the time, even arousing excessively chauvinistic feelings, was only natural. Everyone now understood that by conceiving the new Games on a completely international level and by wishing to situate them on a world scale, I had not only chosen the only practical means of ensuring their continued survival but at the same time had served the best interests of Hellenism."[12]

[11] *Ibid.*, p. 560.
[12] *Ibid.*, p. 511.

He could have added "modern Hellenism," but did not, since he believed that his hosts shared his idealism. He wrote: ". . . during my stay on Greek soil I was particularly pleased to see that my philhellenism was now understood and appreciated by all my good Greek friends."[13] Coubertin went on to say that the one tribute that touched him more than any other was the dedication of a marble seat in the Panathenaic Stadium in his honor. It was a revival of an ancient custom in which the name of a beneficiary of the games was carved in gold on the back of a seat.

In the following years, there were more signs of Coubertin's reconciliation with the Greeks. In March 1935, he gave a long speech in Paris, with the Greek ambassador to France in attendance, recounting the history of the Olympics and their ancient Greek underpinnings. When he came to discuss the 1896 Olympics, he was effusive in his praise and declared that they were a momentous occasion. Coubertin was also appointed an honorary member of the Greek government delegation and delivered a major speech on sports reform to the League of Nations in Geneva in 1930. His "Charter for Sports Reform" stemmed from his growing concern in his final years to preserve the purity of sport. The speech advocated a return to the classical roots of sport and included the substitution of "super stadiums" that were designed to house "spectacular athletic meetings" with "buildings after the style of modernized Ancient Greek Gymnasiums." At the meeting, he was accompanied by his friend, Chrysafès, the Greek Olympic official.

The Olympic movement began treating the Greeks as rightful heirs to the classical tradition. The stadium in which the 1928 games in Amsterdam were held included another display of the classical Greek legacy of using fire in religious and sporting activities: a tall tower, atop of which a flame was lit. The stadium's architect, Jan Wils, received an award for the edifice, appropriately named the "Tower of Marathon." Coubertin and the Dutch hosts also came up with the idea of the Greek team marching first in the parade of national teams at the opening of the Amsterdam games. Along with the tradition of the torch relay from Olympia to be inaugurated in 1936, this practice became a permanent feature of the Olympics and was considered by outsiders to be a symbolic nod toward ancient Greece. As far as the Greeks were concerned, however, this honor reflected on modern Greece. In the official report of the Greek delegation to Amsterdam, Michaël Rinopoulos wrote that being given first place in the opening parade of nations "invigorated our

[13] *Ibid.*, p. 512.

national pride, and the performance of our athletes was excellent as a result."[14]

At the 1932 games in Los Angeles, the organizers adopted the ritualistic and ceremonial aspects of the previous Olympiad. The Greek team marched first in the opening parade of nations, and a choir sang the *Olympic Hymn*. Of the three articles included in the souvenir program, one was about the games in antiquity. These initiatives are not surprising, as there was a long tradition of philhellenism in the United States; coincidentally, a year earlier, the American School of Classical Studies in Athens had begun major excavations at the foot of the Acropolis. The Greeks did not stop to think whether the organizers were honoring ancient or modern Greece, as it was all the same to them. One of the most comprehensive Greek histories of the modern Olympics claims that Greece was honored at Los Angeles more than at any previous Olympiad.[15]

The circumstances in which the Greeks arrived in Los Angeles are a reminder of the stark contrast between the glories of ancient Greece and the prosaic reality of its modern counterpart. In fact, the Greek team almost did not make the long trip to California to witness the accolades: the country was suffering an economic crisis and the bankrupt government was unable to fund the trip. The funds were raised privately in Greece and among the Greek American community. The team was made up of only ten athletes, the smallest group that ever competed for Greece at the Olympics. Four of the ten athletes were Greek Americans, two of them members of the Greek American Athletic Club of New York. The Greeks had a few modest successes: Geōrgios Zerbinēs came in fourth in freestyle and fifth in Greco-Roman wrestling, while Iōannēs Farmakidēs also came in fifth in Greco-Roman wrestling: overall, an underwhelming set of results, but understandable given the circumstances in Greece and the long distances traveled.

ATHENS, 1934: THE IOC'S FORTIETH ANNIVERSARY

The IOC's choice of Greece as the venue for the celebration of the fortieth anniversary of the Olympic movement's founding congress in 1894 confirmed the country's growing importance in the movement. This was the first such commemoration to take place at a venue other than the IOC's

[14]HOC Minutes, 38th meeting, October 29, 1928.
[15]Skiadas, *100 chronia neoterē . . .*, p. 258.

headquarters. The tenth anniversary had been marked in Paris and the thirtieth had taken place in Lausanne, to which the IOC had moved after the First World War, which had prevented any events taking place on the twentieth anniversary. Needless to say, the Hellenic Olympic Committee did all it could, both to link the fortieth anniversary to a celebration of the classical past and to advertise the proposed Classical Games. The heavy overlay of classical themes throughout the IOC's visit to Greece was probably a welcome diversion from the controversy over the Berlin Olympiad due to open in two years. The IOC was headed at the time by Count Henri de Baillet-Latour, a Belgian member since 1903, who was elected as Coubertin's successor in 1925 and remained in that position until his death in 1942. The IOC clearly did not object to the incessant harking back to antiquity during its visit, although Baillet-Latour used his public speeches to defend the modern Olympic spirit. Somewhat less of a philhellene than Coubertin, he appeared more focused on the IOC's concerns with the dangers posed by politics, commercialism, and the dilution of amateurism; nevertheless, he also lauded the classical spirit in his public appearances.

The eleven-day commemoration began on May 16, 1934, the day the IOC formally opened its thirty-first session in one of the most imposing neoclassical buildings in Athens, which houses the Academy of Athens, a self-selecting assembly of Greece's most prominent intellectuals. In opening the proceedings, President Baillet-Latour was happy to report progress on the two main issues that concerned the IOC: the concession of "guarantees" required of the German Olympic Committee as a prerequisite for holding the games in Berlin; and the problem of "semi-professionalism." The rest of his brief remarks outlined the IOC's other achievements; he would save his praise for ancient Greece for more public occasions.[16] But Coubertin's message (he was too infirm to travel to Athens) was brimming with praise for both ancient and modern Greece.[17] After the opening session, the IOC, along with the Greek president, leading government figures, and foreign ambassadors, attended an event organized by the Greek National Theater. It began with the male Choir of Athens's rendition of the *Hymn to Apollo*, which Coubertin had incorporated into the proceedings of the founding congress at the Sorbonne, followed by performances of Aeschylus' *Persians* and Euripides' *Cyclops*.

[16]HOC Archives, k62/f8/e18/May 16 1934/Speech by IOC President Baillet-Latour.
[17]*Ibid.*, k62/f8/e11; Pierre de Coubertin, "À mes amis hellènes."

The classical theme of the visit continued over the following days. On the afternoon of the second day—in another gesture of deference—the IOC visited the main cemetery in Athens, where it paid its respects to past leaders of the Greek Olympic movement, including Iōannēs Chrysafēs and Dēmētrios Vikelas. This was followed by a visit to the recently restored Acropolis and an official dinner hosted by the mayor of Athens. On the third day, the morning working session was followed by an excursion to Poseidon's temple at Sounion and to the site of the battle of Marathon, with a reception at the Greek foreign ministry concluding the day's proceedings. The fourth day was just as busy, although the IOC's morning session lasted only two hours. The IOC assembled at the Panathenaic Stadium to witness the unveiling of a *stele* that honored Coubertin's revival of the games (all previous Olympiads were inscribed on it). The organizers reluctantly agreed not to list the 1906 interim Olympics, but HOC vice-president Nikolaos Athanasiadēs did not miss the opportunity in his short address to claim that sport had always been considered a national institution in Greece.[18] The highlight of the day was a special ceremony on the Acropolis after dusk. The date and time were chosen because of a full moon that night. The ceremony included a reading of excerpts from a text that embodied French nineteenth-century philhellenism, Ernest Renan's "Prayer on the Acropolis." The emotionally delivered rendition, by actress Elenē Papadakē of the National Theater, moved many of those in attendance to tears.

Renan's text was emblematic of the organizers' wish to revive the romantic philhellenism of the nineteenth century and ignore the more recent ambiguous, if not critical, views of Western intellectuals regarding Greek antiquity. Renan idealized the Acropolis, writing that, until he saw it, he had "believed that perfection was not of this world." This was no longer a commonly held view. As we have noted, twentieth-century intellectuals such as Virginia Woolf had a less romantic attitude to modern Greece's actual embodiment of ancient Greece. One of Virginia Woolf's close friends, British women's activist Ethel Smyth (1858–1944), was irritated by Greece and unimpressed with the ancient sites when she visited the country in 1927. Smyth wrote that the ruins in Olympia were "more painfully archaeological than ever."[19] Another brand of intellectual, British writer Evelyn Waugh (1903–1966), wrote about his travels in the Mediterranean in a way typical of

[18]*Ibid.*, k62/f8/e24/May 19, 1934/Speech by Nikolaos Athanasiadēs.
[19]Ethel Smyth, *A Three-Legged Tour in Greece: March 24-May 4, 1925*, William Heinemann, London, 1927, p. 109.

his work, which was utterly unromantic about the countries and ancient sites
he visited. In his introduction to the 1947 reissue of Waugh's *Labels: A
Mediterranean Journal* (originally published in 1930), Kingsley Amis (still a
student at the time) noted, "It must have been a refreshment in 1930, as it is
now, to come a cross a travel book totally free of Mediterranean mystique, of
any implication that the author is condescending to reveal some hint of his
feeling for the ancient cradles of our culture."[20]

One wonders what these authors would have thought of the reenactment
of the Classical Games sponsored by the IOC in Greece. The IOC attended
the event on May 20, after several museum visits in the morning. The reenactment itself was preceded by a great deal of pomp. In the afternoon, the
members of the IOC and HOC greeted the Greek president at the entrance
to the Panathenaic Stadium. Three bands struck up the Greek national
anthem, followed by a procession of the flags of all the member-nations of
the IOC. As the flag-bearers marched past, the bands played the *Olympic
Hymn* accompanied by the Choir of Athens and no less than 3,600 boys and
girls representing all of Athens's high schools. Speeches followed, and
Iōannēs Makropoulos, Greek minister for education and religion, described
the IOC members as pilgrims who had come to Greece to worship the
Olympic spirit. The minister paid tribute to Coubertin and described the
revival of the games not merely as an important moment in the history of
sport, but as a defining event for the history of humanity since it represented
the restoration of the Olympic ideals.[21] The rest of the IOC's engagements in
Greece consisted of a four-day grand tour of the Peloponnese, with an itin-
erary that combined the major tourist stops, including the region's foremost
archeological sites: Corinth, Agamemnon's supposed tomb at Mycenae, the
ancient theater at Epidaurus, the town of Sparta and the nearby Byzantine
settlement at Mystras, and, of course, Olympia, where the IOC officially
closed its proceedings and ended its visit.

THE CLASSICAL GAMES

The reenactment of the Classical Games was the boldest attempt on the
part of the hosts to invest the IOC's thirty-first session with images of ancient
Greece. Iōannēs Chrysafēs (1873–1932) was the prime mover behind Greece's

[20]Robert Eisner, *Travelers to an Antique Land*, University of Michigan Press, Ann Arbor,
1991, p. 183.

[21]HOC Archives, k62/f8/e25/May 19, 1935/Speech of Iōannēs Makropoulos.

ultimately doomed effort to revive the so-called Classical Games. Chrysafēs was as much of an idealist as his friend Coubertin, and he was passionately engaged in persuading the Greek and international Olympic movements that the true spirit of the games could be rediscovered by recreating those of antiquity. He had studied at the University of Athens and obtained a degree in mathematical physics, but went on to become a certified trainer, working under Iōannēs Fōkianos. Chrysafēs was a man who pursued causes passionately, and he combined his enthusiasm for promoting physical education with a fervent nationalism. Early in his career as a physical-education teacher and sports administrator, he campaigned unsuccessfully for the introduction of Swedish-style exercises in the school curricula in place of the more static "German/Swiss" style of exercise. He had fought as a volunteer in the Greek uprising in Ottoman-controlled Crete in 1896, returning briefly to attend the Olympic Games. The following year, he fought in the Greek-Turkish war. At the turn of the century, he traveled abroad, frequently picking up valuable information about the latest developments in physical education and sports culture. He went to Sweden and then Paris, where he addressed an international conference on physical education. Chrysafēs was involved in organizing the interim Olympics in 1906, and he led the Greek delegation to the 1908 and 1920 Olympiads. Just before reenlisting in the Greek military to fight in the Balkan Wars, he had the satisfaction of seeing the government finally adopt a Swedish-based exercise curriculum in the schools. Chrysafēs published several books on physical education, ranging from historical studies on its theory and practice in ancient Greece to textbooks on Swedish methods and manuals designed for Greek schools.

Chrysafēs was a romantic, and he campaigned to restore what he considered to be the true spirit and form of sport in antiquity. He was thus attracted to the movement that opposed keeping records of athletic performances. This movement had become popular in Greece in 1896, the year that Chrysafēs published his views. They echoed the critique of recordkeeping emanating from the sports culture of central Europe and Scandinavia, which supported physical development over the pursuit of records. Competing for the sake of records, according to Chrysafēs, was detrimental to physical development and forced athletic clubs to focus exclusively on their ablest members. Chrysafēs's opposition to records was a lost cause, however, since "record-oriented" sport soon prevailed in Greece as it did everywhere else.[22]

---

[22]Koulouri, *Athlētismos kai opseis . . .* , pp. 123–124.

Chrysafēs's drive to restore forms of track and field to those of antiquity appeared to gain broader acceptance in 1925. Initially, he advocated the inclusion of these events in the Olympics. The Greek organizers of the interim games of 1906 had taken the liberty to include such events without the IOC's approval. Chrysafēs was the force behind the reintroduction of the discus throw used in antiquity, which was different from the conventional discus throw, at the unofficial Olympics in Athens in 1906 and the London games of 1908. The classical style involved throwing the discus upward, and had been extrapolated from studying classical texts and depictions, which, needless to say, caused a great deal of debate. In its meeting after the Paris Olympics, the IOC rejected the Greek plan. Its members politely pointed out to the Greek delegates that their proposal went against the committee's intentions to limit the number of sporting events in the Olympics, and that, in any case, differing opinions over the classical discus throw would raise too many complaints and conflicts.[23] Undeterred by this setback, Chrysafēs outlined his views on the Classical Games at an Olympic congress on education, held in conjunction with the IOC session in Prague in 1925. He talked about his vision of recreating the ancient Greek gymnasium and organizing the Classical Games in Greece between each Olympiad. The IOC allowed him to express his views because Coubertin shared many of his "purist" concerns. The two also shared an enthusiasm for restoring the ancient Greek (municipal) gymnasium as a public space for learning, exercise, and socialization.[24]

Coubertin's visit to Greece in 1927 provided Chrysafēs with a singular opportunity to publicize his concept. Coubertin attended a meeting of the HOC that year at which Chrysafēs submitted his proposal. At the meeting, the honored guest gave his support to a project that would reinvigorate the spirit of the Olympics, but he recommended that the Classical Games be restricted to events that were not part of the program of the Olympic Games. The HOC went ahead with its plans and, at the Amsterdam Olympiad of 1928, formally announced that the first Classical Games would be held in Athens in 1930. They would comprise three "Hellenic foot races," the discus and javelin throws, wrestling, and the pentathlon. The project received worldwide publicity and the Greek diaspora press was one of its most enthusiastic advocates. One Greek American monthly noted that "the Scandinavian and German athletes, who are keenly interested in the promotion of

---

[23]Manitakēs, 100 chronia neoterou . . . , p. 459.
[24]Skiadas, 100 chronia neoterē . . . , pp. 263–264.

classic games, have already shown a lively interest in the success of these games."[25]

Unfortunately, the ripple effect of Wall Street's crash in 1929 meant that the Greek economy experienced a severe downturn. The government, pleading lack of funds, postponed the games: they had to wait until 1934. While the games' postponement in 1930, and Chrysafēs's death in 1932, did not derail them, it robbed them of momentum and of the clarity of the original concept. Given the economic strictures on launching the games, the HOC reached a compromise: they would be "reenacted" during the IOC visit to Greece in 1934. It was a risky project, as researchers had yet to come up with satisfactory information about the precise ways in which sporting events were held in antiquity. Thus, while the Greek committee was very clear about what the Classical Games could offer Greece and the ailing Olympic movement, it was less clear, in Chrysafēs's absence, about what they entailed in practice.

The Hellenic Olympic Committee saw the Classical Games as augmenting both Greece's specific place in the Olympic movement and, more generally, its international status. The HOC invoked Greek national interests while soliciting help from the Greek government. The Greek sports world of the interwar period was acutely aware of how far Greece lagged behind other countries within the Olympic movement. Those feelings were captured well in a memorandum written in 1934 by Kōnstantinos Geōrgakopoulos, a member of the Hellenic Olympic Committee. The purpose of the memorandum was to solicit the help of the Greek ministry of education in the HOC's attempt to organize the Classical Games, which were the last chance for Greece, "the mother of Olympism," to "preserve her rights over her beautiful, spiritual child," wrote Geōrgakopoulos. It was too late to hope that Greece could maintain its privileged position over the modern Olympics, he explained.[26]

The rhetoric about Greece acquiring an important position in the Olympic movement, and enhancing its international standing more broadly, was never substantiated by Geōrgakopoulos or by any other advocate in the 1930s: it was, quite simply, a deeply held ideological principle. There was actually no concrete proof that either goal was being realized, unless one

---

[25]"Greeks Planning to Revive the Classic Olympic Games," *The Ahepan*, November 1929, p. 15.

[26]HOC Archives, k62/f3/e6, Geōrgakopoulos to minister of education, April 18, 1934.

considers the mere presence of the IOC in Greece as a major international occasion for the country. What in effect was happening was that Greek spokesmen were echoing the views of a growing number of voices that, in the debates over Greek identity, supported its continuity from antiquity to modernity. Even there, however, one may doubt the effectiveness of the rhetoric, as the country was shaken at the time by a number of social problems aggravated by the economic crisis of the early 1930s. Still, the country's parlous social and political state at the time did not seem to prevent Geōrgakopoulos and company from waxing lyrical about modern Greece and the Olympics—indeed, perhaps it even encouraged him.

The organization of the Olympics in Athens in 1896 and 1906 "had embedded the idea of holding the Games in the conscience of the civilized world," but this happy consequence for the rest of the world had a negative outcome for Greece, Geōrgakopoulos's memorandum noted. This was because "the technology demanded by the contemporary international games, and their complex organizational requirements, rendered the Panathenaic Stadium in Athens and the other Greek athletic facilities inadequate." Moreover, the memorandum added, the Greek state was now incapable of shouldering the considerable financial burdens involved in organizing international Olympics. This situation, Geōrgakopoulos continued, concerned the HOC because "the Greek athletic world cannot remain a mere spectator or anonymous participant of a magnificent athletic *fête* that grew and developed in Ancient Greece and was revived thanks to the heroic efforts and sacrifices of modern Greece."[27]

When the HOC president, Iōannēs Drosopoulos, wrote to the Greek minister of military affairs requesting his assistance in providing draftees, he was candid about Greece's vested interests. Stressing the significance of the reenactment, Drosopoulos wrote that "this reenactment will determine the restoration of the Classical Games, which will provide our country with the opportunity to continue this beautiful tradition of our ancestors, and will also bring about a significant influx of tourists." Those goals, he emphasized, were in the Greek national interest; by helping to realize them, the army would be continuing the glorious tradition of its ancestors.[28] The HOC's memorandum to the ministry of education drawn up by Geōrgakopoulos echoed these arguments, claiming that the Classical Games would allow

[27] *Ibid.*, k62/f3/e6, Geōrgakopoulos to minister of education, April 18, 1934.
[28] *Ibid.*, k62/f4/e12, HOC to ministry of military affairs, April 20, 1934.

Greece to assume the "position in civilization created by our ancestors" as well as benefit the national economy.[29]

Publicly, the Hellenic Olympic Committee touted the Classical Games as a way to restore the "true spirit" to international sport. A memorandum submitted by the HOC at the IOC session in 1934 restated many of Coubertin's—and the IOC's—concerns about the erosion of the games' founding principles. The primary worry was that the pursuit of records overshadowed the value of winning: athletes were focusing more on breaking records than on victory. The memorandum blamed this trend on modern technological changes that made measurements more exact but also more complicated and difficult to follow. In contrast, the ancient Olympics involved raw speed and strength unaided by technology, and the goal was victory, celebrated without regard to the achievement of a record-making performance. The simplicity of ancient sport, the unalloyed contest between human beings and natural forces, and the moral and spiritual dimension to athletic competition, were at the core of the revival of the Olympic Games. It was this spirit that the HOC wished to restore by establishing games modeled strictly on the athletic competitions of antiquity.[30]

Unfortunately, the reenactment of the Classical Games, hastily prepared and superficially choreographed, fell flat. The competitions were held as faithfully as possible to those of antiquity. The "athletes" wore loincloths and were barefoot, and the races started when a stretched rope was lowered in front of the runners. As some observers pointed out, however, many facets of the ancient games, such as wrestling and the high jump, were unknown. And the use of army draftees, who were essentially acting rather than competing, meant that the ancient spirit was not conveyed effectively.[31]

SPORT AND POLITICS

The IOC's endorsement of the Classical Games went beyond the routine manipulation of ancient Greece for the purpose of highlighting the historical pedigree of the Olympics. This was a time when debate was raging over whether or not, following Adolf Hitler's accession to power in 1933, the 1936 Olympiad scheduled for Berlin should take place in that city. A large part of

[29] *Ibid.*, k62/f3/e6, Geōrgakopoulos to minister of education, April 18, 1934.
[30] *Ibid.*, k62/f3/e7, memorandum on the Classical Games, May 1934.
[31] Skiadas, *100 chronia neoterē . . .* , pp. 272–273.

the athletic community throughout the world had expressed its opposition to holding the games in the German capital. In the United States, where those protests were pronounced, the country's most important sporting authority, the Amateur Athletic Union, voted in late 1933 for a boycott of the 1936 games unless the Nazi regime reversed its discriminatory policies toward Jewish athletes. This thorny issue was all but swept under the rug by the IOC in 1934, at least in terms of its public pronouncements. Indeed, the "Hellenization" of the games provided the perfect smokescreen for IOC officials to try and turn the public's attention elsewhere.

Actually, the return to classical roots was more than a smokescreen; it gave the IOC the excuse to present itself as being committed to the so-called "purity" of the ancient games, which were, predictably, presented as unsullied by political considerations. Keeping the Olympics "free of politics" was—and remained—the IOC's strategy whenever it faced embarrassing circumstances such as the one it confronted on the eve of the 1936 games, namely, dealing with the oxymoronic concept of "Nazi Olympism."

The Classical Games provided an ideal venue for Baillet-Latour to pontificate about the purity of the games and duck the issue of the compatibility of the "Olympic spirit" with Nazi Germany. In his speech prior to the opening of the Classical Games, Baillet-Latour spoke about the threat to the spirit of the Olympics from several factors, including politics, jealousies and overriding ambition among certain sports administrators, commercial calculations, growing emphasis on winning rather than on participating, and the undermining of the principles of amateurism and physical education. Physical education, Baillet-Latour emphasized, had, "as its purpose, to endow a race [sic] of people with a strong organism that provided healthy males with the necessary balance between the cerebral and the physical, a balance that enabled them to be cool-headed and face the difficulties of life." He added that, in a moral sense, sport taught people to respect authority. Baillet-Latour also touched on politics, albeit in an oblique and nominal reference to the growing controversy over the upcoming Olympics. He stated that "physical education . . . cannot have a political, religious or linguistic coloring,"[32] a move designed to underline the IOC's "apolitical" attitude.

For their part, the Greeks seemed to be oblivious to the controversy over the Berlin games, let alone the IOC's manipulation of the ancient "spirit." With the exception of a single letter by an American Jewish organization

[32]HOC Archives, k62/f8/e18/Discours du Président du CIO/29 Mai 1934.

explaining its opposition to the games in Berlin, the available documents in the HOC's archives do not include any other material on this topic. As for newspaper commentary, it was limited to reports of the controversy around the world. Further research on Greek attitudes is required, but until more light is shed on Greek views, it does seem as if Greek pride over the recognition of the ancient past obscured the sinister and manipulative sides of the celebration of the ancient spirit in Athens.

* * *

Coubertin's turn to the classical roots of the Olympics in the wake of the First World War, an era identified with the rise of modernity, is not surprising. Eric Hobsbawm—who coined the phrase, "invented traditions"—wrote that "they are responses to novel situations which take the form of reference to old situations."[33] Grateful for Coubertin's initiative in integrating ancient Greek symbolism—and, as a result, modern Greece—into the Olympic movement, Greece relaxed pressure on the issue of becoming the permanent venue and realigned its Olympic policy to exploit the movement's return to antiquity. The Greeks were quick to understand that Coubertin and other like-minded colleagues on the IOC saw ancient tradition as a useful counterbalance to the ills besetting the movement; they therefore designed their role as the repository of ancient Greek culture, and sport, appropriately. This was not always easy or even effective, as we have seen. Nonetheless, Greece was—or, rather, thought it was—back in the international Olympic picture, and that was a significant asset for a small country without international stature on any other front. Regrettably, this process came with a heavy moral cost at a time when the rise of the Nazis would not persuade the IOC to move the games away from Berlin. Classical roots—and, by extension, modern Greece— became unwilling accomplices to the IOC's spurious claim that the Olympics did not take politics into account.

The Greeks showed their gratitude to Coubertin in the ceremonies held in Olympia after his death. The founder of the modern Olympics died in Switzerland on September 2, 1937. Coubertin had requested that his ashes be sprinkled on the sacred grove in Olympia, but, without explanation, his family decided to bury his body and, instead of his ashes, sent his embalmed heart to Greece. In a carefully organized, simple, and solemn ceremony

---

[33]Eric Hobsbawm and Terence Ranger, editors, *The Invention of Tradition*, Cambridge University Press, Cambridge, 1983, p. 2.

attended by the HOC, government representatives, and Crown Prince Paul of Greece, his heart was interred under the *stele* that commemorated his role in founding the modern Olympics.

CHAPTER 5

GREECE AND THE BERLIN OLYMPIAD

AT EXACTLY 11:30 AM ON JULY 20, 1936, a combination of lenses and mirrors concentrated the rays of the sun into a single beam, igniting a chemical mixture at the bottom of a large silver bowl on the site of ancient Olympia: the Olympic flame had been lit. "High Priestess" Koula Pratsika, resplendent in her short white tunic and sandals, knelt to light the torch. Followed by eleven other young women portraying maidens of the temple, she walked, torch held aloft, toward an altar manufactured for the occasion, reciting parts of Pindar's Olympic odes. The torch was successfully transferred to the altar and, as its flames leapt upward, the women stood at attention while photographers steadied their cameras. A runner prepared to receive the torch. The symbolic journey of the torch, from Olympia to Berlin, was the most significant event invoking Greece as the *locus classicus* of the Olympic Games between the world wars.

Indeed, the most controversial games of the twentieth century served to establish a lasting connection between modern Greece and the Olympics. The so-called "Nazi Olympics" involved not only a brazen attempt to celebrate Aryan superiority but also a homage to the Olympic movement's classical heritage. Hitler was initially dubious about holding the games in Berlin. He was nevertheless persuaded to embrace them, partially as a result of a group of German classicists, heirs to a distinguished scholarly and philhellenic tradition. The combination of the Nazi penchant for spectacle and mass rallies was wedded to what was originally conceived as a celebration of classical Greek sport, and the result was an unprecedented display of the ancient Greek heritage at the Berlin Olympiad. Although Greece was never granted the right to host the games permanently, the Berlin games established it as the permanent source of Olympic ritual.[1]

[1]Richard Mandell, *The Nazi Olympics*, University of Illinois Press, Urbana, 1987, is the standard study of the 1936 Olympics and the main source on this subject for this chapter.

The International Olympic Committee, in what was the most heavily debated—and debatable—decision in its history, decided to proceed with the games in Berlin despite growing international protests in Europe and the United States and even the announcement of alternative, "people's" Olympics in Barcelona (in then-Republican Spain) supported by antifascist and socialist parties. The considerable body of literature on these games reflects a consensus that the Nazis treated them as a propaganda exercise, and that the IOC was complicit in that process, although authors differ among themselves over the extent of the IOC's responsibility.[2] While it is true that the IOC forced Hitler to make some concessions, these were relatively minor compared to the political content and symbolism of the 1936 Olympiad.

The Greek state, which controlled the Hellenic Olympic Committee, was therefore a willing participant in the German-Nazi appropriation of ancient Greece in the context of the 1936 games. The country's political life had begun a gradual slide into conservatism in the early 1930s when a series of developments saw the demise of Venizelos's Liberal party, the ascent of the conservative Populist party, and, finally, the restoration of the monarchy in 1935. This meant that Greek governments during this period wedded the concept of modern Greek continuity with the ancient past to the service of the authoritarian regimes they favored. This also entailed considerable tolerance for the policies of the newly established Nazi regime. Thus, Athens welcomed the feelers put out by Berlin concerning German plans to give the 1936 games a distinctly classical Greek accent, and the Greeks were ready to provide assistance in that venture. Indeed, the months prior to the Olympics witnessed the steady rise of the political fortunes of General Iōannēs Metaxas, who believed in a strong state, harbored a metaphysical sense of nationalism rooted in ancient Greece, and also happened to be a germanophile. Greece had experienced considerable political and social unrest during the first months of 1936 when King George II turned to Metaxas and appointed him prime minister in April. Less than four months later, on August 4, Metaxas engineered a coup and established himself as dictator, the

[2] Aside from Mandell, the English-language sources include Arnd Krüger, "The Olympic Games of 1936 as the Fifth German Combat Games," in Roland Naul, editor, *Contemporary Studies in the National Olympic Games Movement*, Peter Lang, Frankfurt, 1977, pp. 153–175; Findling & Pelle, *Historical Dictionary . . .*, pp. 84–92; Guttmann, *The Olympics . . .*, pp. 53–71; Maurice Roche, *Mega Events and Modernity: Olympics and Expos in the Growth of Global Culture*, Routledge, New York, 2000, pp. 108–122; Alfred E. Senn, *Power, Politics and the Olympic Games*, Human Kinetics, Champaign, 1999, pp. 50–63.

Παναθηναϊκὸν Στάδιον   Athènes.   Le Stade.

A postcard depicts the Panathenaic Stadium during the 1906 interim Olympics in Athens;
© A. Pallis and Cie, Athènes.

The Greek team enters the stadium during the inaugural ceremonies of the Antwerp Olympiad in 1920.

Young women from the Lykeion tōn Ellēnidōn place wreaths on the flags of the IOC member-nations, May 1934; © Fōto Spor (*Athens*).

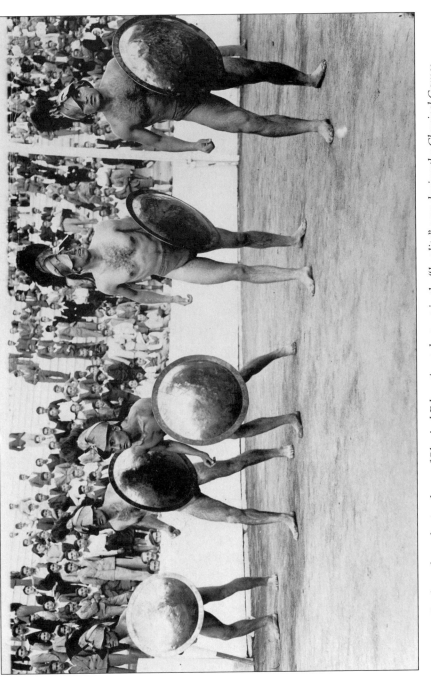

Students from the Academy of Physical Education take part in the "hoplite" race during the Classical Games

In ancient Olympia, kneeling "priestesses" receive the flame that will be transported to the Berlin Olympiad, July 1936; © Iōannēs P. Tselepēs (Pyrgos).

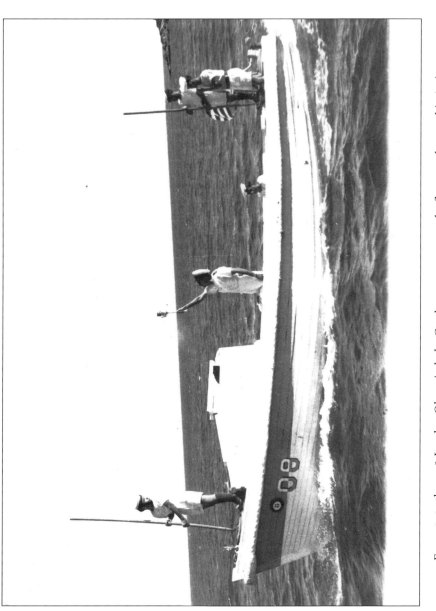

En route to the 1948 London Olympiad, the Greek navy transports the flame to the warship Astinx

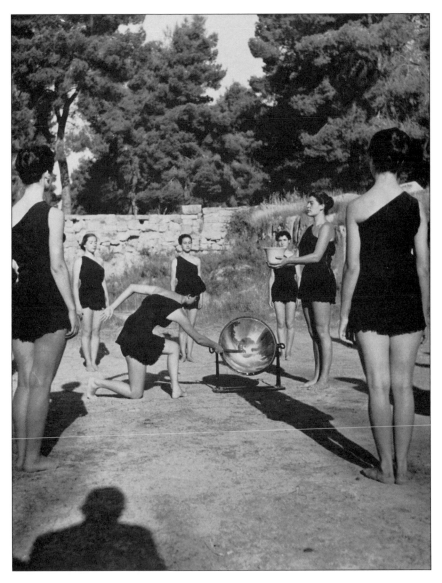

In ancient Olympia, "High Priestess" Xanthippē Pēcheōn lights the flame that will be transported to the Helsinki Olympiad, June 1952; © Ēnōmenoi Fōtoreporter.

"Hoplites" ritually "obstruct" torchbearer E. Marino from entering the Acropolis in a ceremonial moment from the torch relay prior to the Melbourne Olympiad, November 1956; © Adelfoi Megalokonomou.

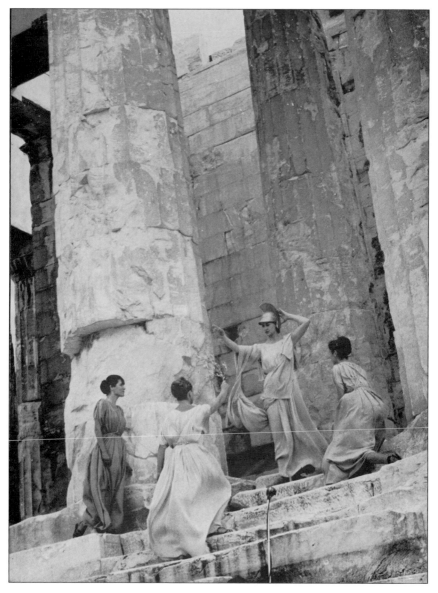

The "Goddess Athena" (actress Maria Kazazē) gives an olive branch to a "priestess" (actress Aleka Katselē) in a ceremony on the Acropolis prior to the Melbourne games, November 1956; © Adelfoi Megalokonomou.

In the presence of Crown Prince Constantine, the Olympic flame is transferred to containers (in the center of the photo) for its first airborne trip (to Melbourne) November 1956. © Adelfoi Flōrou.

A runner carries the Olympic torch to Athens airport en route to the winter Olympics in Grenoble, December 1967; © K. Megalokonomou, Ellēnika Fōtografika Nea.

The "priestess" (actress Nora Katselē) raises the flame in ancient Olympia
prior to its relay to the Mexico City Olympiad in 1968;
© *K. Megalokonomou,* Ellēnika Fōtografika Nea.

The HOC meets on January 21, 1975, with Deputy Minister Achilleas Karamanlēs (center, facing the camera, hands on table). HOC vice-president Tzōrtzēs Athanasiadēs sits next to him, on the left, while HOC president Apostolos Nikolaidēs sits on his other side, on the right. Next to Nikolaidēs is HOC second vice-president, Dēmētrios Xerouchakēs and, next to the latter, the committee's general secretary, Nikos Filaretos; © K. Megalokonomou, Ellēnika Fōtografika Nea.

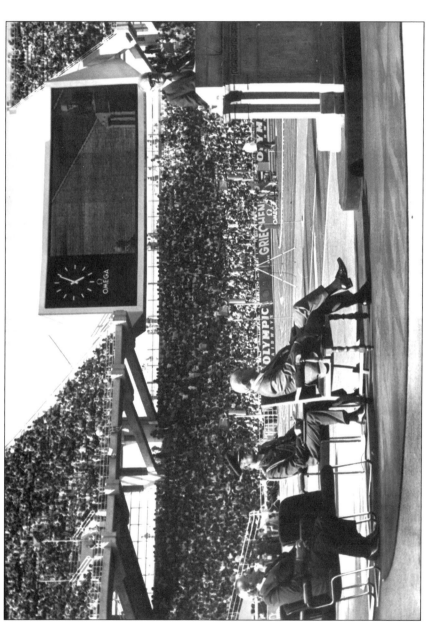

Greek president Kōnstantinos Karamanlēs (at the head of the seated group) during the Olympic Stadium's inauguration, 1982; © K. Megalokonomou, Ellēnika Fōtografika Nea.

A series of stamps issued in 1967 with five different athletic themes, including two Olympic ones; © Philatelic Directorate, Hellenic Post Office.

A series of Olympic stamps issued for the 1980 Moscow Olympiad, with various depictions of ancient stadiums; © Philatelic Directorate, Hellenic Post Office.

A series of Olympic stamps issued for the 1984 Los Angeles Olympiad, with ancient Greek themes; © Philatelic Directorate, Hellenic Post Office.

A series of Olympic stamps issued for the 1992 Barcelona Olympiad, with contemporary athletic themes; © Philatelic Directorate, Hellenic Post Office.

head of a quasi-fascist regime that claimed inspiration from ancient Sparta. With Metaxas in power from April 1936 onward, it is not surprising that Berlin was guaranteed all the help it needed to embark on its manipulation of the ancient Greek spirit. As was the case in earlier decades, any international recognition of Greece's ties with its past was regarded positively in Athens. That this recognition in this case came from the Third Reich does not appear to have caused undue concern in Greece. Even potential critics of the alliance with the Nazis were too distracted by the waves of strikes and police violence that swept through Greece's urban centers during the first six months of the year.

Kōnstantinos Th. Dēmaras, a young academic, was among the very few observers not caught up in the widespread enthusiasm over Greece's role in the Berlin Olympics. Appropriately for a scholar who would become an authority on the Greek Enlightenment, Dēmaras was critical of the religious content surrounding the torch-lighting and relay, which had been among the new features of the games conceived by the German organizers and had involved considerable input from Greece. In a newspaper article, Dēmaras noted that these somewhat hyperbolic and theatrical religious ceremonies connoted the sun-worshiping cults that, he wrote, were the source of the original use of fire in ancient times. He added that, by including such elements in the games, the organizers were unintentionally strengthening the idolatrous displays of Hitler's regime in Germany. Dēmaras also pointed out that if the purpose of the ceremonies was to celebrate the spirit of ancient Greece, the ancient ideal of a healthy mind in a healthy body also had to be evoked. As such, the Olympics should celebrate the intellect as well as athletics.[3]

Dēmaras's was unfortunately a solitary voice reminding his compatriots that a cultural affinity with classical Greece did not, necessarily, have to serve an authoritarian logic. Indeed, throughout most of the twentieth century, ultra-conservative thinkers in Greece had blithely harnessed the spirit of ancient Greece, and the supposed continuity between modernity and antiquity, to right-wing political agendas. Liberal and left-wing thinkers, in contrast, ceded this ground to their ideological adversaries by not proposing a counter-discourse that linked classical traditions to democratic and progressive principles. This cultural climate dominated through the mid-1970s and

---

[3] Kōnstantinos Th. Dēmaras, "Olympiaka" ["Regarding the Olympics"], *Eleutheron Vēma*, July 26, 1936.

began to change only during the last quarter of the century, when a democratic and European-oriented Greece produced perspectives that broke the right-wing monopoly on the Greeks' understanding of their classical heritage. The Hellenic Olympic Committee was affected accordingly, and its own relationship to the ancient Olympics and their meaning would change only in the latter part of the twentieth century with the demise of the more traditionalist generation of leaders.

THE GERMAN-GREEK CONNECTION

The Nazis orchestrated the recognition received by Greece at the 1936 games, but they were able to legitimize their plans with the help of a long tradition of German philhellenism and study of ancient Greece. E. M. Butler, a Cambridge scholar, described this relationship as "the tyranny of Greece over Germany." The list of German intellectuals enthralled by Greek antiquity consists of several major thinkers, including, of course, Johann Winckelmann, Goethe, Heine, and Nietzsche. They were among many, however, whose interests and work reflected an almost obsessive preoccupation with ancient Greek culture.[4] Winckelmann, in fact, was the first to suggest excavations be undertaken at Olympia.

Heinrich Schliemann (1822–1890) initiated excavations at several important sites and, by doing so, paved the way for others to begin explorations at Olympia. Schliemann, a German merchant, began his study of archeology late in life. After marrying a Greek woman several years his junior, he then proceeded to make a series of stunning, albeit controversial, archeological discoveries at Troy and Mycenae. In his own way, he was the heir to the long and distinguished German philhellenic tradition. According to Butler, "the exaggeration, the excess which is discernible in the attitude to Greece of one great German after another from Winckelmann onward, found its supreme manifestation in Schliemann."[5] Yet, Schliemann was also an opportunist of sorts, using his discoveries to turn himself into an international celebrity even as fellow archeologists disputed his exaggerated claims.

Schliemann wanted to explore ancient Olympia, but the Greek government granted permission to German archeologist Ernst Curtius (1814–1896), professor of ancient history at Berlin. Curtius was less flamboyant and more

---

[4] E. M. Butler, *The Tyranny of Greece Over Germany*, Macmillan, New York, 1935.
[5] *Ibid.*, p. 304.

orthodox in his approach to excavations. The excavation of Olympia between 1875 and 1881 was the first large-scale continuous excavation in Greece made possible through international contracts: it was financed by the German government and managed by a board of directors in Berlin. Curtius was only the first among his compatriots to begin excavating at Olympia, having worked hard to generate support for the project from the Reichstag. He invoked philhellenic sentiment and a belief that investment in culture would deflect decadence and materialism from Germany. When he arrived in Olympia, it was under the terms of a negotiated deal between the German and Greek governments. None of the artifacts could leave Greece except for duplicates; a small museum was to be built on the grounds; and the German government could recoup the costs of the dig by selling reproductions. The costs were indeed astronomical, and while Bismarck was forced to terminate excavations in 1880, the seeds of scholarly cooperation had been planted.

Some of the most distinguished German archeologists also worked in Olympia, including Wilhelm Dörpfeld (1853–1940) and Adolf Fürtwangler (1853–1907, and father of Wilhelm, the celebrated conductor), who developed a bitter rivalry over the dating of ancient artifacts, including some found at Olympia. German archeologists excavated the central part of the sanctuary, including the major structures visible today: the Temple of Zeus, the Heraion, the Metroon, the Bouleuterion, the Philippeion, the Echo Stoa, the Treasuries, and the Palaestra. Among the most important finds were the sculptures from the Temple of Zeus, the *Nike* of Paionius, the *Hermes* of Praxiteles, and numerous bronzes. As the German Archaeological Institute's Website explains, "the goal of this undertaking was the scientific investigation of the site, not—as was normal up until that time—the attainment of exhibition pieces for the homeland of the excavators."[6]

On the occasion of the Berlin Olympics, the German institute decided to begin a new round of excavations. Coubertin had given the project his enthusiastic support. The work started in 1937 and continued with digs begun earlier on the south wall of the stadium, the south hall, the bath complex, and the gymnasium. Among the finds were the stone weights used by athletes to gain momentum in the long jump and the statue of an athlete starting his race; obviously, however, the most spectacular outcome of this round of excavations was the unearthing of the entire stadium, a task that involved

[6]"Olympia;" Athens Section, German Archaelogical Institute, http://www.dainst.org/index_548_en.html.

shifting 40,000 square meters of earth and stones (although further excavations would not reconstitute the stadium in its present form until after the Second World War).[7] Meanwhile, classicists in Germany were busy envisioning ways in which the Berlin Olympiad might showcase the parallel between modern Germany and ancient Greece.

On the eve of the Olympics, it was Hitler himself who encouraged a more explicit manifestation of the ties between Germany and ancient Greece. Berlin was a city of monumental, neoclassical buildings and museums with significant pieces of ancient Greek art. Planning a grandiose rebuilding of Berlin, Hitler had turned to architect Albert Speer, an admirer of the classical Greek style. Their long-term plans were never completed, but Speer designed the Zeppelin Field in Nuremberg, used by Hitler for his Nazi rallies, to imitate the horseshoe style of the Panathenaic Stadium in Athens. With regard to the Olympics, rituals designed to evoke the customs of Greek antiquity, such as the torch relay, parts of the opening ceremony, and an exhibition of ancient Greek art in Berlin, would not have been possible without the approval of the Führer himself.[8]

THE TORCH RELAY

The torch relay is a unique and captivating buildup to the Olympic Games and one of their most recognizable rituals. It was enacted for the first time at the 1936 Olympics. It was just one of many symbolic practices that the German organizers included in order to make a memorable and special event, and its creation exemplified the ways the German initiative resonated in Greece. Germany's Carl Diem (1882–1962), another devotee of ancient Greece, came up with the idea of the torch relay and received enthusiastic support from fellow members on the German Olympic Committee. When the IOC approved the project, Alexandros Filadelfeus, a member of the Hellenic Olympic Committee, suggested that the flame be lit at the temple in Olympia.

In conceiving this plan, Diem drew attention to the use of flames and torch processions that the Olympic movement happened to share with the authoritarian and fascist movements of interwar Europe. Events that

[7]Berthold Fellman, "The History of the Excavations at Olympia," *Olympic Review*, 1973, pp. 109–118.

[8]For Hitler's classicist esthetics, see Frederic Spotts, *Hitler and the Power of Aesthetics*, Overlook Press, New York, 2003.

involved lighted torches in a procession or race—sometimes a relay race—had been part of both religious festivals in antiquity and the ancient Olympics. The *lampadēdodromies* involved runners carrying a flaming torch while simultaneously attempting to outpace their competitors and keeping the flame alit. The practice, originally a religious act honoring a god, developed into a form of competitive sport. The presence of a flame at the altar in ancient Olympia during the athletic events symbolized peace and friendship. The modern Olympics had included the use of fire and flaming torches from the time of the 1896 games, when a procession of torches had taken place after dusk. Four years later, the design on the winners' medals included a torch. A torch procession was also included in the interim Olympics in 1906. But it was the emphasis on symbolism and tradition during the interwar period that introduced more dramatic uses of fire in the Olympics. The 1928 games in Amsterdam had their Tower of Marathon, while the organizers of the Los Angeles games had created a kind of altar at the entrance to the stadium where a flame burned during the course of the event. The flame at the Los Angeles Coliseum became the unofficial emblem of the 1932 games and featured in many photographs and drawings in newspapers and magazines.

The use of a torch and indeed the inception of a torch relay cannot be considered as unalloyed evocations of ancient Greek practices, however. Torchlit processions had become a staple of the Nazis in Germany and of other fascist movements throughout Europe. The symbolism was inescapable, but none of the major accounts of the preparations leading to the Berlin games suggest great concern over this among sports administrators or commentators in those European states that remained democratic at the time. When, during the IOC session in Greece in May 1932, the German Karl Ritter von Halt, conveying Diem's views, proposed a torch relay from the sanctuary in Olympia to Berlin for the city's Olympiad, the proposal was well received. In 1935, the IOC formally approved the idea, paving the way for the first torch-lighting ceremony that took place in July 1936.

Many have speculated that Diem's torch relay was a Nazi-inspired plan; even if it were not, however, the concept's obvious connection to the symbols used by the Nazis and fascists should have been damning enough. Richard Mandell, author of the classic study on the Berlin Olympics, describes Diem as "the greatest sports historian and most profound theorist of sports education" and notes that he was not a party member, although he admired the

Nazis' achievements before the war and cooperated with them, thinking that he was turning German classicism into a mass movement.[9] Still, one cannot help but notice the frightening correspondence of the use of torches by the Olympic and Nazi movements, and the apparent unwillingness of anyone within the Olympic movement to prevent the plan from being implemented.

The IOC's approval spurred copious planning and preparation. Diem was eager to model the relay on ancient Greek practice and sought advice from his colleagues in order to get as close to the original methods as possible. Georg Karo (1872–1963), a classicist and former director of the German Archaeological Institute in Athens, informed Diem that the ancients used faggots of narthex stalks; he added, however, that that material would be unreliable if the flame was to be kept burning for the twelve consecutive days needed for the relay from Olympia to Berlin. With the help of chemists, therefore, Diem designed a modern version of the torch that relied on incendiary magnesium, and he enlisted the help of the Krupp firm to manufacture the torches to be used in the relay. Another German industrial giant, optical manufacturers Carl Zeiss of Jena, produced the reflectors that Koula Pratsika would use to gather the rays of the sun and light the flame at Olympia. Needless to say, Hitler's government spared no effort to ensure the smooth and unobstructed passage of the relay through each country.[10]

The Greek government and the Hellenic Olympic Committee were just as concerned as their German counterparts about the relay's success, and their eagerness to ensure it must be interpreted as something more than merely doing their duty. To date, no information has surfaced indicating that anyone in the government or the HOC had second thoughts about Greece's role in the torch relay. Certainly, the Olympic committee could have resisted any pressure from the government since, after the restoration of the monarchy in 1935, the HOC's new president was Crown Prince Paul, following in the footsteps of his father, Constantine. In actuality, both government and HOC appear to have done all in their power to secure the success of the project, unconcerned with the problem that, by doing so, they were cooperating with Hitler's Germany. Thus, the railroad station at the small village of Olympia was spruced up and the streets and public areas received additional electrical lighting. The village also gained additional telephone and telegraph lines, and postal facilities were improved. The police solved the problem of

[9]Mandell, *The Nazi Olympics*, p. 85.
[10]*Ibid.*, pp. 130–132.

lack of available accommodation by obliging the local residents to provide beds for visitors.[11]

The torch relay afforded the Greek organizers the opportunity to indulge their own penchant for harking back to antiquity. The solemn ceremony surrounding the lighting of the flame in the Altis, the sacred enclosure of the excavated temple at Olympia, was meant to evoke ancient practices. The female dancers of the elite *Lykeion tōn Ellēnidōn* dance troupe, dressed in short, beige-colored costumes, were the only ones to enter the sacred site around the altar. Pratsika was at their head, followed by Elenē Dragoumē, Liza Dragoumē, Annē Frangiadē, Rena Koimisē, Dora Loundra, Maria Loundra, Aleka Mazarakē, Nonē Papageōrgiou, Maria Panagiōtopoulou, Loulou Pesmatzoglou, and Elsa Vergē. After the high priestess gently transferred the flame from her torch to the fire altar at the temple, her entourage recited Pindaric odes.

The lighting of the fire altar was followed by several speeches, shortened because the midday July sun was blazing down on the crowd of guests and spectators. The local mayor delivered a brief speech and then a brief message by Coubertin was read; he had been too infirm to travel to Greece for the occasion. To the delight of the Greek crowd, Coubertin sang the praises of ancient Greece yet again. He described Olympia as "a most illustrious place" and described the Olympic movement as forging ahead "under the aegis of an eternal Hellenism that has not ceased to light the way for the centuries and whose ancient solutions remain today as applicable as they ever were." Coubertin's words were followed by speeches by the Greek government's representative, Kōnstantinos Geōrgakopoulos, and the German ambassador. They both stressed the significance of Greek antiquity to the present, as well as the close relations between Greece and Germany. Geōrgakopoulos's speech echoed the idea that the site itself had inspired the members of the IOC to dream up the torch relay during their visit to Olympia in 1934.[12]

Kōstas Kondylēs, who lit the torch at the fire altar, was a muscular youth clad in a loincloth. Kondylēs was the first of the 3,069 runners, each running one kilometer, who would transport the flame from Olympia to Berlin's Olympic stadium over a period of twelve days. The longest country segment was the 1,108 kilometers across Greece. The distance would have been shorter today because of improved roads, but the route in Greece was lengthened

---

[11]Skiadas, *100 chronia neoterē . . .*, pp. 299–300.

[12]"Apo tēn Archaian Olympian exekinēse chthes to ieron fōs" ["The Sacred Light Set Off Yesterday from Ancient Olympia"], *Eleutheron Vēma*, July 21, 1936.

because the relay needed to pass through Athens. After Greece, the relay wended its way through Bulgaria, Yugoslavia, Hungary, Austria, Czechoslovakia, and, finally, Germany, where it traveled for 267 kilometers north to Berlin.

There were ancient-style ceremonies at several stops as the flame proceeded north from Olympia toward the Greek-Bulgarian border. Hundreds of people lined the roads from Olympia to Athens. After meandering through the Peloponnese, the flame arrived in Athens on the afternoon of the next day, July 21. A large crowd assembled at the edge of the capital, on the road that linked it with Piraeus, where the runner who arrived lit the torch of the first Athenian runner. After a few tantalizing seconds and the lighting of the Athenian torch, a new round of cheering and straining against the police cordon was unleashed. In just over ten minutes, another torchbearer was making his way up the hill of the Acropolis. On either side of the road leading up to the ancient monuments, *euzones* (Greek royal guards) stood with the flags of all fifty countries taking part in the Berlin Olympiad. The so-called sacred rock was about to witness its first pseudo-pagan religious ceremony in almost two thousand years.

It involved three male actors of the Royal Theater dressed as *hoplites* (foot soldiers) and another, Nikolaos Rozan, dressed as the high priest of the temple. Rozan appeared at the Propylaea, the entrance to the Acropolis, where he received the torch before making his way toward the Parthenon, walking through a group of young female dancers (supposedly the temple's virgins) who rained rose petals on his path. As the "high priest" approached the altar and lit the flame, two priestesses on either side bowed and fell to their knees, while others placed wreaths around the altar. Rozan then retraced his steps to the entrance of the Parthenon, flaming torch still in hand. At the entrance, he addressed the runner who would take the torch, telling him to announce to humanity that "the Olympic spirit has not died. . . . [T]he Olympic flame will continue to enlighten the peoples of the world as long as they meet in contests that are peaceful, noble and beautiful. . . . [F]rom the depths of the centuries and from the temple of Pallas Athena [the Parthenon] and from the sacred rock of the Acropolis, I bless the athletes of the world who will participate in the XIth Olympiad of Berlin."[13]

The deliberate inclusion of the Acropolis in the torch relay, and the

[13]"Ē iera flox ekinēsasa ex Olympias diēlthe chthes panēgyrikōs ek tou asteos tēs Pallados Athēnas" ["The Sacred Flame that set off from Olympia Passed Through the City of Pallas Athena in Celebration"], *Eleutheron Vēma*, July 22, 1936.

special ceremony that was held there (repeated when the flame was on its way to Melbourne for the 1956 Olympiad), was calculated to enmesh the primary symbol of ancient Greek civilization into the symbolic meaning of the Olympics. Strictly speaking, the Acropolis was totally unrelated to the games held in ancient Olympia, but this was a mere detail that everyone was prepared to overlook in the overheated atmosphere of ceremonialism. After all, the Acropolis had featured in the events related to the 1896 and 1906 games in Athens, as well as in the IOC's meeting in 1934. Now, thanks to the torch relay, it became an organic part of the theatrical proceedings.

There was more to follow: the flame was taken to the Panathenaic Stadium where Greece's King George and members of the government attended another event at which athletes and "priestesses" combined to celebrate the Olympic spirit. Photographs show the stadium, with a capacity of 70,000-plus, almost full. The next day, the relay arrived at the ancient site of Delphi, where another ceremony took place. The torch-relay events were well attended, with large crowds at the ceremonies in Olympia, Corinth, Athens, and Delphi, and thousands lining the roads to see the torch make its way northward through central Greece and beyond, to the city of Thessalonikē.

The lighting of the torch and subsequent relay was a relatively short part of Leni Riefenstahl's classic documentary on the Berlin Olympics, *Olympia*, but it set the stage for the entire work, while her presence in Greece at the time added to the glamour of the occasion. The sheer novelty of filmmaking and the large size of Riefenstahl's entourage, not to mention her capricious demands of everyone involved, attracted almost more attention than the relay itself. The German filmmaker did not shoot a conventional documentary about the flame-lighting ceremony and relay (or the rest of the games, for that matter). Instead, she conveyed a fantastic image that evoked ancient grandeur—she favored showing the torchbearers in ancient settings, for example—and, toward that purpose, she improvised by focusing on ancient sites not necessarily connected to the Olympics (such as Delphi). At Olympia, she chose to depict a different altar for the lighting of the flame, as she deemed it more "filmic." At the ceremonies in Delphi, Riefenstahl became the center of attention when she accepted the invitation of one of the torchbearers to dance Greek dances with him in the stadium and ended up on the shoulders of Greek athletes, carried around the stadium to the applause of the assembled crowd.[14]

[14]Cooper C. Graham, *Leni Riefenstahl and Olympia*, The Scarecrow Press, Metuchen, 1986.

Greek writers, meanwhile, myopically saw the Olympic torch as a symbol of peace transmitting the spirit of ancient Greece to the rest of the world, especially to Germany. At the ceremonies in Olympia, Geōrgakopoulos told the assembled crowd: ". . . you have witnessed a sacred ceremony in which all the peoples of the world are included, have faith in the Olympic Spirit which free men, friends of peace and founders of a great and immortal civilization created." The poet Geōrgios Anninos wrote an ode entitled "Olympia 1936 AD," in which he spoke of a spirit of peace emanating from an ancient Greek sanctuary and becoming instilled, via the Olympic flame, in "Teutonic bodies."[15]

The successful conclusion of the Greek segment of the relay was a source of pride for many Greek observers. The Athens daily, *Eleutheron Vēma*, editorialized that the success must have reassured all who had expressed doubts about the project's feasibility, mainly because of the poor quality of Greek roads. Others had been concerned that Greek attitudes and (in)discipline would not sustain the relay's organizational requirements. Nonetheless, the editorial continued, thanks to the dedication of the organizers, the support of many young people, and the population's widespread interest and attendance, the project was successful.[16]

With most of the public distracted by the country's severe social and political upheavals, not many people appeared to have had time to react critically to the glowing reports of the Greek press, and the newspapers in Athens continued to cover the torch relay in a celebratory manner. The accolades to ancient Greece invoked by the relay as it made its way through Europe were a source of great pride to the Greeks. The German hosts inevitably outdid all other countries. In anticipation of the flame's entry into Germany, the mayor of a town on the German-Czech border invited the Greek students in Dresden to raise the Olympic flag at the border post. Dresden was the first large city to receive the flame in Germany, and its authorities organized an especially grandiose welcoming ceremony held in a large open space. The mayor made a special point in his speech to salute the Greek journalists present, who received an ovation from the crowd.[17]

The success of the torch-lighting and relay in 1936 led to their continua-

---

[15]Skiadas, *100 chronia neoterē* . . . , pp. 300–303.

[16]"Semeiōmata" ["Notes"], *Eleutheron Vēma*, July 25, 1936.

[17]Geōrgios Androulidakēs, "Ē teletē afixeos tēs Ieras Flogos eis Dresdēn—exeretikai timai eis tēn Elladan" ["The Ceremony of the Arrival of the Sacred Flame in Dresden: Extraordinary Honors for Greece"], *Prōia*, August 2, 1936.

tion in the Olympic Games from that time onward. As Olympics historian John MacAloon has noted, however, the flame relay has changed meaning over time. Some see it as a democratic counterpart to the elitist nature of the opening ceremonies in the host-city stadiums, which are attended only by the well-connected and wealthy. But more recently, the commercialization of the torch relay has shorn it of any hint of "democracy." A parody of its original inception, the opening event in its entirety is, today, a celebration of nothing more than itself, or at best of those who financed it, the natural result of a flood of money, self-interest, and political manipulation.[18]

While the dramatic transformation of the torch's symbolism through the present is easy to recognize, it is also true that the particular symbolism it acquired in 1936 was especially sinister, in that it legitimized the Nazi Olympiad. We have already seen how the recreation of the ancient spirit during the IOC's visit to Athens in 1934 helped sanitize the IOC's unwillingness to grapple with the political and moral issues associated with holding the games in Berlin. The torch ceremony is yet another example of how this modern institution acquired an ancient aura that overshadowed pressing contemporary political opposition. The Olympic movement depicted itself as a timeless, tradition-bound institution that was therefore untouched by the particular political dynamics of the present: in 1936, this self-justification validated the constructed continuity between antiquity and the Berlin games. In the event, modern Greece became a willing accomplice to this manipulative strategy.

THE OPENING CEREMONY

The opening ceremony of the 1936 games has gone down in history as a grotesque celebration of the Nazification of the Olympics. Hitler, in his brown Storm Trooper uniform, was the center of attention for a good part of the proceedings. After his grandiose entry into the packed, 110,000-capacity stadium, flanked by dignitaries including the IOC, the parade of athletes began led by the Greek team. A heretofore rarely used Olympic salute (an open palm held to the side) resembled that of the Nazis and echoed the eerie similarities between the two movements that had been evoked by the use of

[18]John MacAloon, "Olympic Ceremonies as a Setting for Intercultural Exchange," in Miquel De Moragas, John MacAloon, and Montserrat Llines, editors, *Olympic Ceremonies: Historical Continuity and Cultural Exchange*, IOC, Lausanne, 1996, pp. 29–43.

torches. Indeed, teams belonging to countries with pro-fascist regimes employed what was obviously the Nazi version of the salute, to the delight of the crowd. The German team, as hosts, brought up the rear of the parade. As they entered, marching eight abreast in perfect order, "Richard Strauss' huge orchestra dropped the innocent march they had been playing and launched into the familiar phrases of 'Deutschland über alles' and the 'Horst Wessellied [the Nazi anthem].' Almost the entire stadium rose instantly to freeze into the 'Heil Hitler' position and stayed that way."[19]

In what surely qualifies at best as willful blindness and, at worst, sheer awe at the Nazi display, the Greek press downplayed the obvious ideological manipulation of these games and concentrated instead on the "glory" they reflected on ancient Greece. The press maintained this posture throughout the Olympics, expressing varying degrees of admiration for the organization of the games and the host city more generally. Greek journalists visiting Berlin naively believed that the ancient spirit of the Olympics had somehow neutralized the sinister aspects of the Nazis. A week before the games opened, a Greek correspondent claimed that Greece had already achieved a victory in Berlin. The proof was that nationalist socialist imagery on the city's streets and public buildings had given way to Olympic symbols. The fact that the five Olympic rings had displaced the swastika, Chrēstos Kavafakēs wrote, was yet another sign of the power of the spirit of Greek antiquity.[20] A report on the front page of *Eleutheron Vēma* mentioned Radio Berlin's announcement that the arrival of the flame in the German capital was a reminder of the ancient Greek concept of competing not for money but for virtue—but the report passed over without comment the radio station's further statement that Germans welcomed the flame with their hearts and their arms raised in a Nazi salute. The Greek press, on the whole, fell into the trap of admiring the revival of ancient Greece but blatantly ignoring its underlying, and manifest, political exploitation.[21]

The August 2 headline on one of the Athens dailies proudly announced: "The XIth Olympiad Opened in Berlin with a Grandiose Acclamation of the Ancient Greek Spirit." Another headline described the Olympic flame

[19]Mandell, *Nazi Olympics . . .*, p. 150.
[20]Chrēstos A. Kavafakēs, "Ē nikē tēs Ellados eis to Verolino" ["Greece's Victory in Berlin"], *Eleutheron Vēma*, July 22, 1936.
[21]"To Verolinon ypedechthei me synginēsē kai enthousiasmon to Apollōneion Fōs tēs Olympias" ["Berlin Welcomed the Apollonian Light of Olympia with Emotion and Enthusiasm"], *Eleutheron Vēma*, August 2, 1936.

welcomed by Berlin as an "immortal symbol and lesson given by the Greeks," omitting the adjective "ancient." These sentiments encapsulated the way most Greek observers saw the opening ceremony of the Berlin Olympics. As always, the pole position of the Greek team elicited great pride: "First came the Greek athletic team. The Greek flag appeared suddenly against the dark background of the tunnel. There was Greece, not only with the memories of its great past, but also with its present strengths. . . . Greek antiquity was parading but with it came Louēs clad in the traditional dress and the bravery of Greece that began in 1821. And after Greece came everyone else in alphabetical order. . . ."[22] The parade's ending, with the rousing entry of the German team, led to the spectacular entry of the last relay runner into the Olympic stadium and the lighting of the altar, which strained the crowd's emotions even further. Needless to say, the moment gave rise to a new round of articles in the Greek press brimming with national pride.[23] The enthusiasm of the Greek press for Greece's prominence in the opening ceremonies was such that Hitler's invocation of the ancient Greek spirit of the Olympics in his speech to the IOC was reported with no political criticism, even by the liberal press. The events that followed included a performance by the *Lykeion tōn Ellēnidōn*; a veteran activist for women's issues in Greece, Kallirroē Parren, led the handpicked forty-member group that had traveled from Athens.

One of the most memorable moments of the opening ceremony came when Spyros Louēs was presented to Hitler, an encounter that epitomized the way both the German and Greek sides cooperated with each other to lend the opening ceremony its grandeur. Louēs, a national hero in Greece, had traveled with the Greek athletes and taken part in the parade. The old athlete, dressed in traditional Greek dress, flanked by German athletes (including boxer Max Schmeling), and with tears of emotion streaking his tanned and wrinkled face, offered Hitler an olive branch. It was a highly symbolic—and, in retrospect, profoundly sad—moment that captured the confluence of Hitler's Germany and Metaxas's Greece through the Olympic Games.

[22]Chrēstos Kavafakēs, "To Athlētikon Stadion tou Verolinou" ["The Athletic Stadium of Berlin"], *Eleutheron Vēma*, August 4, 1936.

[23]Nikolaos Lanitēs, "Ē Lampas eis to Verolinon" ["The Torch in Berlin"], *Eleutheron Vēma*, August 7, 1936.

GREECE'S ATHLETIC PERFORMANCE

The Athens correspondents noted that Greece's "privileged" moment in the sphere of ritual at Berlin failed to obscure the country's less-than-impressive athletic status. The issue of the country's inability to field a competitive team in the Olympics was unavoidable. The more attention lavished on Greece in the ceremonies, the more Greek observers became acutely aware of how poorly their country would do in the sporting contests themselves. A few days before the games opened, a Greek journalist tried to place the role of Greek athletes in its proper perspective. "Our participation in the Olympic Games is not a sporting expedition in pursuit of victories, it is the fulfillment of a duty," sportswriter "Geo" wrote in a major Athens daily. "When other countries send their athletes to the Olympics without any great chance of success," he continued, "it would not be proper for Greece, the inheritor of the Olympic tradition, to be absent from the international playing field with the excuse that it did not have athletes strong enough to win." The writer underscored that the true purpose of the Olympics was participating, not winning. Nonetheless, he ventured to suggest that there were a few Greeks who could place in the top ten in their respective competitions.

Geo went on to mention marathoner Stylianos Kyriakidēs (1910–1987), whose good form suggested that he could finish well. The Cypriot-born Kyriakidēs had won the marathon in the Balkan Games of 1934 in Zagreb, breaking Louēs's Greek record, which had stood since 1896.[24] There was less optimism in the case of discus-thrower Nikolaos Syllas (1914–1986), who was not in very good form, although he was "a fighter" (sometimes it was the best fighters rather than the record-holders who won in the Olympics, Geo added hopefully). A third track-and-field athlete, Chrēstos Mantikas, competing in the 400-meter hurdles, would face difficult opponents, including US record-holder Glenn Hardin, who had won silver in Los Angeles, and Canada's John Loaring, a future Commonwealth Games winner.[25] The legendary Mantikas had won four gold medals in the 110-meter hurdles, 400-meter hurdles, 4x100-meter relay, and 4x400-meter relay at the first Balkan Games in Athens in 1930, and he virtually monopolized the 400- and 110-meter hurdles in the Balkan Games throughout the 1930s. In 1934, Mantikas had won a bronze

[24]For a biography of Kyriakidēs, see Nick Tsiotos & Andy Dabilis, *Running With Pheidippides: Stylianos Kyriakides, the Miracle Marathoner*, Syracuse University Press, Syracuse, 2001.

[25]Geo, "Ti tha petychoun oi ellēnes athlētai?" ["What Will the Greek Athletes Achieve?"], *Eleutheron Vēma*, July 12, 1936.

medal in the 400-meter hurdles during the first-ever European athletics championships in Turin.

Another Greek hopeful in Berlin was Domnitsa Lanitou, the first Greek female to compete in track and field in the Olympics, who would run in the 80- and 100-meter sprints. Lanitou was born in Cyprus in 1915 and became involved in sports at the age of twelve. She moved to Greece in 1931, but experienced many obstacles in her effort to continue her career because of a general unwillingness to accept female athletes: there had even been some objections to Lanitou going to Berlin. Although Lanitou would also compete in the London Olympiad in 1948, it would be years before female athletes became an integral part of Greek Olympic teams.

Within a week, Geo discussed the question of the likeliest winners as a way of putting the disadvantages of Greek athletes in broader perspective. His concern with their performance reflected a particularly strong sense among Greek observers that sport in Greece was underdeveloped, but it also mirrored views about what made winners in sports contests. Modern-day competitive sport, Geo wrote, was the privilege of only a few advanced countries, which confirmed their predominance at every international meet. Greece lagged behind, but so did other more developed countries such as Germany, France, and the Latin countries (of South America and southern Europe). The majority of winners spoke English, according to Geo, indicating that it was not only a question of body type, in this case northern European, but also of a particular sporting culture. More than anything else, Geo concluded, English-speaking athletes—English, Irish, and American, in particular— possessed a competitive spirit, matched only by certain Scandinavians, which combined enthusiasm, self-control, and a granite-like will, and contributed toward countless victories in international competitions.[26]

In Berlin, it was non-track-and-field athlete Angelos Papadēmas who gained the highest position of all Greeks with a fourth-place finish in the automatic pistol-shoot. The best results in track and field were Mantikas's sixth place in the 400-meter hurdles and Syllas's sixth place in the discus throw. (Mantikas had to content himself with dominating the Balkans until the Second World War forced him to stop competing altogether. Syllas would come in first in the discus throw at the British athletic championships in 1937 and 1939 and would return to Olympic competition after the war.) As for

---

[26]Geo, "Poioi kerdizoun eis tous Olympiakous Agōnes?" ["Who Wins in the Olympic Games?"], *Eleutheron Vēma*, July 20, 1936.

Lanitou, she reached the Olympic semifinals. Hopes for a medal remained, however, because Kyriakidēs was to compete in the marathon on the games' last day. A good showing by a Greek in the marathon would be a wonderful addition to the honors Greece had received in the ceremonial part of the 1936 Olympiad. Not since Louēs's triumph in 1896 had the Greeks had anything to cheer about in this most symbolic of all races. Kyriakidēs told Greek journalists that he was well prepared and felt confident, which only raised expectations. Kyriakidēs's style was to hold back and finish strongly, and he managed to stay close to the leaders for the first part of the race, meaning that he had a realistic chance of overcoming them toward the end. However, Argentinean Juan Carlos Zabala, gold-medalist in the marathon in Los Angeles, set an extraordinarily fast pace to the run, by all appearances vying for a new record. Around the thirty-first kilometer, Englishman Ernest Harper and Korean Sohn Kee-chung (who was running as part of the Japanese team, under the name of Kitei Son, as Korea was then under Japanese occupation) caught up with Zabala. By that time, it was too late for Kyriakidēs, who had ignored his coach's advice to adopt a faster pace. While Sohn became the first athlete to complete the marathon in less than two and a half hours, Kyriakidēs finished eleventh in a field of fifty-six.

Kyriakidēs's performance failed to bring a Greek fairy-tale ending to the Berlin marathon, and Greece had still not won a medal since the 1912 games in Stockholm. Several voices calling for renewed effort to develop Greek sport were raised as the XIth Olympiad came to a close. Almost all the Greek newspapers recommended renewed efforts to improve the state of Greek sport. In many cases, the critique broadened to include Greek culture in general. *Eleutheron Vēma* editorialized that Greece could not hope to match the leading sports powers in the world, but it could return to the distinctions its athletes had gained in the first few Olympiads. It would not be inconceivable for Greece to become a "Finland or a Sweden of the South," the newspaper commented, referring to countries that did enjoy a measure of success in the Olympics without predominating. For that to happen, the editorial continued, Greece had to stop improvising, as it did in all its activities, and adopt a disciplined system of preparation. Since Greece could not hope to emulate the sporting powers such as the United States or Japan, it should implement the vision of the late Chrysafēs, who had hoped that Greece would follow the gymnastics-based philosophy of the Swedes. With gymnastics as its core, a plan for developing Greek sport should strive, first of all, to inculcate the athletic spirit in the population in the broadest manner possible, with records and individual excellence a secondary concern. Only after "the nation" embraced sport as part of its daily regimen of body and soul, the editorial concluded, could the "land that created" sport compete with other peoples in producing records and champions.[27] Next to the vigorous spread of gymnastics, other recommendations included government initiatives to improve diet and introduce after-work recreation programs.

* * *

In the standard work on the Berlin Olympiad, sports historian Richard Mandell concludes with a discussion of the impact of the games on Nazi Germany and their broader implications for sport around the world. The grandiose setting, the high level of organization, and the strong showing by German athletes enabled the regime to use the success of the event to consolidate its grip on power domestically and legitimize itself internationally, its exclusion of Jewish athletes notwithstanding. In a broader sense, the 1936 games were also important, Mandell notes, because they marked the end of athletic individualism and sport as mere play and ushered in a new era of regimented training and performance. In this new era, sport became a contest invested with mythological and political import, and a way for nations and ideologies to compete with each other.[28]

The impact of the 1936 games on Greece's role in the Olympic movement was politically useful but morally damaging. The emphasis on ancient Greek themes remained a feature in future Olympic Games, the most dramatic example being the retention of the torch relay from Olympia to the host city. The Greeks were flattered by the attention the Germans paid to ancient Greece, and they were overawed by the games' spectacular organization. Fears about Germany's future plans were put aside, as were sensitivities about German domestic sports policies, namely, their antisemitism. Basking in the limelight created by the Nazis' use of ancient Greek symbols, the Greeks left the games confident about their future but also concerned about enhancing their chances of achieving better results on the sporting field itself. Yet they had failed to recognize the costs of Greece's moment in Berlin's limelight. The ancient spirit had been appropriated politically by the Nazis so as to establish

[27]"Orthon kai praktikon ideōdes" ["A Correct and Practical Ideal"], *Eleutheron Vēma*, August 17, 1936.
[28]Mandell, *The Nazi Olympics . . .*, pp. 285–290.

the connection between the supposedly Aryan super-race and classical Greece. Caught somewhere in the middle of this theater of the absurd, modern Greeks became passive collaborators.

The Greek-German encounter in 1936 had a dramatic and human postscript. Kyriakidēs, the Greek marathoner, spent the Second World War in Athens, when the Greek capital was under German occupation. Late in the afternoon one day in the spring of 1943, a German patrol blocked off the street on which he was walking near his house in the Chalandri area, detaining all the men and questioning them about the recent killing of German soldiers by the Greek resistance. The danger of being randomly arrested and executed in reprisal for such acts of resistance was always present, but Kyriakidēs had to take the risk of moving about in order to secure food for his family. In this instance, when the soldiers searched his pockets, they discovered to their surprise a pass for the Berlin Olympiad issued by the German government and signed by Diem. Their attitude toward him changed immediately, and they released him. The next day, he learned that some of the men who had been apprehended with him had been executed. A few days later, the Germans paid him a respectful call at home, and even brought him some supplies of food.[29] This time, the Olympics had overshadowed Nazi policies, and the life of a great Greek athlete was saved. Kyriakidēs survived the war and went on to win the Boston marathon in 1946.

[29]Tsiotos and Dabilis, *Running with Pheidippides* . . . , pp. 113–121.

CHAPTER 6

OLYMPIA AND THE COLD WAR

T HE HOC HAD SCHEDULED an important meeting for the afternoon
of October 28, 1940. The agenda included the future of the Classical
Games and the establishment of an Olympic Academy in Olympia: the two
topics were linked. Disillusionment with the performance of the ancient version of track and field in 1934 led to discussions about whether the preservation of the games' ancient heritage might be better served through study
rather than practice. Ideas about an institute for Olympic study had been
floated as early as 1927, when Coubertin had visited Greece. In a proposal
submitted jointly to the HOC with Diem in 1938, Iōannēs Ketseas, a member
of the Greek committee, had suggested establishing an Olympic Academy.
The two men would indeed play a central role in establishing this academy in
the early 1960s. A visit by Diem to Nazi-occupied Greece in 1942 was evidently not held against him later by the Greeks, and, at the end of his life, he
was able to demonstrate his passion for sport in an environment that was
uncomplicated by politics. The HOC approved the concept and passed it on
to the IOC, which signaled its own approval the following year. Now, the
Greeks could begin thinking in practical terms.

Iōannēs Ketseas (1887–1965) took part in the 1906 interim Olympics and
became the longest serving member of the HOC in the twentieth century.
Ketseas represents, in many ways, the older generation of HOC leadership
that shaped the committee's work through the 1960s. As a royalist, he person-
ified the committee's ties with the palace and had a very traditionalist and
conservative view of the classical heritage. Ketseas was appointed to the HOC
in 1927 and chosen as a member of the IOC in 1946, serving as a member in
both committees continuously until his death in 1965. His views on the
Olympic movement typified the conservative tendency of venerating antiquity rather than conceiving of it as something to be adapted to the needs of
modern society. Possession of the appropriate ideological *bona fides* coupled

with a deeply felt passion for the Olympic movement enabled Ketseas to play an instrumental role in spurring the Greek state to support the efforts to create the Olympic Academy. Ketseas's speeches would certainly qualify as an example of what critically minded Greek intellectuals call *progonoplēxia*—literally, being struck by ancestors—that is, a didactic invocation of an idealized ancient Greek culture. In a speech in 1964, inaugurating the International Olympic Academy's fourth session, Ketseas cited Diem's speech in Nazi-occupied Athens in 1942 as a model for regarding the ancient past. Ketseas told his audience that Diem had "stressed that the views of the ancient Greeks regarding conduct and athletic ideals remain unchanged and valid until our days, without the possible deviations having registered any progress whatsoever." He concluded that, "We owe gratitude to eternal Greece, which taught us the true athletic principles and ideals."[1]

The October 28, 1940, meeting never took place. Greece entered the Second World War that same day, enduring four years of Axis occupation compounded by internecine strife, which, upon liberation in 1944, culminated in a civil war between left and right from 1947 until 1949. Greece was occupied by Nazi Germany and its allies, Italy and Bulgaria, through the end of 1944, a period of hardship that witnessed the emergence of a communist and left-wing resistance movement. Soon, the goal of opposing the Axis became entangled in internal struggles between left and right. Even the sports world was divided. After the country fell to the Axis, the HOC and other sports authorities did very little to help the athletic community cope with the hunger and hardships that affected the population. Into that vacuum stepped a group of left-wing administrators and athletes who formed two organizations, one for athletes and one for coaches, which offered assistance and advice to the sports community. Its leaders included Grēgorēs Lambrakēs, a former marathoner and young doctor.[2] (Lambrakēs became a peace activist after the war, and his peace marches from Marathon to Athens publicized his campaign for nuclear disarmament.)

When the Axis evacuated Greece in 1944, they left a divided country behind them. Left-wing guerrillas, who had borne the brunt of the resistance against the occupation, vied for power with right-wing groups and the old establishment. The conflict tore Greece apart and ended in civil war, during

---

[1] Iōannēs Ketseas, "Inaugural Speech," *Report of the Fourth Summer Session of the International Olympic Academy*, DOA, Athens, 1964, p. 23.

[2] HOC Archives, k 86/f 2/e1/1948.

which the United States replaced the British as patrons of the right when the Truman Doctrine was announced in 1947, a development that contributed to the left's defeat in 1949. In the aftermath, a parliamentary democracy was established, but the country's political orientation was decided not by the ballot but, instead, by a tripartite alliance composed of the right, the monarchy, and an army backed by the United States.

After the events of the 1940s and their political consequences, the Hellenic Olympic Committee's initiatives were taken in a domestic background, reinforced by the larger Cold War, that a leading Greek sociologist has described as "nationalist fundamentalism."[3] Under these conditions, the presumed glories of the Greek "race" and its classical past became a staple of public discourse and a core element of education. It is not surprising, therefore, that the HOC, supported by the government, would do all in its power to try to redirect the international Olympic movement's attention toward a renewed celebration of the games' ancient heritage. This was a difficult task, however, as the movement was caught up in contemporary problems, generated by the Cold War and increasing commercialization, which recourse to "tradition" could not resolve easily. Consequently, the Greeks relied more and more in their struggle on the site of ancient Olympia.

RETURN TO THE OLYMPIC ROOTS

The ideological appropriation of classical Greece by the country's postwar conservative establishment meant that Greece displayed greater eagerness than the international Olympic movement to make Olympia the symbolic headquarters of the modern Olympics. The Olympic Games and the plans for an International Olympic Academy (IOA) had been postponed because of the war. The IOC confirmed its commitment to creating the academy at Olympia during its forty-fourth session in Rome in 1949. The IOA would be established in Olympia, as proposed by the Greeks, and administered by the HOC under IOC auspices. Its founders conceived of the academy as an international cultural center whose mission was "to preserve and spread the Olympic Spirit, study and implement the educational and social principles of Olympism and consolidate the scientific basis of the Olympic Ideal."[4]

---

[3]Constantine Tsoukalas, "Ideological Impact of the Civil War," in John O. Iatrides, editor, *Greece in the 1940s: A Nation in Crisis*, University Press of New England, Hanover, 1981.
[4]*The International Olympic Academy*, IOC, Ancient Olympia, no date, p. 14.

The realization of the Olympic Academy did not take place until 1961, however, because the planned turn toward the Olympic movement's ancient roots was overshadowed by more pressing demands. During the 1950s, Avery Brundage (1887–1975), who became the IOC's president in 1952 (and remained in that position through 1972), was confronted with urgent contemporary problems and had little time to contemplate a return to antiquity. Brundage was a towering figure in US sport, having served as president of the AAU (1928–1935) and of the US Olympic Committee (1929–1953). Brundage first established his reputation as a hard-nosed realist when he had pushed for American participation in the Berlin Olympiad. He believed not only that politics should be kept out of the Olympics, but that he also knew best what was "political" and what was not. He therefore resisted the entry of communist countries into the Olympic movement while also stubbornly trying to uphold its attachment to amateurism.[5]

As he confronted these problems for most of the 1950s, Brundage typically did not invoke Greece in his speeches as often as Coubertin had. During the early Cold War era, it was the politics of the present that predominated, not the symbolism of the past. The superpower contest, and the issue of accepting communist states into the Olympic movement that it generated, entailed an engagement with contemporary politics, not history. This is not to say that the IOC turned its back on the ancient Greek symbolism that had become part of Olympic ritual. On the contrary, it insisted on retaining it, and held a torch relay from Olympia to London for the 1948 Olympiad even though the Civil War was still raging in Greece.

The retention of ancient Greek imagery by the Olympic movement in 1948 sent Greek observers into raptures, in sharp contrast to non-Greek observers who found the symbolism less significant. For example, Greek observers saw the opening of the 1948 games as an occasion to celebrate the continuing relevance of the ancient Greek spirit. The correspondent of the Athens daily *Kathimerini*, Athanasios Sempos, opened his report from London as follows: "Today's opening of the XIVth Olympiad . . . was a true apotheosis of the ancient Greek spirit and a reverent acknowledgment by humanity of the immortal moral values that were born in Greece. . . . [T]he [Greek] blue and white flag was at the head of the parade." In contrast, *New York Times* reporter Allison Danzig emphasized the relaunch of the games after their wartime interruption, a theme highlighted by the major news agencies as

[5]Senn, *Power, Politics . . .* , pp. 112–154.

well.[6] Two years later, Greece's calls for an international gathering to inaugurate the Olympic Academy in 1950 and to discuss the ancient heritage of the games went unanswered. The HOC wrote to eighty national committees, inviting them to an inaugural conference in Greece in 1950, but only four responded, all of them negatively.

The differences between Greece's and the other countries' perspectives on the significance of the ancient heritage were rooted in postwar agendas. For Greece, the ancient past was a way to legitimize its postwar regime. In 1949, Greece emerged from a civil war deeply divided between right and left, a polarization that effectively neutralized the very few centrist proponents of reconciliation. Instead, an anticommunist, pro-American, conservative ruling party perpetuated the divisions spawned in the 1940s, although the threat of a successful communist bid for power had been totally eliminated. The government encouraged the glorification of ancient Greece, a nationalist staple that functioned almost metaphysically, and certainly as a self-aggrandizing myth to cloak contemporary sociopolitical conflicts. The "rehabilitation" of communist political prisoners at an internment camp on the island of Makronēsos included the performance of ancient Greek tragedies with the prisoners as actors. A leading conservative politician described Makronēsos as the "new Parthenon." In schools, ancient Greek subjects—especially grammar—dominated the curriculum.

The ruling government's use of antiquity as an instrument to promote a sense of continuity between modern and ancient Greece, and to denigrate its communist opponents, was evident during the torch-lighting ceremony for the 1948 Olympiad. While almost identical to that of 1936, it was a much less elaborate affair, with fewer foreign dignitaries. At the site—around which armed soldiers were posted—the procession paused briefly before the monument to Coubertin. Chrēstos Zalokōstas—a former athlete, industrialist, and author of fiction, as well as a figure closely associated with the right-wing political establishment—who had been appointed by King George to the HOC in 1935, delivered the main speech. Zalokōstas averred that the torch relay symbolized humanity's course toward attaining the ancient spirit of the Olympics and achieving peace. At the time, however, the relay could not follow the route northward it had traced in 1936 because of ongoing hostilities

[6]Athanasios Sempos, "Ē panēgyrikē enarxis tēs ID Olympiados" ["The Gala Opening of the XIVth Olympiad"], *Kathimerini*, July 30, 1948; Allison Danzig, "King George Opens Olympics for 6,000 from 59 Nations," *The New York Times*, July 30, 1948.

between the government army and communist guerrilla forces. Instead, runners transported the flame to the nearby port of Katakolo on the western coast of the Peloponnese. The villages and the town of Pyrgos on the way were draped with flags, and their inhabitants lined the streets. At Katakolo, the flame boarded the Greek warship *Astinx* (Hastings), which took it north to the island of Kerkyra (Corfu). A day later, the Greek government issued a protest "to sports-loving people of the world" denouncing the communist guerrillas for having planned to disrupt the torch relay by killing a gendarme guarding the *Astinx* while it was anchored at Katakolo. The government based its denunciation on an "intercepted radio program." In a reference to the Soviet Union, which it considered to be allied to the Greek communists, the pro-government *Kathimerini* said it hoped the free peoples of the world would understand that the "Asiatic north" was trying to extinguish the Olympic flame and the spirit it symbolized.[7]

Ideology aside, other developments contributed to Olympia emerging as a useful and accessible symbol for the Olympic movement. The 1950s witnessed improvements in transportation and communication between Athens and the provinces, which made Olympia easier to visit. The road from the town of Pyrgos, to Olympia's west, was improved and extended eastward and over the mountains to the town of Tripolē. The improvements in the railroads meant that trains traversed the winding, mountainous, 220-mile distance from Athens in less than nine hours (admittedly still a taxing journey). The excavation of the temples was completed, and pine trees were planted around the ruins. With its cluster of newly revealed temples, the excavated site began to acquire a picturesque natural surrounding.

It soon also acquired more and more foreign visitors, who began to "discover" Greece through tourism. The 1950s saw the beginning of what would become, in the next few decades, a mass tourist influx to Greece. One of the first Club Med resorts opened on Kerkyra in 1952 as the government began investing in tourist infrastructure. Visitors to Greece once again began to experience the "spirit of place" in and around ancient sites. While their interest in the country was no longer as strictly focused on the classical as that of the nineteenth-century romantics, and had a broader scope, it was just as affecting. It included not only the ancient sites and their natural settings, but also what modern visitors perceived to be the pristine beauties of the Greek landscape in its entirety.

[7]"Apo tēn Olympian" ["From Olympia"], *Kathimerini*, July 18, 1948.

We can think of this new understanding of Greece more specifically as a shift from experiencing the spirit of place to experiencing the spirit of the landscape. In richly documenting the post-Second World War reinvention of Greece, David Roessel cites Stephen Spender, who, in 1954, wrote that philhellenes were no longer concerned with romanticism's efforts to rediscover the ancient within the modern Greeks, but were, instead, engaged in a "rediscovery of the classical by way of modern Greece"—by way of Greek landscape, to be precise.[8] This landscape became a central concern after the Second World War in the work of writers such as Lawrence Durrell and Patrick Leigh Fermor and was shared by Greek writers such as Nikos Kazantzakēs and Geōrgios Seferēs.

Indeed, while several European writers experienced the Greek landscape as a Dionysian and wild *topos*, as Roessel notes, Olympia managed to retain its dignity. Several foreign travelers wrote about the peacefulness and beauty in and around the area. An English couple, experienced travel writers, described their visit around the time of the Olympic Academy's inauguration in lyrical terms: "It is a delight to wander through the grove of Olympia, and inspect the columns and marbles of a past age, scattered among the trees and the flowers in a setting of singular loveliness. . . . [O]ne is not even tempted to evoke the scenes and gatherings of fifteen hundred years ago, for it would seem that this valley has never been more beautiful than it is now. . . ."[9] Similarly, the *Life World Library* volume on Greece wrote that, "Everywhere in Greece one meets with history and welcome. . . . [A]t Olympia the pebbly river, towering pines, olive trees and gentle hills mantled with daisies all conspire to sooth one's soul."[10]

Meanwhile, the IOC had rediscovered its own zeal to establish the Olympic Academy. Although issues of creeping commercialism and preservation of a pure form of amateurism still loomed large on its agenda, Avery Brundage recognized the value of the academy. There was a sense of prestige with which the site of ancient Olympia invested the academy, making it a useful tool in his struggle to restore the games to their original purity. The clearest acknowledgment of Greece's enhanced position came the year the academy opened, when Brundage spoke warmly of the role Greece could play in maintaining and guarding the Olympic spirit. "There is no better place to

---

[8]David Roessel, *In Byron's Shadow: Modern Greece in the English and American Imagination,* New York, Oxford University Press, 2002, p. 253.

[9]Eric and Barbara Whelpton, *Greece and the Islands,* Robert Hale, London, 1961, p. 74.

[10]Alexander Eliot and the editors of *Life, Greece,* Time, Inc., New York, 1963.

accomplish this than in Greece, a truly Olympic country."[11] It was as if, suddenly, the Olympic movement as a whole felt an affinity with the physical space that had fostered the original Olympics, ushering in a new era in which Greece gained importance in a new sense: instead of conveying the old romantic "spirit of place," Greece now offered the place in which a spirit could be imagined.

THE INTERNATIONAL OLYMPIC ACADEMY

The International Olympic Academy opened in Olympia in 1961 and has functioned ever since as the intellectual and spiritual headquarters of the Olympic movement, complementing its administrative seat in Lausanne. The academy, which operates basically as a summer school and retreat, began as the destination of a primitive form of pilgrimage. At the time, it lacked its present rural, campus-like atmosphere, with rows of dormitories arranged in an amphitheater-like shape around the running track on a slope overlooking the ancient site. Prior to 1967, there was no landscaping. Participants in the annual summer sessions lived in tents and held their sessions in the open, under the trees. Photographs from the academy's early days convey a place of rudimentary comfort that did not prevent the early pioneers from showing excitement and enthusiasm at being at the ancient site.

The Greek sporting community had begun the process of trying to consecrate Olympia and anchor it to modern sport before the academy was established. In 1959, Olympia witnessed a Greek athletic event whose success prompted ideas about holding international meets there on a regular basis. The ministry of education, responsible for developing sport in schools and institutions of higher education, organized a cross-country run for Greek students at Olympia that year. The dean of the University of Athens, archeology professor Spyros Marinatos, explained the logic in a letter to the HOC and extended an invitation to it to collaborate on the project: "The meaning of holding this race in the glorious and sacred site of Olympia goes deeper and further than being simply an athletic event. Our wish is for the gathering and the race to take on the character of a pilgrimage and spiritual immersion for the students, who are the spiritual, political, and administrative future of our country in the concept of Olympism, that glorious ancestral achievement." Marinatos added, "the presence of Greek academic leaders

[11]*Kathimerini*, July 18, 1948; *The New York Times*, July 22, 1948.

would constitute a sacred pilgrimage, as well as an obligation of the Greek intellectual world to the ancient athletic traditions so influential throughout the civilized world."[12]

The HOC was happy to support the initiative, and its vice-president, Kōnstantinos Geōrgakopoulos, attended the cross-country event in March. In his speech, Geōrgakopoulos echoed Marinatos's view of Olympia's sanctity and significance. Both men stressed the contemporary value of the heritage of ancient Greece and the exemplary ways it fostered sport in combination with religion and the arts. Within a few months, the ministry and the HOC were exchanging ideas about the feasibility of an international cross-country run at Olympia, as well as additional track-and-field events.[13]

The establishment of this international academy put the Hellenic Olympic Committee back on the map and was a great source of domestic pride. The academy's inaugural session in the summer of 1961 attracted thirty delegates from twenty-four countries. In addition, groups of athletes from Athens and Cologne performed exercises as part of the session's program. The elderly Diem ensured a large German and international presence. As an early proponent of creating the academy, and then-principal of the Cologne *Sporthochschule*, he enjoyed great respect among Greek Olympic officials.

Reflecting the purpose of the academy in many ways, its opening session was combined with the completion of the German Archaeological Institute's excavations of the stadium at Olympia. The Germans had continued excavations through 1942, even as they inflicted a brutal occupation on the rest of the country, and resumed work in 1952, clearing the western part of the stadium adjacent to the cluster of temples at the site. Between 1958 and 1961, they completed the excavation of the stadium, as well the restoration of its original shape and size. Diem was instrumental in raising the required funds in Germany. On June 22, 1961, the IOC and national Olympic committees of Greece and Germany inaugurated the stadium.[14]

The topics of the summer sessions organized by the IOA in the 1960s reflected an emphasis on the games' ancient heritage. The first session was dedicated to the memory of Coubertin, the spirit of Olympism, and athletic training in classical Greece, while the 1962 session included a segment on the

---

[12]HOC Archives/e1/1959.

[13]HOC Archives/March 8, 1959/*Logos ekfōnēthēs ypo tou A' Antiproedrou tēs EOA k. K. Geōrgakopoulou en Archaia Olympia tē 8ē Martiou 1959* [*Speech Made by the First Vice-President of the HOC, Mr. K. Georgakopoulos, at Ancient Olympia on March 8, 1959*].

[14]Fellmann, "Excavations at Olympia . . . ," p. 118.

Olympic spirit examined through ancient sources and a subject during the following year was ancient gymnastics.[15] In 1965, when Brundage attended the session, delegates discussed the history of the Olympics.[16] The list of speakers who gave lectures at the IOA during its first annual sessions included many from abroad who were prominent in the study of both antiquity and sport. Dr. H. Bartels of the German Archaeological Institute had done excavations at Olympia. Oscar Broneer was professor of archeology at the University of Chicago and involved in excavations in Isthmia, another ancient site in the Peloponnese. Werner Korbs was Diem's successor at the Cologne *Sporthochschule*. Paul Vialar was president of France's sportswriters. Bruno Zauli was honorary secretary of the Italian Olympic Committee, organizer of the 1960 Rome games, and president of the European Committee of the International Amateur Athletic Federation (IAAF). Zauli founded the European Cup in track and field in 1965, which was originally named after him but is now known by the name of its commercial sponsor. The Austrian, British, Swiss, and US Olympic committees also sent speakers to the IOA's sessions in the early 1960s.

Many speakers drew comparisons between the practices of the ancients, and the organization of the Olympics in antiquity, with the conditions obtaining at the time. Speaking of the truce that was established in and around Olympia before and after the games were held, Diem noted, "Contrast these rules with the inhumanity of war in the present-day world."[17] The sense of the games' continuity, naturally, was not the monopoly of the academy but was widely shared in Greece. One Greek author published a history of the Olympics that eschewed the distinction between "ancient" and "modern" and began in 776 BCE and concluded in 1964, merely indicating that there had been a 1,500-year break between 393 CE and 1896.[18]

The Greek hosts, who funded the academy's operation, did as much as possible to imbue its summer sessions with ceremony. In 1964, instead of simply holding a reception for delegates in Athens on their way to Olympia,

[15]*Report of the Second Summer Session of the International Olympic Academy*, HOC, Athens, 1962.

[16]*Report of the Fifth Summer Session of the International Olympic Academy*, HOC, Athens, 1965.

[17]*Report of the Third Summer Session of the International Olympic Academy*, HOC, Athens, 1963, p. 91.

[18]Alexandros S. Santas, *Olympia, Olympiakoi Agōnes, Olympionikai 776 px–393mx & 1896–1964* [*Olympia, Olympic Games, Olympic Winners, 776 BC–393AD & 1896–1964*], no publisher, Athens, 1966.

a half day's drive away, the organizers held a meeting on Pnyx Hill, overlooking the Acropolis; every session since then has included such a gathering. Crown Prince Constantine (grandson of his namesake, King Constantine, who had been so involved in the 1896 Olympics as crown prince) attended as many functions of the early sessions as his schedule permitted, while the Greek speakers included distinguished archeologists, classicists, and sports administrators. The hosts ensured that the theme of the games' ancient heritage featured prominently in the events surrounding each session by providing lectures and seminars, and including athletic activities and tourism. Visits to ancient sites in the Peloponnese were an integral part of the IOA's summer sessions. In 1962, for example, after delegates gathered in Athens for a reception, they left for Olympia on buses the next day following a route "intended to give an opportunity for as much sightseeing as possible." They stopped at Mycenae for Agamemnon's "tomb," the Sanctuary of Asclepius, and the ancient theater at Epidaurus. The return journey took a detour to include Delphi, site of the ancient oracle and the quadrennial Pythian Games in antiquity.[19] Visits to those and other sites were part of the regular program of activities in the following years.

Finally, the establishment of shrines dedicated to past figures of the Olympic movement made the academy into a place of historic and symbolic significance. Aside from the monument to Coubertin, where his heart was interred in 1937, another was erected on the grounds commemorating the "joint founders" of the International Olympic Academy, Diem (who died in 1962) and Ketseas (who died three years later). Wreaths are laid at the monuments during every summer session.

The academy, however, is not only a place of symbolism and speeches that seeks to celebrate the ancient spirit; it is also a forum in which concerned individuals, dedicated to the ideals of Olympism, gather every year and exchange views. The summer sessions attract a broad range of sports administrators, sportswriters, teachers, and both graduate and undergraduate students from all over the world. These men and women are, in a sense, the true believers in Olympism. They are committed to preserving the original ideals of the Olympics; toward that purpose, they reflect on the movement's current issues, including corporate involvement and influence, drug control, and the relations between sport and society. Leading IOC officials, experienced sports administrators, and top athletes address the sessions and take part in

---

[19] *Report of the Second Summer Session* . . . , pp. 11–12.

their deliberations. The academy is a useful reminder that there are many people within the sports world who look upon the Olympic movement, despite its flaws, as offering a vision that can counter the worst excesses of commercialism and politics in sport.

GREECE AND THE COLD WAR OLYMPICS, 1948–1964

Greece's efforts to play a major role in the international Olympic movement by emphasizing the necessity and importance of ancient Greek symbolism were handicapped by its incompetence in sport. When plans were underway for the establishment of the Olympic academy, the HOC wrote to the government stressing Greece's need to do better in terms of its athletic record at the games. Without some success on the athletic field, it said, Greece would be unable to acquire greater prominence in the international Olympic movement.

An appraisal of Greek sport on the eve of the establishment of the academy reveals two decades of nearly total neglect. Prewar legislation had shifted a great deal of the responsibility for promoting sport from the Olympic committee to the government. Greece almost did not take part in the 1948 Olympiad because the finance ministry refused to provide funds for athletes to travel to London. The Hellenic Olympic Committee raised the money by appealing for help to Greek shipowners based in London and New York. In his report on the 1948 Olympics, Ketseas, the HOC's general secretary at the time, noted that Greece could not possibly have been absent. He cited three reasons. First, he said, the modern Olympics were "the spiritual child of Greece." Second, Britain and Greece had traditionally had close ties, which included "recent common struggles" (a reference to the 1940s). Finally, Greece could not appear unable to attend because of its ongoing civil war. In the event, Greece managed to send sixty athletes to London in 1948, including one female, Domnitsa Lanitou. They took part in cycling, fencing, rowing, sailing, shooting, track and field, water polo, and wrestling. Wrestlers Nikolaos Birēs and Geōrgios Petmezas came sixth in their categories in Greco-Roman wrestling, the highest positions achieved by the Greek team.[20]

There were fifty-three Greek athletes at Helsinki in 1952, competing in rowing, shooting, soccer, track and field, wrestling, and, for the first time ever for Greece, basketball. Yet again, however, there was little to cheer about.

[20]Skiadas, *100 chronia neoterē* . . . , pp. 342–344.

Iōannēs Koutsēs came sixth in clay-shooting and Syllas, the team's flag-bearer, was ninth in the discus throw. Finally, in the Melbourne games of 1956, Greece won its first medal since 1912. Twenty-seven-year-old Peloponnesian Geōrgios Roubanēs won the bronze in the pole vault (in the next two years, he would break the European record twice). Only twelve Greeks traveled to Australia, and they competed in rowing, shooting, track and field, and wrestling.[21]

In Rome, in 1960, there was a single Greek distinction again, when the *Nēreus*, skippered by twenty-year-old Crown Prince Constantine, won the gold medal in the dragon class. The yacht's other crewmembers were Odysseas Eskintzoglou and Geōrgios Zaïmēs. The entire Greek royal family was present; at the exuberant quayside celebrations, Queen Frederika dunked her gold-medalist son into the water. According to the Associated Press, Constantine bobbed up smiling.[22] Still, none of the other forty-nine athletes from Greece who made the short trip to Rome were able to place in the top six or finals of any event. Public opinion in Athens momentarily ignored the poor general showing of the team, however, and prepared a suitable welcome for Constantine and his crew. They rode in an open-roofed car all the way from the airport to the Tomb of the Unknown Soldier, where the mayors of Athens and Piraeus, the HOC, and the senate of the University of Athens received them. At the Greek frontier, the army cleared part of a minefield in symbolic imitation of the razing of the walls of a city, the ancient custom of welcoming a winner that conveyed the sense that his presence alone was enough for a city to defend itself.[23] The *Nēreus* went to the headquarters of the Greek yacht club, where it has been preserved ever since—outlasting its skipper, who fled Greece in 1967 (after his failed countercoup against the colonels' dictatorship that had seized power earlier that year). Constantine was permanently exiled after the restoration of democracy in 1974, when Greeks voted overwhelmingly in a referendum to establish a republic.

Constantine's victory barely eased the mounting frustration with Greece's athletic performance in the Olympics. Prior to the sailing victory in Rome, the Greek press had reported Greece's poor performance in the other events. The newspapers picked up on this after the celebrations had subsided.

[21] *Ibid.*, pp. 369–370.

[22] "Greek Queen Dunks Son After his Yacht Wins," *The New York Times*, September 8, 1960.

[23] Kōnstantinos G. Kavikēs, *Penies gia to thauma tēs XVII Olympiados* [*Jottings on the Miracle of the XVIIth Olympiad*], Kaiafas, Athens, 1960; Skiadas, *100 chronia neoterē . . . ,* pp. 375–377.

Writers lamented the professionalization of sport on a world scale, but were more critical of the underdevelopment of Greek sport, the lack of public interest and facilities, and the rudimentary nature of physical education in the schools. Fingers were pointed at an administration overburdened by too many inefficient organizations. The government's general secretariat of sports was not doing a good job of promoting school sport; semi-autonomous federations for each sport were doing just as badly trying to produce top athletes; and the HOC was left with the task of engendering interest in the Olympics. An overarching problem was that postwar governments had ignored their responsibility to promote sport and physical exercise in theory as well as in practice.

Greece's poor showing in the Olympics was not the only yardstick used by critics. Greece had traditionally done very well in the Balkan Games, an annual regional track-and-field contest that had begun in 1929. But that was not the case when the games resumed in 1953, after a thirteen-year interruption because of the war and its political consequences in southeastern Europe. Even a cursory glance at the lists of winners and their countries during the 1950s shows that Greece was overtaken by most of its Balkan neighbors.

Another round of complaints reappeared within four years, and the problem was even discussed in parliament. The eighteen-man Greek team—without Constantine this time—did just as poorly in the 1964 Olympiad in Tokyo. This time, the criticism flowed unrestrained in the press. Petros Charēs, an important literary figure, joined the debate and pointed out the contrast between the humiliating sporting results and the honorable achievements of a number of Greeks in literature. Charēs cited the Nobel Prize won in 1963 by Seferēs and the international acclaim for Kazantzakēs, who had died in 1957 (his novel, *Zorba the Greek,* had been made into a successful movie in 1964). Meanwhile, the parliamentary debates recommended changes. A new liberal government (of the Center Union party) had replaced the conservatives, who had ruled uninterruptedly since the war; thus, there was greater willingness to criticize the past. The government suggested innovations that ranged from encouraging more physical education in schools to funding sports facilities throughout the country.[24]

There was a small, bright moment for Greece in 1964, when the flame was transported for the first time to the winter Olympics in Innsbruck,

---

[24]Skiadas, *100 chronia neoterē . . .* , pp. 413–414.

Austria, although Greece's tiny presence at those games made any national pride at the symbolism muted at best. The winter games had taken place for the first time in 1924 at Chamonix, France, but Greece had not been among the sixteen nations participating. The first winter Olympics in which Greece was present, albeit with one athlete, were those in the German resort of Garmisch-Partenkirchen in 1936. Winter sports were emerging meekly in Greece, and the first domestic winter games were held in 1932. After the Second World War, athletes from twenty-eight countries competed in the 1948 winter Olympiad at St. Moritz, Switzerland. Among them was a sole Greek skier who came in 101st in his race. (More recently, the Greek teams have been only a little larger and their finishes only marginally better.)

The country's growing political instability, however, meant that the blueprints conceived in 1964 would not be implemented. It was the former athlete and peace activist, Grēgorēs Lambrakēs, who became the tragic figure in an escalating spiral of violence and political uncertainty. Lambrakēs had been elected to parliament as a member of the major left-wing party, EDA (*Eniaia Dēmokratikē Aristera*, United Democratic Left), and his newfound prominence drew the wrath of extreme right-wing groups that had operated unrestrained since the Civil War. Lambrakēs was assassinated in 1963, an event that inspired the book, *Z*, by Vasilēs Vasilikos, and the movie directed by Costa-Gavras. The assassination precipitated the end of conservative rule in elections that year, but the monarchy, the army, and conservative politicians used their powers to undermine the centrist government in the summer of 1965. A period of domestic political strife followed that allowed a junta of army colonels to seize power and establish a military dictatorship in April 1967.

Only a few days before the colonels' coup, the HOC had organized an Olympic Games Day celebration and tried to use it as a platform to promote the development of sport in the country. The concept of employing the Olympics to boost sport reflects how easily the Greek public identified with the Olympics rather than with sport and physical exercise. Almost two decades after the end of the Civil War, physical exercise in schools remained stunted, as did most of the sports included in the Olympic games. Instead, professional soccer, a sport played by few but followed by thousands, was extremely popular and described as Greece's "king of sports." Another spectator sport, basketball, was also slowly growing in popularity in the country's large cities. The major sports clubs functioned as umbrella organizations, fostering a number of sports in addition to soccer and basketball. The Athens club, *Panathēnaikos*, took great pride in being involved in a record number of sixteen sports in the 1960s, but soccer enjoyed the most attention, resources, and public following. The Olympic Games Day celebrations held in the Panathenaic Stadium in April 1967 were an effort to promote the so-called "other" sports.

The HOC had begun planning the Olympic Games Day celebrations in 1966 and wrote to Brundage soliciting his support. At its forty-second session in January 1948, the IOC had decided that a World Olympic Games Day celebration should be made an annual event of the Olympic movement. The IOC conceived of this event as a celebration in honor of its own founding in Paris on June 23, 1894. The first Olympic Games Day was, therefore, celebrated on June 23, 1948, with the participation of Austria, Belgium, Canada, Great Britain, Greece, Portugal, Switzerland, Uruguay, and Venezuela. When the celebration did not become a regular event, the Greeks proposed a different date and a different kind of celebration. They put forward April 6, the date of the first modern Olympic Games in 1896, and recommended that the celebration involve athletics. In his letter to Brundage, Pyrros Lappas, a member of the HOC and IOC, assured him that notwithstanding the inclusion of an athletic component, "our main purpose is intellectual.... [T]he main purpose of all of us will be to remind the whole world, on the same day and with the most powerful and unanimous show, of the spirit and philosophy of the Olympic Movement, of Olympism and of the Olympic Ideal."[25]

The Olympic Games Day celebration took place on April 6, 1967, and its purpose was to rally support for sport domestically. The Greeks went ahead with the event even though Brundage took no decision as to whether the IOC would make it an international occasion for the Olympic movement as a whole. The program included a message from King Constantine II, the gold-medalist crown prince who had assumed the throne after the death of his father, King Paul I, in 1965. Constantine referred to Coubertin, the games of 1896, the role of his namesake grandfather, and the importance of competing rather than winning. He then called upon the government and athletic organizations to join together in a campaign to develop sport in Greece. Greek athletics, he concluded, should and could gain the distinction

[25] *Programma eortasmou Olympiakēs Ēmeras. VIIou Diethnous Klassikou Marathōniou Dromou, Athlētikōn Agōnōn kai Epideixeōn. Athēnai, 6 Apriliou 1967, Panathēnaikon Stadion* [*Program of the Celebration of Olympic Day: VIIth International Classic Marathon Race, Athletic Contests, and Exercises, Athens, April 6, 1967, Panathenaic Stadium*] Athens, 1967.

in international arenas dictated by the athletic traditions of the Greek nation.[26]

There was also an ongoing public debate on sport, and a lecture by Petros Theodōrakakos, professor of physical education at the University of Athens, outlined its main themes. Theodōrakakos entitled his lecture, "Physical Education, Another Requirement for Technical Progress," a choice of words that conveyed the speaker's modernist approach to his subject. Indeed, his talk included many references to the important role played by physical education in "modern nations," a category in which he included western European and Scandinavian countries as well as Japan and the United States. He also referred to the eighty-five-year-old king of Sweden, Gustav VI Adolf, playing tennis and US president Dwight Eisenhower playing golf. But next to these references, about a third of his talk cited classical Greek authors and the value they had placed on physical education. He used the rest of his lecture to lament the indifference toward sport shown by the Greek government and universities. He noted how American and European universities had made use of a Greek invention, while, in Greece, "the mother of sport and physical education," sport was an afterthought in the educational curriculum. Theodōrakakos called for the creation of sports facilities in "every town, every village, and every neighborhood."[27]

GREECE, THE OLYMPICS, AND THE COLONELS' DICTATORSHIP, 1967–1974

In theory, Greece's role in the Olympic movement was not seriously affected during the seven years the colonels ruled the country. In principle, the basic approach remained the same. For example, when the HOC contacted the municipality of Athens in connection with the torch relay for the 1972 Olympiad, it noted that, "from a Greek point of view, our national goal is the worldwide showcasing of the Greek origins of the Olympic ideals and the underscoring of Greece's active role in the revival and organization of the first international Games of the modern era in 1896."[28] In practice, however, the corrupt and incompetent regime proved unable to develop the country's sports. It tried to manipulate sport in its own interests and trumpeted its

[26] *Ibid.*
[27] HOC Archives/k163/f 12/April 1967/p. 1.
[28] HOC Archives/k265/f 1/January-July 1972/p. 1.

concern for the country's sports culture, but failed to live up to its own rhetoric.

The dictatorship established a centralized system of control, with a government agency—the general secretariat of sports—responsible for all matters relating to sport. It also dismissed all members of committees in charge of sports organizations, federations, and clubs, and began to appoint its supporters in their place, mostly military men or conservative politicians. Since the Olympic committee was already a bastion of conservatism (although not necessarily pro-junta), the regime intervened relatively late, in December 1968. By that time, King Constantine, who had initially supported the coup, had attempted a countercoup that failed and gone into exile abroad, depriving the HOC of its president, Princess Irene, Constantine's sister, who had replaced him when he assumed the throne. The regime found an easy solution by promoting Vice-President Theodosios Athanasiadēs, a retired lieutenant-general, to the post of president and appointing Evangelos Moiropoulos, a former athlete and track-and-field administrator, to a vice-presidential position. Otherwise, the committee's membership remained the same until 1973, when the regime appointed one of its flunkeys, Lieutenant-General Spyridōn Vellianitēs, an outsider with no ties to the sports community, as president.

The regime's all-powerful general secretariat of sports intervened more blatantly in the HOC's affairs than governments had before the dictatorship, and it used Olympic events as a forum to trumpet the regime's "achievements." The Olympic Academy's tenth summer session took on the character of a festive celebration in order to mark the completion of the first decade of its existence. The junta's secretary of sports, Kōnstantinos Aslanidēs, attended the opening session on Pnyx Hill. HOC officials had to toe the line. Epameinōndas Petralias, a member of the HOC since 1961 and its general secretary since 1969, noted the "unshakeable faith" of the Greeks in the Olympic ideals and thanked the "National Government," the general secretariat, and General Secretary Aslanidēs for making the academy "the ideological center of World Sports."[29] The academy's sessions continued uninterrupted until 1974, when a major Greek-Turkish conflict over the island of Cyprus precipitated the collapse of the colonels' regime and the cancellation of that summer's session, which would resume the following year.

[29] *Report of the Tenth Session of the International Olympic Academy*, HOC, Athens, 1970, p. 17.

The year before the coup, 126 participants from twenty-five national Olympic committees, both record numbers, had attended the session. While the numbers dipped during the next two summers, both the number of delegates and national Olympic committees represented—133 and thirty, respectively—were, by 1969, the highest ever.

The dictatorship committed itself to helping sports and began a campaign to endow "every town with a stadium and every village with a training facility"; in practice, however, very little was done, and the beneficiaries of funding were local powerbrokers identified with the regime. The funding received by soccer and basketball owed more to a logic of bread and circuses than to any serious plan to develop those sports from the grassroots. Track and field and other Olympic sports also received help on a selective basis, but with political criteria always paramount.

Consequently, despite the regime's bluster, Greek performance in the 1968 and 1972 Olympiads showed only marginal improvement from previous ones. Forty-eight athletes traveled to Mexico City, among them eight wrestlers. It was in that sport alone that the Greeks did well. Twenty-three-year-old Petros Galaktopoulos won a bronze medal in Greco-Roman wrestling, and two freestyle wrestlers, Othōn Moschidēs and Nikolaos Karypidēs, came in fourth. Pole-vaulter Chrēstos Papanikolaou, who had finished eleventh in Tokyo, placed fourth in Mexico City, breaking his personal record. In the Munich Olympiad of 1972, where Greece sent sixty-one athletes, Galaktopoulos did even better, winning a silver medal; Ēlias Chatzēpaulēs matched that performance by coming second in the Finn-class sailing event. There were a few more good efforts: Chrēstos Iakōvou, the future national weightlifting coach, was fifth in one of the weightlifting categories, and Greek Cypriot Stauros Tziōrtzēs came in sixth in the 400-meter hurdles. Papanikolaou—who had broken the world record in the pole vault in 1970 and was the team's flag-bearer in the inaugural parade—did not do well, finishing eleventh overall.[30]

The Hellenic Olympic Committee met to discuss the Greek team's performance at the Munich games in October 1972, and the conclusions were sobering. Moiropoulos, the committee's vice-president who had led the Greek delegation, noted that the minor improvements made by Greeks in past Olympiads had put greater demands on the team. Before, he told his colleagues, Greece had competed knowing that it had no chance of achieving

[30]Skiadas, *100 chronia neoterē . . .*, pp. 433–436.

anything except, perhaps, an individual breakthrough. Now, the team was expected to do well, not merely to put in an appearance. Despite the relatively good showing by the Greeks, there was evidence of very bad physical and mental preparation on the part of many athletes, according to Moiropoulos. He also questioned the decisions of individual sports federations about whom to send, and pointed to their failure to ensure the readiness of the athletes.[31]

The HOC regarded the assassination of the Israeli athletes at Munich as a desecration of the Olympic spirit, and it condemned the event while agreeing with the decision not to interrupt the games. It did not feel it was in a position to do anything about the situation. Saddled with an undemocratic regime condemned internationally for its treatment of political prisoners, Greece was hardly in any position to take international initiatives. Watching in horror from his exile in Paris as the terrorist attacks against the Israeli athletes unfolded, however, was former Greek prime minister Kōnstantinos Karamanlēs. By the time the next Olympics came around, Karamanlēs would be back in power in Athens, a popular figure widely regarded as the restorer of democracy after the collapse of the dictatorship in 1974. Karamanlēs would feel confident enough to take a major initiative in regard to Greece's relationship to the Olympic movement. In doing so, he would also end the era in which Greece had tried to foster a return to the roots of ancient Olympia and inaugurate a new one.

[31]HOC Minutes, 90th Meeting, October 3, 1972.

CHAPTER 7

GREECE AS THE PERMANENT OLYMPIC VENUE?

T HE LEADERS OF THE GREEK DELEGATION to the 1976 Montreal
Olympiad were busy worrying about yet another poor athletic display
on the international stage—"Montreal was a nightmare for the Greek team,"
declared respected sportswriter Giannēs Diakogiannēs[1]—when they were
suddenly faced with a more pressing problem. Kōnstantinos Karamanlēs had
publicly proposed that Greece become the permanent venue of the summer
Olympic Games without warning or prior consultation with the HOC.
Abruptly and singlehandedly, the Greek prime minister had created a new
environment that would shape Greece's relationship with the international
Olympic movement for the next decade.

Initially, the IOC did not wish to entertain the notion of Greece becoming the permanent site of the games, and it handled the matter as diplomatically as possible in order not to alienate Greece or many others throughout
the world who saw the Greek proposal as a useful recommendation. But the
IOC had to show some interest in 1980, when Britain, the United States, and
several other Western countries announced their boycott of the Moscow
Olympiad because of the Soviet invasion of Afghanistan. Already, there had
been a vigorous international debate about the future of the games, and the
Greek proposal suddenly seemed a reasonable alternative solution.

The debate within Greece, meanwhile, followed the same pattern,
becoming more open and intense in the 1980s with the reciprocal superpower boycotts of the 1980 and 1984 Olympiads. There was the additional
issue of what the Greeks saw as the egregious commercialization of the
Olympics on the part of the organizers of the 1984 games in Los Angeles. At

---

[1]Giannēs Diakogiannēs, "Einai aplo, mas leipei ē sovarotēta" ["It's simple, we lack seriousness"], *Eleutherotypia*, August 5, 1976.

the same time, responding to international demands, Karamanlēs made his initially vague proposal more specific by suggesting a venue near Olympia. The specifics and their implications invited a more focused and controversial debate in Greece. By the mid-1980s, the range of general and particular issues pertaining to the Olympics and Greece's role in them were a major topic of public debate in the country.

Karamanlēs was at the center of Greece's proposal to host the Olympic Games permanently. Alternately gruff and charismatic, and a driving force in Greek political life in the second half of the twentieth century, he did not shy away from adopting forceful positions and ensuring their implementation. He had already been in power for eight turbulent years (1955–1963), but he was to establish himself as one of Greece's greatest statesmen when he returned from exile in 1974 to guide the country's transition from dictatorship to democracy. He was elected prime minister that year and reelected in 1977, serving through March 1980 when he became president of the Greek republic. His first presidential term lasted until 1985, followed by a second one in 1990 that ended with his death in office in April 1993.

The Karamanlēs government took steps to eradicate the dictatorship-era status quo in sport by appointing many new members to the HOC and choosing veteran sports administrator Apostolos Nikolaidēs (1896–1980), who had been part of the Greek team at the 1920 Olympiad, as its president. The government's choice was designed to show that things were changing in the country's sports hierarchy. Nikolaidēs was the country's most experienced sports administrator, having served the track-and-field association as its general secretary from 1932 to 1945 and as its president from 1945 to 1968, when he was removed by the dictatorship. He had also been a member of the HOC from 1953 to 1960, serving as its vice-president between 1955 and 1957. Nikolaidēs had also been a founding member of the Greek soccer federation and the longstanding *éminence grise* of *Panathēnaikos* (reverentially referred to as the team's "Patriarch"), except, again, during the dictatorship, when the junta's appointees to the club's hierarchy had marginalized him. After the dictatorship fell, a total of nine members on the thirteen-member, junta-era committee were replaced. New members included Nikos Filaretos, who had a background in business and became an IOC member in 1981, and Kleanthēs Palaiologos, one of Greece's senior sportswriters, with a longstanding connection to the Greek Olympic movement.

Filaretos and Palaiologos embodied the winds of change sweeping through Greece's Olympic hierarchy. Filaretos brought a deep commitment to the principles of amateur sport to the HOC. As a member of the Olympic Academy's board since 1974, and its president from 1986 to 1993 and again from 1997 to the present, he had often gone on record as a sharp critic of the politicization and commercialization of the Olympic movement. His investment in the IOA showed another form of commitment—and idealism. Namely, to the belief that the new generations of the Olympic movement that attended the academy's sessions could be educated to uphold the purity of the Olympic spirit. Several years ago, he remarked that the best compliment he had ever received about the Olympic Academy was from a German delegate, who told him that it reminded her of the atmosphere in an Olympic village without the competitive tension.[2] As for Palaiologos, although he had taken part in the academy's sessions for many years and was a member of its board, he was not appointed to the HOC until 1974. Palaiologos was a student of the ancient Olympics, with a tendency to focus on what he saw as the humanistic and egalitarian dimensions of the ancient games.[3]

The changes in 1974 included uncoupling Cyprus's sports from those of Greece, a union that had heretofore symbolized the nationalist idea of a cultural Hellenism that included both countries. This had happened even though Cyprus, a former British colony, had become a sovereign state in 1960 after the failure of the movement to unite it with Greece. In one of many signs that the Greek majority on the island still hankered for union with Greece, the Cypriot state permitted the top Greek Cypriot athletes to compete in international meets as members of the Greek national team. The Greek dictatorship went as far as to include a Cypriot team in the Greek professional soccer league. Cyprus only formed its own national Olympic committee in 1974, and the IOC conferred its official recognition four years later.

It is worth noting that while the transition to democracy in 1974 liberated the HOC from the older authoritarian visions of antiquity embraced by some of its former leaders, it did not free it from government control. It could not have been otherwise in a country in which the government plays a very large role in public affairs even in democratic times. Thus, despite Nikolaidēs's stature, he was limited in the initiatives he could take. The

---

[2]Nikos Filaretos interview, *Athlos kai Politismos* [*Sport and Culture*], Volume 6, 2000.

[3]Kleanthēs Palaiologos, "O thesmos tōn Olympiakōn Agōnōn kai o rolos tou stēn pragmatopoiēsē tēs enotētas tou archaiou ellēnismou" ["The Institution of the Olympic Games and its Role in the Realization of the Unity of Ancient Hellenism"], *Leukōma tēs 21ēs Synodou tēs Diethnous Olympiakēs Akadēmias*, DOA, Athens, 1982, pp. 76–83.

governmental oversight body, the general secretariat of sports, retained its predominance, both over sport and the country's athletic preparations for the Olympics.

As Karamanlēs was the driving force behind the idea of Greece as the perennial Olympic site, the intensity with which the country pursued that goal ebbed and flowed with his political fortunes. There was no perceptible change when he moved to the presidency in 1980, which occurred between the reiteration of his original proposal in January of that year and the Moscow Olympics in July, since his New Democracy party remained in power. In the general elections in October 1981, however, the Panhellenic Socialist Movement (PASOK) defeated New Democracy, and Andreas Papandreou became prime minister. Although PASOK loyally supported the proposal, it remained associated primarily with Karamanlēs, which probably made his political rivals a little less enthusiastic in their efforts to keep it alive.

Inevitably, PASOK's victory in 1981 and its subsequent eight-year tenure in power through 1989 affected the outlook as well as the makeup of the HOC. The government began to approach the Olympics in terms of principles closer (ostensibly) to its own heart, such as social transformation and world peace. In early 1985, Lambēs Nikolaou, an accomplished civil engineer who was serving as a technical advisor to Prime Minister Papandreou at the time, was appointed to the HOC and immediately assumed its presidency. He was subsequently appointed to the IOC in October 1986. Nikolaou, a technocrat rather than an ideologue, conveyed the new government's perspective on the Olympic movement in measured tones; in opening the Olympic Academy's twenty-eighth session in 1988, for instance, he said that the "Olympic movement today is the greatest social force on earth; it promotes hope for the consolidation of peace."[4]

Karamanlēs's idea reflected the Greek sense of continuity with the original Olympic Games. Undergirding his proposal was the importance Greeks attached to Olympia as the birthplace of the Olympics, as well as the belief that the location itself would help to revive the Olympic spirit. As such, it was a continuation of the commemorations held in Olympia during the interwar period and of the creation of the academy after the war. Significantly, Miltiadēs Evert, a close political associate of Karamanlēs, saw this proposal as a sign of continuity with another important feature of Greece's relationship to

---

[4]Lambēs Nikolaou, "Address and Opening," *Report of the Twenty-Eighth Session, 29 June-14 July 1988*, DOA, Athens, 1988, p. 34.

the Olympics: the promotion of Greece's European identity. Karamanlēs's vision of Greece, wrote Evert, was to make it the spiritual center of Europe. Prior to laying claim to the Olympics, Karamanlēs had established the European Cultural Center at Delphi (which sponsors events related to the humanities), supported the creation of a cultural center in Athens, and strengthened the Athens Festival, Greece's major international summer arts and cultural event.[5]

There was indeed a correspondence and no contradiction between Karamanlēs's broader European vision and his proposal for the Olympics. Karamanlēs may have headed a conservative government that had been invested deeper in anticommunism than in enhancing Greece's postwar democratic system during his earlier tenure in power that ended in 1963, but when he reentered Greek politics in 1974, it was with a distinct commitment to democratize and Europeanize the country, a process that he believed was intertwined. Indeed, his greatest achievements were the transition to democracy in 1974 and Greece's entry into the European Economic Community in 1981. His proposal that Greece should host the Olympics—however rash and unplanned it was—reflected a sense that Greece had to assert itself and assume the responsibility of salvaging an international institution whose origins were Greek. It was, in a sense, an echo of the old Hellenic internationalism that Greek leaders had displayed with regard to the Olympics at the turn of the twentieth century.

THE MONTREAL OLYMPIAD AND KARAMANLĒS'S PROPOSAL

Sandwiched between the assassination of the Israeli athletes at the Munich games in 1972 and the boycotts of the Moscow and Los Angeles games, the political problems of the Montreal Olympiad in 1976 are often overlooked. It is important to recall those problems, as they were a major force behind Karamanlēs's proposal. Indeed, the efficiently organized Montreal games are remembered for the legacy of economic difficulties they bequeathed the city rather than for their organizational success in athletic terms.

The first political issue to cast a shadow over the Montreal games involved the accommodation of both the People's Republic of China (PRC) and the Republic of China (ROC or Taiwan), which ended with the

[5]Miltiadēs Evert, *Karamanlēs o anamorfōtēs* [*Karamanlēs, the Renovator*], no publisher, Athens, 1983, p. 172.

Republic of China withdrawing from the games. The Canadian government had already recognized the People's Republic, as had the United Nations, but the IOC had not resolved its attitude toward the "two Chinas." The same applied to the United States: President Richard Nixon had visited China in 1972 and upgraded US-PRC trade relations, but the United States would not officially recognize the PRC until 1978. Meanwhile, just before the games, Pierre Trudeau's government refused to allow ROC officials and athletes into Canada. A major crisis loomed, pitting the host country against both the IOC and the United States, which was obliged to back its Taiwanese allies and spoke of boycotting the event.

A last-minute compromise resolved the problem, but the other political crisis, involving the African states, proved irreparable. African sports leaders had demanded the expulsion of New Zealand from the Olympic games because its national rugby team, the "All Blacks," had gone on a playing tour of South Africa, which was excluded from the Olympic movement at the time because of its apartheid regime. Although rugby was not an Olympic sport, Africans and non-Africans alike were outraged because the tour had taken place in the aftermath of a bloody massacre of black civilians, including many children, in Soweto, South Africa, in June 1976. The IOC did nothing, however, and more than twenty African teams and a number of other Third World nations withdrew from the Olympiad. Seven African countries had already decided not to send teams to Montreal.

This tense situation, which worsened when a Soviet fencer was caught cheating, unleashed a worldwide debate on the games' future, leading Karamanlēs to issue his proposal toward the end of the Olympiad. Days before Karamanlēs made his statement, Bill Bradley, a basketball player for the New York Knicks, trumped him. Bradley had captained the US basketball team at the Tokyo Olympiad in 1964. In an op-ed piece in *The New York Times* on July 12, 1976, Bradley outlined his views about the Olympics, beginning his article with an eerily prophetic scenario that spoke of a US boycott of the Moscow Olympics in 1980. To prevent the degeneration of the Olympics, Bradley proposed five reforms: jettisoning the concept of amateurism, which was outdated; eliminating team sports because they simulated war games; making the Olympics more participant-oriented; awarding all participants a medal, but eliminating the silver and bronze medals and awarding a gold medal only to someone who had broken a previous gold-medal record in the respective Olympic sport (Bradley thought this would make athletes compete against a standard, not another athlete or nation); and advising that "the Olympics . . . be situated permanently in Greece, the country of their origin." All nations competing in the games would have to contribute toward funding the new facilities. Spoiling the effect somewhat, Bradley confused Olympia with Mount Olympus (which is several hundred miles north of the site of the ancient Olympics): "Every four years, the world's youth would return to Mount Olympus in a spirit of friendship to compete in the finest athletic installation in the world," Bradley concluded. The article was reprinted in the Greek press, with Olympia being substituted for Mt. Olympus.[6]

On July 31, Karamanlēs wrote to IOC president Lord Killanin, proposing that Greece become the permanent host of the Olympic Games in response to the crisis in which they found themselves. He listed the problems that he believed threatened the very existence of the games: political and racial conflicts that undermined the idealist nature of the Olympics and led to boycotts such as the recent one; increased commercialization; growing costs that eliminated small countries as potential venues; an overemphasis on winning that generated chauvinism; and, finally, the lack of the truce that had existed during antiquity. The solution, according to Karamanlēs, lay in directly associating the games with the place in which they had originated, which amounted to reiterating the older view that the ancient Greek spirit inhered in the land that bred it. He told Killanin: "The revival of the Olympic Games in their ancient birthplace (but also in the site where the modern Games began in Athens in 1896) not only will achieve a high degree of symbolism. In addition, the institution will get rid of the corrupt elements that have accumulated within it and threaten its existence. A rigorous and simple athletic spirit will be restored . . . [and] political, nationalist and non-sporting exploitation will be banished."[7]

The proposal became front-page news throughout the world, and many media organizations treated it seriously, if not positively, and letters to newspapers in several countries hailed the idea. The London *Times* carried a front-page article supporting Karamanlēs. Not surprisingly, the Republic of

---

[6]Bill Bradley, "Five Ways to Reform the Olympics," *The New York Times*, July 21, 1976; *Kathimerini*, July 27, 1976.

[7]"Proposal for the permanent holding of the Olympic Games in Greece," www.karamanlis-foundation.gr; Gianna Panousakē, "To orama tou K. Karamanlē gia tēn anaviōsē tou Olympiakou Ideōdous" ["K. Karamanlēs's Vision for the Revival of the Olympic Ideal"], *Athlēsē kai Koinōnia*, Volume 22, 1996, pp. 22–29; *Kathimerini*, August 1, 1976.

China's Olympic committee applauded the idea, insinuating that the Moscow games might be cancelled—and prompting *Pravda* to reassure its readers that the proposal did not affect the 1980 games. There were also skeptics, however, such as *Le Monde*'s Athens correspondent, who called the proposal interesting and generous, but utopian.[8]

Lord Killanin was considered a more flexible administrator than his predecessor, Avery Brundage, whom he replaced in 1972 at the Munich Olympics. He, too, was obviously experienced in matters of international sport, having joined the IOC as Ireland's representative in 1952 and becoming vice-president in 1968. His views on amateurism were not as deeply held as those of Brundage, which led to changes in eligibility. But the Karamanlēs proposal was an even more difficult issue, and he reacted with caution. Nikos Filaretos was a leader of the Greek delegation to Montreal, and he remembers Killanin's unenthusiastic expression when HOC member Epameinōndas Petralias formally handed him Karamanlēs's letter. From that expression alone, Filaretos foresaw that the proposal would not be accepted.[9] The IOC president sent back a short and cautious reply stating that the IOC would take Karamanlēs's proposal into account when it discussed its longer-term plans, which, however, was not something he anticipated happening in the near future. The IOC's more immediate goal, Killanin added, was to decide on the venue for the 1984 Olympiad.

In Greece, meanwhile, the proposal was greeted warmly, not only because it drew international attention to the country, but also because the contemporary troubles faced in Montreal clashed with the sense of tradition that Greeks had tried to impart to those particular games. The torch-lighting ceremony in 1976 had taken place at Olympia with the usual pomp, and included the minister to the prime minister (and his nephew), Achilleas Karamanlēs, as well as members of the Montreal organizing committee. Furthermore, the HOC had moved the celebration of Olympic Games Day from April 6 to July 15 to combine it with the handover of the Olympic flame to the Canadians at a ceremony in the Panathenaic Stadium. Greek president Kōnstantinos Tsatsos attended the event, as did government officials, and it included readings of Pindar's Olympic odes, a parade of representatives of Greek sports clubs, and the torch's arrival from Olympia.

Asked their reactions to Karamanlēs's proposal, leading members of the Hellenic Olympic Committee naturally endorsed it, but managed to strike a

[8] Skiadas, *100 chronia neoterē . . .*, pp. 452–453.
[9] Author's interview with IOC member Nikos Filaretos, June 2001.

note of caution for those who could read between the lines. President Niko-laidēs prefaced his remarks by saying that he had had the opportunity to study the matter in depth, and expressed his support, but stressed the need for Greeks to rally around the proposal so as not to show disunity in the eyes of international observers. Vice-President Tzōrtzēs Athanasiadēs said he thought the games should take place in Athens, not Olympia. It was left to committee member Angelos Lembesēs to raise some doubts, commenting that implementing the proposal would entail a long struggle and require enormous effort, and adding that he did not think it was feasible for the games to take place in Olympia.[10]

It should also be noted that the invocation of ancient traditions was not universally endorsed in Greece. In the new, post-1974 conditions, many historians and intellectuals began to disparage what they saw as ancestor-wor-ship, a formalistic attachment to ancient Greece that was no more than wish-ful thinking. This was part of a broader trend of exploring the roots of Greece's relative underdevelopment, which had been exposed by the disintegration of the country's shaky postwar democracy in 1967. For a while at least, many of the country's leading historians and social scientists, a number of whom had just returned from exile abroad after the junta's collapse in 1974, engaged in an earnest debate over Greece's backwardness and cultural identity.[11]

The historian Nikos Svorōnos (1911–1989) offered one of the most sophisticated critiques of the continuity thesis between ancient and modern Greece. While he endorsed the concept of continuity with the classical past on a cultural—primarily linguistic—level, Svorōnos considered it to be just one of several elements in forming modern Greek identity. Furthermore, he pointed out, the modern Greek state's often justified sense of insecurity, caused by economic and political intervention by outside powers, prompted many thinkers to compensate by overemphasizing the continuity theory over all other elements of Greek identity. In turn, political leaders, fearful of the domestic social tensions generated by outside intervention, found that the idea of continuity with the ancient past functioned as a convenient ideolog-ical cloak for authoritarian government.[12]

[10]*Eleutherotypia*, August 3, 1976.
[11]For a representative collection of essays from the proceedings of a conference on Greek identity held at the Panteion University in Athens in 1981, see D. G. Tsaousēs, editor, *Ellēnis-mos kai ellēnikotēta* [*Hellenism and Greekness*], Estia, Athens, 1983.
[12]Nikos G. Svorōnos, *Episkopēsē tēs neoellēnikēs istorias*, Themelio, Athens, 1977, pp. 22–24.

Immediately after the Montreal games, the HOC met to engage in the routine lamentations about yet another poor Greek Olympic showing. The Greeks had not been expected to do well, and an Athens newspaper subtitled an article on the team traveling to Canada, "first in the parade, extras in the sports." Among the thirty-seven athletes, weightlifter Nikos Ēliadēs came in fifth, Anastasios Boudourēs was sixth in the Finn-class sailing event, and wrestler Geōrgios Chatzēiōannidēs was seventh—the worst results since 1964, and a reminder of the incompetence of the dictatorship's policies toward sport from 1967 to 1974. Discussion about the more immediate causes of the bad outcome by Greek athletes resulted in a wide-ranging critique of the ways sport was organized in Greece. Committee members disparaged the role of the sports federations and the way they ignored proper preparation of athletes by not adhering to rigid criteria of selection. There was even guarded criticism of the government's supervisory body, the general secretariat of sports.

As the HOC was thus engaged in dealing with the consequences of Greek failure in competition, it was the government, not the committee, which followed up on Karamanlēs's proposal, although it did not get very far. When the HOC met to discuss the proposal in August, it discovered that the government planned to supervise the initiative. The minister to the prime minister informed the Greek committee that he would be assembling a separate committee under his direction in which the HOC would have a few representatives. This new committee did not do much, however, as became evident when an IOC member, Mohamed Mzali from Tunisia, arrived in Athens charged by the IOC to investigate the proposal. Mzali asked how far the Greeks had gotten with their plans. Achilleas Karamanlēs responded with his own request that the IOC send the Greeks a set of demands they could work on. As Killanin put it, "the scheme was found to be so impractical that there was no report on the question."[13]

The Karamanlēs proposal appeared to be dying a slow death when the IOC did not discuss it in its eightieth session in Athens in May 1978. The reason, according to Killanin, was that the Greek side had not produced any additional and specific proposals. This created the impression that the original proposal had been shelved; meanwhile, the death of Petralias, who had been a member both of the HOC and IOC and had been handling the matter, led to a breakdown in communications between the latter and the for-

---

[13]Lord Killanin, *My Olympic Years*, William Morrow, New York, 1983, p. 152.

mer. In the event, the IOC decided that the 1984 games would be held in Los Angeles.

The Greeks regrouped at this point, and there is evidence that they refashioned their arguments to address the practical objections voiced against their proposal. The move away from a romantic image of ancient Olympia and toward the issue of the concept's technical feasibility was evident in an op-ed piece that appeared in *The New York Times* in August 1979, written by Helen Vlachos, the editor and publisher of the Athens daily *Kathimerini.* Her choice of that particular newspaper was due to the relative weight of American views and to the fact that the winter Olympics were scheduled to take place in Lake Placid, New York, six months later. She devoted most of her article to outlining exactly how the Greek site would operate. The plan would involve "all the competing nations to come and build their own pavilions and to contribute in the building of all necessary installations." She asked, "why not build a new Olympia, somewhere in the vicinity of the ancient but living presence of old Olympia?" Vlachos referred to the pastoral advantages of the place, saying, "Greece would offer the site— one of the most beautiful, the most peaceful on the small planet earth— under populated [*sic*], unpolluted, with a year-round mild climate, near the sea, in the heart of the Peloponnese, where nature has staged its best settings upon a human scale." But, she quickly added, "an airstrip would tie Olympia with all the world, welcoming all races, colors and creeds, wholly democratic, and free as much as possible from today's invading commercialism."[14]

The *Times* applauded the proposal's formulation by Vlachos. Two days later, it noted in an editorial that, "Mrs. Vlachos may be overly optimistic in maintaining that the pure air and harmony of Ancient Olympia would somehow impart a new spirit to the Games, but the Olympic spirit is now so flawed that any change would probably be an improvement and this change is the best imaginable." The editorial went on to say that, "The case for returning the Olympics to Greece permanently seems just, sensible and compelling. It is just because the Olympic flame was first lit in Greece in 776 BC. It is sensible because creating a permanent home for the Games would be a one-time expense. And it is compelling because such a site would eliminate competition among governments, cities and networks to make the Games bigger, costlier and grimmer."[15]

[14]Helen Vlachos, "Return the Olympics to Greece Permanently. They Started There," *The New York Times*, August 12, 1979.

[15]"A Greek Home for the Games," *The New York Times*, August 14, 1976.

GREECE AS A PERMANENT SITE AND THE WESTERN BOYCOTT OF 1980

The West's boycott of the Moscow Games in 1980 gave the Karamanlēs proposal new life. The Soviet invasion of Afghanistan in December 1979 was the catalyst that transformed growing Western apprehension about holding the Olympics in Moscow into an outright boycott. The boycott was a weapon wielded by US president Jimmy Carter, British prime minister Margaret Thatcher, and other Western politicians to strike at the Soviets politically; it was not an initiative designed to uphold the integrity of the Olympics. Indeed, the boycott in many ways undermined the cause of preserving the games' purity. Karamanlēs, who reintroduced his idea, opposed the West's boycott.

In January 1980, Karamanlēs reiterated his proposal during the ceremonial laying of the cornerstone of the Olympic Stadium that Greece was building just north of Athens, partially in anticipation of claiming the right to host the games on their centenary in 1996. In his speech, he condemned both the Soviet invasion as well as talk of a retaliatory boycott of the Moscow Olympiad, and he drew the conclusion that the international climate lent further justification to his proposal. Karamanlēs sent Killanin another letter at the end of January 1980 in which he stated that Greece would offer a site at Olympia for the games to take place and help resolve the problems that plagued them. "I hope you agree with me, Mr. President," Karamanlēs wrote, "that Greece, perhaps more than any other country, has a right to be concerned with the increasing use of the Olympics for political and non-sporting purposes."[16]

In an attempt to address at least some of the many questions raised by the original offer, this new version was more detailed and specific. Karamanlēs stated that Greece would provide a venue for the games in Olympia that could become an international and neutral zone with the help of an international agreement guaranteeing the zone's independence and the IOC's overall responsibility for the athletic activities taking place there. Moreover, he added, Greece would be happy to discuss any other demands the IOC might have. Upon hearing that Killanin had expressed doubts about Greece's ability to host a neutral zone because of its supposed political instability, Karamanlēs sent a second letter. In it, he rightly scorned as baseless the

---

[16]Skiadas, *100 chronia neoterē* . . . , pp. 453–455.

idea that Greece was plagued by political instability, and he pointed out that a neutral zone would be preferable to holding the games in countries with totalitarian regimes of either the right or the left.

Killanin's response was much more positive this time, at least compared to his reaction to the original proposal. In May 1980, he appointed a committee of IOC members to examine the matter in greater detail. Louis Guirandou-N'Diaye, from Côte d'Ivoire and a member of the IOC since 1969, was its president; its members were Pedro Ramírez Vázquez, an internationally renowned architect from Mexico, James Worrall of Canada, Philipp von Schoeller of Austria, and Greece's Nikolaos Nēsiōtēs. Guirandou-N'Diaye visited Olympia with Karamanlēs and reported back to the IOC meeting in Moscow in July 1980 that he believed it was feasible to hold the games in Kaiafas, a coastal location close to ancient Olympia. He had toured the area in a helicopter, accompanied by Karamanlēs and Nēsiōtēs, for the purpose of locating potential sites around but not within the actual site of ancient Olympia, which the Greeks wished to leave untouched in planning a permanent venue. Guirandou-N'Diaye's report did not make an impact on Killanin, who in any case was stepping down from his post at the IOC's eighty-third session, held in conjunction with the games in Moscow. He admitted in his memoirs that, "From the outset I was never a supporter of this idea, but I appointed a committee of inquiry."[17] (Many years later, Guirandou-N'Diaye was implicated in the Salt Lake City bribery scandal. Following an IOC investigating commission recommendation, he was issued a "serious warning" in early 1999; he died in June of that year.)

In the meantime, there was considerable support for Karamanlēs's proposal in several Western countries, especially those considering a boycott of the Moscow games. Both the US senate and the European parliament backed the plan. Bill Bradley, who had suggested Greece become the permanent site in 1976 when he was a basketball player, was now a US senator, and he brought the issue to the upper house of Congress. Support also came from Australian prime minister Malcolm J. Fraser and former secretary of state Henry A. Kissinger. *The New York Times* endorsed the idea of a permanent site in several editorials and columns. In January 1980, for example, the newspaper commented that, "The summer Olympics need a permanent home in a more neutral setting. Logic and sentiment argue for Greece."[18] As the

---

[17]Killanin, *My Olympic Years . . .* , p. 152.
[18]"Tossing the Olympic Javelin," *The New York Times,* January 17, 1980.

debate continued, Greece and Switzerland emerged as the likeliest candidates for a permanent site, Switzerland offering the political stability and neutrality that Greece apparently lacked, according to some observers.

Despite Killanin's unenthusiastic attitude, Greek hopes were buoyed not only by Guirandou-N'Diaye's visit and the reaction of public opinion around the world, but also because Greece had gained some attention with a few successes at the Moscow Olympiad. In his speech at the Olympic Stadium earlier in the year, Karamanlēs had spoken about Greece's efforts to improve its presence in sport, which included Greek distinctions on the international level. Thus, it was especially gratifying when the forty-two-athlete team returned with three medals. Twenty-eight-year-old Cretan Stelios Mygiakēs won the gold medal in the featherweight class in Greco-Roman wrestling, while Geōrgios Chatzēiōannidēs, another featherweight and the son of Greek Civil War refugees in Soviet Kazakhstan, won the bronze medal in freestyle wrestling. The three-man crew of the Greek Soling-class sailboat, Anastasios Boudourēs, Anastasios Gavrilēs, and Aristeidēs Repanakēs, won the bronze medal.

Yet not all Greeks enthusiastically backed Karamanlēs's proposal, and a great deal of skepticism was voiced in Athens. A panel discussion organized by the Athens-based Greek Society in July 1980 reveals the range and type of issues that concerned those who weighed the proposal's pros and cons. The panelists included a technical consultant to Prime Minister Geōrgios Rallēs, who had replaced Karamanlēs in May after the latter's election as president of the republic. The other members were Marina Chaidopoulou-Adams, a landscape architect, Angelos Chōremēs, director of classical antiquities at the ministry of culture, Igor Degalin, a professor of urban planning at the University of Athens, and Giannēs Marinos, editor of the respected weekly economic review, *Oikonomikos Tachydromos*.

The panelists discussed the numerous effects of building the required infrastructure and sports facilities on the archeological site at Olympia and on the surrounding region of the western Peloponnese. They also considered issues of heritage—and whether contemporary Greece could claim ancient Greece as its heritage—as well as the real nature of the original Olympics and to what extent the ancient games could be a model for the modern world. The panelists agreed that the integrity of the site at ancient Olympia had to be preserved, whatever happened in the future. The possibility of building facilities in the surrounding region also raised some alarm due to environmental concerns and the existence of as-yet-unexplored places of potential archeological value. Chōremēs discussed the underlying assumptions of Greek historical continuity and described them as popularly held conventional wisdom rather than historical fact (but nonetheless significant). There was greater diversity among the panel in characterizing the ancient games as economically or religiously driven, and the extent to which one could regard the modern games as their continuation.

Nikolaos Nēsiōtēs (1925–1986), the member of the IOC committee studying the feasibility of Greece as a permanent site, was in the audience, and he took the floor to clarify the IOC's current assessment of the issue. Nēsiōtēs was an important force in the HOC and the Olympic Academy whose career ended tragically in a fatal automobile accident while he was driving to Olympia in August 1986. He was a former swimmer and basketball player who had gone on to become a professor at the University of Athens. Nēsiōtēs became president of the Olympic Academy in 1977 and a member of the IOC in 1978. In a comprehensive and thoughtful intervention, easily the most valuable contribution to the evening's discussion, Nēsiōtēs gently allayed many of the panelists' fears and concerns. He explained that Olympia would remain untouched. With regard to the surrounding area, he clarified that there were no definite plans and that preliminary discussions had considered limiting the permanent installations to the main athletic facilities, temporary buildings, trailers, and even campgrounds for office space and accommodation. Nēsiōtēs defended the idea of the modern games as a continuation of the original ones, albeit in spirit rather than in fact. Finally, he stressed that the IOC's deliberations were at a very early stage and that its assessment of the pros and cons of the Karamanlēs proposal would proceed carefully and methodically and take into account the many concerns raised.[19]

The Samaranch presidency and the Karamanlēs proposal

Upon his election as president of the IOC, Juan Antonio Samaranch took on the task of resolving the debate about a permanent site—and doing so with the consummate diplomatic skill that would ensure he stayed in his position for the next twenty-one years. In other words, while Samaranch appeared to

---

[19]*Prooptikes gia tē monimē diexagōgē tōn Olympiakōn Agōnōn stēn Ellada* [*Prospects for Permanently Holding the Olympic Games in Greece*], Ellēnikē Etaireia, Athens, 1980.

become much more engaged in the issue than was his predecessor, his role, ultimately, was to defuse it in a way that caused the least conflict. He was helped by the success of the Los Angeles Olympiad, notwithstanding the Soviet retaliatory boycott, and Greece's reorientation toward its candidacy for the centenary Olympiad of 1996. Even more important, many national Olympic committees, international sports federations, and IOC members had, in the meantime, come out against the idea of a permanent site, which had in a sense become associated with the boycott.

During his first few years in office, Samaranch made several moves to show his continued interest in Greece as a permanent site at some time in the future. At the eighty-fourth IOC session in September 1981, Samaranch said that the matter would be examined in detail even as the IOC was awarding the 1988 games to Seoul. Greece submitted its proposal formally at the Olympic congress held in Baden-Baden. In November, the IOC commission, headed by Guirandou-N'Diaye, returned to Greece on a factfinding mission. In September 1982, Samaranch attended the inauguration of the Olympic Stadium in Athens on the opening day of the European track-and-field championships held at the stadium. Karamanlēs naturally took the opportunity to reiterate his proposal on that very public occasion.

Samaranch's delicate treatment of the Greek proposal demonstrated how the IOC also valued the ancient symbolism of the games. As a former sports official of Francisco Franco's dictatorship, Samaranch understood the extravagant use of political symbolism. Samaranch had, of course, reconstructed himself in the post-Franco era as a democratic politician, but his political apprenticeship made him much more sensitive to the significance of the Greek proposal than had been the case with his predecessor, Killanin, or, for that matter, the other senior IOC officials. Accordingly, Samaranch deftly played along with the proposal, managing never to come out strongly either for or against, biding his time and leaving all possibilities open. The respect with which the Greek officials treated him is proof of his diplomatic skills. Samaranch was also familiar with finance, coming from a wealthy business family in Barcelona, and he would go on to become president of Catalonia's largest financial institution (while still presiding over the IOC). If his instincts told him that the games' economic well-being would be threatened by a permanent move to Greece, he chose not to tell his new Greek friends.

There was not much activity around the proposal for the next year, but the issue suddenly flared up in Greece during the preparations for the 1984

Los Angeles games. Despite the boycott by the Soviet Union and several of its allies, the Los Angeles Olympiad proved to be an economic, rather than a political, milestone in the history of the Olympics. In the wake of grave economic problems suffered by Montreal, no Western government was prepared to guarantee the financial resources that hosting the 1984 games would entail. In the event, Los Angeles had been the only candidate city for the XXIIIrd Olympiad, but the bid had been underwritten not by city authorities but a private group of entrepreneurs. The IOC had to revise its charter to accept this novel arrangement. Headed by businessman Peter Ueberroth, the Los Angeles Olympic Organizing Committee (LAOOC) proceeded to organize the first privately funded Olympiad by raising millions of dollars from a glittering array of corporate sponsors.

Reaction to Ueberroth's strategy was strongly negative in Greece, particularly regarding the LAOOC's plan to sell kilometers along the torch-relay route. Historically, individual runners had transported the flame the length of a kilometer. To raise money for charity, the organizers stipulated that companies or individuals could run in the relay only if they paid a $3,000 participation fee. Greek public opinion was scandalized by what most observers described as a desecration of the purity of the Olympic spirit. Anti-American sentiment, shared by many Greeks, also came into play—a legacy of active US support of the colonels' dictatorship and tacit American support for Turkey's subsequent invasion and occupation of Cyprus. This skepticism also derived from a suspicion of corporate motives and, in a country that saw support for sport as a duty of government, even opposition to private funding of sport.

For a while it looked as if the Greeks, in protest, would not permit the flame to travel from Olympia to Los Angeles. When the HOC notified Samaranch in November 1983 that it was considering taking this action, Ueberroth countered that he would use the flame burning at IOC headquarters in Switzerland. Subsequently, however, the LAOOC agreed to halt remaining sales of kilometers (by that time, it had already raised $11 million); in regard to the LAOOC's strategy, Ueberroth also tried to argue that it should have used the word, "contribution," instead of the term, "sponsorship," which had, unfortunately, led the Greeks to assume that the flame would be exploited for commercial gain.[20] But the Greeks were not placated (or fooled, depending on one's point of view), confirming both their passion for the Olympics and their hostility toward American corporations, no matter how the latter try to mask their intentions.

[20]"Torch Dispute is Ended," *The New York Times*, March 21, 1984.

In April 1984, the prospect of the traditional torch-lighting ceremony was dimmed substantially when the Federation of Greek Amateur Athletic Clubs barred its members from participating in the torch relay from Olympia to Athens, the municipal councils of several towns en route decided to boycott the occasion, and even the municipality of Olympia was said to be considering demonstrations designed to prevent the relay.[21] At this point, Ueberroth—named "Man of Year" in January 1985 by *Time* magazine, which described him as "an impresario embodying the renewed American spirit"— made an astonishing revelation: two Swiss students had secretly lit the flame at ancient Olympia and transported it to IOC headquarters in Lausanne. If the Greeks did not agree to the lighting ceremony, he would use the fraudulently secured flame.

The Greek side finally relented. As a sign of continuing protest, however, the Greek government and the HOC kept the ceremonies to a bare minimum, with only a brief speech by Nēsiōtēs at the torch-lighting. There was no relay from Olympia to Athens, since the flame was transported to the Greek capital by helicopter and then placed on a special White House airplane to be flown to New York, where it began its long journey through thirty-three states to Los Angeles—the first time in history that no runner had carried the flame on Greek soil.[22]

The reactions to the LAOOC's campaign of corporate sponsorship and the last-minute boycott by the Soviet Union and another thirteen countries, the result of the ongoing Cold War between the two superpowers, served to galvanize Greek opinion around Karamanlēs's proposal. Kōstas Laliōtēs, PASOK's undersecretary for youth and sport, was representative of this change when he spoke during the opening ceremony of the Olympic Academy's twenty-fourth session in July 1984. Laliōtēs had spoken alongside Karamanlēs at the inauguration of the Olympic Stadium in 1982, but had not mentioned the proposal to hold the games permanently in Greece. This time, however, things had evidently changed. As did the other speakers, including Samaranch, Laliōtēs referred to the crisis the games were experiencing yet again and added, "Greece has responded to the demands of our times. The inspired proposal and initiative of the President of the Greek Republic, Mr. Constantine Karamanles, is quite well known, as is the fact that many

[21]Mario Modiano, "Greeks call off flame lighting ceremony," *The Times* [of London], April 27, 1984.

[22]For Ueberroth's account, see his memoir, Peter Ueberroth with Richard Levin and Amy Quinn, *Made in America: His Own Story*, William Morrow, New York, 1985.

national and international organizations have supported this proposal. The Government of our country has supported, from the very first, the initial proposal and is now renewing and reaffirming the inspiring and hospitable invitation of Greece to have the Olympic Games organized and staged permanently in their country of birth. We are sure that the recognition of Greece as the permanent seat of the Olympic Games will enhance the principles, values and the spirit of Olympism and bring them closer to today's complex reality."[23]

There is a double irony in Laliōtēs's praise of the proposal made by Karamanlēs, his ideological adversary. At a time of sharp political differences between PASOK and New Democracy—PASOK refused to support Karamanlēs when his presidential term ended the following year—the shared sense of the important role Greece could play in the Olympic movement brought the two sides together. Alas, days later, the Los Angeles Olympiad would score a tremendous public-relations success and suddenly make hosting the games more appealing. This, coupled with the failure of the boycott to undermine the games, signaled that the Olympics were emerging from their crisis. This was the death knell for Karamanlēs's proposal.

The abrupt end of dialogue on the games' permanent move to Olympia probably saved the IOC the embarrassment of having to reject the Greek idea. The site of the ancient games functioned smoothly as the Olympic movement's symbolic ancestral home: its "Mecca," according to Brundage. But Karamanlēs's proposal, and specifically the choice of Olympia as the venue for the modern Olympics, upset the carefully maintained balance between the Olympic movement's myths and its reality. The Greek prime minister had evidently forgotten that Greece was no more than a mythical (and myth-making) landscape for the Olympic movement. The IOC did not associate Greece with the type of wealthy and modern country that could guarantee organizational and financial success for the Olympics. But Lord Killanin had been far too polite to articulate that type of Olympic *Realpolitik* and offered kind words instead—as well as an appropriate epitaph for the Greek proposal: "The debate that this created showed that there are people, outside the movement, who are eager to see the Games sustained as a cornerstone of peace and goodwill. Because of that I am deeply grateful to Karamanlis for pursuing the concept."[24]

[23] *Report of the 24th Session of the International Olympic Academy, July 4–19, 1984*, IOA, Athens, 1984, p. 32.

[24] Killanin, *My Olympic Years . . .*, p. 153.

CHAPTER 8

ATLANTA 1996 AND HOW GREECE LOST THE CENTENARY GAMES

C OCA-COLA DEFEATS THE PARTHENON: that was how the Greek press greeted the IOC's choice of Atlanta over Athens for the 1996 Olympiad. While it is true that the enormously influential corporate interests lined up behind Atlanta's bid played a role in the outcome, the Greek campaign also contributed to the result. Atlanta's victory over Athens, the sentimental favorite, was surprising, and it came after a closely fought battle. Athens had been the early frontrunner, but, as the campaign unfolded, the other candidate cities began catching up as Athens tried to transform the main thrust of its bid in order to outflank its rivals. But this was not easy. During the previous decade, in their proposal that their country host the Olympics permanently, the Greeks had shown an ability to enrich tradition-based arguments with practical elements that addressed more contemporary concerns. The enormity of the centenary as a selling point, as well as their own obsession with continuity with the past, overwhelmed the Greeks, however, and limited their capacity to address growing unease about Athens's ability to run the games efficiently.

The story of Athens's bid for the centenary Olympiad encapsulates the Olympic movement's concerns and overall state in the 1980s. Anxious over the economic and organizational viability of the games and impressed by corporate influence, the Olympic movement was prepared to reject history and tradition, and embrace the high-tech image of a New World Olympiad. As self-evident as these observations seem in retrospect, the Greek bid was, remarkably, unable to grasp their significance and tailor its platform accordingly. Scholarly studies of bids by cities to organize Olympiads after the financial success of the Los Angeles games in 1984 have focused on particular cities.

They have examined the positions of supporters and opponents of the respective bids, their arguments and tactics, and the way advocates ultimately presented a bid in the final stage of the selection process. These studies include Christopher R. Hill's examination of two British bids (those of Birmingham for the 1992 games and Manchester for 2000), Helen Jefferson Lenskyj's investigation (into Toronto's failed 1996 bid and Sydney's successful 2000 bid), and a monograph by Ian Jobling (also on Sydney's bid for the 2000 games).[1]

While there are no studies on the bidding process as a whole for the 1996 games, Atlanta's bid has come under scrutiny because of bribery allegations from a number of sources. Investigations in 1999 involved officials of the Salt Lake City committee (which had successfully bid for the 2002 winter games) bribing certain IOC members with cash and gifts worth hundreds of thousands of dollars. In his exposé of Olympic corruption, journalist Andrew Jennings devoted several pages to the 1996 games. He suggested that the Atlanta committee exploited the presence of the Martin Luther King Center in its city and relied on the Coca-Cola company to wine and dine and offer generous gifts to certain members of the IOC.[2] After news of the Salt Lake City scandal broke in early 1999, members of the Atlanta bidding committee admitted to having given gifts in excess of the $200 limit to several IOC members. Melissa Turner, a reporter for *The Atlanta Journal-Constitution,* produced a series of articles detailing the activities of the organizing committee and its president, Billy Payne, but her emphasis was on the period after Atlanta was awarded the 1996 games.[3]

ATHENS BIDS FOR THE 1996 GAMES

"I am sure that holding the Games here on their 100th anniversary of their modern revival will provide an opportunity to reinvest the Olympic spirit

---

[1]Hill, *Olympic Politics . . . ,* Chapter 5; Helen Jefferson Lenskyj, *Inside the Olympic Industry: Power Politics and Activism,* SUNY Press, Albany, 2000, Chapter 4; Ian Jobling, "Bidding for the Olympics: Site Selection and Sydney 2000," in Kay Schaffer and Sidonie Smith, editors, *The Olympics at the Millennium: Power Politics and the Games,* Rutgers University Press, New Brunswick, 2000, pp. 258–271.

[2]Andrew Jennings, *The New Lords of the Rings,* Simon and Schuster, New York, 1996, pp. 133–143.

[3]Melissa Turner, "Inside the '96 Olympics/Day 1, Billy Payne: Hero of the Hard Sell," *The Atlanta Journal-Constitution,* August 6, 2000. In keeping with the new, post-1984 direction of the Olympics' corporatization, Payne was not only president of the Atlanta bid committee, but also its "CEO."

with its ancient origins and reconfirm its principles." With those words, spoken at a commemoration of the modern Olympics' ninetieth anniversary, Prime Minister Andreas Papandreou launched Greece's bid for the 1996 Olympiad. Papandreou was an unlikely political figure to be leading a major sporting initiative. Totally uninterested in sport but with a surfeit of populist charisma, he could afford to stay away from the VIP seats in soccer and basketball stadiums that afforded less popular politicians easy access to some popular recognition. In a sense, however, this was not a sporting initiative by any strict definition: it was an exercise in identity politics. The decision to use the anniversary to announce Greece's bid for the centenary Olympiad confirmed that this project was conceived in terms of appealing to the old Greek staples of identity, tradition, and history. Here, of course, Papandreou was at his best, cleverly appropriating conservatism's stock beliefs and exploiting them for his ostensibly socialist agenda. Prior to Papandreou, the more traditional Greek left had always treated classical Greece with the suspicion it reserved for the core values of the right.

In the four and a half years between the declaration of Greek intent and the IOC meeting in September 1990 that would decide among the candidate cities, the Greek campaign encountered several obstacles. The procedural ones had to do with the way the bid was administered, and particularly the extent of government involvement in leading it. The organizational hurdles related to hosting and administering the games included ensuring a suitable urban environment and infrastructure as well as producing the necessary range of facilities to guarantee the Olympiad's smooth and efficient running. On the whole, the organizers overlooked these problems due to their abundant faith in the basic claims of the Greek bid. They believed that the IOC, and the rest of the world for that matter, would readily support their arguments that Athens should get the 1996 games in the name of history and tradition. Indeed, for the first few years, the Greeks limited themselves to that argument and did not emphasize any other virtues in their bid. Typical in this respect was a Greek parliamentary motion, offered in April 1986 in conjunction with Papandreou's statement and designed to support the bid, which passed unanimously. The motion opened with the statement that Greece was the birthplace of the Olympic ideals, that the games had a history of a thousand years in Greece, and that the centenary of the modern games would be in 1996. Therefore, reflecting the sentiments of the entire Greek people, the parliament supported the HOC's proposal that the 1996 games take place in

Athens. Recourse to history had gone from being an essential principle to becoming a mere fig-leaf, which the Greeks hoped would compensate for their bid's technical deficiencies—although international observers were already describing Athens as the "sentimental" favorite that, nonetheless, had to contend with technically superior bids from several rival cities.

Unfortunately, it was only in the summer of 1989 that the bidding committee, renamed "Athens '96," finally acquired a semblance of political autonomy. The involvement of national governments with local city authorities is an essential feature of any effective bid by a city; in Greece's case, however, and for a long time, the bid appeared to be run by the government. The first committee established in 1986, for example, included the prime minister, the speaker of parliament, the mayor of Athens, the leader of the opposition, government ministers, and representatives of all major political parties, as well as the president of the HOC. This arrangement ensured that politics would disrupt or at least interfere with the committee's work. There may not have been another alternative at the time, since government is centrally involved in virtually all Greek civic affairs, but the drawbacks of this practice in the case of the bidding procedure soon became evident.

The clash between the PASOK government and the municipality of Athens came first. In a surprising result, the conservative New Democracy candidate, Miltiadēs Evert, defeated PASOK's Melina Merkourē in October 1986 in the mayoralty election. Evert immediately proceeded to fight for a bigger role for the municipality on the bidding committee, and, having failed to do so satisfactorily in his opinion, withdrew from the committee for the first six months of 1988. He agreed to become involved again only two months before the Greek bid was to be presented at the Seoul Olympics, the *quid pro quo* being that the municipality would become the "joint-bidder." The second enormous problem arose in June 1989, when PASOK lost the parliamentary elections but no other party won a clear majority. An unprecedented coalition between New Democracy and the Communist Party of Greece (*Kommounistiko Komma Elladas*, or KKE) formed a fragile government, and the country went to the polls twice again before New Democracy was able to gain a workable parliamentary majority in April 1990. These changes affected Greek momentum and the Greek presentation at a crucial IOC session in Puerto Rico in August 1989. It was then that the committee was reorganized and named "Athens '96," with representatives of the government, the city, and the HOC.

The organizational problems facing Athens were well known long before the summer of 1989. When the bid was launched in 1986, there was considerable opposition from within Greece. Left-wing parties and several intellectuals raised doubts about Athens's ability to host the Olympiad, citing the enormous costs, the lack of transport, the city's overcrowded urban landscape, and, last but not least, the smog that choked it. The environmentally based objections were serious and well founded. The deterioration of the quality of life in Athens lay in a combination of factors. The city had undergone a massive influx of migrants from the provinces in the postwar era, and the population of greater Athens multiplied exponentially from 600,000 to four million in only thirty years. Poor planning led to crowded neighborhoods and congested roads, made worse by the economic prosperity and lower fuel prices of the early Eighties, which brought more cars into the city. The existence of only a single subway line made traffic problems even worse. All this, combined with the physical environment—Athens lies in a valley ringed by mountains in three directions, with the sea to its south—helped produce acute pollution. Beginning in the early 1980s, a Los Angeles-type of photochemical smog made its appearance. In 1988, at Liosia, one of the northern Athens suburbs, the eight-hour average ozone concentration exceeded the threshold of danger prescribed by the European Community. The authorities placed limits on traffic and took other measures, but the smog persisted.

Its serious environmental objections notwithstanding, however, the left's exclusive emphasis on this issue was typical of its ambivalence toward the return of the Olympics to Greece. For the strongest element within the left, the KKE, the issue was relatively simple and clear-cut. In principle, the party supported the Olympics in a way that reflected its alignment with Soviet-style, Marxist-Leninist ideology. The Olympics enabled the so-called socialist countries to demonstrate their superior form of social organization through excellence on the sporting field. As far as Greece was concerned, the party maintained the general critique of Western ways of running sport, namely, the trend toward commercialism and agendas that ignored the needs of ordinary people. But for the other left-wing parties and unaffiliated leftists, most of whom did not share the KKE's admiration for the Soviet system and its instrumentalist view of the Olympics, things were far more complicated. The concept of Greek continuity from the classical to the modern era was always a thorny one for leftist intellectuals, who were quick to criticize what they saw as *progonoplēxia* and the political exploitation of the continuity theory, without producing a sustained counter-discourse that could articulate a lucid stance on the Olympics. Some on the left rejected the whole idea, while others believed that the games' content could be changed on the basis of a different reading of Greek antiquity. Ultimately, however, no clear view emerged. Thus, the left was limited to sniping at collateral targets, such as the bid's insufficient environmental planning.

THE CAMPAIGN INTENSIFIES

One can look at the Greek campaign as unfolding over two periods. The Seoul Olympiad of 1988, at which the cities preparing bids for 1996 made presentations, brought the early phase to a close. It had begun on a very confident note with Papandreou's announcement in April. With Samaranch present, the Greek prime minister declared, somewhat presumptuously, "I believe Greece is entitled to have this honor," adding, "I appeal especially to the International Olympic Committee and to its honorable president, Mr. Juan Antonio Samaranch, personally for this." The IOC president responded, "I will try as hard as I can to bring the Games to Athens in 1996."[4] The words spoken at this gathering marking the ninetieth anniversary of the modern games typified the early optimism that accompanied the Greek bid. Greece was invoking history and laying an almost proprietary claim to the centenary games, believing tradition entitled it to host them. Samaranch went along with the Greek claims and did not abandon that posture, publicly at least, until the IOC met in Tokyo in September 1990.

Within a few months, Toronto joined the fray when its city council voted unanimously in August 1986 to bid for the centenary games. The city's mayor, Art Eggleton, traveled to Lausanne in October of that year to observe firsthand how things worked. The 92-member IOC was convening its ninety-first session to choose a host city for the 1992 summer and winter Olympiads. The Toronto organizing committee, unlike the Greeks, had based its preparations on the Los Angeles model by soliciting considerable investment from the private sector. Still, with the memories of the financial losses suffered by Montreal, there was some opposition in Canada to Toronto's bid, including from a local group working toward returning the Olympic Games to Greece. Moreover, the bid's organizers decided to consult with a wide range of the

---

[4]Mario Modiano, "Athens Claiming their Birthright," *The Times* [of London], April 16, 1986; *The Toronto Star*, April 16, 1986.

city's constituencies. This move, coupled with several serious and competing media outlets, contributed to a very open and controversial debate about the merits of holding the games in Toronto.

There was much less debate of any kind in Athens. This was partially due to Greek conventional wisdom that the Olympics are indeed part of the nation's heritage. With the greater part of the population endorsing them, a rejection of the return of the games to Athens, even on technical grounds, would be perceived as a blow to the collective sense of national identity—and a rejection of the "responsibilities" accruing therefrom (protecting the so-called purity of ancient Olympic traditions from the manifold evils of political and economic interests, for example). Also, it has to be said that public life in Greece is not structured in a way that allows open and unrestrained debate, especially if it entails criticism of policies deemed to be in the "national interest." Put another way, civil society is less developed in Greece than it is in other Western democracies, and the state and political parties wield a great deal of influence over the media, while unaffiliated citizens' groups are a rarity, even now. To this day, all these factors combine against the type of open debate on the Olympics that one repeatedly witnesses in other developed countries. (As pointed out, even the Greek left, a potentially forceful critic of the games, adopted an indirect critique citing environmental concerns rather than directly questioning the very need for the Olympiad.)

The Greek committee was also present in Lausanne in October 1986 to "get a reading on" the atmosphere as Barcelona was awarded the 1992 summer Olympiad over Paris. The Greeks then pushed Athens's candidacy for the next games along predictable lines. In what one Toronto newspaper described as a slick color pamphlet, the Greek committee echoed the basic refrain of its claim: the belief in the inherent right of Greeks to stage the 1996 games in order to celebrate the centenary where the institution was revived. The leaflet included segments from Samaranch's speech in Athens, in which he had said that he hoped everyone present at the time would meet again in a decade to celebrate the centenary.[5]

In the early fall of 1987, a full three years before the IOC's decision was due, there were grounds for guarded optimism in Athens. In January, there had been so much concern with the slow pace of the preparations that Lambēs Nikolaou, the HOC's president, had spoken out publicly about the

---

[5]Laurie Monsebraaten, "Athens Beats Toronto Off Blocks With Bid to Host 1996 Olympics," *The Toronto Star*, October 16, 1986.

need to cover a lot of ground within the next six months. His fellow HOC and IOC member, Nikos Filaretos, also echoed Nikolaou's concerns and told *The New York Times*, "We have to stop putting all our hopes on our ancient and modern historical ties to the Olympics, believing that this automatically entitles us to the golden Olympiad. Such illusions have been responsible for our tragically slow start."[6] Yet a few months later, government officials were striking more optimistic tones. Pollution and the other urban issues remained, but the construction of sports infrastructure was progressing, and international reactions to Athens's bid were positive. The government was spending money upgrading sports facilities; it also invited international bids to expand the facilities around the Olympic Stadium to include a velodrome, a sports hall, outdoor swimming pools, warm-up tracks, tennis courts, and a press center. At a European sports conference held in Athens, former champion—and Olympic gold-medalist—runner Sebastian Coe from Britain was among several celebrities who expressed themselves favorably regarding Athens's chances. The undersecretary of sport, Sēfēs Valyrakēs, claimed that he encountered no negative reactions to Greece's bid when he had traveled abroad to promote it.[7]

The representatives of the Greek bid had clearly shifted tone in 1987, having become aware of concerns being voiced about their ability to raise funds to complete necessary construction. Without abandoning the tradition-oriented core of their arguments, committee members traveling abroad focused on the issue of funds. For example, retired general Euangelos Savramēs was in Indianapolis for the first world indoor track-and-field championships to lobby IOC members and talk to newspaper reporters. Savramēs argued forcefully that Greece already had the necessary funds for road improvements and new facilities. He also explained that security at Athens airport and elsewhere would be under the strict control and supervision of the ministry of public order.[8] The Greek bid took a step forward in the summer of 1988, soon after the mayor of Athens rejoined the campaign. Papandreou formally announced the Greek bid on June 29 at a dinner for Samaranch and other IOC members at the ancient *agora* in Athens. Samaranch was in the Greek capital to open the Olympic Academy's twenty-eighth summer session. Upon his arrival, the IOC president echoed his earlier support by

[6]Paul Anastasi, "Greeks' Plans for Olympiad are Imperiled," *The New York Times*, January 19, 1987.
[7]Pat Butcher, "Athens ready for 1996 Games," *The Times* [of London], October 6, 1987.
[8]Al Sokol, "General Carries Torch for Greece," *The Toronto Star*, March 10, 1987.

saying, "If you work hard, I can tell you Athens will be the host country. . . . I don't think the other candidates should worry you."[9]

In his speech, Papandreou said that the 1996 games would be an Olympiad of "peace and civilization," and that all Greeks supported Athens's bid. Until that moment, the association of the 1996 games with "peace and civilization" had been one of the few concessions made by the Greeks in acknowledging the relevance of the Olympics to the present—although there was, of course, a double meaning to the term, since a truce from warfare was part of the ancient Olympics. At the same time, peace was a favorite buzz-word of the country's ruling party and was probably intended for domestic consumption and for the ears of non-Western states. The next day, Sama-ranch and Melina Merkourē, Greece's minister of culture, laid the corner-stone for the velodrome and other facilities to be built around the Olympic Stadium.

By the time of the Seoul Olympics in September 1988, Atlanta and Man-chester had joined Athens and Toronto in bidding for the 1996 Olympiad, and all four candidates were in Korea to make their case. An Australian city was also going to bid, but the final choice had not yet been made. George Papandreou, the prime minister's eldest son, headed the Greek delegation that traveled to South Korea to make the case for Athens. He had been appointed minister of education in a government reshuffle and, since the undersecretary of sports reported to him, his father decided to step aside and allow him to lead the organizing committee (Merkourē remained its execu-tive head). Among the four candidate cities, Athens and Atlanta were the most visible in Seoul, although their representatives adopted entirely differ-ent tactics. Still in the early phase when sentiment overshadowed close assess-ments of efficiency and capability, the Greeks pushed their case with a frontrunner's confidence. In contrast, the Atlanta Organizing Committee (AOC) played the role of underdog. The city's mayor, Andrew J. Young, and Billy Payne, a real estate lawyer who would make a short presentation to the IOC, had led a group of business, civic, and political leaders to Seoul. The Atlanta representatives openly admitted that their city was a long-shot and that they hoped to be competing again for the 2000 games, after gaining experience in the bidding process and having learned about the IOC and how it worked.[10] Young's comments about the meeting between the IOC and the

[9] *Ta Nea,* June 30, 1988.

[10] Larry Copeland, "Atlanta Team to Begin Marathon Bid to get Summer Games in '96," *The Atlanta Journal-Constitution,* September 9, 1998.

AOC were typical in that respect. "We just went in there and stammered and stuttered and smiled," he said.[11] Kevin Gosper, an Australian sports official who was to be closely involved in Melbourne's bid, which was announced in November of that year, has written that Atlanta's tactics lulled its competition into complacency. "They told us early on they had come into the bidding as a warm-up for 2000 or 2004. Their rhetoric rubbed off on us and made us believe that they weren't a really serious candidate this time around."[12]

The main public event for the Greek delegation was a press conference that concluded with a reception and the distribution of shoulder bags bearing the slogan, "Athens '96." George Papandreou's remarks combined references to history and tradition with arguments about Athens's ability to host the games in terms of infrastructure and security. He added that measures such as controls on industry and automobile emissions would resolve the problems posed by smog. "Tradition is our strongest asset," he conceded, "but we cannot overlook the other details." A reporter from the *Toronto Star* was more than impressed: "Papandreou was the perfect diplomat. Humbly, he refused to knock Toronto or Manchester or anybody else. And at the end of a bravura performance he had tallied heavily. Athens had consolidated its hold on first place."[13]

Papandreou, however, had failed to impress the men from Atlanta. The AOC left Seoul believing that "Athens can be beaten, though not necessarily by Atlanta." They conceded that Athens remained the sentimental favorite but noted that Papandreou had acknowledged the need for revamped telecommunications and transport networks. The AOC and the correspondent from *The Atlanta Journal-Constitution*, Ed Hinton, dwelt on these deficiencies, which they believed would adversely affect Athens's chances. Meanwhile, they found that there was support for Atlanta from the Soviet Union and the other eastern European countries because of their ties with the Atlanta-based Turner Broadcasting System. Andrew Young was also very well regarded among leaders of African nations. Finally, the AOC drew encouragement from the advice it had received from the representatives of Lillehammer, the Norwegian city that was the IOC's surprise choice to host

[11]Ed Hinton, "Atlanta Makes its Case in Seoul to Host '96 Olympics," *The Atlanta Journal-Constitution*, September 13, 1988.

[12]Kevin Gosper with Glenda Korporaal, *An Olympic Life: Melbourne 1956 to Sydney 2000*, Allen & Unwin, St. Leonards, 2000, p. 224.

[13]Jim Proudfoot, "Athens Widens its Lead in Footrace with Toronto," *The Toronto Star*, September 19, 1988.

the 1994 winter Olympiad. They told the Americans that they had scored their upset by developing strong personal contacts with as many IOC members as possible, rather than with "power politics, showmanship or gimmicks." In fact, Atlanta had used every tactic enumerated above extremely well in its fight to win the nomination from the US Olympic Committee and was now planning to use them all again in its bid for the 1996 games.[14]

George Papandreou, meanwhile, left Seoul with a more realistic understanding of the task ahead. The experience had been an eye-opener. He told the Greek press that witnessing the ways in which the Korean hosts had dealt with the logistical problems of organizing the Seoul games showed the Greeks how much they still had to do in order to present a persuasive case. "We have some basic advantages" over the other cities, he told them, "but we have to intensify the rate of our preparations" and make a great effort.[15] That particular statement, which spoke volumes and was reported alongside the news of the successful press conference, went almost unnoticed.

The second and more difficult phase of the Greek bid began after the Seoul Olympiad, when the bidding for 1996 entered its final stage. The deadline for submitting formal applications to the IOC was April 1989, leaving eighteen months for the candidates to make their cases and the IOC to assess them before the final choice was announced in September 1990. Already, by late 1988, with the Seoul Olympics out of the way and the choice for the 1994 winter games already made, all eyes were on the cities bidding for 1996. The international press was scrutinizing their claims more carefully and critically, and their respective representatives were weighing their own chances against those of their rivals. As such, the post-Seoul atmosphere had not strengthened the Greek case. The biggest issue was financial. The press reported that the Greek estimates, which foresaw a very narrow profit as compared to those of the other cities, had not budgeted for security. This was a serious matter, particularly because of the notorious Greek terrorist group, November 17. An Athens newspaper reported that Prime Minister Papandreou had vetoed an additional series of cultural activities for the games in order to relieve the budget. There were even reports of the Greeks hiring Peter Ueberroth as a consultant. With those types of stories appearing in the international press, the Greek organizing committee began a campaign of damage control by

---

[14]Ed Hinton, "The Battle for 1996," *The Atlanta Journal-Constitution*, September 19, 1988; Ed Hinton, "The Atlanta Olympic Watch," *The Atlanta Journal-Constitution*, September 28, 1988.

[15]*Ta Nea*, September 16, 1988.

producing a set of persuasive budgetary figures, official assurances about infrastructure, and reminders that most of the athletic facilities were ready. For good measure, the committee released another glossy pamphlet with color photographs and suitable statements from Nikolaou and Valyrakēs.[16]

The cracks appearing in the Greek façade encouraged its rivals, including Melbourne, the city chosen by the Australian Olympic Committee over Brisbane and Sydney to compete for the 1996 Olympiad. Kevin Gosper, the committee's head and a member of the Melbourne bidding committee, has suggested that, beyond those cracks, the Athens campaign suffered from internal procedural problems: "Athens was not doing a good job selling itself and its lobby team had lots of problems. . . . Samaranch was getting advice . . . that the Greek capital could be a logistical disaster for the Centennial Games." After visiting Athens, Gosper went away "believing they [Athens] could be beaten."[17]

The other cities also stepped up their activities, and the Manchester committee chose to tackle the issue of the centenary head on, suggesting the separation of the celebrations from the actual games. "Britain," the committee asserted, "with impeccable Olympic credentials has a role in the celebration which it is keen to fulfill."[18] Featuring prominently in the Manchester committee's material were William Penny Brookes's Olympic Games from the nineteenth century. The committee was not averse to invoking Coubertin either, and it stated that, following the games, the facilities would be turned over to the public, which would honor one of the baron's guiding principles, namely, that everyone, regardless of social class, have the chance to take part in physical recreation.

The Greeks submitted their bid formally to the IOC in January 1989, retaining their primary emphasis on tradition and history. The actual file was the size of a bulky briefcase and contained three volumes, totaling 1,100 pages, and six videocassettes. The material included historical and contemporary data about Athens, answers to the standard twenty-three questions posed by the IOC to each candidate city, and data about the different sports and their venues. Within eight months, however, the Greeks were scrambling to persuade the IOC that their preparations would be complete by 1996. This new round of damage control occurred in Puerto Rico in August 1989, at the

---

[16]P. Skeggs, "Athens' late run," *Sun*, December 8, 1988.

[17]Gosper, *An Olympic Life . . .* , p. 223.

[18]*Manchester 1996—The British Olympic Bid*, MOBC, Manchester, 1990, p. 10.

IOC's last session before the crucial decision in Tokyo the following year. Meanwhile, elections in Greece had brought down PASOK and yielded the makeshift coalition headed by conservatives and supported by communists. The new administration tried to address the problem of political interference by creating a new organizing committee, "Athens '96," which included representatives from the private sector as well as the HOC, the government, and the municipality of Athens. Its president was Spyros Metaxas, of the internationally known brandy distillery, and Loukas Kyriakopoulos, a civil engineer and former advisor on urban planning to Karamanlēs, was vice-president.[19]

The IOC met at a luxury hotel on Condado Lagoon, just west of San Juan. The picture-perfect surroundings, from the palm trees lining the lap pool overlooking the lagoon to the elaborate waterfall in the hotel lobby, did not lessen the pressure surrounding the meeting. Each delegation had a hospitality suite to wine and dine the IOC before formally presenting the merits of its case in an hour-long presentation (in addition to a combined presentation and press conference for the international media). The gathering outside San Juan was crucial to the bidding process because it was the only time the IOC delegates would come together before making their final decision. Each candidate city devoted enormous resources to the occasion, notwithstanding limits imposed by the IOC (such as the $200 cap on gifts) in an attempt to scotch rumors that its members were open to lavish treatment that degenerated into bribery. This was a decade before the Salt Lake City scandal obliged the IOC to overhaul the selection system and apply even stricter limits. The approaches used by the cities vying for the games varied. Atlanta's representatives arrived with the biggest delegation, seventy persons. The thirty-strong Melbourne group came bearing a bid book that cost a million dollars, arranged for the local English-language paper to include a four-page inset promoting its bid, and then deposited copies of the paper outside all the guests' hotel rooms. In contrast, the Manchester delegation kept to its low-key approach, without any elaborate literature or gifts, saying that the IOC delegates were inundated and never sure of who gave them what.[20]

The Greek delegation's approach backfired in two ways. First, its attempt

[19]When Athens '96 submitted its candidacy, the other members of the committee were Geōrgios Andreadēs, Dēmētrēs Diathesopoulos, Geōrgios Kandelēs, Kōnstantinos Liaskas, and Iōannēs Triantafyllidēs.

[20]Ed Hinton, "Athens Gets Rolling in its Bid for '96: IOC Hears Greeks' Unity Cry, Vows to be 'Ready,' " *The Atlanta Journal-Constitution*, August 30, 1989.

to present a unified political front (to allay fears that domestic politics would undermine Greece's ability to continue preparations) did not work. Intent on making a show of political unity, the thirty-one-person delegation to Puerto Rico had representatives from all the major political parties, headed, because of the recent election results, by New Democracy. They included Miltiadēs Evert, who had moved from the mayoralty of Athens to the ministry of health, and the internationally known composer, Mikēs Theodōrakēs (who, however, was a communist). Many of the politicians were new, unfamiliar faces; even worse, in the view of London *Times* correspondent David Miller, there were too many Greek spokesmen, which confused those in attendance and blunted the message.[21]

Second, the Greek invocation of history and tradition miscarried. A leader of the Athenian delegation stated that Greece had a right to host the games because of history, and nations owed it to Athens to hold the games there. But Gosper interjected that no city had a right to host the games and every city had a right to bid for them. Representatives from other cities agreed, and some reporters implied that some of the delegates from Athens had used an arrogant tone. Although this was not the first time the Greeks had made such statements, the challenge offered by Gosper and others showed that the climate had changed, and that issues of funding and completion of facilities and infrastructure had tarnished Athens's image and strengthened its rivals' claims. One should also add that the leaders of the Greek delegation lacked the charisma of George Papandreou, who had done much better a year earlier in Seoul as Athens's main spokesman. In any case, and unbeknown to the Greek delegation, the tide was already turning against it. The Atlanta and Toronto delegations, taking advantage of their relative proximity to San Juan, arranged for visits of IOC members to their respective cities; AOC chairman Billy Payne arranged for private jets to whisk twenty-four IOC members to Atlanta. Back in his hotel room overlooking Condado Lagoon, Payne still insisted that his city was the underdog, even after Andrew Young had made a resonant pitch for Atlanta by associating its spirit with that of Martin Luther King, Jr.[22]

If anything, and despite a recent spate of economic woes, confidence was mounting in Greece that Athens would be awarded the 1996 Olympiad. An

[21]David Miller, "Alarm over support for Athens," *The Times* [of London], August 11, 1990.
[22]Ed Hinton, "Young Counters Athens' Dramatic Appeal to IOC: Olympic Speech Wins Points With Press," *The Atlanta Journal and Constitution*, August 29, 1989.

elaborate set of celebrations was arranged to coincide with the announcement sometime in the early afternoon of September 18, 1990. Large screens were placed in centrally located Constitution Square in downtown Athens to beam live coverage from Tokyo, and a parade of athletes through Athens and several evening concerts were planned. Local authorities throughout the country were geared to put up flags on public buildings, which would be lit in the evening, and schools scheduled special celebrations. While Prime Minister Kōnstantinos Mētsotakēs, elected in April, had recently announced a series of austerity measures—resulting in a string of strikes that, on the eve of the decision, affected Olympic Airways, buses, trains, banks, and hospitals—most people did not see these events as influencing the IOC's decision-making process, nor did they let them impinge on the overwhelming sense of optimism.

Meanwhile, in Tokyo, the Greek delegation headed by Mētsotakēs engaged in one last round of lobbying that echoed the earlier, more self-assured phase of its bid. The Greek presence was aggressive and bold. The main thrust of the arguments in favor of Athens remained history and tradition, although committee representatives were also prepared to tackle the more mundane issues of budgeting and organization. For instance, Kyriakopoulos had spoken confidently about Athens's ability to raise money and complete the necessary infrastructural work in an interview just before he left for Tokyo, but several influential voices at the meeting questioned Athens's preparedness. Richard Pound, an IOC member from Canada and a member of its executive board, told reporters that, but for tradition, Athens would probably not have been a viable candidate. Pound's statement was a closer reflection of the IOC's thinking than Samaranch's self-serving support for Athens, according to David Miller of *The Times*.[23]

Unconcerned about flouting the IOC's new rules on spending, or about the limit on a candidate city that restricted its entertainment to no more than five IOC members at a time, the Greek embassy in Tokyo reportedly *fêted* at least fifteen IOC members. The occasion was a reception, three days before the vote, at which internationally renowned singer Nana Mouskouri performed. The next day, Metaxas, along with a group of Greek American businessmen, offered a three-day Greek island cruise for 15,000 athletes and officials after the games if Athens won its bid. The Greek presence at the Shin Takanawa Prince Hotel complex impressed a newspaper reporter from

[23]David Miller, "Alarm over support . . ."

Melbourne, who wrote that "the Athens lobby has performed strongly in the meeting halls and corridors of Tokyo." Six elegant hostesses tending to the Greek display suite were "handing out gifts and inviting visitors, journalists and IOC members to a nearby hotel for free drinking, dancing and eating."[24]

At about 9:45 pm, Samaranch walked onto the stage of the Shin Takanawa Prince Hotel's convention center with the rest of the IOC filing in behind him. As they took their places, Nikolaou fixed his gaze on the Greek prime minister, who was in a front row of the auditorium, and gave him a negative sign by nodding his head upward. Surprised, the Greek delegation tried to make eye contact with the other two Greek members, the former king, Constantine, and Nikos Filaretos. The presence of the former king on the IOC was a delicate issue for Greece after the abolition of the monarchy. Since then, he had remained on the body, but not as a Greek representative. In any case, this was an occasion in which the former monarch and the current republic shared common ground. Constantine and Filaretos wore similar, noncommittal expressions on their faces. Samaranch stepped up to the microphone and announced that Atlanta had won. The enormous screens in Athens focused on the Greek prime minister standing next to his wife and the deputy prime minister. All three were visibly stunned, as were the other members of the Greek delegation. The sentimental favorite had lost, and the festivities in Athens were canceled.

Greek voices in Tokyo and Athens were quick to blame the corporate interests that had lined up behind Atlanta and helped "steal" the centenary Olympics away from their birthplace. Former minister of culture Melina Merkourē uttered the most quoted phrase about Coca-Cola defeating the Parthenon. Several other Greek officials echoed that view. Initially at least, no member of the Greek delegation was able to reflect critically on whether Greece had been deficient in persuasively conveying its ability to overcome the problems of security, smog, transport, and funding for the remaining athletic facilities. Nikolaou said that the Greeks had made no mistakes, while Mētsotakēs, evidently still concerned with the issue of Greek political unity, stated that "we were united" in defending the efforts of the Athens bidding committee.[25]

[24]M. Franklin, "Drowning in Olympic Spirit," *The Herald*, September 17, 1990; Simon Barnes, "Greece come up trumps with sentimental card," *The Times* [of London], September 11, 1990.

[25]Nikētas Gavalas, "Kaname to kathēkon mas" ["We Did Our Duty"], *Kathimerini*, September 19, 1990; Pantelis Kapsēs, "Ē *Coca-Cola* Nikēse tēn Istoria" ["Coca-Cola Defeated

An editorial in *Kathimerini* the next day was one of the few sober and critical voices raised in Greece in the aftermath of the decision in Tokyo. After mentioning that it had raised the issue several times earlier, the newspaper observed that the overwhelming presence of politicians on the organizing committee had skewed its activities, yielding many more events geared toward domestic consumption rather than to internationally oriented efforts. The editorial, entitled "Unprepared and Irresponsible," noted that the Tokyo delegation included "half the government," along with a large number of representatives of the other parties. The introverted assumption of the relevance of domestic politics to Greece's bid, it added, dominated even last-minute efforts. As an example, it cited a press conference by the two candidates for mayor of Athens, Merkourē and Antōnēs Tritsēs, given in Tokyo for the benefit of Greek journalists at a time when international contacts were crucial to Athens's chances.[26]

It was obviously too early for Greek detachment. For the moment, there was anger and frustration among most Greek observers and in public opinion. With time, however, more sober and critical assessments would emerge. In a newspaper article in 1996, Ēlias Sporidēs, a sportswriter who had been on the bidding committee, offered a number of reasons for Athens's failure. He began by speculating on the IOC's odd voting patterns, such as the votes that went to Belgrade in the first round not going to Athens later, as expected. But then he went on to concede that Athens's bid had been run in an amateurish and disorganized way (although he did not elaborate).[27] While short on specifics, more and more critical voices were raised, aimed at Greek incompetence rather than Coca-Cola. During Athens's bid for the 2004 Olympiad, officials routinely mentioned that Athens's earlier attempt had been deficient, complacent, and unable to address obvious weaknesses high on everyone's list, such as security, smog, and transport.

CENTENARY CELEBRATIONS

Instead of celebrating the centenary in conjunction with the Olympic games,

History"], *Ta Nea*, September 19, 1990; Nikos Asēmakopoulos, "Atlanta-*Coca-Cola*," *Eleutherotypia*, September 19, 1990.

[26]"Aproetoimastoi kai aneuthynoi" ["Unprepared and Irresponsible"], *Kathimerini*, September 19, 1990.

[27]Ēlias Sporidēs, "Ē exagora psēfōn gia tēn (chamenē) Chrysē Olympiada" ["The Bribed Votes for the (Lost) Golden Olympiad"], *To Vēma*, April 14, 1996.

Greece marked the occasion with a special set of events on Olympic Games Day, April 6, which inevitably evoked a return to the past. Soon after Athens was denied the 1996 Olympiad, the IOC made public its intention to offer the Greeks an olive branch by including some form of Greek involvement in the centenary games. Holding the marathon of the 1996 Olympics in Greece was one of the ideas floated at the time. Ultimately, the IOC decided to celebrate the centenary separately from the actual games.

By that time, Greece was bidding for the 2004 Olympiad, which became a sub-theme of the festivities. The centenary celebrations included a special IOC session at Olympia and several events in Athens. The event at Olympia included the ceremonial lighting of the torch, which took place on March 30 with all the usual pomp, and unfolded in the presence of Samaranch, members of the IOC, members of the Atlanta organizing committee, and Hillary Clinton, representing the president of the United States. The First Lady, accompanied by her daughter, Chelsea, had arrived in Greece a day earlier to tour the Acropolis and the ancient Athenian *agora*. Despite fears of the Atlanta organizers that the Clintons' presence would detract from the actual purpose of the gathering, the ceremony went well and delivered the type of "spirit-of-place" effect that philhellenes had experienced in the past. The managing director of communications of the Atlanta committee, C. Richard Yarbrough, wrote that the lighting of the flame "was one of the most extraordinary experiences" of his life. The Americans were certainly overawed by their surroundings and the occasion. A little before convening at the temple, the Atlanta group, along with the Clintons, "held hands, said a little prayer, cried a few tears of joy." Reflecting on the event four years later, Yarbrough noted, "To see the ceremony . . . was to be mentally transported back in time. . . . I look back to that trip to Olympia and say that all of the meanness and pettiness of Olympic Games planning was made bearable by that one incredible event. I still get emotional thinking about it."[28]

The centenary's commemoration continued on April 5, when the HOC organized a formal meeting at the Old Parliament Building in Athens and gave awards to the president of Greece, Kōstēs Stephanopoulos, to IOC president Samaranch, and to the mayor of Athens, Dēmētrēs Avramopoulos. The highlight of the centenary celebrations, however, was a recreation of the first Olympic Games held—where else?—at the Panathenaic Stadium. This

---

[28]C. Richard Yarbrough, *And They Call Them Games*, Mercer University Press, Macon, 2000, pp. 151–152.

involved contests in all the sports from the 1896 Olympiad, using the rules that had been in force a century earlier. The participants were athletes from the nations that had participated in 1896, and, in order to maintain historical accuracy, the winners received a silver medal and those coming in second a bronze medal, as well as an olive wreath for all medalists. In a reversal of the usual sequence, the Olympic flame arrived at the stadium at the conclusion of the events, on its way to a tour of Greece, before going on to Atlanta.[29]

The willingness of the Greek government and the HOC to invest time and money in these celebrations can easily be derided by cynics, but one would do well to recognize their value to the Olympic movement. The concept of "invented traditions" is widely accepted as an important feature of modern national and international institutions. Students of the Olympic movement are well aware of the significance of rituals and symbols in its history. The centenary celebrations were yet another reminder that Greece plays a unique role in fostering as well as hosting such events, a role that is integral to the viability of the modern Olympics.

Greek sports at the Atlanta Olympiad

During his stay in Athens for the centenary celebrations, Samaranch had told his hosts that recent athletic successes by Greece would help its bid for 2004. He said he was aware that a Greek soccer club had scored an important victory in the European Champions league, and that the same club's basketball team had reached the final four of the Euroleague, the European basketball championship. Samaranch added that he had also noticed that Greek athletes had distinguished themselves internationally in weightlifting, track and field, and sailing. Indeed, 1996 turned out to be an excellent year for Greek sport. The *Panathēnaikos* basketball team won the European championship, while the *Panathēnaikos* soccer team reached the semifinals of the European Champions league. Greek athletes had already done very well in the more traditional Olympic sports at the time of Samaranch's visit to Athens, but they were saving their best for Atlanta.

In view of the gap between Greece's sporting presence and its ceremonial role in each Olympiad, it is ironic that the major breakthrough by Greek athletes should have occurred in 1996 at Atlanta. It was said at the time that

[29]N. A. Kōnstantopoulos, "Athēna: Meres tou 1896" ["Athens: Days of 1896"], *Kathimerini*, April 6, 1990.

Australia's compensation for Brisbane not being selected to host the 1992 summer games was an extraordinary showing by the country's athletes in Barcelona that year. Something similar happened at the centenary games, at which Greek achievements were unprecedented (with the exception of the 1896 games). A great deal of hard work took place before the Greeks could impress on the athletic field in Atlanta, however, and it entailed restructuring the way athletes were chosen for the Olympics, as well as systematic efforts by administrators and coaches backed by government funding and assistance. These changes began to take effect in the 1980s. The Olympic committee prevailed over the sports federations and began gradually imposing stricter standards and criteria for selecting athletes.

In 1984, Greece had sent a relatively small delegation to Los Angeles, a total of thirty-three, including the water-polo team. There had also been fewer administrators than usual. The largest group was the wrestlers, and it was in Greco-Roman wrestling that Greece gained its only medals. Twenty-five-year-old Peloponnesian Dēmētrēs Thanopoulos won the silver medal in the middleweight category. In his third Olympics, Charalambos Cholidēs—born in 1956 in Tashkent in the Soviet Union of Greek parents who were political refugees from the Civil War—won the bronze medal in the bantamweight category. Brothers Geōrgios and Panagiōtēs Poikilidēs came in fourth in the heavyweight and super-heavyweight categories, respectively. Mygiakēs, the hero of the Moscow games, was eliminated early, while another Greek hope, javelin-thrower Anna Veroulē, who had won gold in the women's javelin throw in the European Games in Athens in 1982, was also disappointing in Los Angeles, as were the other Greek track-and-field athletes.

At a December 1987 meeting, the HOC decided to adopt even stricter criteria in selecting athletes, and it pledged to resist pressures from the sports federations and even the government. This was a positive step: by making the selection process more difficult, the HOC was not only challenging Greek athletes to fight harder for the honor of representing their country, but promoting a more competitive frame of mind among those athletes who made the final cut. In the short term, however, the HOC's newfound assertiveness ran into opposition and led to friction with the track-and-field federation and government members on the eve of the Seoul Olympiad. Deputy minister Roula Kaklamanakē resigned her post, protesting the exclusion of her nephew, boardsailor (windsurfer) Nikos Kaklamanakēs, from the team. Ultimately, fifty-seven athletes traveled to South Korea but returned with very little. The sole Greek medalist was Cholidēs, who won the bronze in the bantamweight category in Greco-Roman wrestling.

The Greek results in the Barcelona Olympics in 1992 signaled the gradual improvement in Greek sport and served notice of future success. The Greek team returned with two gold medals, neither in wrestling, the only sport in which there had been some success in the past. The first came in the women's 100-meter hurdle race, where twenty-seven-year-old Voula Patoulidou became the surprise winner ahead of LaVonna Martin of the United States and Bulgarian sprinter Yordanka Donkova, the world recordholder. The favorite, American Gail Devers, winner of the 100-meter race, stumbled after hitting a hurdle. This was the first medal ever won by a Greek woman in track and field, and it reflected the steady development of women's sports in Greece over the previous decade.[30]

When Patoulidou was born in 1965 in a village near Flōrina in northern Greece, Greek female athletes were not good enough to qualify for Olympic events. The Greek state, moreover, did little to encourage them. Domnitsa Lanitou had participated in 1936 and again in 1948, but she was the exception to the rule. Then, in 1976, long-jumper Maroula Lambrou and javelin-thrower Sofia Sakorafa went to the games in Montreal and to the Moscow games four years later. Soon, spreading sports facilities throughout the country, and growing recognition of the need to develop female athletes, paid dividends. The big breakthrough came in the European games of 1982 in Athens. Anna Veroulē won the gold and Sakorafa the bronze in the women's javelin throw. With Sakorafa injured in 1984, Veroulē went to Los Angeles along with a hurdler, Elisavet Pantazē. A record ten female athletes traveled from Greece to Seoul in 1988, six in track and field, three in gymnastics, and one in shooting. That same year, in Calgary, skier Thōmaē Lefousē became the first Greek female to take part in a winter Olympiad.[31]

Patoulidou herself excitedly interpreted her great moment in broader, national, and modernizing terms, rather than as simply a victory for Greek female athletes. In the ecstatic rush in the aftermath of her victory, she spontaneously uttered a phrase that became famous instantly, and much quoted, in Greece, although some publications chose not to print it in full.

---

[30]For Patoulidou's account, see her biography, Voula Patoulidou, *Ekrēxē Psychēs* [*Burst of Spirit*], Kastaniōtēs, Athens, 1997.

[31]For a review of the evolution of women's track and field in Greece, see Eleutherios Skiadas, *Gynaikeios athlētismos stē synchronē Ellada* [*Womens' Sports in Modern Greece*], Lavyrinthos, Athens, 1998.

Patoulidou described her feat as something she had done "Gia tēn Ellada, re gamōto," which can be (loosely) translated as "For Greece, for fuck's sake!" The phrase has since become synonymous with a humorously expressed but still exuberant sense of self-sacrifice and patriotism. In her autobiography, which closes with that axiom, Patoulidou explains that she spent some childhood years in Germany, where her parents had emigrated temporarily. There, she became aware of two different images of Greece: the backward nation envisaged by foreigners and the developed nation of which Greeks demanded foreign acknowledgment. All her life, she had wanted to find a way to raise her country's esteem in the eyes of the world, which she managed to do at last by winning her gold medal. At that moment, in which she "restored pride and dignity to every Greek," she couldn't help but utter her famous maxim.[32]

Pyrros Dēmas won the other gold for Greece in the light-heavy weight category in weightlifting, and his victory reflected two developments in that sport. The first was the arrival in Greece of ethnic Greeks from eastern Europe after the collapse of communism. Dēmas was born of Greek parents in Albania and moved to Greece in 1990. Meanwhile, the Greek weightlifting federation that brokered the move had been busy strengthening the sport over the previous decades, which was the second factor in Greek progress. Several other ethnic Greek weightlifters went to Greece with Dēmas, and they would make their impact on the 1996 games. The Greek successes in Atlanta may not have been entirely surprising: there had been long-term planning for the 1996 games in the expectation that they would be held in Athens. Still, Greek athletes exceeded all expectations. They won eight medals in Atlanta, five in weightlifting. Pyrros Dēmas repeated his triumph in Barcelona by winning gold in the light-heavyweight category. Dēmas set a world record by lifting 865.25 pounds and became the thirteenth lifter to win gold in two consecutive Olympics. Kachi Kachiasvili, a naturalized Greek born in Georgia who had won the gold in Barcelona for the post-Soviet Commonwealth of Federated States, won the gold in Atlanta in the first heavyweight category. Middle-heavyweight Leōnidas Kokkas won the silver, as did Valerios Leōnidēs, a featherweight, and Leōnidas Sampanēs, a bantamweight. Both Kokkas and Sampanēs were ethnic Greeks born in Albania, and Leōnidēs was an ethnic Greek born in Russia.

Other medals won in Atlanta were a gold in boardsailing by Nikos Kaklamanakēs, a gold in the floor exercises of artistic gymnastics by Iōannēs

[32]Patoulidou, *Ekrēxē Psychēs* . . . , pp. 575–577.

Melissanidēs, and a silver in the women's high jump by Nikē Bakogiannē. The victories by Kaklamanakēs and Melissanidēs were the first ever for Greeks in these sports, while Bakogiannē became the second Greek female to win a medal in track and field. Like Patoulidou, she had grown up in the provinces, where she began her career, and moved to Athens at seventeen to continue her training.

The Atlanta medalists returned on a specially chartered Olympic Airways jumbo jet to a tumultuous welcome in Athens, in which the present was honored as much as the past. The athletes rode from the airport to the Panathenaic Stadium in open-top army jeeps along streets lined with cheering fans raining olive branches and flowers onto the procession. At the stadium, a string of dignitaries made patriotic speeches before the athletes addressed the crowd and dedicated their medals to Greece. Compared to the events held in the stadium four months earlier, the celebrations for the return of the athletes marked a shift—unremarked on at the time—to an emphasis on contemporary Greece, its national spirit, sports policies, and the skills of its top athletes. In Greek terms, it signified an important move away from an almost exclusive connection between sport and antiquity toward an acknowledgment of modern Greek capabilities.

CHAPTER 9

WINNING AND ALMOST LOSING THE 2004 ATHENS OLYMPIAD

A
S THE GREEK MEMBERS OF THE IOC followed President Samaranch onto the stage of the Palais de Beaulieu in Lausanne on September 5, 1997, they must have felt a sense of *déjà vu*, although the outcome would be better than it had been in Tokyo seven years earlier. The gathering in Lausanne to choose the host city for the 2004 Olympiad was entirely different from the one in Tokyo. There was no Greek prime minister waiting expectantly in the front rows of the auditorium this time: Kōstas Sēmitēs had decided not to travel to Lausanne, but went to Thessalonikē instead, where he inaugurated the city's annual international trade fair. Sēmitēs's absence indicated that Greece was less inclined to pursue the 2004 games as desperately as it had the centenary Olympiad. Thus, the Greek delegation was not headed by the prime minister this time, but by the newly appointed president of the Athens 2004 bid committee, Gianna Angelopoulou-Daskalakē. As a woman and former conservative deputy, Angelopoulou had been a surprise choice on the part of Sēmitēs, who had replaced the ailing socialist party leader Andreas Papandreou as prime minister in early 1996. She had been included on the New Democracy ticket in 1989 thanks to the support of party leader and fellow Cretan, Kōnstantinos Mētsotakēs, and as a result of a successful career in the law firm of New Democracy deputy Nōndas Zafeiropoulos. Soon after her election to parliament, she obtained a divorce from her first husband, Parthenēs, and married millionaire businessman Theodōros Angelopoulos. She did not seek reelection in the 1993 elections when Papandreou's PASOK defeated Mētsotakēs's New Democracy.

Angelopoulou's appointment by Sēmitēs represented a sea change in Greece's approach to this bid in comparison to its earlier attempt to host the centenary games. Sēmitēs was known as a technocrat, and the passing of the baton from Papandreou to him in 1996 signaled a shift away from ideology to modernization and efficiency. As such, Greece launched its bid for 2004 by stressing its ability to organize the games efficiently while keeping the allusions to history and tradition in the background. The choice of an able person unaffiliated with the governing party—indeed, who was a member of the opposition—delivered a strong message: Sēmitēs favored capable hands, irrespective of political outlook.

How Athens won the 2004 games

The bidding process for 2004 was different from those in previous years. First of all, the IOC decided to announce its choice seven rather than six years before the games were to take place, so as to give the winning city adequate time to prepare. Second, there was a new set of rules. In 1994, at its 102nd session, the International Olympic Committee decided to split the selection procedure into two phases. In Phase I, the IOC evaluation commission prepared a report, which was released to the public, and then formed a panel to select the finalist cities on the basis of that report. The panel included the IOC's executive board (minus those members whose countries were submitting bids), representatives of the national Olympic committees, and a representative of the international federations (the international nongovernmental organizations to which the relevant national federations are affiliated and which are recognized by the IOC as administering one or more sports at an international level). The IOC would then announce a shortlist of candidate cities; in this case, the announcement was scheduled for March 1997. In Phase II, the IOC would visit the finalist cities before voting. The selection of the host of the 2004 Olympiad would take place by secret ballot at the 106th IOC session to be held in September 1997 in Lausanne.

From the outset, the new Greek bid was manifestly oriented toward addressing the infrastructural issues that had prevented Athens from being awarded the games in 1996. The Greek bidding committee submitted its application to the IOC in August 1996, stressing that its contents proved that Athens was ready to host the games. Petros Synadinos, who directed the compilation of the application material, told Greek reporters that it contained "45 maps, 115 architectural plans, 257 photographs, and 453 tables" designed to respond to the IOC's nineteen criteria for evaluating each candidate city's capacity to organize the games. Seventy-five percent of the athletic facilities were complete.[1] Gianna Angelopoulou stated that "all the thorns that deprived us of the Olympics in 1996 have been eradicated. Transport and communications that were sectors with problems are now factors working in our favor. We have solutions such as the Athens subway, the new airport, the ring road north of Athens, mobile telephones, and, above all, we possess excellent athletic facilities."[2]

The IOC began planning for 2004 immediately after the Atlanta Olympiad. Thomas Bach, a German member of the IOC's executive board, arrived in Athens in late October 1996 to lead the nineteen-strong evaluation commission on a three-day visit. The Greek government received the commission at Zappeion Hall. Deputy Foreign Minister George Papandreou, Undersecretary of Sports Andreas Fouras, Mayor Dēmētrēs Avramopoulos of Athens, and members of the Hellenic Olympic Committee and the Athens 2004 committee were also present. At a press conference later, Bach, the commission's president, outlined the procedure for evaluation but gave no hint of the group's first impressions of Athens. "We are honored to be in the country which gave birth to the Olympic Games," Bach said. "The Olympic spirit is present more than ever before and the Olympic spirit is one of the criteria for a candidate city."

Bach was appropriately guarded in his comments and also stated that the commission needed three full days to draw conclusions. At the final press conference, he added, "We will talk about our first impressions but not about our conclusions. . . . We will give a fair and objective report. We ask 600 questions to each city and evaluate nineteen criteria, including the Olympic village, transport, and protection of the environment and security. Our visit has two (equal) aspects: the first half involves the discussions with the candidate committee and the second is the visits to installations."[3] Bach kept his word and talked only about the committee's impressions rather than its conclusions, but he sounded encouraging nonetheless. He said that the "committee [had] ascertained that the candidacy of Athens is supported by the overwhelming majority of the Greek people. Additionally, there is support from businessmen and political bodies." He commented positively on the program

---

[1]"Etoimoi gia to 2004," *To Vēma*, September 15, 1996.

[2]Marilē Margomenou, "Ē Athēna mesa se enan fakelo" ["Athens in a Folder"], *To Vēma*, August 18, 1996.

[3]"Athens Formally Receives IOC Evaluation Commission," Athens News Agency, October 16, 1996.

of cultural events that was being planned and concluded by saying that "we appreciate the guarantees of the government and the opposition for the candidacy of Athens."[4]

The next round of formal contacts came in November, when all candidate cities made presentations to the IOC's executive committee at the IOC's general assembly in Cancun. A joint Athens News Agency and Agence France Presse report on these presentations shows evidence of some bias. The report mentioned that "observers at the International Olympic Committee's general assembly session have described Athens' candidacy for the 2004 Olympic Games as the best of all eleven cities contesting the world's largest sporting event, followed by those of Istanbul and Seville. The Lille candidacy was described as a pleasant surprise, as was that of Buenos Aires, while those of Rio de Janeiro and Stockholm were described as 'without mistakes.' By contrast, the presentations of St. Petersburg, San Juan, and especially Rome, considered one of the favorites, were viewed as disappointing, while that of Cape Town was considered to have excessively relied on the personality of South African President Nelson Mandela."[5] Yet again, the Greeks made their case by emphasizing infrastructure, although they mentioned Greece's special role in the Olympic movement. In the presentation's main segment, Angelopoulou talked about Athens's sports facilities and the other projects already under construction. She was followed by Marton Simicek, the Athens 2004 public relations director, who spoke about the international academy in Olympia and its significance to the Olympic movement throughout the world. Simicek's father, Otto, had moved to Greece from Poland in the 1930s to coach track and field and ultimately became the academy's dean.

Before the IOC met in March to whittle down the number of cities, the release of its preliminary findings led to complaints from some cities and even some angry infighting among rivals. The report of the evaluation commission was expressed in diplomatic language, but nonetheless conveyed the potential weaknesses of several cities quite clearly. It mentioned the atmospheric pollution in Athens, the crime rate in Cape Town, the traffic problems in Istanbul, the lack of a large-capacity airport in Lille, and the opposition in Stockholm to holding the games there. Soon after the IOC made its evaluations public, Istanbul sent a five-page rebuttal addressing what it considered

[4]"IOC Evaluation Committee Finds 3 Strong Advantages to Athens' Bid," Athens News Agency, October 29, 1996.

[5]"Athens' Candidacy File for 2004 Olympic Games Garners Widespread Praise," Athens News Agency/Agence France Press, November 18, 1996.

to be mistakes in its evaluation. The head of the bid committee, Yalcin Aksoy, described the evaluation as "an injustice"; Sinan Erdem, the president of the Turkish Olympic Committee, called the procedure "unfair."[6] The Cape Town committee unofficially claimed that Rome's representatives were trying to undermine South Africa's candidacy, ostensibly because Rome, a favorite, felt threatened because Cape Town was emerging as a sentimental favorite. The Italians retaliated by saying they had nothing to worry about. The Russian government came to the defense of St. Petersburg's bid by saying that it deserved to be awarded the games for political reasons irrespective of its economic weaknesses.

The Greek bid committee evidently prepared very well for its scheduled presentation in March in Lausanne. Days before the eleven candidates gathered at IOC headquarters, the Greeks sent the other ten committees an olive branch as a gesture of good will. Traveling to Lausanne, the Greek committee was composed of an unusually small number of less than twenty-five members. The members who spoke during the twenty-minute audiovisual presentation to the IOC's selection committee presided over by Swiss member Marc Hodler knew which topics to address and what type of questions would be handled by each. Angelopoulou said that the group had prepared for everything, even the way they would greet the IOC committee. The preparations paid off. Greek IOC member Nikos Filaretos commented that his colleagues went up to him after its conclusion, nodding and saying, "Excellent."[7]

Athens was the first of the five finalists to be announced, since the names were read alphabetically, along with Buenos Aires, Cape Town, Rome, and Stockholm. The representatives of St. Petersburg were the only ones from the eliminated cities who had believed they had a chance and were visibly despondent. The others, representing Istanbul, Lille, Rio de Janeiro, San Juan, and Seville, were more or less prepared for the inevitable. After the outcome, the Greeks were elated but measured and businesslike in their comments. Angelopoulou confirmed that Athens's bid for 2004 was unfolding on a different level from the one for 1996. At the core of the new bid was a will "to make a different impression than we did last time." Synadinos spoke of the need for the Greek effort to remain focused in the months ahead, to maintain contact with the IOC, and to continue working on the financial issues.

---

[6]"Race to Host 2004 Games Turns Sour," Associated Press, March 5, 1997.

[7]Marilē Margomenou, "Pōs ē Athēna bēke stēn pentada" ["How Athens Made it Into the Five"], *To Vēma*, March 3, 1997.

Within days, Kōstas Liaskas, a civil engineer, president of the Technical Chamber of Greece, and future vice-president of the Athens 2004 committee, spoke in Athens about the range of public works being launched there. Work had begun on the new airport, the subway, and ring roads. There were plans for a regional railway and tramlines. The introduction of natural gas was one of several environmentally conscious measures for reducing the city's atmospheric pollution by 25 percent by 2004. Liaskas told *The New York Times*, "The last time the bid was more emotional, more symbolic, many Greeks believed that it was a good bid because of our history. This bid is more realistic. We are making an effort, as much as possible, to speak less and do more."[8]

When the five finalists returned to Lausanne in September 1997, Rome was considered to be a bit ahead of Athens, but Cape Town was the sentimental favorite. Buenos Aires was an outsider, happy to have made the final cut but regarded as an unlikely host because of economic instability in Argentina. Argentinean president Carlos Menem's vigorous support of the bid, and the city's very good transportation infrastructure, did not sufficiently outweigh the economic obstacles. Stockholm was also considered a long-shot because of substantial domestic opposition. Days before the final selection process began, a bomb exploded at Ullevi Stadium in Göteborg, the very venue where the soccer matches would take place if Sweden won its bid, and previous attacks on Swedish sports facilities had been the work of a group opposed to the Olympics. Olof Stenhammar, the head of the Swedish bidding committee, tried to put on a brave face by saying that his team was busy lobbying in the final days. Although Samaranch stressed that the IOC would not be swayed by such acts of violence, the incident did not help Stockholm's diminishing chances.

Rome's bid resembled that of Athens in the sense that it stressed the advantages of the city's sports facilities and the country's organizational capabilities. Raffaele Ranucci, the director of the Roman bid committee, was quoted as saying, "it's beautiful to have the Colosseum, but it's not enough."[9] Rome's bid had the mixed blessing of possessing an outspoken advocate, Primo Nebiolo, an Italian IOC member and president of the International Amateur Athletic Federation. While attending the world athletic championships in Athens that summer, Nebiolo had criticized the very low

[8]Celestine Bohlen, "In 2004, Will the Glory Be Greece's, or Rome's?" *The New York Times*, March 7, 1997.
[9]*Ibid.*

attendance during the competition's first days and suggested that it would damage Athens's chances in September.

Cape Town was the sentimental favorite because of South Africa's recent abolition of apartheid and people's feelings that Africa deserved to be awarded the games for the first time in Olympic history. Nelson Mandela's active support of the bid lent it credibility and helped to defuse concerns over crime, organizational inexperience, and political instability. At Cape Town's final presentation, Mandela would ask IOC members to give Africa's march to the new future the impetus it deserved. Ultimately, however, the contest came down to Athens versus Rome, although Cape Town's bid remained strong in the eyes of the public. William Hill, the bookmakers, announced a day before the vote that late support for Cape Town among bettors had cut its price from 4–1 to 11–8. Rome remained the odds-on favorite at 4–5, with Athens running third at 7–2. Stockholm lagged behind at 9–1, while Buenos Aires was at a distant 80–1. Buenos Aires was eliminated first, followed by Stockholm, and then Cape Town.

Athens won the games, prevailing over Rome in the final and deciding vote with the surprising score of 66–41. Athens achieved its victory because it was able to reassure the committee that its infrastructure and organizational ability could support the games. It beat out Rome thanks to a sense of guilt left over from 1996 and because of the impressive performance of Angelopoulou. Carlos Ferrer, an IOC member from Spain, said that after the transportation and technology problems in Atlanta, some of his colleagues had felt guilty about not having awarded the centenary Olympiad to Athens. Once Athens had proved capable of conducting the 2004 games as well as any other candidate, they felt some indebtedness to the city. *The Times* of London noted, "the IOC righted the wrong perpetrated when it sent the Games to the soulless American city of Atlanta. Heavy with guilt, it awarded them for the year 2004 to Athens."[10]

When Samaranch announced Athens's victory, the members of the Greek group in the auditorium "embraced and began waving the blue and white national flag. They chanted 'Gianna, Gianna' in recognition of Angelopoulos-Daskalaki, the lawyer and charismatic head of the Greek delegation that is credited with running an outstanding campaign."[11]

[10]Rob Hughes, "Olympic Games come home as Athens flame burns again," *The Times* [of London], September 6, 1997.

[11]John Goodbody, "Athens triumphs in battle to host Olympics in 2004," *The Times* [of London], September 6, 1997.

Observers lavished praise on Angelopoulou in the aftermath of Athens's selection. A *New York Times* reporter wrote that "the winning bid was orchestrated" by Angelopoulou, whose "skills in holding together dissonant groups and her ability to get the message out that Athens wanted to earn the Games, not be handed them, were critical in swaying the IOC vote in Greece's favor."[12] An admiring British reporter remarked, "The winner for Athens is a woman. Gianna Angelopoulos is 41, a mother of three, a lawyer, a politician and a charming and a formidable lady indeed. Yesterday, holding the stage for three quarters of the fifty-five minutes allotted to the presentation, Angelopoulos, so elegant in white and adorned in pearls, proved that womanhood could be the pearl of this highly political decision-making, even in this predominantly male club."[13] Without the recourse to history and tradition that had blunted the effectiveness of its earlier effort, Athens's bid for 2004 reflected a fresh perspective on Greece's relationship to the Olympic Games.

EARLY COMPLACENCY: 1998

If Greece's success in Lausanne was an example of lessons learned from previous disappointment, the early phase of preparations for 2004 was an example of lessons unlearned. The dissolution of the bidding committee meant that the initiative for the preparations fell to the government. Even though the government created a supposedly autonomous organizing committee, cabinet ministers retained overall responsibility and supervision. Consequently, all major decisions became entangled in turf wars between ministries that assumed responsibilities for different aspects of the preparations. At the same time, the opposition exerted pressure on the government in an attempt to influence the makeup of the organizing committee. The opposition was also quick to point out areas in which preparations lagged. Decision-making became mired in the public sector's labyrinthine bureaucracy and, since the government retained overall control, many initiatives had to wait until unrelated political crises were resolved.

As in all cases of cities preparing for an Olympiad, the IOC played a supervisory role, monitoring progress and prodding organizers when

[12]Jere Longman, "Athens Wins a Vote for Tradition, and the 2004 Olympics," *The New York Times*, September 6, 1997.
[13]Rob Hughes, "Olympic Games come home . . ."

necessary. Publicly, the IOC prefers to exude confidence in the hosts, and one has to read between the lines of its officials' platitudes at the press conferences staged at the end of their site visits. Samaranch especially tended, in the Greek case at least, to strike a reassuring tone of confidence, while the IOC members charged with the hands-on monitoring were a little more candid. Press reports, with access to inside information and off-the-record remarks, usually offered a more realistic picture.

The government took its time in forming an organizing committee. In late January 1998, only days before the opening of the winter Olympics in Nagano, it finally announced the appointment of Stratēs Stratēgēs as director of the Athens 2004 organizing committee (ATHOC). Stratēgēs, born in the Greek capital, was a former New Democracy deputy with a doctorate in economics and maritime law from the London School of Economics. In selecting him, Sēmitēs obviously wished to convey the same message he had in appointing Angelopoulou, namely that the committee's leadership would go to someone qualified and not necessarily a PASOK loyalist. The number-two post in ATHOC, that of managing director, went to Kōstas Bakourēs, chairman of Ralston Energy Systems Europe S.A., the European arm of the St. Louis-based Eveready Battery Company. Bakourēs, born in a village outside Tripolē in the Peloponnese had an MBA from DePaul University in Chicago and had begun his career with the Esso Pappas petroleum company in Greece before moving to Eveready in 1970. The other appointees to the committee were the undersecretary of sports, Petros Sgouros, Athens mayor Dēmētrēs Avramopoulos, and the Greek members of the IOC, Nikos Filaretos and Lambēs Nikolaou. At the same time that the government created this group, however, it also announced the establishment of two other committees: a national committee headed by the country's president and consisting of representatives of a wide range of parties and organizations, which was scheduled to meet only two or three times a year and was thus designed as a symbolic gesture of broad inclusion; and a second, "interministerial," committee that was far from symbolic and included all government ministers whose particular areas of responsibility would be affected by the preparations.

Suspicions that government ministers would overshadow Stratēgēs's Athens 2004 committee were confirmed almost immediately. As the government was announcing the names of Bakourēs and the other members of ATHOC, government ministers were making a range of statements about the

Athens games at a conference at Zappeion Hall.[14] Kōstas Laliōtēs, minister for the environment, town planning, and public works, and responsible for the construction of the city's infrastructure and athletic facilities, said that many projects were already underway, while the required studies and plans were ready for others. Andreas Fouras, the deputy minister of sports, spoke about the Olympiad's financial administration, and stressed that the relevant bill passed by the government assured full accountability of all those engaged in preparations. Members of the government who could not attend the conference, meanwhile, sent messages. The environment was the main theme in the message sent to the conference by Sēmitēs himself; among other things, he said that the quality of the games would not be judged solely by how much their negative impact had been minimized, but also on the actual improvement in the character and infrastructure of Athens through the appropriate projects. Greece's European Union commissioner, Chrēstos Papoutsēs, also sent a message to the conference in which he proposed that a special energy center for the games be established in Athens with EU funds to study new energy needs and propose solutions on administration and energy conservation.

As ATHOC came together in the government's shadow in 1998, the Hellenic Olympic Committee found itself on the margins of Greek Olympic affairs, although it had *ex officio* representation on the organizing committee. The IOC's rules mandated a separate committee to organize a host city's preparations, with the national committee simply participating. On paper, therefore, there was nothing unusual in the arrangements in Athens. As we have seen throughout this account, however, the HOC had always seen itself as the guardian of the authentic Olympic spirit. Despite the HOC's political coloring throughout most of the twentieth century, its leading members had acted in good faith to preserve both Olympic tradition and what they considered to be the games' aspect of "pure sport." Their protest against the commercialization of the Olympic torch relay by the Los Angeles organizing committee in 1984 was a striking example of the HOC's sense of duty toward tradition. Now, without anyone really noticing, as this was how things were done after a city was awarded the games, the HOC withdrew to the background. Judging by what would soon follow, it could be said that tradition did the same thing.

[14]The conference was organized by the World Network of Environmental Science and Technology in cooperation with the International Institute of Environmental Research and the Athens daily *Eleutherotypia*, and was entitled "Olympic Games, City and Environment."

Stratēgēs gave his first press conference (jointly with Fouras) upon his return in mid-February from Nagano, but his comments were quickly eclipsed by the conflict that broke out in parliament over staffing his committee. The president of ATHOC reported that his meeting with Samaranch had been cordial, and he went on to say that "there were no fears" about Greece's ability to rise to the challenge. The atmosphere was quite different in the Greek parliament, where the government submitted a bill that included the ratification of Stratēgēs's committee and other measures connected to the Olympics. It was fiercely criticized by the opposition, not on its merits as an organizational blueprint but on the basis of the government's criteria for appointing officials and allocating funds. Speaking for New Democracy, deputy Fanē Pallē-Petralia said that her party would vote against the legislation because it "transform[ed] 2004 from a national goal, and incentive for growth, into a hothouse of scandals." She added that the bill did not meet the three conditions for successful games: transparency, unanimity, and effectiveness. The *rapporteurs* of the three parties to the government's left (the KKE, Coalition of the Left, and Democratic Social Movement) expressed serious reservations regarding environmental consequences, commercialism, and the composition of ATHOC, and said that they would vote against the bill. In the end, however, the bill passed thanks to PASOK's handy majority in the chamber.[15]

The parliamentary debate disclosed the government's point-man: Minister of Culture Euangelos Venizelos, in whose ministry the deputy ministry of sport resided. Venizelos led the government in the debate and was the spokesman for the ministerial committee. It was Venizelos, for example, who emerged from a meeting of that committee in May 1998 to reassure reporters that "the venture is a great one, it is a national affair. No haste, no last-minute improvisation and no waste of effort or money can be excused. We are working in a very systematic and disciplined manner ... yielding results."[16] Venizelos was also in charge of a "Cultural Olympiad" that was supposed to run in tandem with the games but actually began in 2000. It entailed a cultural program based in Olympia, Delphi, and Epidaurus coordinated by the ministry and organized by other institutions such as the European Cultural Center of Delphi, the National Theater, the State Theater of Northern Greece, and the

---

[15]"Government, Opposition Clash Over 2004 Bill," Athens News Agency, February 12, 1998; "Discussion on Draft Bill Complete," Athens News Agency, February 13, 1998.

[16]"Government Says Preparations for 2004 Olympics on Target," Athens News Agency, May 20, 1998.

National Gallery. Finally, Venizelos was also in charge of mobilizing the Council of Hellenes Abroad (*Symvoulio Apodēmou Ellēnismou,* or SAE). This umbrella group is run by wealthy diaspora Greeks, but is subsidized by the Greek government. Venizelos said that the SAE would participate in a "National Council for the 2004 Olympiad" made up of a five-member committee headed by SAE president Andrew Athens. The minister came up with yet another plan, organizing a "Young Expatriates' Olympiad" to be held regularly in Thessalonikē. Without being specific, Venizelos said that the involvement of diaspora Greeks in the Olympiad's preparations would be crucial to its success.

Meanwhile, another member of the ministerial committee, Deputy Foreign Minister George Papandreou, was fully involved in a project designed to promote the revival of the concept of the Olympic truce. During the ancient Olympics, warfare was suspended around the time of the games to permit athletes to travel to Olympia and return to their cities safely. In its modern form, the idea was for a ceasefire on global conflict during the period of the Olympics. Implementing such a project was an ambitious goal, but one that had garnered the support of the IOC and other international organizations. Papandreou had taken on the task of exploring the feasibility of an Olympic truce long before any Greek committee had been established. In November 1997, he discussed the idea with UNESCO's director-general, Federico Mayor, in Paris. In January 1998, Papandreou met with Samaranch in Lausanne. The IOC's president announced his support and agreed with the proposal to establish a truce center in Olympia. In May of that year, Papandreou described the proposed center in Olympia as a place that would provide a neutral ground for dialogue and mediation, "where all sides could have contacts in pursuit of peace and friendship among peoples."[17]

When Samaranch visited Athens in September 1998, he appeared to encourage the wide range of initiatives planned by the Greek organizers. He signed agreements to establish a "Cultural Olympics" institute at Olympia and to enable collaboration between the Olympic Games Museum in Olympia and the museum at the IOC's headquarters in Lausanne. Samaranch declared that, "The texts we signed were an important beginning for the 2004 Games." He added that he had always supported the idea of the games having two dimensions, athletic and cultural, and that the 2004 games

[17]"King Juan Carlos Backs 'Olympic Truce' Headquarters Proposal," Athens News Agency, May 28, 1998.

in Athens would have a third, the historical. The IOC president also met with the Greek prime minister, with Bakourēs, Stratēgēs, Papandreou, and Venizelos present. After the meeting, Venizelos observed, "It was an exceptionally friendly working meeting. We are very optimistic because we have the advantage of time and are working within the framework of the contract signed with the IOC last year in Lausanne. Everybody's optimism about a [*sic*] successful Games is based not only on good organization but also because [*sic*] we will introduce a cultural Olympiad and the Olympic Truce."[18]

Yet not all observers shared Venizelos's optimism, noting that, in the year that had elapsed since the city had been awarded the games, and despite the wide-ranging initiatives, not much work had actually been done on the necessary athletic facilities. An article in *Ta Nea*, an Athens daily sympathetic to PASOK, pointed out that despite government assurances that it was keeping to a timetable, hard work would have to begin very soon if the current pace was to be maintained. It also pointed out that many plans were only at the blueprint stage, including those for the Olympic village, the equestrian center, the rowing center, and the facilities for baseball, softball, beach volley, and the indoor facility for handball, fencing, judo, and volleyball. The article noted, moreover, that several venues had been changed, which could lead to unanticipated delays.[19]

A CRISIS LOOMS: 1999

By the time the IOC and the Greeks met again formally in February 1999, dramatic changes had occurred. In December 1998, IOC member Marc Hodler alleged publicly that the Salt Lake City committee that bid successfully for the 2002 winter games had bribed several IOC members. The idea that many IOC members were prone to bribery and other illicit emoluments was already part of worldwide conventional wisdom, but Hodler's accusations sent shock waves through the Olympic movement. A crisis loomed when it became obvious that they were also likely to be proven true. In Athens, Venizelos called a meeting of the Hellenic Olympic Committee and ATHOC to discuss the situation, and pronounced himself fully satisfied with

[18]"Protocol Signed for Establishment of 'Cultural Olympics' Institute," Athens News Agency, September 3, 1998.

[19]Dēmētrēs Dontas, "Olympiakoi Agōnes: Ē Athēna den echei xefygei apo to chronodiagramma gia ta erga" ["Olympic Games: Athens is Not Behind the Timetable for the Facilities"], *Ta Nea*, September 3, 1998.

the progress on Olympic projects, as well as with ATHOC's accountability. Construction on most sites would begin in 2001, he said; he also accused the "naysayers" who focused on delays of "humiliating" Greece.[20] Buoyed by the knowledge that the Olympic scandals had not affected ATHOC, the Greeks looked forward to a factfinding visit by an IOC delegation within a few days.

Venizelos would not remain the minister in charge of preparations for long, however, as he was soon appointed to another ministry—although he would return to his Olympic responsibilities in a few months, most probably because Sēmitēs realized that he was indispensable in that position. Venizelos combined the traditional style of a Greek minister—headstrong and forceful—with an ability to appear considerate toward those around him, even his opponents. Throughout the preparations, he managed to balance carrots and sticks, pushing things through without alienating too many people. Venizelos's velvet-glove style contrasted with the administrative manner of many of his ministerial colleagues, past and present, and enabled him to lead as well as motivate a complicated network of power relationships surrounding the preparations. (Kōstas Bakourēs spoke openly about the negative consequences of the government's role in an interview published in early 1999. A year after leaving his corporate position in Switzerland and returning to Greece, Bakourēs admitted that the Greek bureaucracy's "degree of ineffectiveness was worse" than he had anticipated, with "a complete lack of a sense of urgency, an inability to make decisions"; he concluded, "The government has more power than I would have liked.")[21]

On February 16, 1999, only three days after the IOC met with Venizelos, and almost three thousand miles away, Turkish commandos apprehended the most wanted man in Turkey, Abdullah Oçalan, as he was making his way from the Greek embassy in Nairobi to the airport in Kenya's capital. Oçalan had been wandering from country to country for several months after being expelled from Syria, where he had established his headquarters and directed the struggle of the Kurdish minority in Turkey. The Kurdish leader, a hero to his people but a terrorist to the Turks, had shuttled around Europe trying to find sanctuary. The countries that refused to offer it to him did so because they did not wish to disrupt relations with Turkey or be accused of

---

[20]"Venizelos Satisfied with Progress, Transparency in Olympic Projects," Athens News Agency, February 13, 1999; Dēmētrēs Dontas, "Apo to 2001" ["From 2001 Onward"], Ta Nea, February 13, 2002.

[21]Gregory A. Maniatis, "Ringmaster: An Exclusive Interview With the CEO of Athens 2004," Odyssey, January-February 1999, pp. 40–42.

harboring an insurgent who condoned armed struggle. The news that he had found asylum in its Kenyan embassy was a major diplomatic embarrassment for Greece, especially after it was discovered that Oçalan might have entered the country illegally more than once during his travels. Kenya expelled the Greek ambassador for sheltering the Kurdish leader without its knowledge and, two days later, the Greek ministers of foreign affairs, the interior, and public order resigned over the matter.

The IOC members arrived in Athens a day before the resignations to find the country in considerable political turmoil over the Oçalan affair. Jacques Rogge, president of the coordinating committee (and Samaranch's successor in 2001 as IOC president), and Gilbert Felli, the IOC's liaison with the international sports federations, met the next day with Mayor Avramopoulos and Venizelos. That very day, the prime minister accepted the resignations of his ministers and reshuffled the cabinet, moving Venizelos to the ministry of development and appointing Elisavet Papazōē to the ministry of culture. George Papandreou was promoted from deputy to full minister of foreign affairs. The visit began with meetings between the IOC and all the political parties. Then, Rogge and Felli went about the more serious business of visiting and learning about the sites.

The press conference given by Rogge and Felli at the end of their visit provided the first hint of growing concern about the pace of preparations. Rogge sounded the optimistic notes, leaving Felli to sound the alarm bells, albeit delicately. Felli commented on the IOC's supervisory role, which entailed working with the host city with a goal of adhering to original plans as much as possible. Whenever necessary changes were made, Felli said, they usually entailed additional delays, raising concerns over the completion of works. He noted that the organizers were as yet unsure of the location of the Olympic village and the equestrian center, that the rowing-center project was still caught up in the courts, and that there were still no suitable venues for baseball, hockey, and softball.[22]

Although Athens was not implicated in any financial or bribery scandal, and the IOC appeared to be emerging more or less unscathed from the Salt Lake City situation, Felli's comments cast a pall over the preparations, which prompted different reactions from the government, opposition, media, and the IOC itself over the next few months. Government critics and other

---

[22]Dēmētrēs Dontas, "Anēsychia gia erga" ["Concern About Projects"], *Ta Nea*, February 20, 1999.

observers highlighted the problems looming on the horizon and also spoke of friction between the organizing committee and the government. With Venizelos now at the ministry of development, the government missed his self-confidence and emphatic dismissal of criticism. In the event, Sēmitēs stepped in himself and cast Greece's preparation in the broader context of the country's modernization. In May, at the inauguration of the HOC's new headquarters—a six-story, marble-and-glass building facing the Olympic Stadium in northern Athens—he said that Greece was forging ahead and gave its imminent accession to the European Monetary Union as an example. Samaranch, who also attended the event, offered what would be one of several rounds of reassuring comments about the IOC's views of the preparations.[23]

Within weeks, there was an anticipated crisis when Stratēs Stratēgēs resigned as president of ATHOC. As a close friend of the exiled Greek royal family, Stratēgēs had wished to travel to London in July, to attend the wedding of Alexia, the daughter of the former king, Constantine. The government instructed Stratēgēs not to make the trip because he was considered "a political person," in other words, a paid civil servant, and the Greek government had no formal relations with the royal family. Stratēgēs responded by handing in his resignation, "for personal reasons," and leaving for London, telling reporters that he was now "a free citizen." In his letter to the prime minister, he also said that he hoped his replacement would be able to continue working "unhindered" and with the required urgency.[24]

Stratēgēs's resignation shattered the façade of confidence and optimism surrounding the preparations. Opposition spokespersons, reporters, and media commentators suggested that the resignation was the inevitable outcome of the conflict between ATHOC and the government. Although the government's foes claimed that preparations were in dire straits because of mismanagement, Papazōē insisted that preparations remained on track. It took several days for Sēmitēs to appoint a replacement, as he waited to consult with Samaranch, who was due in Athens later that month for the opening of the Olympic Academy's summer session. Upon hearing in Lausanne of Stratēgēs's resignation, Samaranch apparently indicated that Greece might need a minister for the Olympics in order for ATHOC to begin working

[23]"Samaranch Satisfied with Progress Over 2004 Games," Athens News Agency, May 26, 1999.
[24]Manōlēs Mauromatēs, "Paraitēsē vomva gia to 2004" ["Resignation Bombshell for Athens 2004"], Ta Nea, July 7, 1999.

efficiently. After consulting in Athens, however, Samaranch and Sēmitēs decided that in view of mounting opposition in Greece, ATHOC's new leader should not be a political figure. Ultimately, Sēmitēs appointed Panagiōtēs Thōmopoulos, the deputy governor of the National Bank of Greece; Thōmopoulos retained that post while serving as president of the organizing committee. In a gesture designed to appease conservatives, Sēmitēs also created the post of vice-president and appointed former New Democracy deputy and ATHOC member Nikē Tzavela to the post.

From that point onward, the periodic visits of IOC members to Athens and their contacts with the organizers unfolded under a cloud of concerns and even doubt about whether the athletic venues, let alone all the planned projects, would be completed in time. The next round of meetings, site inspections, and press conferences came in late September and early October. Rogge's coordinating committee arrived first, along with Samaranch, and then the entire IOC executive committee descended on Athens for a meeting. The series of contacts began with the unveiling of the 2004 Olympiad's official logo, a white circular olive branch on an azure background. The two sides then got down to business. The official statements were considerably less ebullient; acknowledging that they were tackling a series of difficulties, the IOC expressed satisfaction over the efforts being made, saying that the two sides were in full agreement over the issues that needed to be addressed.

"I cannot imagine the Games will not be held in Athens"

In January 2000, Rogge was sounding distinctly more cautious about progress in Athens, saying, "I believe that whatever problems exist will be overcome. It's imperative, however, for there to be greater flexibility in the moves being taken, as well as for more rapid decisions by the organizing committee. You must overcome the problem of bureaucracy."[25] He added that certain changes in related legislation were also necessary. The next day, following Rogge's remarks, the conservatives attacked the government. Speaking in parliament, Giōrgos Orfanos, New Democracy's representative on sports issues, said that these comments by a leading IOC official proved the

---

[25]"IOC-Athens 2004-Rogge," *Athens News Agency*, January 27, 2000; Manōlēs Drakos, "Ypainigmoi apo to klimakio" ["Insinuations from the Delegation"], *Eleutherotypia*, January 28, 2000.

government's "hamfistedness" in managing the preparations. He added that Rogge's statement was "a slap in the face for the government, as well as for the non-existent 2004 Organizing Committee, confirming our concerns over the insignificant to negative results of preparations so far to hold the Olympic Games. The responsibility lies completely and exclusively with the Prime Minister for his choices, which have resulted in the international humiliation of our country. It's time for the 'group' of inept party and related opportunists to go, because they have now become dangerous." Following a government announcement that, as public works minister, Kōstas Laliōtēs was taking responsibility for all building projects related to the Olympics, New Democracy unleashed yet another widely publicized broadside. Its leader, Miltiadēs Evert, said the move proved that the government had been misleading public opinion about the extent of delays.

The announcement in February that national elections would be held in April virtually sealed the fate of the preparations. With PASOK and New Democracy running neck and neck in opinion polls, the government turned its attention to the electoral race. It was perhaps typical of the government's concern with domestic politics at this time that a trip abroad by ATHOC's leaders to meet with the IOC did not include politicians. The trip was to Sydney, where the IOC was undertaking its last-minute inspection six months before the 2000 Olympiad. When the Greek committee made its presentation, a satellite link-up was arranged so that Papazōē and Fouras could participate. The electoral campaign, meanwhile, led to a moratorium on IOC statements regarding preparations. Anything the IOC said publicly could be misconstrued as trying to influence the outcome. At any rate, given the unpredictability of the result on April 9, it is hard to imagine that the members of the government involved in the preparations would have taken time out from campaigning during this time. PASOK ended up winning the elections with a wafer-thin majority, but the honeymoon period that had insulated the government from the IOC was over.

About ten days after the ballot, Greek sports fans settled in front of televisions in their living rooms or in cafes around the country to watch the *Panathēnaikos* basketball team defeat Maccabi of Tel Aviv in the final game of the Euroleague, the European basketball championship. Four years earlier, when *Panathēnaikos* had made it to the Euroleague's final four on its way to winning the tournament, Juan Antonio Samaranch had mentioned its good performance along with several other good showings by Greek sports teams. Now, two and a half years after Athens had won the right to hold the 2004 games, he was not in a charitable mood. He came out of a meeting with the Greek organizers in Lausanne on April 20 and delivered an unprecedented public rebuke. He said that the Athens games were in the worst organizational crisis faced by an Olympic city in his twenty-year tenure. Samaranch declared that he had told the Greeks that organizing the Olympics involved three phases: green, when everything is going smoothly; yellow, when there are "many problems"; and red, when the "Games are in danger. I told them we are at the end of the yellow phase." He then continued: "If from now until the end of the year there are no drastic changes, we will enter the red phase. They [the Greeks] need to make important changes as soon as possible. This kind of organization is not delivering the results we expected. With four years before the Games, it's time the government takes the responsibility they have to take." Samaranch would not say what the IOC would do if Athens failed to shape up by the end of the year. He played down the possibility of stripping the games from Greece. "I cannot imagine the Games will not be held in Athens," he said. "We hope after this warning all the things will be in the right way.... I am sure and optimistic there will be these changes very, very soon." Samaranch said he wondered again whether the Greeks should appoint a government minister who would be exclusively in charge of them.[26]

Richard Pound, the Canadian vice-president of the IOC, was characteristically blunter about the problems and Athens's prospects of retaining the games. He said the Greeks were "running out of time," and that moving the games was technically feasible. "It would have to be a major crisis," Pound added. "Yes, we can do that. But you're better off dancing with the girl you brought than changing midstream. We did it when Denver backed out of the 1976 Games. We cast about and found Innsbruck. It can be done, but we sure don't like to do it. It's not good for us, it's not good for Greece and it's not good for the Games."

Jacques Rogge, as head of the IOC panel that was supervising the Greek preparations, tried to be the most diplomatic of the three Olympic leaders. He said that the Greeks had to speed up decisionmaking, and listed problems in accommodations, traffic, security, communications, construction, venues, and infrastructure. "What is needed is a bit more sense of urgency and to understand the scope of the games. Our partners do not understand what the

[26]Stephen Wilson, "Shape Up, IOC Warns Athens," Associated Press, April 21, 2000.

games are. The whole structure must be revamped." Rogge added that there was no contingency plan for moving the games. "We feel that's not needed," he said. "It would be unfair to the Greeks. We are finding backup plans within the organization."[27]

Stunned government officials in Athens launched a desperate damage-control operation that would last several days and leave most of public opinion unconvinced that "things were not that bad." The next day's newspapers gave the comments of the IOC leaders full coverage and translated the metaphor of the traffic lights used by Samaranch into the cards used to penalize soccer players, yellow for a warning and red for an ejection. Headlines announced that the IOC had shown Greece a yellow card, or that it was threatening it with a red one. Along with its report, *Ta Nea* published an interview in which Samaranch said he had warned Greek officials privately about the dangers of the delays, but to no avail. Government spokesman Dēmētrēs Reppas said that Greece would respond to the situation and overcome whatever problems lay in the way, adding that the prime minister was going to take full charge of preparations. Giōrgos Floridēs, who had replaced Fouras as deputy minister of sports, also said that Greece would respond and added confidently that the games would be perfectly organized and a milestone in the history of the Olympics.

A more realistic assessment came from Theodōros Pangalos, who had been appointed minister of culture after the elections. As an influential member of the government, Pangalos would not mince his words or offer bland reassurances. He had been out of the cabinet since the Oçalan crisis in 1999, when he had resigned as foreign minister. Sēmitēs had obviously brought him back into the cabinet because he wanted a political heavyweight in the post responsible for the Olympics. Pangalos admitted that there were problems with the preparations and blamed the dysfunction on the ministerial committee. The new minister of culture said that the committee should be "upgraded" to comprise full ministers, instead of their deputies, and that his ministry should be given clear, overall responsibility. The creation of a ministry for the Olympics would not work in Greece, he believed. Apparently without thinking that it contradicted his view that the ministerial committee should be upgraded, Pangalos also said that ATHOC was the main vehicle for

---

[27]Manōlēs Drakos, "Kitrinē karta stēn Olympiada" ["A Yellow Card for the Olympics"], *Eleutherotypia*, April 21, 2000; Manōlēs Mauromatēs, "Sēma kindynou" ["Danger Sign"], *Ta Nea*, April 21, 2000.

the organizational effort and that the government should help free it from all bureaucratic impediments.[28]

When the IOC had issued its rebuke in late April, Rogge had noted that the Greeks had somehow lost the dynamism they had shown when Athens was bidding for the games and that they had to rediscover it somehow. The prime minister evidently took those words to heart. On May 10, he surprised most of the country by announcing the appointment of Gianna Angelopoulou to the post of president of ATHOC. The ministerial committee unanimously supported the appointment. Using an analogy calculated to have effect, Sēmitēs said that the government would move with the same urgency it had shown months before, when an earthquake struck the environs of Athens. The prime minister said he would chair a newly established Olympic Preparations Coordinating Committee that would also include the cabinet's top ministers and the 2004 organizing committee's leadership, namely, Angelopoulou and managing director Kōstas Bakourēs. In order to forestall any misunderstanding, Pangalos reiterated that the organizing committee would be autonomous, and that the government would offer all its help and support.[29]

After her triumph in Lausanne in 1990, the woman who had led Athens's successful bid returned to private life, working in her family's business and raising her three children in London. When the first president of Athens 2004, Stratēgēs, resigned, rumors had raged in Athens about Angelopoulou taking over the committee. A newspaper reported that even though she was a friend of the royal family, she had not attended the wedding over which Stratēgēs had relinquished his position (although reports indicated that her husband had attended). Another report claimed that Angelopoulou had declined Sēmitēs's offer to replace Stratēgēs because she had been concerned about the degree of government control over ATHOC.

Angelopoulou almost certainly lobbied to upgrade the position of president of ATHOC before accepting the post, and Sēmitēs willingly made concessions. Angelopoulou wàs a popular choice, a respected administrator and, in the words of her outgoing predecessor, Thōmopoulos, "a dynamic

---

[28]Dēmētrēs Dontas, "Analamvanei to thema prosōpika" ["He is Taking Over Personally"], *Ta Nea*, April 26, 2000.

[29]"Angelopoulou-Daskalakē Tapped as New 2004 President," Athens News Agency, May 11, 2000; "Aifnidiasmos me tēn Gianna" ["Surprise with Gianna"], *Eleutherotypia*, May 11, 2000.

woman." Yet even she, who had achieved so much in Greece's male-domi-
nated political world, could not singlehandedly challenge the structural predominance of government over the preparations for the Olympics. Three
months after her appointment, she was signing "memoranda of cooperation"
with the general secretariat of sports and Laliōtēs's public works ministry
regarding projects for the games. The agreements, approved in advance by
the prime minister, defined "the competencies of both sides," or, in plain English, drew lines in the sand to prevent turf wars and strengthen the hand of
ATHOC.

(ATHOC's need to coordinate its initiatives with the general secretariat
of sports reflected the government's continued interest in closely monitoring
all issues relating to Greek sport. In that sense, PASOK proved no different
from Karamanlēs's administration, although Papandreou created a deputy
ministry to run sport, while retaining the secretariat. Between 1974 and 1985,
the general secretariat of sports (*genikē grammateia athlētismou*), the government body responsible for administering sport, was under the jurisdiction of
and answered to the deputy minister of the government's "president"—
which is to say, the deputy to the prime minister—who had overall responsibility for "youth and sport." In 1985, PASOK placed the general secretariat
under the jurisdiction of the ministry of culture and also created a deputy
minister of culture responsible for sport. What all this meant in the end for
the 2004 Olympiad was many more cooks to spoil the broth because the hierarchy now included the minister of culture, deputy minister of culture
responsible for sport, and general secretary of sports. All three were peering
over Angelopoulou's shoulders—as was the ministry of public works.)

The team of close collaborators that Angelopoulou gathered around her
confirmed her preference for technocrats over politicians. Petros Synadinos,
who had been a part of the group that led Athens's successful bid for the
games, replaced Bakourēs as managing director. The managing director,
Giannēs Spanoudakēs, who was appointed in March 2001, had spent the previous twelve years as a senior manager for Dow Chemical, rising to the position of global business director in 1996. Spyros Kapralos, a former swimmer
and water-polo player who took part in the Los Angeles Olympics in 1984 and
then followed a career in international banking, was appointed executive
director of ATHOC in May 2000. The second executive director, Kōstas
Liaskas, joined ATHOC as its construction expert. He had headed the Greek
Technical Chamber since 1988 and had served as minister of public works in

two caretaker administrations. In addition to having been on the bid team for the 1996 games, the fifty-eight-year-old Liaskas had served as vice-president of the 2004 bid committee. Finally, the third executive director, Marton Simicek, an experienced sports administrator, had a background in insurance and management. The HOC's president, Lambēs Nikolaou, was also appointed to ATHOC's leadership as the group's vice-president, but he had the limited role of filling in for Angelopoulou as a figurehead on formal occasions.

If anyone thought the technocrats would not be beholden to the government, all they had to do was read between the lines of an Athens News Agency report soon after Angelopoulou's appointment. There was an obvious clue: the prime minister had appointed all of ATHOC's executive board. Reppas dropped another hint, stating that the government's parting with Bakourēs had been amicable, and that the government would use him again "in good time." Best of all was the final comment in the agency's report. "Observers note," it ventured bravely, "that the reshuffle represents a strengthening of Angelopoulos-Daskalaki's position." Commentary, it should be said, was (and remains) rare for a news agency that is nothing more than a government mouthpiece. Indeed, the agency had systematically suppressed reports of the IOC's criticisms of the preparations. Clearly, it now felt that the situation merited comment—although it said nothing about the government's relationship to the committee.[30]

Yet Gianna Angelopoulou's return in May 2000 far from guaranteed a happy ending to the preparations or even that they would be soon put back on track. When Samaranch sounded the alarm bells, he helped Greece's political leadership understand that time was running out. If Greece was to prove modern and competent enough to host the Olympics successfully, the public sector's bureaucratic snail's-pace would have to speed up, and efficient practice would have to live up to the rhetoric of modernity. A parallel obstacle for the Greeks was the thorny issue of commercialism, which now pervaded the Olympics. Since the 1980s, the Olympics had been increasingly tied to corporate interests, which had become a structural reality in the movement. The "selling of the five rings" was accepted practice after the Los Angeles Olympiad.[31] Somehow, Angelopoulou would have to straddle the contradiction of continuing to sell the rings to major corporations while

[30]"Athens 2004 Organizing Committee Gets New Board," Athens News Agency, June 23, 2000.

organizing "traditional games" in a country proud of its heritage and ambivalent about multinational corporations. These tasks, however, were dwarfed by the even more difficult challenge of working with government officials and civil servants to keep the preparations from strangling in endless red tape.

[31]See Robert K.Barney, Stephen R. Wenn, and Scott G. Martyn, *Selling of the Five Rings: The IOC and the Rise of Olympic Commercialism*, University of Utah Press, Salt Lake City, 2002.

CHAPTER 10

COUNTDOWN TO ATHENS 2004

A BOMB EXPLODED IN THE PORT OF Piraeus on June 29, 2002. It sounded the death knell of Greece's notorious November 17 terrorist group, which had successfully eluded the authorities for twenty-seven years, assassinating twenty-three people and committing a string of armed robberies. At the core of the Olympic movement's fears about security in Athens was the threat posed by this group, which had targeted foreign diplomats, the US military, and Greek businessmen and politicians alike. On that day in Piraeus, a November 17 operative was seriously injured when a bomb he was carrying went off prematurely in his hands. In custody, the man provided volumes of information to the authorities that enabled them to arrest most of the group's members in July and also uncover caches of arms and documents, yielding additional data about November 17's activities. While police pursued the remnants of the terrorist network, Gianna Angelopoulou informed the IOC in late August that the group no longer posed a threat to the 2004 games, although, naturally, she added, the organizers would not relax their vigilance regarding security.

In March 2003, the accused members of November 17 went on trial in Athens, but ATHOC was too busy by then putting out other fires to remind anyone that the security fears concerning the Athens Olympiad had been assuaged. In the nine or so months that had elapsed between the breakthrough against terrorism and the trial, preparations had continued their precarious roller-coaster ride. The IOC alternated between praise and threats, the relationship between the organizing committee and the government oscillated from hot to cold, and even the normally cordial relations between the organizers and Lausanne had become strained.

While fears about security were allayed considerably by the antiterrorist drive in the summer of 2002, serious concerns over delays on construction of infrastructure and sites remained. An announcement by the Greek government in July 2002 that some planned sports venues would not be built because they were too expensive and that alternative facilities would be used in 2004 merely confirmed what everyone had known all along. Although seventy-five percent of the required venues were in place when Greece was awarded the games in 1997, the construction of the remaining ones had proceeded slowly. This was either because resources had been diverted toward much-needed transport and other infrastructural work, or because of lack of funds, or because of politics. In any case, the "seventy-five percent" bandied about as the official figure was misleading in that a number of different facilities had to be constructed in separate locations in and around Athens, a fact which made the "twenty-five percent" remaining more daunting. This new construction included an international broadcast center, a press center, indoor sports arenas in the districts of Nikaia, Galatsi, and Anō Liosia, the equestrian and shooting centers in the town of Markopoulo (outside Athens), the rowing/canoe/kayak center on the coastal area of Schinias near Marathon, and a series of outdoor facilities at the site of the old airport at Ellēnikon and the neighboring sports center of Agios Kosmas, southeast of central Athens. Furthermore, the existing seventy-five percent required considerable upgrading, which included installing a roof at the main stadium and rebuilding Karaïskakēs Stadium in Piraeus.

At the core of the delays lay the country's economic fragility, its bureaucracy, and its chronically uninhibited politics. Greece will be the smallest country to host the Olympics since Finland in 1952 (the larger but not stronger Mexican economy had faced similar strains in 1968), and the weight of the financial demands placed on Athens have now become abundantly evident. For the development of sports facilities and Olympics-related projects, the games' total budget was projected at $4.9 billion, with the Greek state contributing $3 billion, the European Union $700 million, and the rest coming from private sources. Political realities complicated and slowed preparations. Despite Angelopoulou's dynamic leadership of ATHOC, the government held on to many organizational responsibilities, especially those related to building the transportation network and athletic venues. Worse, the perennial game of musical chairs among top ministers continued unabated after Angelopoulou assumed her post. The ministry of culture, which bore the major responsibility for preparations, had changed hands in late 2000 for the fourth time since Greece had been awarded the games three years earlier. The minister of public works, who had been placed in charge of construction projects, was also replaced in late 2001. By that time, the clock seemed to be ticking furiously. The Sydney Olympics were over, and both government and organizers were feeling the pressure and pushing preparations forward. Remarkably, despite Athens's perennial inability to build venues in a timely manner, both the government and ATHOC continued their efforts to impart a special Greek flavor to the 2004 games. In the event, the results were mixed.

SYDNEY 2000

The euphoria generated by Angelopoulou's appointment to the Athens 2004 organizing committee evaporated within a few months when Greeks witnessed the smoothness and efficiency of the Sydney Olympiad in September 2000. The 1996 games had been so poorly organized that the Greeks knew they would be able to improve on the inefficiency of the transportation system and delayed transmission of results that gave the Atlanta Olympiad such a bad name. The Australians did such an outstanding job of organizing the Sydney games, however, that they inadvertently, and abruptly, raised the bar for Athens.

On the eve of the Sydney Olympiad, there was reason for guarded optimism in Athens. Under Angelopoulou, ATHOC had signed several agreements with government ministries designed to give it greater flexibility in its operations. In late August, members of the IOC commission overseeing the preparations made a brief visit to Athens, after which Jacques Rogge proclaimed himself satisfied enough to withdraw the so-called "yellow card" that Samaranch had "shown" Greece four months earlier. The efforts in the Greek capital had gained momentum and Greece was back on track, although there was no time to idle. Rogge said, "We must not add pages to the calendar. Time is passing swiftly," and, he added, the organizers faced a "marathon that must be run at sprinting speed." Rogge concluded that the basic elements of the preparations had been set on firm foundations, and he underscored the personal interest shown by Prime Minister Sēmitēs and the now excellent relations between the government and ATHOC.[1]

By the time of the closing ceremony in Sydney, Angelopoulou had to strain to offer assurances that the 2004 games would emulate the

---

[1]"Greece Back on Track, but Still Has to Beat the Clock for 2004, IOC Delegation Says," Athens News Agency, August 26, 2000.

extraordinary success of the 2000 Olympiad. As Angelopoulou and Mayor Avramopoulos received the Olympic flag at the closing ceremony, as is the custom for the representatives of the next host city, they listened as Samaranch described the 2000 games as "the best so far." It was an expression he had used in the ceremony in Barcelona (his home town), but not in Atlanta. All eyes were now on Athens. Asked a few days later by NBC, the US television network that had the broadcast rights to Athens 2004, whether Sydney's success was daunting, Angelopoulou responded with a mixture of reassurances and allusions to the special Greek character of the next Olympics. She said that the accomplishments of the Australian organizers were an inspiration to the Greeks, who would "seek to give the world Games that are good for the athletes and for the audience, for everyone, combining the Olympic heritage with ultra-modern installations."[2]

The optimistic façade shattered in less than a month, when the underlying tension between the organizing committee and government ministers burst to the surface in mid-October. Kōstas Liaskas, the organizing committee's technical director, clashed publicly with Laliōtēs, the minister of public works, who had not wished to grant the committee the right to hire public-works consultants of its own choice. The outcome of the clash between the minister and the technocrat held no surprises. Prime Minister Sēmitēs granted Liaskas the courtesy of a brief meeting and then announced his dismissal from the committee for having made statements that were "incompatible" with his position. The next day, one newspaper described the event as the government delivering "a clear message" to ATHOC.[3]

To the embarrassment of the Greeks, Rogge issued a public call for a "truce" between ATHOC and the government. He also asked for greater governmental involvement and initiative on speeding up preparations. Angelopoulou did not react publicly to Rogge's wakeup call, an indication that she supported it and considered it only inasmuch as it was addressed to the government. In contrast, Pangalos, the minister of culture, and Laliōtēs issued firm but polite rebuttals to the effect that the preparations were in fact proceeding smoothly, indirectly denying any rifts between them and ATHOC.

Liaskas's self-immolation forced ATHOC and the government to

[2]"Gianna Angelopoulou-Daskalaki Interviewed on the Prospects of the Athens Olympics in 2004," Athens News Agency, September 30, 2000.

[3]Maria Daleanē, "O Laliōtēs 'Ediōxe' ton Liaska" ["Laliōtēs 'Ousted' Liaskas"], Ta Nea, October 19, 2000.

acknowledge their split publicly and try to breach the rift. Within days, an announcement that Angelopoulou, Laliōtēs, and Pangalos would have "their first private meeting" in order to iron out differences confirmed what observers had known all along: namely, that the two ministers were unhappy about ceding power to the committee and its leader. Signs of conflict had first appeared when Pangalos had decided at the very last minute not to travel to the Sydney games. Later, he confirmed that he had stayed behind because he had refused to approve what he considered to be excessively high salaries for ATHOC. Shortly thereafter, government sources leaked information to the media concerning the supposedly exorbitant sums Angelopoulou had spent in Sydney on a reception and for other activities designed to publicize the Athens Olympiad. ATHOC responded that the expenses were less than those incurred by government delegations during similar trips. Media concerns were clearly politically directed: the media almost never question routinely lavish expenses incurred by the Greek government in the name of promoting so-called "national" issues abroad.

Angelopoulou and the ministers emerged from their meeting with the usual reassurances, but their comments were not persuasive. They did not fool the IOC. Richard Pound stated that the troubles with Athens's preparations were very serious, rating them "9 on the scale of 10." The Greeks reacted assertively, announcing that preparations would proceed more rapidly and that by the time Rogge arrived for his next scheduled visit in late November, he would find the situation dramatically improved. But the façade of unperturbed self-confidence received another blow when Liaskas announced that he would ask the Supreme Court to investigate his firing by the prime minister. He told the media that there were too many chiefs trying to run the preparations and also gave the impression that several ministers responsible for many of the Olympiad's works did not understand the importance of working with ATHOC. "I do not have any indications that there is a change of attitude and significant progress," Liaskas said. "I hope everything goes well." He added that he thought that some ministers had not understood "the full meaning of this effort. There are of course attempts, but there are just too many bosses for one Olympiad," he concluded.[4]

Iōannēs Pyrgiōtēs, an MIT-trained architect, replaced Liaskas on ATHOC's executive committee. It was a safe promotion "inside the fold" of

[4]Lisa Orkin, "Former 2004 Official says Government must Cooperate in Olympic Preparations," Associated Press, November 11, 2000.

someone who was already a member of ATHOC's board and who had also worked with Angelopoulou on the bid committee. Pyrgiōtēs had been a consultant to the ministry of public works from 1983 to 1988; if anything, therefore, he was bound to be sensitive to the difficulties that resulted from ATHOC's relationship with Laliōtēs.

A semblance of order was restored by late November. For once, Greece's political unpredictability made a positive contribution to preparations. Pangalos, outspoken as always, was dismissed as minister of culture for publicly criticizing Greece's foreign policy. The prime minister reappointed Venizelos to his old ministry, marking his return to the post he had held when Greece was awarded the games in 1997. In contrast to Pangalos, Venizelos appeared to be much more willing to tolerate ATHOC's autonomy. Although the conflict between government officials and ATHOC was far from over, Angelopoulou could now rely not only on the prime minister's support but also on that of the minister in charge of preparations. This was probably one of the reasons that Rogge, visiting Athens at the end of the month, made very positive statements about the progress that had been made. He was careful to note that time had been lost in the past and that the organizers would have to work against the clock, but he praised the progress that had been achieved.

Yet, just as it seemed that the tension between ATHOC and the government was abating, a crisis broke out within the committee, and Petros Synadinos was its next victim, along with the committee's media strategist, Yiannis Roubatis. They resigned in early December 2000, ostensibly, as always, for "personal reasons." According to press reports, Synadinos felt he had been marginalized by Angelopoulou, who had gone along with government measures giving her some of his responsibilities. His resignation was yet another blow to ATHOC's prestige. One report described it as the outcome of a civil war that had raged within the committee, while another spoke of two years of "human sacrifices" in ATHOC.[5] It was a further sign of how the government saw Angelopoulou as the personification of ATHOC when it took three months to replace Synadinos with Giannēs Spanoudakēs in March 2001.

The two months of organizational turmoil brought to an end in November 2000 by Rogge had contrasted with the optimism of the Greek athletic

---

[5]Manōlēs Drakos, "Amoivaia Perifronēsē" ["Mutual Disrespect"], *Eleutherotypia*, December 5, 2000; Geōrgios Lakopoulos, "To 2004 Trōei ta paidia tou" ["2004 Devours its Children"], *To Vēma*, December 12, 2000.

community in the wake of the Sydney Olympiad. In sporting terms, the 2000 games were the best ever for Greece. Its athletes returned with thirteen medals, almost as many as Greece had won in total since 1896. Several medals won by the weightlifters were expected, but those in track and field were a pleasant and notable surprise. This was especially the case with sprinter Kōnstantinos Kenterēs, who was ranked outside the top twenty in the 200-meter dash. After running fast in the qualifying rounds, he entered the final confidently, although still an outsider. In the race, the 27-year old Kenterēs was a meter behind the three 100-meter finalists—Trinidad & Tobago's Ato Boldon, Britain's Darren Campbell, and Obadele Thompson from Barbados—who were contesting the lead into the straightaway. Campbell momentarily surged ahead, only to see Kenterēs suddenly charge past him and maintain his lead until he spread out his arms in victory at the finish line. The American sprint duo of Coby Miller and John Capel, also favorites, trailed home in the seventh and eighth spots. Kenterēs got hold of a Greek flag from a spectator and went off on his victory lap. His win was so unexpected that the normally reliable organizers had neglected to arrange for an interpreter at the end of the race, and Kenterēs's coach had to step in. "People may be surprised, but I knew I was going to win," he said, "It was do or die for me tonight." Greece had finally arrived at the top table of athletics. "I was not scared of anyone. I knew I could outrun them." At the official post-race press conference, Kenterēs was asked how it felt to be the first white man to win the 200 meters since Pietro Mennea in 1980, but wisely chose to misunderstand the question. "Mennea was a great athlete," he replied through an interpreter, "but I have my own personality."[6]

Greek track and field had already scored several successes, most notably when Aikaterinē (Katerina) Thanou came second to world recordholder Marion Jones in the final of the 100 meters. Unlike Kenterēs, the twenty-five-year old Thanou was expected to do well; indeed, she was considered the only threat to the American, Jones. After finishing ninth in Atlanta in 1996, Thanou had shown remarkable improvement, winning bronze medals in the European championship of 1998 and the world championship the following year. There were two more silver medals for Greece, both going to women. Anastasia Kelesidou came in second in the discus, behind Belarus's Ellina Zvereva, who, close to forty years old, became the oldest female Olympic

[6]Richard Williams, "Athenian's fast ascent defies Campbell charge," *The Guardian*, September 29, 2000.

gold-medalist in track and field. Thessalonikē-born Kelesidou, twelve years younger, had won the silver medal in the world track-and-field games a year before the Sydney Olympiad. Greece's champion javelin-thrower, Mirella Manianē-Tzelilē, won the other silver medal. (Manianē-Tzelilē, an Albanian, had moved to Greece and married Greek weightlifter Giōrgos Tzelilēs; she had won the gold in the world championship in 1999.)

Meanwhile, the Greek weightlifters continued their impressive performances in Sydney. Pyrros Dēmas, in the 77–85-kilogram category, and Kachi Kachiasvili, in the 85–94-kilogram category, won gold medals again. They joined Turkey's champion, Naim Suleymanoglu, as the only three weightlifters in history to win three straight Olympic medals. Viktōr Mētrou very narrowly missed the gold in the 69–77-kilogram category, and Leōnidas Sampanēs also won a silver in the 56–62-kilogram category. Finally, in what was the first appearance of women's weightlifting in the Olympics, Iōanna Chatzēiōannou won a bronze medal in the 58–63-kilogram category.

The rest of the Greek distinctions came with a gold medal in *tae kwon do* by Michaēl Mouroutsos, a silver medal in the rings event in gymnastics by Dēmosthenēs Tampakos, and a bronze medal by the women's team in rhythmic gymnastics. Also, Amiran Kardanōf, a Russian-born member of the Greek wrestling team, finally ended a long period of Greek frustration in wrestling by winning the bronze medal in freestyle. It was the first medal for Greek wrestling since Cholidēs had won the bronze in Seoul in 1988. (Prior to Seoul, of course, it had often been the case that the only medals won by Greeks were in wrestling, whether freestyle or Greco-Roman.) Medals aside, there were several impressive results by Greek athletes that confirmed the advances made by Greek sport. A three-man cycling team was fourth in a sprint event; Greco-Roman wrestler Kōstas Thanos also came in fourth, losing his last bout in overtime. Several Greeks came in fifth: Aretē Athanasopoulou and Alexandros Nikolaidēs in *tae kwon do*, Tigran Ouzlian in boxing, Stella Tsikouna in the women's discus throw, and Aftantil Xanthopoulos in freestyle wrestling.

2001: NEW FEARS

Jacques Rogge was elected president of the IOC in July 2001, and the news of his election brought relief and satisfaction in Athens. The Greeks had established a good working relationship with Rogge during his tenure as head of the IOC committee overseeing the 2004 preparations. In contrast, officials in Athens would have not been as happy if two of Rogge's rivals, Canada's Richard Pound or South Korea's Un Yong Kim, had won. Pound had been outspoken about the problems facing Athens, while Kim was unknown (but reputedly able to operate behind the scenes).

The run-up to the IOC's presidential elections had given ATHOC a honeymoon of sorts during the first six months of 2001, although it still had to contend with the pressures exerted by the government. None of the presidential candidates wished to cause undue alarm by sounding too negative about the preparations. If anything, the IOC's attitude has always been that "the show must go on"; indicating otherwise does not behoove any IOC presidential aspirant, under any circumstances. The government, however, was concerned with the rising costs, and the issue came to a head in May. Finance Minister Giannos Papantōniou told the press that the organizers could not simply keep on increasing the budget for the games every time they met with the government. A meeting at the time revealed a great deal of tension between the two sides, with reports of Venizelos clashing with Angelopoulou and threatening to resign.[7] Within a week, the rift was repaired, and both ATHOC and the government launched a public-relations exercise to promote the games.

Upon assuming the IOC's presidency, Rogge adopted a much stricter attitude toward the Greeks. By September 2001, in Athens at the conclusion of his first visit as president, he was sounding like Pound, warning that "despite all the work that has been accomplished, the task ahead for the construction sector is unparalleled in the history of Greece and time is ticking away."[8] He had accompanied Denis Oswald, the IOC executive member from Switzerland who had taken over from Rogge as head of the IOC committee monitoring the Athens games. They jointly headed a 44-member panel that fanned out across the capital to take a closer look at many planned venues that remained on the drawing board less than three years before the scheduled start of the Olympiad. Work had begun on the Olympic village and rowing center, but there was no progress on at least eight other venues, including the sailing and equestrian centers, as well as the wrestling hall and gymnastics arena. Oswald, meanwhile, was also very explicit about his concerns with

[7]Geōrgios Lakopoulos, "Ē Panakrivē Olympiada" ["The Exorbitant Olympiad"], *To Vēma*, May 20, 2001.

[8]"Statement of the IOC President Following his Visit to Athens," IOC press release, September 26, 2001.

the state of preparations, and called for acceleration in the work and better cooperation between ATHOC and the government ministries. The IOC as a whole called for Greece's "national spirit" to "deliver."[9]

In the wake of the September 11, 2001, terrorist attacks, security concerns loomed large. The IOC's more immediate anxieties were over the 2002 winter Olympics in Salt Lake City, but security was discussed during the visit to Athens. In an attempt to reduce rising unease over the budget while also responding to the new fears over security, the IOC and ATHOC claimed that they would implement increased security measures without adding to the cost of the games. But the IOC also offered financial assistance to Athens if security costs increased. The issue of security prompted Rogge to revert to his earlier, reassuring mode, and he told reporters that both he and Oswald had participated in the last "innocent" Olympics, in Mexico in 1968, and had witnessed the increasing security concerns that had affected the Olympics since that time. Increased security, however, Rogge added, had never detracted from the success of the Olympic Games.[10] (No one apparently noticed Rogge's astonishing amnesia: the Mexico City Olympiad was marred by a bloody attack on protesting students by the authorities in Mexico City just before the games opened. In any case, the term, "innocent," is simply inappropriate for an institution so deeply enmeshed in a net of political and economic interests.)

A new round of financial strictures and broader political concerns confronting the Sēmitēs government had caused this latest bout of finger-pointing over delays in the preparations. Observers attributed the failure to meet economic targets and pledges for reform to a political crisis in the governing party. After a politically hot summer, it scheduled an emergency convention in mid-October to decide whether Sēmitēs would remain as its head. A possible defeat for the prime minister would have led to his resignation and probably thrown the government into chaos. Meanwhile, Greece's failure to meet many budget targets in 2001 threatened to curtail some public works and infrastructural projects, including roadwork needed for the games.

Sēmitēs prevailed over his critics at the party convention, and he emerged stating that the preparations for the Olympics were Greece's first priority. Meanwhile, the ratification of his undisputed leadership gave him enough momentum to proceed to yet another reshuffling of ministerial

[9]"Road and Venue Construction Remain Top Issues in Athens," IOC press release, September 28, 2001.

[10]Maria Daleanē, "Echei Apantēseis" ["It Has Answers"], *Ta Nea*, September 27, 2001.

posts. The changes affected preparations in two ways. First, Sēmitēs relieved Kōstas Laliōtēs of the public works ministry he had held since 1993 and appointed Vasō Papandreou in his place. Second, he appointed six deputy ministers—of defense, development, health, culture, public order, and education—whose primary responsibility was to assist the preparations in their respective ministries. Government sources stated that the prime minister's aim was to send a message to the IOC and to his fellow citizens that the effort to organize the games was the most important one for the country. Furthermore, government circles asserted that Sēmitēs would personally take control of coordinating preparations, but this time with better "tools," as all six deputy ministers were chosen because of his trust in them and their willingness to work in the direction determined by him. Venizelos, who retained his post as minister of culture, also retained overall responsibility for preparing the games, while Vasō Papandreou, as public works minister, would continue Laliōtēs's work. The year ended on a slightly optimistic note, as Oswald reported some progress upon visiting Athens again in November. The IOC official was careful to stress that delays remained and that schedules were tight, but he also said that preparations had finally hit "cruising speed." Still, while Oswald expressed his relief that construction of the Olympic village was finally underway, he also voiced concerns over how slowly the government was tackling the problems of accommodations and transportation.

2002: GOOD NEWS ON TERRORISM, BAD NEWS ABOUT THE VENUES

The breakthrough in the pursuit of November 17 in 2002 overshadowed the increasing worries about the delays in completing the athletic venues in Athens. Nonetheless, as September 5—the fifth anniversary of the games' awarding to Greece—approached, the elimination of the terrorist threat was becoming old news as the issue of venues gained the front pages. The breakup of November 17 neutralized a serious threat to the games, but security concerns remained. The planning and funding of an antiterrorist plan continued, and it was clear that Greece would spend a record amount to provide adequate security for the games. To be sure, the police had successfully pursued November 17, and this reflected positively on the government, but it did little to allay fears about construction delays. Only days before the first November 17 terrorist was apprehended in June 2002, Denis Oswald concluded his second visit to Athens that year by issuing yet another warning about mounting delays.[11] The organizers had assured Oswald that they would resolve problems relating to the venues at the old airport at Ellēnikon by the time he returned in June; this was not the case, however. Contracts relating to the construction of an artificial whitewater course for canoe and kayak, basketball arenas, and baseball diamonds had not been signed when Oswald did return. Delays on other projects, meanwhile, meant that several international sports federations were expressing concerns that there would be no time to hold crucial trial events before the Olympics opened.

In August 2002, the organizers managed to hold a successful two-week sailing regatta, the first test for 2004, and the event's smooth organization contributed to a climate of optimism. The IOC praised the work of the Greeks, although it had clashed with them a few weeks earlier after the government had announced, unilaterally, that it would be reducing the scope of some venues. These included facilities to be built on the site of the old airport and the venue of the soccer final, Karaïskakēs Stadium. The stadium, built in 1968, was supposed to have been refurbished, but the government announced that there would be no time to complete the work by 2004. Buoyed by the success of the sailing event in August, Gianna Angelopoulou spoke confidently about 2004 on September 5. She was able to point to the work done on the Olympic village, which was ahead of schedule. Other positive signs included the progress made in other venues such as the special weightlifting center being built in the Piraeus suburb of Nikaia, as well as on roadbuilding around the city. Yet the venues planned for the old airport remained an open question, as did a tramline to connect that site with the city's center. Beyond these core issues, the organizers appeared confident that the campaign to enlist the required 60,000 volunteers to work during the Olympiad was advancing, and they also believed that the plan to promote an Olympic truce was gaining support globally. Indeed, construction delays notwithstanding, both government and organizing committee appeared enormously pleased with the progress being made on the "soft" Olympic issues, such as Greece's own input into the games, which included upholding Olympic traditions, returning the games to their roots in terms of creating a less glitzy event, and linking the games to peace and an Olympic truce.

The International Olympic Committee had decided to revive the ancient

---

[11]"Progress Witnessed by IOC Delegation Visiting Athens," IOC press release, June 27, 2002.

concept of the Olympic truce in 1992, with the view to protecting, as far as possible, the interests of athletes and sport in general, and to contributing to peaceful and diplomatic solutions to the conflicts around the world. Greece, both as host of the 2004 games and heir to their ancient traditions, plays an important role in the campaign. Its interest epitomizes the deep-seated belief among many Greek government and sports officials that the ancient legacy of the games can be brought to bear on current affairs. This view is shared by a sizeable segment of Greek public opinion and reflects the view of continuity between ancient and modern Greece. The campaign itself typifies the willingness of Greek governments to undertake global initiatives in the name of the relevance of classical Greek traditions to contemporary world affairs. (A decade or so ago, for example, Greece launched a campaign to mark the anniversary of the establishment of democracy in ancient Athens.) The statement issued by the truce campaign opens as follows: "The concepts of the Olympic Games and of the Olympic Truce or 'Ekecheiria,' meaning the ceasing of hostilities during the duration of the Games, are inextricably linked." It goes on to explain that, "throughout the duration of the Olympic Truce, from the seventh day prior to the opening of the Games to the seventh day following their closing, conflicts ceased, allowing athletes, artists and spectators to travel to Olympia, participate in the Olympic Games and return to their homelands." It continues by calling for the introduction of a similar truce during all modern Olympics.[12]

One should not rush to dismiss the truce campaign as a preposterous public-relations ploy. Any literal application of the concept of Greek continuity might strike most people as very strange, if not ridiculous; moreover, suggesting that the truce established during the ancient Olympics can somehow be implemented today stretches credulity. Yet one should bear in mind that the truce provides potent symbolism, which international organizations committed to peace might find attractive. The United Nations has endorsed the creation of a truce committee, and a number of heads of state, prime ministers, and personalities from around the world support the campaign. Since 1993, the UN general assembly has repeatedly expressed its support for the IOC by unanimously adopting a biannual resolution (the year before each summer or winter Olympiad) entitled "Building a Peaceful and Better World Through Sport and the Olympic Ideal." The United Nations has

[12]"United Nations General Assembly adopts Olympic Truce with unprecedented unanimity," http://www.olympictruce.org/html/news.html.

invited member states to observe the Olympic truce individually or collec-
tively, and to seek, in conformity with the goals and principles of the UN
charter, to settle all international conflict through peaceful and diplomatic
means.[13]

Admittedly, the project has attracted only elite support and has yet to be
tested in terms of broader appeal. Indeed, there was evidence in October 2002
that it could not appeal broadly when a Greek and Turkish soccer club met
for the first time ever in a game of the UEFA Cup, a European tournament.
The presidents of both teams, *Fenerbahçe* and *Panathēnaikos*, pledged their
support of the truce initiative in a pre-game ceremony attended by the Greek
and Turkish foreign ministers. When they walked onto the field on their way
to the VIP section, however, they found themselves in the midst of a cauldron
of noise as a small section of visiting Greek fans exchanged insults and
nationalist slogans with Turkish fans. The Greeks even threw broken seats at
the official party.

The Athens 2004 organizing committee, in a gesture meant to express its
support for the truce campaign and popularize it, suggested to the IOC that
the torch relay in 2004 go around the world—indeed, that the Olympic flame
travel through areas of conflict, spreading the message of peace. When Greek
foreign minister George Papandreou spoke of this plan in a session at the
Olympic Academy in 2001, a member of the audience inquired if the relay
route would be designed so as to go through areas in which conflict had
already broken out or, instead, areas of tension, since actual conflict resolution might be beyond the symbolic abilities of the Olympic flame. Papandreou answered that the route was still under discussion, but he conceded
that the project entailed several difficulties.

2003: THE CLOCK IS TICKING

Whatever the attendant complexities of the traditional aspects that were
being introduced into the 2004 games by the host nation, they paled into
insignificance when compared to the very real problem of construction
delays that continued to plague Greece in early 2003, a mere eighteen months
before the games' opening in August 2004. The contrast was exposed dramatically in early 2003. In January, Rogge visited Athens and came away with a
positive impression of the progress of preparations. A highlight of his visit

[13] *Ibid.*

was the unveiling of the 2004 Olympic torch, a design that combined steel with olivewood, simultaneously symbolizing Greek modernity and tradition. Olive trees are, of course, indigenous to Greece and the entire Mediterranean region, and olivewood is laden with symbolism. In fact, according to legend, Athens took its name from the goddess Athena when its citizens chose her gift of an olive tree over Poseidon's offer of a steed.

Another happy and symbol-laden occasion during Rogge's visit came when the organizers announced their plan to give the 2004 torch relay a global scope. Rather than have the shortest relay ever, from Olympia to Athens, the 2004 Olympics would witness the longest ever, with the flame leaving Olympia and circumnavigating the globe for thirty-five days. Beginning in May, the route would pass through all the cities that had hosted summer Olympics in the past, as well as Beijing, the next host, and a number of other cities with "cultural significance," including Cairo, Cape Town, Lausanne, New York, and Nicosia. It would then return to Greece and pass through every prefecture before arriving in Athens in August, for the opening of the games. This megaproject would involve a record number of torchbearers, estimated at ten thousand. The IOC's executive committee approved the plan "unanimously and enthusiastically."[14]

The announcement that Coca-Cola would be underwriting this global relay, along with electronics manufacturer Samsung, the media outlet Eurosport, and Greek construction company Gefyra, went almost unnoticed by the Greek media. Sometime between that moment when the games were awarded to Greece and that other moment when urgency set in about preparations, Greek fears about commercialism evaporated. It probably helped that the Sēmitēs government had launched a drastic program to privatize state companies in the name of Europeanization, triggering growth in the private sector. At least the more extreme expressions of anti-commercialism had evidently gone the same way as the socialist rhetoric of Sēmitēs's predecessors. Considering that Greeks were, until recently, among the leading critics of the games' commercialism, the new, more "realistic" attitude toward paying the piper may signal a sea change in attitudes. This would also mean the disappearance of an important voice within the Olympic movement against the incursions of financial interests. To be sure, the new Greek attitude would not condone the type of fundraising involved in the torch relay

[14]"First ever global torch relay route approved by the IOC," ATHOC press release, February 21, 2003.

of the Los Angeles Olympiad in 1984, but it is hard to see where the Greek side will draw the line in the future. Greece had always countered commercialism by recourse to government and the public sector. But with the gradual erosion of Greece's vast public sector, anti-commercialism may be losing its financial base and could well begin to wither away. There is, finally, the problem of the accelerated pace at which the Olympics are being commercialized. Samaranch's tenure witnessed the enormously successful pursuit of the corporate sector as a major partner in financing the games. But the infusion of corporate capital is altering the games, which is to say that after the question of where the Olympics are headed comes the question of whether Greece can follow.[15]

Six weeks after Rogge's visit, the warm glow of the symbolic use of the torch in the interests of world peace gave way to the cold light of *Realpolitik*. Rogge told an IOC executive meeting in late February about his concerns regarding the delays in construction in Athens and the fear that there would be no time to hold some crucial test events. He also openly worried about the organizers' sluggishness in making security arrangements. Rogge nonetheless explained that all this did not mean that the games would not take place in Athens. Making light of the situation, he concluded by telling reporters that the pace of Athens's preparations reminded him of the music in the movie, *Zorba the Greek*, which began slowly, but picked up speed as it went along.[16] Still, the Greek government reacted strongly, claiming that the work was on schedule, although several press reports pointed to a range of delays; Venizelos responded that things were under control while government spokesman Tēlemachos Chytērēs blamed the latest delays on court challenges that, he said, would be overcome.

Protests by local residents against building some venues, along with criticism of the projects' environmental consequences, represented real, albeit small-scale, opposition to the Olympics from a segment of the Greek public. Clearly, not everyone living in and around Athens accepted the idea of the Olympics as a grand celebration of the spirit of ancient Greece. Ultimately, however, neither local nor environmental protests could stop the Olympiad since the organizers had taken care to present an environmentally responsible case and, wherever they could, use the courts to overcome opposition.

[15]The most comprehensive account of Olympic commercialism, especially under Samaranch, is Barney, Wenn, & Martyn, *Selling the Five Rings* . . . .
[16]Jonathan Fowler, "IOC Chief to Athens: Get Moving," *USA Today*, February 22, 2003.

Indeed, the need to modernize the city's transport networks—to "Euro-peanize" the city, according to some—and the fact that new venues were strategically distributed throughout normally overlooked suburbs of the city, made it difficult to launch sustained and across-the-board opposition to the works or, by extension, to the whole idea that Athens should host the games. In fact, local protests were not the real cause of the delays. The Associated Press, for example, reported that there were still major delays at the sports complex planned for Athens's old airport, which included a basketball arena and fields for softball, baseball, and field hockey. The wrestling venue and the facilities for modern pentathlon and badminton were also far behind schedule. Moreover, at least two of seven planned media villages were in danger of being scrapped, which would result in relocating 600 journalists. There was also no contract to upgrade the swimming facilities, as well as delays in renovating most existing facilities. The IOC was also reportedly worried that a steel-and-glass dome designed by Spanish architect Santiago Calatrava for the main stadium would not be built in time for the test events.[17]

Significantly, while the government protested Rogge's intervention, Angelopoulou took the opportunity to voice her own concerns. ATHOC's president said that no one should have been surprised by Rogge's remarks and that the preparations were close to breaking-point, with a need for everyone to work even harder because any slowdown would jeopardize them.[18] Observers wondered whether her statement was meant as a gentle nudge designed to push the government to accelerate its work. It was no secret that the organizing committee and ministers in charge of preparations had spent weeks bickering over a budget shortfall in "overlay" projects, such as new signage and additional seats and facilities at existing stadiums.

Public, rhetorical nudges are part and parcel of Olympic politics, and it was a sign of the urgency felt by the IOC that another of its members picked up on Rogge's theme, but did so much more bluntly. In March, IOC vice-president Kevin Gosper was reported by Australia's *Herald-Sun* newspaper as saying that the Olympic body was considering installing its own staff in senior positions on the Athens organizing committee because construction work was lagging so far behind. He then added, "Athens runs the risk of being the distressful meat in the sandwich between two great Games (Sydney 2000 and Beijing 2008)." Although he had clearly overstepped the unwritten rules

[17]Associated Press, March 2, 2003.
[18]*www.sport.gr/news/030224/2004.asp.*

of rhetorical pressure, Gosper was playing bad cop to Rogge's good cop, a role played earlier by Richard Pound. Predictably, Athens responded furiously, spearheaded by Angelopoulou, who contacted Rogge and described Gosper's comments as unacceptable. An explanation by the Australian official followed in which he said he'd been misquoted—but the point had been made.

Subsequent developments followed the script: a meeting between government ministers and ATHOC executives presided over by Prime Minister Sēmitēs resolved differences and reaffirmed a common commitment to push ahead. The meeting was, once again, described as having taken place in an "excellent climate and will for cooperation among all parties involved." More specifically, the meeting discussed the IOC's issues and concerns. Reports indicated that the talks included very practical matters such as redirecting the installation of equipment in venues still under construction with an eye to satisfying the games' requirements rather than any longer-term vision of facility use after 2004. In appropriately diplomatic language, it became clear that the government would curtail the involvement of local authorities in site and infrastructure construction across the greater Athens area. The topic of volunteers offered a positive note, as organizers expected the total number of applications for 60,000 places to reach 100,000.[19]

THE RACE TO THE FINISH

With less than twelve months before the games' opening on August 13, 2004, a general pattern to the preparations became obvious. A part of the original infrastructure plans submitted by Greece would not be completed and would be scaled down. In some cases, more makeshift arrangements would be made, such as refurbishing existing facilities rather than building new ones, or holding test events in locations other than those to be used during the games. To what extent these shortcuts would detract from the Olympiad remained unclear. In addition, central issues such as Athens's traffic problem and the inadequate number of hotel beds would be dealt with at the very last minute. Thanks to the relatively extensive powers enjoyed by the state in Greece, one could expect the government to take a more direct role in decisionmaking as time ran out. The IOC would most likely continue to play cat-and-mouse with Athens, applying pressure throughout the final preparations.

[19]"Athens 2004 President presents the preparations for the 2004 Olympic Games to the 115th IOC session," ATHOC press release, July 3, 2003.

When an IOC delegation visited Athens in mid-July 2003, it ascertained that preparations had been stepped up, as entire parts of the city looked like building sites. Crews were working twenty-four hours a day on some venues. The IOC inspectors seemed happy with preparations at the coastal areas of Falēron and Agios Kosmas, slated to host the sailing events, and said significant progress had been made with the two indoor fields at Ellēnikon, the venue for baseball, softball, and basketball, as well as the canoe and slalom events. According to reports, the IOC team expressed some reservations about whether these sites would be ready for test events in January and February 2004. They were also concerned that the Olympic swimming venue, rising up near the main stadium, would not be ready in time for test events in April 2004. The reviewers were reportedly happy with progress made on the rowing center at Schinias and the Olympic complex in Goudi, where the modern pentathlon and badminton events would be held. The major concerns were over renovating Karaïskakēs Stadium and installing the steel-and-glass roof over the main Olympic Stadium, since the IOC worried about the work interfering with the test events scheduled for both venues. As the IOC delegation departed, a sense that everything would be ready, albeit at the last moment, prevailed through the city, although nobody wished to entertain the possibility of an emergency derailing preparations.

It is worth remembering that the 2004 Olympiad's organizational aspects will not be the sole factors defining its success or failure, and that tradition-laden games, and their effectiveness, will also determine the ways they are experienced and remembered. Rogge has noted several times that Athens can be expected to do only so much in terms of the technical aspects of the games, given the realities and long history of the modern Olympic landscape—the troubled landscape, he could have added. What Athens can offer instead is history and tradition, the IOC president has said many times. It is clear that the Greek hosts will spare no effort to invoke the games' classical roots and employ symbols to remind the world of this institution's traditions. A good example of ATHOC's commitment to impart an ancient Greek flavor to the 2004 Olympics is its successful effort to redesign the medals awarded in each event. Since 1928, the gold, silver, and bronze medals have depicted a permanent logo on one side and a design by the host city on the other. The IOC's permanent logo included a structure strongly resembling Rome's Colosseum, which the Greeks wished to replace with an ancient Greek structure. The Greeks succeeded in gaining the IOC's approval to do so in July 2003. Needless to say, the explanations offered by Angelopoulou and Nikolaou glossed over the replacement of a Roman image with a Greek one and emphasized the fact that the old design showed the goddess Nike seated next to the exterior of the Colosseum-like building, while, in reality, Nike was always shown in Greek antiquity as flying.

In presenting the new medal designs, Angelopoulou explained that Nike was worshipped as the personification of victory in the ancient stadium as well as on the ancient battlefield, with Zeus sending her to earth to crown winners. Historical research, she said, showed that the goddess was always represented as "winged," full of movement and dynamism, descending from heaven either to sing praises for a victory, or offer libations, or crown a winner. The best-known of several statues and vases in which the goddess is represented in this way is, of course, the winged *Nike* of Samothrace in the Louvre, she added. The new design corrected this oversight, therefore, by depicting Nike flying into a stadium—which, in this case, happened to be the Panathenaic Stadium in Athens, site of the 1896 games.[20]

There were other controversies, however. A particularly strange one ensued over the uncomfortable encounter between the oldest sporting institution in the world and the world's oldest profession. The municipality of Athens announced that it would be regulating the city's brothels in anticipation of the Olympiad, but the plan was misunderstood as a proposal to increase prostitution rather than clamp down on unlicensed brothels in anticipation of the rise in demand for sexual services that has been evident at every recent Olympiad. The Church of Greece protested, as did some Athens prostitutes (in a small demonstration outside a government building). The uproar took on an international dimension when Sweden's deputy prime minister and equality minister, Margareta Winberg, persuaded fellow ministers in Norway, Finland, Iceland, Estonia, Latvia, and Lithuania to join her in expressing their "abhorrence" at the implied exploitation of women. Denmark declined to sign on, describing the protest as "childish." Meanwhile, the Athens organizing committee prudently declined to comment, leaving the municipality to try and explain itself—as it did, quite convincingly, under Mayor Dora Bakogiannē, the first woman ever elected to the post (and a conservative at that).

The media circus over the brothels had been preceded by claims that

---

[20]"Athens 2004 President presented in Prague the Medals for the 2004 Olympic Games," ATHOC press release, July 2, 2003.

organizers were putting pressure on municipal authorities in and around Athens to do something "drastic" with the Greek capital's many stray dogs, whose presence threatened the country's image (if not quite the smooth running of the games). Meanwhile—and much more relevantly—when certain Olympic test events held in August 2003 ran into problems, observers became even more skeptical about the 2004 games. These events included rowing, archery, canoe/kayak, beach volleyball, cycling, and equestrian competitions staged at the venues that would host the respective Olympic contests the following year. The biggest problems occurred in connection with the rowing event at Schinias, which was, in fact, the world junior championship in the sport. Before the event even began, the eighty-strong German team suffered salmonella poisoning at its hotel in the nearby town of Nea Makrē and had to drop out of the competition. Then, the second day of races had to be canceled because of very strong seasonal northerly winds (known as *meltemia*) blowing that day. Since the Schinias rowing site was newly constructed, it raised questions about the quality of planning that had gone into the project. There were also difficulties because of wind at the archery event held in the Panathenaic Stadium. At a press conference, representatives of the IOC, ATHOC, and the rowing federation all defended the facility at Schinias and praised its state-of-the-art functionality.[21] But the opposition daily *Kathimerini* remained unconvinced, writing the next day that the several boats capsized by the wind had made for a shipwrecked test event. The normally staid conservative newspaper playfully wondered whether all that had happened was the "revenge" of the warriors of Marathon for the organizers' hubris in building a rowing facility on the site of the ancient battle.[22]

Against the background of a chorus of criticism by the international media, the IOC stepped in and praised the organizing committee for its "successful running of the test events." IOC member Denis Oswald, speaking at a press conference in Athens, said that the IOC was satisfied with the committee's work, as well as with that of municipal and national authorities. He noted the organizers' flexibility in responding to problems that arose and offering solutions, and he also praised the enthusiasm and commitment of the Greek volunteers.[23] Regarding the volunteers, praising them was the least

[21]Geōrgios Rousakēs, "Meltemi . . . aisiodoxias ["A *Meltemi* of Optimism"], *Ta Nea* August 8, 2003.

[22]"Ē ekdikēsē tōn Marathōnomachōn" ["The Revenge of the Marathon Warriors"], *Kathimerini*, August 8, 2003.

[23]IOC press release, August 19, 2003.

he could have done, as they had suffered through a major breakdown in their transportation arrangements.

In what was turning into a pattern in the fall of 2003, the IOC again strongly backed ATHOC in the wake of speculation in the international press about security "lapses" in Athens that threatened the smooth running of the 2004 games. Allegations that the organizers were falling short of introducing adequate security defenses against a possible terrorist attack during the Olympics had been standard fare in press reports from the time Athens had won the games. Inevitably, as concerns about preparations for the games increased with only a year left before the opening, security concerns also escalated. In Australia, a country whose media consistently covered the Athens preparations, a newspaper report in mid-August 2003, as the countdown to the opening day of the 2004 games had passed the 365-day mark, spoke about delays in preparations and lax security measures.[24] In late September, the *Washington Post* carried an extremely critical article on security in Athens on its front page. The report claimed that "an August [security] test revealed serious, if correctable, deficiencies." The piece went on to cite disparaging remarks by American and Israeli analysts and officials about the Greek attitude toward security. For some of those interviewed, there was, apparently, a geographical determinism to Greece's problems, which were therefore inherent, reinforced by unspecified poor policing of its borders. As the article put it, "With a long coastline dotted with scores of islands, close proximity to the Balkans [*sic*] and lax immigration policies, Greece has long had a reputation as a haven for terrorists."[25]

Before examining the inevitably vigorous rebuttals issued in Athens, it may be useful to pause and consider the motives behind the media criticism, which was not limited to the stories mentioned above. Putting aside the possibility that the alleged security lapses were leaked to the press by parties seeking to pressure the organizers into taking more measures (or purchasing more surveillance equipment), one has to weigh the media's commercial interests. The Olympics are big business, not least for the media. With public interest in the events rising steadily in the months preceding the games, the media inevitably seek to satisfy the demand for stories. It was at Mexico City in 1968 that Roone Arledge, the legendary producer for ABC Sports

[24]Peter Fray, "Athens lunges towards the finishing line," *Sydney Morning Herald*, August 13, 2003.
[25]Gregory L. Vistica, "For Athens Olympics, A Security Gap: Tests Show Porous Defenses, Reports Cite Planning Breakdowns," *Washington Post*, September 27, 2003.

(and, later, News), revolutionized television coverage of the Olympics by approaching the event not merely as a news story but as a mixture of news, entertainment, high drama, and stories focused on the personalities of the athletes. Arledge ultimately became the first television producer to receive the Olympic Order, awarded by the IOC's executive board to someone who has rendered outstanding services to the Olympic cause. This new way of depicting the Olympics reached new heights with documentary filmmaker Bud Greenspan, whose work has been described as "wrapping heart-touching, if somewhat schmaltzy, tales of Olympic bravery around up-close footage."[26] The print medium was soon echoing this approach to the games, and it is not surprising that its treatment of the slow-moving preparations in Athens has been embellished and exaggerated. In the haste to report boats capsizing because of *meltemia* lashing the facility at Schinias, for example, many writers conveniently forgot that Sydney had experienced similar mishaps during its test events, including a whale swimming into the sailing course and low-flying jets screaming over an equestrian event, terrifying the horses.

ATHOC, supported by the IOC, responded instantly to media charges. In its press release, it declared that the security effort during the test events "was recognized with very positive comments by the IOC president, in recent statements, by all the Olympic Movement, as well as by the US secretary of state and the US ambassador in Athens." And it added, forcefully: "Beyond any fantastic scenarios and hyperbole there is only one reality: Greece is preparing with great effort to organize totally safe Olympic Games in 2004."[27] Rogge lent ATHOC a helping hand a few days later when he told reporters he believed the Athens games would be "exemplary."[28] On October 16, Angelopoulou made a public presentation of the games' security program jointly with the ministry of public order and the Greek police. ATHOC's president explained that, while security was a major priority for her committee, ATHOC did not have sole responsibility for it, since it was collaborating with the IOC, the ministry of public order, and the Greek police, as well as with several other countries. She mentioned a consortium of seven nations: Australia, France, Germany, Israel, Spain, the United Kingdom, and the

---

[26]Bob Ford, "Olympics Video Merits A Gold in Sugarcoating," *Philadelphia Inquirer*, December 18, 1998.

[27]"ATHOC Responds to Washington Post's Criticism Over Games' Security," Athens News Agency, September 28, 2003.

[28]"Culture Minister and IOC President Discuss Olympic Games Preparations," Athens News Agency, October 3, 2003.

United States. This collaboration, she concluded, made for an "unprecedented level of international cooperation on Olympic Security."[29]

Angelopoulou's invocation of a collective, international responsibility for security, and the IOC's immediate support on that score, points to an eleventh-hour alliance between Athens and Lausanne. We should bear in mind that ultimately the IOC is as invested in the success of the XXVIIIth Olympiad as are the organizers and host nation. By mid-October 2003, with three hundred days left until the opening of the games, it was too late to adopt the Samaranch scare tactics and pull out a yellow card or even threaten the Greeks with a red card that would signal a move to a different venue. As time runs out, it is probably Avery Brundage's statement that "the Games must go on!"—uttered in the wake of the terrorist attack in Munich in 1972—that current IOC head Jacques Rogge has in mind. As they can only go on in Athens at this point, the IOC's tactic in the fall of 2003 was to keep any real worries away from the public eye and limit its publicly expressed concerns to nonessential aspects of the preparations, such as completing the roof on the Olympic Stadium.

While ATHOC no longer had to worry about public criticism from the IOC, the fall of 2003 brought a newly sharpened form of domestic censure. For most of the period since 1997, when Greece was awarded the games, New Democracy had gravitated between acknowledging their "national importance" and maintaining a critical stance toward the PASOK government's deficiencies in preparing for them. But with national elections on the horizon, the party's leader, Kōstas Karamanlēs (the late Greek president's nephew), and the head of its "section" on the Olympics, deputy Fanē Pallē-Petralia (who is also an HOC member), amplified their criticisms, prompting the pro-New Democracy press to follow suit. In a series of statements issued between early September and mid-October 2003, Petralia engaged in an across-the-board partisan critique of the government, accusing it of being responsible for the lag in preparations, over-budgeting, and exploiting the games for political purposes.[30]

[29]ATHOC press release, October 16, 2003.

[30]See, for example, "Dēlōsē tēs ypeuthynou tou tomea Olympiakōn Agōnōn kas Pallē-Petralia schetika me tēn poreia tēs Olympiakēs proetoimasias" ["Statement of the Head of the Olympic Games Section, Mrs. Pallē-Petralia, Regarding the Course of Olympic Preparations"], New Democracy press release, September 3, 2003, and "Dēlōsē tēs ypeuthynou tou tomea Olympiakōn Agōnōn kas Pallē-Petralia anaferomenē stēn episkepsē tou prōthypourgou sto kleisto gymnastērio tēs Nikaias" ["Statement of the Head of the Olympic Games Section, Mrs. Pallē-Petralia, in Reference to the Prime Minister's Visit to the Indoor Sports Arena in Nikaia"], New Democracy press release, October 10, 2003.

The government and ATHOC, backed by the IOC, could afford to ignore the barrage of New Democracy press releases, but they had to confront the negative publicity in the international press regarding preparations. Criticism abroad cut deeply in a country that was seeking international stature by hosting the Olympics. Publicly at least, the ministry of culture and ATHOC appeared to be unperturbed, blaming what they described as (unspecified) "foreign interests" and "agendas." There was obviously some consternation privately, as indicated by the forceful and comprehensive statement on security that Angelopoulou had made in mid-October. The organizers were also careful to continue to produce good news about the preparations, as, for example, when Secretary-General Kofi Annan warmly welcomed the resolution submitted by Greece to the United Nations in late September calling for a truce during the 2004 Olympics.

In the end, as the media around the world enjoy a field day with all the stories about the wide range of unresolved issues, the clock continues to tick for Athens. Very soon, roughly 17,000 athletes and official escorts, 8,000 members of the so-called Olympic family, 3,000 judges and referees, 20,000 journalists, and two million visitors will arrive in Greece's capital for the XXVIIIth Olympiad. It will be the ultimate test of Greece's ability to balance an Olympics steeped in tradition with one run efficiently. Only if it satisfies the prerequisites of games run more or less according to the specifications of the modern, electronic age will the organizers' promotion of ancient Greek symbolism during the twenty-eighth Olympics in Athens in August 2004 help contemporary Greece preserve its privileged place in the Olympic movement of the twenty-first century.

AFTERWORD

THE 2004 OLYMPIAD is a major turning-point in the relationship between Greece and the Olympic movement. It also constitutes an unusually significant moment in the relations of both the country and the movement to the ancient origins of the Olympic Games, especially because contemporary Greece has inherited—which is to say is the custodian of—the physical space in which the ancient culture that produced the Olympics flourished. To examine how these multiple relationships have unfolded since the first modern Olympiad in Athens in 1896 is to appreciate the enormous difficulties in maintaining a balance among them all.

The Greek role, which has been the focus of this study, shows both consistency and fluctuation over time. The constant has been Greece's wish to realize a dual identity: heir to ancient Greece on the one hand, and modern, developed, "European" country on the other. This has meant that the temptation to overplay the advantages of tradition has always been curbed by the need to satisfy the requirements of modernity. It has not been easy to keep this balance. Initially, the Greek claim to hosting the Olympics permanently led to tension between Baron Pierre de Coubertin and Athens. As a result, modern Greece fell out of the Olympic movement's good graces until the global disaster of the First World War made the movement realize how desperately it needed to return to the games' ancient roots if it were to survive. Coubertin then turned to ritual, tradition, and a celebration of the games' ancient heritage in order to bolster the Olympics. By the interwar period, Greece had abandoned its claims to become the permanent site of the Olympic Games, which meant that Coubertin could call upon the modern Greeks to participate in—and therefore legitimize—the invocation of the ancient Olympics. Greece was only too happy to oblige at a time when its social tensions threatened to upset the country's established order. Thus, recourse to the idea of the continuity between modern Greece and its ancient, glorious past functioned as a "unifying" force (or as a disorienting one, for many Greeks at least) and, naturally, as a counter-discourse to modernist and socialist challenges to the status quo.

The period between the two world wars witnessed the emergence of the central role of ancient Greek symbols in the elaborate choreography of ceremonial that is now such an intrinsic part of the summer and winter Olympics. The lighting of the torch in Olympia followed by the relay to the host city; the burning of the Olympic flame at the stadium throughout the games; the ancient Greek images portrayed on the posters, stamps, and official publications of each Olympiad; the entrance of the Greek flag and team at the head of all other teams in the opening ceremony: all this *posturing* was introduced during the interwar years. Admittedly, some ceremonial archaizing did not survive, such as the so-called Classical Games of the 1930s, but that was only because it took time to learn that antiquity was best exploited through metaphor and symbol rather than literally and reflexively.

The Nazi embrace of the Olympics and of their ancient origins, undoubtedly the Olympic movement's political and moral nadir, served—in only apparent paradox—to strengthen the role of modern Greece in the games. The German organizers went out of their way to associate the Berlin games in 1936 with the traditions of Greek antiquity. The torch-lighting followed by the relay were the most spectacular rituals introduced by the organizers. The IOC, and the HOC, not only approved of but collaborated with this manifest ideological appropriation, choosing to ignore its sinister political connotations.

The period following the Second World War eventually brought a different sense of tradition, focused more on the actual physical space of Olympia rather than on ideological assumptions about the meaning of antiquity. But even this felicitous situation for Greece did not last long because the Olympic movement was weakened by disputes rooted in the Cold War and the transformation of sport into entertainment. Those trends distanced the games from their purportedly pure origins in antiquity and opened the door for Greece's reappearance as the guardian of authentic Olympic tradition. In 1976, Greece volunteered to be the games' permanent home, and even considered locating the necessary facilities near or around Olympia. The IOC responded to this proposal almost as coolly as it had in 1896, although even more international voices were raised in favor of the Greek proposal this time than in the previous century.

After almost a decade of uncertainty, the Olympics survived not because of the sanctuary offered to them by the Greeks in Olympia but because the IOC chose to sell the games to corporate capital, following the success of the first corporate-funded games in Los Angeles in 1984. Wrongly assuming that tradition still mattered, Greece's bid for the centennial games of 1996 offered only history, but little organizational efficiency; under the circumstances, it was inevitable that it would lose out to Atlanta's corporate bid. The weaknesses of the Atlanta Olympiad gave Greece a new lease on life; the country finally gained the right to host the 2004 games by offering technocracy as well as tradition.

The 2004 Athens Olympiad involves the same pitfalls for Greece's relationship with the international Olympic movement that it has faced since 1896. Greece has to balance celebrating—as only it can do—the games' heritage with ensuring that they run efficiently: an enormous task considering the projected last-minute completion of preparations. Ultimately, holding the games in Athens in 2004 challenges Greece to find the right equilibrium between past and present.

* * *

The success or shortcomings of the Athens Olympiad are not the sole defining criteria of Greece's future role in the Olympic movement, however, because Greece's part is much broader than administering the actual XXVIIIth Olympiad in August 2004. Greece's responsibility in—and to—the movement is to uphold the invented tradition of continuity between the modern games and the ancient ones. The international Olympic movement that fosters this myth has proven to be an extremely durable institution. If nothing else, it has survived the twentieth century. That is, two world wars; the Cold War; fascism, Nazism, and Stalinism; and nationalist ideologies so grotesque that they remain indistinguishable from genocide and ethnic cleansing: all of these humanly created horrors specifically aimed at destroying the kind of human universalism the Olympics sought to cultivate. In our own day, the resonance of the Olympics' ancient origins—a siren song for so many nineteenth-century romantics—remains almost as powerful as ever. Despite a supposedly countercultural hegemony in late twentieth- and early twenty-first-century life—which includes, prominently, the decline of classicism and even the "killing" of Homer—the truth is that the world retains its fascination with the ancient (or at least mystical) origins of the Olympics, and continues to respond to the reproduction of Coubertin's invented tradition. The answer to the question, "Who needs the Greeks?" is thus a simple one: the Olympic Games.

The Olympic movement has not only survived, it has changed radically through the past century—which is why it needs to hold on to ancient Olympia, even if only symbolically. In the face of political exigencies, financial need, and, perhaps most relevantly, the prospects of enormous financial gain, the purity of the Olympics (which, in any case, never existed in the *real* ancient past) has, of course, been compromised. It is not surprising, however, that even the Nazis tried to appropriate Greek antiquity, or that the International Olympic Academy was established in Olympia at the height of the Cold War. IOC president Jacques Rogge has responded to questions about the viability of the games in Athens by pointing out that, whatever happens, they will be steeped in their historical origins.

Which brings us back to modern Greece, and to its willingness to act out the mythological script it has been called to follow by the international Olympic movement, watched approvingly by millions of people around the world who are still fascinated by the Olympics and their ancient origins. Ever since its establishment almost two centuries ago, modern Greece has merged a deeply seated sense of continuity with ancient Greece into an equally deeply felt belief that it is part of a "civilized" (that is, developed) Europe. Coubertin invited Greeks to play both roles in the context of the international Olympic movement; in doing so, he inflated the collective ego of a proud but marginalized, and small, European nation. Coubertin himself became the first victim of the Greeks' overzealousness; ultimately, however, the Greeks found their appropriate place as the guardians of tradition, even to Coubertin's satisfaction.

Eventually, Greece grew tired with its limited role as curator of ancient Olympic traditions while the games went from crisis to crisis in the postwar era, and it pressed its claims to protect not only the Olympic past but its present. But these claims required that the country produce *bona fides* well beyond the ability to preserve the ancient site at Olympia or organize solemn torch-lighting ceremonies. Above all, Greece had to guarantee the efficiency and technological sophistication required to host contemporary games. It took a while for the international community to be persuaded.

Upon winning the 2004 games, Greece promptly forgot why, and how, it did. Its officials carelessly, naively, announced a no-frills, back-to-the-ancient-basics Olympiad. Perhaps one can't blame these proud heirs to antiquity for reacting instinctively like curators of ancient relics who are suddenly thrust into the international limelight. But the IOC would have none of that—and almost overnight, a new Greek rhetoric of technological capabilities and pragmatic understanding of the enormous financial burdens involved in hosting the games replaced any serious talk about "pure" Olympics. Commercialism and corporate capital, which the Greeks had complained about so loudly in the past, suddenly became integral parts of the preparations. In the past, Greeks had always tempered their modernizing and Europeanizing tendencies with an aversion to corporate and unbridled capitalism (a stance they could afford thanks to the traditionally central roles of the state and public sector in Greek society). This attitude appears to be melting away now, and the embrace of corporate sponsorship is now justified as yet another way for Greece to adapt to the demands of modernity. With the economy on a steady but painful road to privatization, and brand-name consumerism pervasive in Greek society, no one seems to mind.

Still, in an attempt to salvage some of its pride in its past, and live up to its initial declarations, Greece included certain purportedly "pure" elements in its Olympic preparations. The campaign to promote an Olympic truce, a project endorsed by the IOC (albeit halfheartedly), has gained momentum. Its practical results remain to be seen, but no one can fault the Greeks for trying to turn this ideal into something more tangible. By contrast, the so-called Cultural Olympiad, a series of artistic events to celebrate human creativity on an international scale, has buckled under the weight of its own pretensions.

A successful Olympiad requires not only good organization, but also large crowds at hand to cheer on the athletes and confirm the popularity of the competitions. When they were pursuing the games, former IOC head Juan Antonio Samaranch had told the Greeks that they had to improve their performance in sport itself. People will always turn out to cheer for the home team, and Samaranch was laying the ground for more Greek athletes in major sports, as well as for Greek teams competing in sports with relatively little following in Greece. Here, the Greeks have surprised even themselves: thanks to a sustained development program over the past couple of decades, Greece has become a major international force in several track-and-field events, as well as in weightlifting and a number of other individual and team sports. Greece's willingness to measure itself against the most developed countries in the world has allowed it to embrace all types of sports, unfamiliar to its people until now but part of Olympic competition. In an ironic twist, a former US military base's recreational diamond became the field of dreams for the fledgling sport of Greek baseball. Before it was closed a few years ago, the base had been the object of vehement political protests, along with other US military facilities in the country. That a former US ambassador in Athens divided his time during his tenure between tackling political expressions of anti-Americanism and assisting the growth of Greek baseball is emblematic of how much the Olympic connection is transforming Greece.

The games *will* go on, although they will experience reforms,[1] but as long as the Olympic movement needs the ideological legitimacy provided by ancient traditions, Greece will remain an important part of it. The games will go on simply because there are too many interests tied up in their preservation, and, until now at least, modernity and change have not precluded the celebration of ancient origins. Let us also not forget the movement's dedicated foot-soldiers, who gather every summer at the International Olympic Academy, or the (tens? hundreds? of) millions of people around the world: all of them still believe, somehow, that the institution of the Olympic Games is a vehicle for containing, if not reversing, the gross excesses of modern sport. And, finally, of course, there is contemporary Greece itself: its contribution to the Olympic movement is a given because the games are part of the heritage of the classical past, and thus, one way or another, a core element of Greek identity.

[1]See John A. Lucas, *Future of the Olympic Games,* Champaign, Human Kinetics, 1992.

The International Olympic Movement and its Governing Structure

THE INTERNATIONAL OLYMPIC COMMITTEE (IOC) is an international, nongovernmental, not-for-profit organization, and the Olympic movement's supreme authority, founded by Baron Pierre de Coubertin on June 23, 1894. The IOC organizes the Olympic Games, promotes the principles of Olympism, and chooses the cities that host the games. The IOC's members are individuals who act as its representatives in their respective countries, and *not* as delegates of their country within the IOC. There are currently 125 members, as well as 21 honorary members and four "honor" members. The members meet annually at the IOC session. The executive board, founded in 1921, comprises the IOC president, four vice-presidents, and ten other members. The IOC's members elect the president by secret ballot.

PRESIDENTS OF THE IOC

Dēmētrios Vikelas, Greece, 1894–1896
Pierre de Coubertin, France, 1896–1925
Henri de Baillet-Latour, Belgium, 1925–1942
J. Sigfrid Edström, Sweden, 1942–1952
Avery Brundage, United States, 1952–1972
Lord [Michael Morris] Killanin, Ireland, 1972–1980
Juan Antonio Samaranch, Spain, 1980–2001
Jacques Rogge, Belgium, 2001 to the present

GREEK IOC MEMBERS

Dēmētrios Vikelas, 1894–1899
Alexandros Merkatēs, 1899–1925
Geōrgios Averōf, 1925–1930
Nikolaos Politēs, 1930–1933
Angelos Volanakēs, 1933–1963 (he had served earlier as a member from
    Egypt)
Iōannēs Ketseas, 1946–1965
Constantine of Greece, 1963–1974 ("honor" member thereafter)
Pyrros Lappas, 1965–1980
Epameinōndas Petralias, 1975–1977
Nikolaos Nēsiōtēs, 1978–1986
Nikos Filaretos, 1981 to the present
Lambēs Nikolaou, 1986 to the present

The NATIONAL OLYMPIC COMMITTEES (NOCs) promote the basic principles of the Olympic movement within each nation. NOCs work toward developing athletes and sport in their respective countries, and are responsible for sending the national teams to the Olympics. The NOCs also supervise the preliminary selection of potential bid cities: a candidate city must first win the selection process of its own country's NOC before it can compete against those of other countries.

The ORGANIZING COMMITTEE OF THE OLYMPIC GAMES (OCOG) is responsible for preparing and organizing the Olympic Games in each city. It is formed by the country's NOC, effectively in collaboration with the IOC and the respective nation's government. After it is formed, it adopts its own name (Athens 2004 Organizing Committee, for example), communicates directly with the IOC, and ceases to function with the completion of the Olympiad it has organized.

The INTERNATIONAL FEDERATIONS (IFs) are international, non-governmental organizations that administer one or more sports globally and are recognized as such by the IOC. The national federations that administer these same sports in their respective countries are affiliated to the IFs, which are independent of the IOC but are obliged to ensure that their statutes, practices, and activities conform to the Olympic Charter.

The OLYMPIC CHARTER is the codification of the IOC's "Fundamental Principles, Rules and By-laws." It governs the organization and running of the Olympic movement and sets the conditions for celebrating the Olympic Games. It defines Olympism as "a philosophy of life, exalting and combining in a balanced whole the qualities of body, will and mind. Blending sport with culture and education, Olympism seeks to create a way of life based on the joy found in effort, the educational value of good example and respect for universal fundamental ethical principles."

Source: "Organisation," http://www.olympic.org/uk/organisation/index_uk.asp

APPENDIX 2

THE HELLENIC OLYMPIC COMMITTEE

T HE HELLENIC OLYMPIC COMMITTEE dates its origins to November 1894, when a committee met to discuss the organization of the 1896 Athens Olympiad. The honorary chairmen were Crown Prince Constantine and Pierre de Coubertin, who was visiting Athens at the time. Its deliberations were inconclusive, however, and a royal decree in January 1895 established a new committee that met the same month. In 1899, the government reconstituted the group, known as the *Epitropē Olympiakōn Agōnōn* (Olympic Games Committee), as a permanent body. The committee was responsible for organizing the so-called interim Olympic Games held in Athens in 1906. The HOC administers the torch-lighting ceremony at Olympia, a feature of the summer Olympics since 1936 and of the winter Olympics since 1964. In 2000, the committee changed its name to *Ellēnikē Olympiakē Epitropē* (Hellenic Olympic Committee).

HOC PRESIDENTS

Crown Prince Constantine 1895, 1899–1913 (assumed the throne in 1913)
Crown Prince George, 1914–1917
Miltiadēs Negropontēs, 1918–1920
Crown Prince George, 1921–1922; as King George II, 1922–1923
Geōrgios Averōf, 1924–1930
Iōannēs Drosopoulos, 1930–1936
Crown Prince Paul, 1936–1948; as King Paul I, 1948–1952
Kōnstantinos Geōrgakopoulos and Iōannēs Ketseas, 1953–1954
Crown Prince Constantine, 1955–1964
Princess Irene, 1965–1968
Theodosios Papathanasiadēs, 1969–1973
Spyridōn Vellianitēs, 1973–1974

Apostolos Nikolaidēs, 1974–1976
Geōrgios "Tzōrtzēs" Athanasiadēs, 1976–1983
Angelos Lembesēs, 1983–1984
Antōnios Tzikas, 1993–1996
Lambēs Nikolaou, 1985–1992 and 1997 to the present

HOC General Secretaries

The HOC's general secretary has always been a critical post, especially before 1974, when the positions of committee president and vice-president were filled *ex officio* by the head of state or a government official.

Spyridōn Lambros, 1901–1917
Michaēl Rinopoulos, 1918–1921, and 1924–1935
Geōrgios Streit, 1921–1923
Iōannēs Ketseas, 1935–1953
Vasileios Leōntopoulos, 1953–1960
Pyrros Lappas, 1961–1968
Epameinōndas Petralias, 1969–1974
Nikos Filaretos, 1974–1984
Geōrgios Vechos, 1985–1988
Dionysēs Gangas, 1993–1996
Dēmētrēs Diathesopoulos, 1989–1992 and 1997 to the present

Source: "History of the HOC," http://www.hoc.gr/en/info/history.asp.

APPENDIX 3

MEDALS WON BY GREEK ATHLETES

ATHENS, 1896

Silver medals (first place): 10
Cycling, marathon: Aristeidēs Kōnstantinidēs
Fencing, sportsmen's saber: Iōannēs Geōrgiadēs
Fencing masters' foil: Leōnidas Pyrgos
Gymnastics, rings: Iōannēs Mētropoulos
Gymnastics, rope climbing: Nikolaos Andriakopoulos
Shooting, pistol at 25 meters: Iōannēs Frangoudēs
Shooting, rifle, at 200 meters: Pantelēs Karasevdas
Shooting, rifle, at 300 meters: Geōrgios Orfanidēs
Swimming, sailors' 100 meters: Iōannēs Malokinēs
Track and field, marathon: Spyros Louēs

Bronze Medals (second place): 18
Cycling, one-lap race: Stamatios Nikolopoulos
Cycling, two kilometers: Stamatios Nikolopoulos
Cycling, 100 kilometers: Geōrgios Kōlettēs
Fencing, sportsmen's saber: Tēlemachos Karakalos
Gymnastics, horizontal and parallel bars, team event: Nikolaos
    Andriakopoulos, Spyros Athanasopoulos, Petros Persakēs,
    Thōmas Xenakēs
Gymnastics, rope climbing: Thōmas Xenakēs
Shooting, pistol at 25 meters: Geōrgios Orphanidēs
Shooting, rifle at 200 meters: Panagiōtēs Paulidēs
Shooting, rifle at 300 meters: Iōannēs Frangoudēs
Swimming, 500 meters freestyle: Panagiōtēs Pepanos
Swimming, 1,200 meters: Iōannēs Andreou
Swimming, sailors' 100 meters: Spyridōn Chazapēs
Tennis, men's singles: Dēmētrios Kasdaglēs

Tennis, men's doubles: Dēmētrios Kasdaglēs and Dēmētrios Petrokokkinos
Track and field, discus throw: Panagiōtēs Paraskeuopoulos
Track and field, shot put: Miltiadēs Gouskos
Track and field, marathon: Charilaos Vasilakos
Wrestling, Greco-Roman: Geōrgios Tsitas

Third place: 18
Fencing, saber: Periclēs Pierakos-Mauromichalēs
Gymnastics, horizontal bar: Petros Messas
Gymnastics, rings: Petros Persakēs
Gymnastics, vaulting horse: Aristovoulos Petmezas
Gymnastics, parallel bars, team event: Iōannēs Chrysafēs, Philippos
    Karvelas, Dēmētrios Loundras, Iōannēs Mētropoulos
Shooting, military revolver: Nikolaos Morakēs
Shooting, pistol at 25 meters: Nikolaos Maurakēs
Shooting, rifle, at 200 meters: Nikolaos Trikoupēs
Swimming, 500 meters: Eustathios Chōrafas
Swimming, 1,200 meters: Eustathios Chōrafas
Track and field, men's 800 meters: Dēmētrios Golemēs
Track and field, marathon: Spyros Belokas
Track and field, pole vault: shared by Euangelos Damaskos and Iōannēs
    Theodōropoulos
Track and field, shot put: Geōrgios Papasiderēs
Track and field, triple jump: Iōannēs Persakēs
Weightlifting: Sōtērios Versēs
Weightlifting, single-handed: Alexandros Nikolopoulos
Wrestling, Greco-Roman: Stefanos Chrēstopoulos

St Louis, 1904

Gold medals: 1
Weightlifting, two-handed lift: Periclēs Kakousēs

Bronze medals: 1
Track and field, discus throw: Nikolaos Geōrgantas

INTERIM OLYMPICS, ATHENS, 1906

Figures vary regarding these games because the Greek hosts counted Greeks living in the Ottoman empire, British-ruled Cyprus, and Egypt as Greeks. Some of these competed as members of the city-based teams of Izmir and Thessalonikē. Finally, there also was an unusually broad range of events.

Gold: 8
Fencing, saber, individual, one hit: Iōannēs Georgiadēs
Gymnastics, rope climbing: Geōrgios Alimprantēs
Rowing and sculling, sixteen-man naval rowboats: Crew of naval cadet
   school at Poros (Iōannēs Agmimēs, Andreas Drivas, Iōannēs Geōrgas,
   Iōannēs Kairarēs, Dēmētrios Kakousēs, Paulos Karagiozēs, Kōnstantinos
   Kefalas, Iōannēs Lafiōtēs, Iōannēs Loukas, Isidōros Michas, Argos
   Mylōnas, Michaēl Mouratēs, Michaēl Sōkos, Iōannēs Pilourēs, Chrēstos
   Tsirigōtakēs, Petros Veliōtēs [cox])
Shooting, pistol at 25 meters: Geōrgios Orphanidēs
Shooting, dueling pistol at 25 meters: Kōnstantinos Skarlatos
Tennis, ladies' singles: Esmē Smyrniōtē
Track and field, stone throw: Nikolaos Geōrgantas
Weightlifting, two-handed clean-and-jerk: Dēmētrios Tofalos

Silver: 13
Fencing, saber, team event: Iōannēs Geōrgiadēs, Triantafyllos
   Kordogiannēs, Menelaos Sakorafos, Chrēstos Zorbas
Fencing, saber for masters, individual: Iōannēs Raïsēs
Rowing and sculling, six-man naval rowing boats with coxswain: Crew of
   warship *Spetsai* (Dēmētrios Balourdos, Dēmētrios Daēs, Nikolaos
   Dekavalas, Nikolaos Karsouvas, Paulos Kypreos, Spyros Vesalas,
   Kōnstantinos Misonginēs [cox])
Rowing and sculling, sixteen-man naval rowing boats: Crew of warship *Ydra*
   (Stamatios Diomataras, Iōannēs Dolas, Iōannēs Fasilēs, Iōannēs Grypeos,
   Euangelos Chaldeos, Euangelos Kanarakēs, Michaēl Katsoulēs, S.
   Lemonēs, Geōrgios Nikoloutsos, Kōnstantinos Niōtēs, Nikolaos Stergiou,
   Iōannēs Tsirakēs, Kōnstantinos Papagiannoulēs, Iōannēs Papapanagiōtou,
   Petros Pterneas, Xenofōn Stellas, Iōannēs Milakas [cox])
Shooting, clay trap, single shot: Iōannēs Peridēs
Shooting, clay trap, double shot: Anastasios Metaxas

Shooting, military revolver at 20 meters: Alexandros Theofylakēs
Tennis, gentlemen's doubles: Iōannēs Ballēs and Xenofōn Kasdaglēs
Tennis, ladies' singles: Sofia Marinou
Tennis, mixed doubles: Geōrgios Smyrniōtēs and Sofia Marinou
Track and field, discus throw, freestyle: Nikolaos Geōrgantas
Track and field, discus throw, Greek-style: Nikolaos Geōrgantas
Track and field, tug-of-war: *Peiraïkos Syndesmos* team representing Greece
  (Kōnstantinos Lazaros, Spyros Lazaros, Geōrgios Papachrēstou,
  Geōrgios Psachos, Vaseilios Psachos, Panagiōtēs Trivoulidēs, Antōnios
  Tsitas, Spyros Vellas)

Bronze: 13
Fencing, épée for masters, individual: Iōannēs Raïsēs
Soccer: Thessalonikē team (Giōrgios Vaporēs [goalkeeper], Nikolaos
  Pindos, Antōnios Tegos [fullbacks], Iōannēs Kyrou, Geōrgios Sōtēriadēs
  [halfbacks], Iōannēs Abbot, Antōnios Karagiōnidēs, Dēmētrios
  Michitsopoulos, Iōannēs Saridakēs, Vaseilios Zarkados [forwards])
Gymnastics, rope climbing: Kōnstantinos Kozanitas
Rowing and sculling, six-man naval rowboats with coxswain: Crew of
  warship *Ydra* (Dionysios Chrēsteas, Dēmētrios Grous, P. Lomvardos,
  Geōrgios Maroulēs, Nikolaos Fotinakēs, Dēmētrios Souranēs, Petros
  Mexas [cox])
Shooting, military revolver at 20 meters: Geōrgios Skotadadēs
Shooting, pistol at 25 meters: Aristeidēs Rangavēs
Shooting, pistol at 50 meters: Aristeidēs Rangavēs
Tennis, ladies' singles: Eufrosynē Paspatē
Tennis, mixed doubles: Xenofōn Kasdaglēs and Aspasia Matsa
Track and field, 1,500-meter walk: Kōnstantinos Spetsiōtēs
Track and field, 3,000-meter walk: Geōrgios Saridakēs
Track and field, high jump: Themistoklēs Diakidēs
Track and field, stone throw: Michaēl Dōrizas

LONDON, 1908

Silver: 2
Track and field, javelin throw: Michaēl Dōrizas
Track and field, standing long jump: Kōnstantinos Tsiklētēras

Bronze: 1
Shooting, trap: Anastasios Metaxas

STOCKHOLM, 1912

Gold: 1
Track and field, standing long jump: Kōnstantinos Tsiklētēras

Bronze: 1
Track and field, standing high jump: Kōnstantinos Tsiklētēras

ANTWERP, 1920

Silver: 1
Shooting, military revolver at 30 meters, team event: Alexandros
    Theofilakēs, Iōannēs Theofilakēs, Geōrgios Mōraïtinēs, Iōannēs Sappas,
    and Geōrgios Vafeiadēs

MELBOURNE, 1956

Bronze: 1
Track and field, pole vault: Geōrgios Roubanēs

ROME, 1960

Gold: 1
Sailing, dragon class: Crown Prince Constantine (captain), Odysseas
    Eskintzoglou, Geōrgios Zaïmēs

MEXICO CITY, 1968

Bronze: 1
Wrestling, Greco-Roman, 70-kilogram category: Petros Galaktopoulos

MUNICH, 1972

Silver: 2
Sailing, Finn class: Ēlias Chatzēpaulēs
Wrestling, Greco-Roman, 74-kilogram category: Petros Galaktopoulos

Moscow, 1980

Gold: 1
Wrestling, Greco-Roman, 62-kilogram category: Stelios Mygiakēs

Bronze: 2
Sailing, Soling class: Anastasios Boudourēs, Anastasios Gavrilēs, and
  Aristeidēs Repanakēs
Wrestling, freestyle, 62-kilogram category: Geōrgios Chatzēiōannidēs

Los Angeles, 1984

Silver: 1
Wrestling, Greco-Roman, 82-kilogram category: Dēmētrios Thanopoulos

Bronze: 1
Wrestling, Greco-Roman, 57-kilogram category: Charalambos Cholidēs

Seoul, 1988

Bronze: 1
Wrestling, Greco-Roman, 57-kilogram category: Charalambos Cholidēs

Barcelona 1992

Gold: 2
Track and field, women's 100-meter hurdles: Voula Patoulidou
Weightlifting, 82.5-kilogram category: Pyrros Dēmas

Atlanta 1996

Gold: 4
Gymnastics, men's floor exercises: Iōannēs Melisannidēs
Boardsailing, mistral category: Nikos Kaklamanakēs
Weightlifting, 84-kilogram category: Pyrros Dēmas
Weightlifting, 99-kilogram category: Kachi Kachiasvili

Silver: 4
Track and field, women's high jump: Nikē Bakogiannē

Weightlifting, 59-kilogram category: Leōnidas Sampanēs
Weightlifting, 64-kilogram category: Valerios Leōnidēs
Weightlifting, 91-kilogram category: Leōnidas Kokkas

SYDNEY 2000

Gold: 4
Tae kwon do: Michaël Mouroutsos
Track and field, men's 100 meters: Kōnstantinos Kenterēs
Weightlifting, men's 85-kilogram category: Pyrros Dēmas
Weightlifting, men's 94-kilogram category: Kachi Kachiasvili

Silver: 6
Gymnastics, rings: Dēmosthenēs Tampakos
Track and field, women's 100 meters: Aikaterinē Thanou
Track and field, women's discus throw: Anastasia Kelesidou
Track and field, women's javelin throw: Mirella Manianē-Tzelilē
Weightlifting, men's 62-kilogram category: Leōnidas Sampanēs
Weightlifting, men's 77-kilogram category: Viktōr Mētrou

Bronze: 3
Gymnastics, rhythmic, women's team event: Eirēnē Aindilē, Eva
    Christodoulou, Morfoula Dona, Kleonikē Geōrgakopoulou, Maria
    Geōrgatou, Chara Karyamē, Anna Polatou
Weightlifting, women's 63-kilogram category: Iōanna Chatzēiōannou
Wrestling, freestyle, 54-kilogram category: Amiran Kardanōf

Sources: Bill Mallon, *The 1906 Olympic Games: Results for All Competitors in All Events, with Commentary*; Bill Mallon and Ture Widlund, *The 1896 Olympic Games: Results for All Competitors in All Events, with Commentary*; Eleutherios Skiadas, *100 chronia neoterē ellēnikē istoria*, Ta Nea, Athens, 1996; http://www.hoc.gr/games/greekhistory/medals.asp; http://www.olympic.org/uk/athletes/results/search_r_uk.asp.
    Discrepancies in the weightlifting categories are the result of changes introduced in 1992. The crisis of drug-taking to enhance performance in the sport prompted authorities to change weight classes so that the record-book could be started anew—a procedure that was repeated at the 2000 Sydney games.

ATHENS, CANDIDATE CITY

A THENS HAS BEEN A CANDIDATE CITY to host the Olympic Games five times. In 1896, it was the only city considered by the IOC to host the first games, and the Greek capital was the obvious choice for the interim Olympics of 1906. After the Second World War, the HOC proposed that Athens host the 1952 Olympics but withdrew its application before the IOC could consider it; the country was in no position to undertake such a responsibility after a decade of war. The next Greek application would be for the 1996 games on the centenary of the Olympics.

THE 1996 CANDIDACY

The Hellenic Olympic Committee declared Athens's candidacy to host the 1996 games on June 20, 1988. The *Organization for the Candidacy of the Olympic Games/Athens '96* was formed in September 1989. The IOC met at its ninety-sixth session, held in Tokyo on September 18, 1990, to choose among six cities: Athens, Atlanta, Belgrade, Manchester, Melbourne, and Toronto. The IOC voted in successive rounds, eliminating the city with the least votes in each subsequent round. Athens lost to Atlanta in the fifth and final round by 51 votes to 35. Athens had been ahead in the voting through the second round, the two cities tied in the third round, and Atlanta finally went ahead in the fourth round.

The voting was as follows, by rounds:

	1st	2nd	3rd	4th	5th
Athens	23	23	26	30	35
Atlanta	19	20	26	34	51
Belgrade	7	—	—	—	—
Manchester	11	5	—	—	—
Melbourne	12	21	16	—	—
Toronto	14	17	18	22	—

THE 2004 CANDIDACY

Eleven cities expressed an interest in hosting the 2004 games: Athens, Buenos
Aires, Cape Town, Istanbul, Lille, Rio de Janeiro, Rome, St. Petersburg, San
Juan, Seville, and Stockholm. The IOC selected five finalists: Athens, Buenos
Aires, Cape Town, Rome, and Stockholm. The election to choose the winning
bid took place on September 5, 1997, at the 106th IOC session in Lausanne.
Athens won in the fifth round of voting with 66 votes against 41 for Rome. In
this case, the second round was a "tie-breaker" between Buenos Aires and
Cape Town to determine which city would be eliminated, as they had tied for
least votes in the first round. Athens led from the beginning and retained its
lead to the end.

The voting was as follows, by round:

	1st	*2nd*	*3rd*	*4th*	*5th*
Athens	32	—	38	52	66
Buenos Aires	16	44	—	—	—
Cape Town	16	62	22	20	—
Rome	23	—	28	35	41
Stockholm	20	—	19	—	—

Source: "Athens 2004: Election" http://www.olympic.org/uk/games/athens/
election_uk.asp; Eleutherios Skiadas, *100 chronia neoterē ellēnikē istoria; Ta Nea*, Athens, 1996.

APPENDIX 5

THE INTERNATIONAL OLYMPIC ACADEMY

I NAUGURATED ON JUNE 14, 1961, and located at Olympia, the IOC's International Olympic Academy (IOA) functions as an academic center for studying the Olympic movement and promoting its ideals. The IOA operates under the auspices of the IOC, while the HOC is responsible for its administration.

The IOA is an institution that regards the traditions of the Olympic Games, both ancient and modern, as a basis on which sport can play a positive role in fostering universal friendship and cooperation. It describes its aims as preserving and spreading the Olympic spirit, and consolidating "the scientific basis of the Olympic ideal, in conformity with the principles laid down by the ancient Greeks and the revivers of the contemporary Olympic Movement, through Baron de Coubertin's initiative."

The IOA's primary educational activity is administering an annual summer school attended by "young participants," that is, persons between the ages of twenty and thirty-five from around the world who are nominated by their country's national Olympic committees. In 1970, the IOA added summer sessions focused on "Olympism" that were meant for a broader range of participants, including graduate students, teachers, sports administrators, and sportswriters.

The IOA's grounds cover 250 acres on the slopes of the hills overlooking ancient Olympia. Its facilities include a modern conference center and a library of 10,000 volumes on subjects relating to sport and the Olympics. There are also several sports facilities, as sports activities are an integral part of the IOA's summer sessions.

The "Coubertin Grove," which is on the academy's grounds, enables the IOA to play a role in the ritualistic and symbolic promotion of "Olympism." The grove contains the marble *stele* that commemorates Coubertin and contains his heart, which was interred there in 1937. A smaller *stele* honors the IOA's founders, Carl Diem and Iōannēs Ketseas. Each summer session begins

with a ceremony at the grove and wreath-laying to honor these three important figures of the Olympic movement. In addition, the first runner in the
quadrennial torch relay from ancient Olympia carries the flame to the grove,
in homage to Coubertin, before proceeding on the route that will end in the
city of that year's Olympiad.

The IOA also administers the Museum of the Modern Olympic Games,
which is located nearby, in the town of Olympia. The museum was the brain-
child of Geōrgios Papastefanou-Provatakēs (1890–1978), a collector of
Olympic stamps and memorabilia. Papastefanou purchased a former school
building in Olympia in 1961 and established a museum designed to showcase
his collections. Three years later, he turned the museum over to the HOC but
remained as its director. The museum underwent extensive refurbishing and
was expanded between 1968 and 1972, thanks to government funding. The
IOA assumed its administration in 1972.

Sources: *The International Olympic Academy*, IOC, Ancient Olympia, no date; Vasilikē
Tzachrēsta, *Mouseio Synchronōn Olympiakōn Agōnōn* [*Museum of the Modern Olympic
Games*], HOC and IOA, Athens, 2000.

SOURCES CITED

1. PRIMARY SOURCES

The primary sources used in this study consist of material in the Hellenic Olympic Committee's archives and include unpublished correspondence and memoranda as well as copies of published documents such as programs of events and speeches by HOC and IOC officials. Each document used is cited according to the reference system adopted by the archives, a sequence of letters indicating the box ("k"), folder ("f"), and document ("d"), followed by a number. The minutes of HOC executive-committee meetings are kept separately in the archives and referenced as HOC Minutes. I consulted a range of archival sources and executive-committee minutes between the years 1905 and 1972.

2. BOOKS, PAMPHLETS, AND JOURNALS

Barney, Robert K., Wenn, Stephen R., and Martyn, Scott G. *Selling of the Five Rings: The IOC and the Rise of Olympic Commercialism*. University of Utah Press, Salt Lake City, 2002.

Bastéa, Eleni. *The Creation of Modern Athens: Planning the Myth*, Cambridge University Press, Cambridge, 1999.

Beaton, Roderick. "Romanticism in Greece," in Porter, Roy, and Teich, Mikulas, editors, *Romanticism in National Context*, Cambridge University Press, Cambridge, 1988.

Bosanquet, Mrs. R. C. *Days in Attica*, Macmillan, New York, 1914.

Buruma, Ian. *Anglomania*, Random House, New York, 1998.

Butler, E. M. *The Tyranny of Greece Over Germany*, Macmillan, New York, 1935.

Butler, Miss Maynard. "The Olympic Games," *Outlook*, Volume 53, May 30, 1896.

Chrysafēs, Iōannēs E. *Oi synchronoi diethneis Olympiakoi Agōnes*, Athens, 1930.

Clark, Ellery H. *Reminiscences of an Athlete*, Houghton Mifflin, Boston, 1911.

Clogg, Richard. *A Concise History of Greece*, Cambridge University Press, Cambridge, 1992.

Coubertin, Pierre de. *Olympism: Selected Writings*, edited by Muller, Norbert, International Olympic Committee, Lausanne, 2000.

Coubertin, Pierre de *et al. Les Jeux Olympiques*, Charles Beck, Athens, 1896.

Curtis, Thomas P. "High Hurdles and White Gloves," *The Sportsman*, Volume 12, July 1, 1931.

Dēmaras, Kōnstantinos Th. *Ellēnikos Romantismos* [*Greek Romanticism*], Ermēs, Athens, 1982.

Dyreson, Mark. *Making the American Team: Sport, Culture, and the Olympic Experience*, University of Illinois Press, Urbana, 1998.

Ē engainiasis tēs B' periodou tōn Olympiōn [*The Inauguration of the Second Period of the Olympics*], Athens, 1870.

Eisner, Robert. *Travelers to an Antique Land*, University of Michigan Press, Ann Arbor, 1991.

Eliot, Alexander, and the editors of *Life. Greece*, Time, Inc., New York, 1963.

Ellēniko Lexiko, Ekdoseis Armonia, Athens, 1991, fifth edition.

Espy, Richard. *The Politics of the Olympic Games*, University of California Press, Berkeley, 1981.

Evert, Miltiadēs. *Karamanlēs o anamorfōtēs* [*Karamanlēs, the Renovator*], no publisher, Athens, 1983.

Fellman, Berthold. "The History of the Excavations at Olympia," *Olympic Review*, 1973.

Filaretos, Nikos. Interview, *Athlos kai Politismos* [*Sport and Culture*], Volume 6, 2000.

Findling, John E., and Pelle, Kimberly D. *Historical Dictionary of the Modern Olympic Movement*, Greenwood Press, Westport, 1996.

Freud, Sigmund. "A Disturbance of Memory on the Acropolis," in *Collected Papers*, Volume V, The Hogarth Press, London, 1950.

Gallant, Thomas W. *Modern Greece*, Arnold/Oxford University Press, New York, 2001.

Giannakēs, Thōmas V. *Zappeies kai synchrones Olympiades* [*Zappeian and Modern Olympiads*], Athens, 1993.

Gosper, Kevin, with Korporaal, Glenda. *An Olympic Life: Melbourne 1956 to Sydney 2000*, Allen & Unwin, St. Leonards, 2000.

Goumas, Nikos, *et al.*, editors. *Ē istoria tou Panathēnaikou 1908–1968* [*The History of Panathēnaikos, 1908–1968*], Alvin Redman Hellas, Athens, 1969.

Graham, Cooper C. *Leni Riefenstahl and Olympia*, The Scarecrow Press, Metuchen, 1986.

Guttmann, Allen. *The Olympics: A History of the Modern Games*, University of Illinois Press, Urbana, 1992.

Hargreaves, John. *Freedom for Catalonia? Catalan Nationalism, Spanish Identity and the Barcelona Olympic Games*, Cambridge University Press, Cambridge, 2000.

Hill, Christopher R. *Olympic Politics*, second edition, Manchester University Press, Manchester, 1996.

Hobsbawm, Eric, and Ranger, Terence, editors. *The Invention of Tradition*, Cambridge University Press, Cambridge, 1983.

Holmes, Burton. *The Olympian Games in Athens, 1896*, Grove Press, New York, 1984.

Holt, Richard. *Sport and the British: A Modern History*, Oxford University Press, Oxford, 1990.

Jennings, Andrew. *The New Lords of the Rings*, Simon and Schuster, New York, 1996.

Jobling, Ian. "Bidding for the Olympics: Site Selection and Sydney 2000," in Schaffer, Kay, and Smith, Sidonie, editors, *The Olympics at the Millennium: Power Politics and the Games*, Rutgers University Press, New Brunswick, 2000.

Kardasēs, Vasilēs. *Katalogos istorikou archeiou Olympiakou Peiraiōs* [*Catalogue of the Historical Archives of Olympiakos Piraeus*], Dokimes, Athens, 1997.

Kavikēs, Kōnstantinos G. *Penies gia to thauma tēs XVIIēs Olympiados* [*Jottings on the Miracle of the XVIIth Olympiad*], Kaiafas, Athens, 1960.

Kayalis, Takis. "Logotechnia kai pneumatikē zōē" ["Literature and Intellectual Life"], in

Hadziiosif, Christos, editor, *Istoria tēs Elladas ston Eikosto Aiōna: Mesopolemos 1922–1940* [*History of Greece in the 20th Century: Interwar Period, 1922–1940*], Volume B2, Vivliorama, Athens, 2002.

Ketseas, Iōannēs. "Inaugural Speech," *Report of the Fourth Summer Session of the International Olympic Academy*, DOA, Athens, 1964.

Lord Killanin. *My Olympic Years*, William Morrow, New York, 1983.

Kokkinos, Geōrgios, and Fournarakē, Elenē. "... peri tēs sōmatikēs anagennēseōs tou ethnous ēmōn" ["... on the physical regeneration of our nation"], *To Vēma*, March 17, 1996.

Koulouri, Christina. *Athlētismos kai opseis tēs astikēs koinōnikotētas. Gymnastika kai athlētika sōmateia 1870–1922* [*Sports and Aspects of Bourgeois Socialization: Gymnastic and Athletic Clubs, 1870–1922*], IAEN, Athens, 1997.

————. "Voluntary Associations and New Forms of Sociability: Greek Sports Clubs at the Turn of the Nineteenth Century," in Carabott, Philip, editor, *Greek Society in the Making 1863–1913*, Ashgate/Variorum, Aldershot, 1977.

————, editor. *Archeia kai istoria tēs Epitropēs Olympiakōn Agōnōn* [*Archives and History of the Hellenic Olympic Committee*], Athens, DOA, 2002.

Krüger, Arnd. "The Olympic Games of 1936 as the Fifth German Combat Games," in Naul, Roland, editor, *Contemporary Studies in the National Olympic Games Movement*, Peter Lang, Frankfurt, 1977.

Lambros, Spyridōn. *Logoi kai arthra 1878–1902* [*Speeches and Articles, 1878–1902*], Sakellariou, Athens, 1902.

Lefas, Giannēs. *Panagiōtēs Soutsos*, Athens, 1991.

Lekkas, Ēlias. *Istoria tēs AEK* [*History of AEK*], Alexandrēs, Athens, 1996.

Lenskyj, Helen Jefferson. *Inside the Olympic Industry: Power Politics and Activism*, SUNY Press, Albany, 2000.

Leontis, Artemis. *Topographies of Hellenism*, Cornell University Press, Ithaca, 1995.

Linardos, Petros N. *D. Vikelas. Apo to orama stēn praxē* [*D. Vikelas: From the Vision to the Act*], EOA, Athens, 1996.

Liverēs, Giōrgos. *1894–1994. Ē istoria tēs Epitropēs Olympiakōn Agōnōn tēs Ellados* [*1894–1994: The History of the Hellenic Olympic Committee*], HOC, Athens, 1995.

Llines, Montserrat. "The History of Olympic Ceremonies," in Moragas, Miquel de, MacAloon, John, and Llines, Montserrat, editors, *Olympic Ceremonies: Historical Continuity and Cultural Exchange*, IOC, Lausanne, 1996.

Lucas, John. "American Involvement in the Athens Olympian Games of 1906," *Stadion*, Volume 6, 1908.

Lucas, John A. *Future of the Olympic Games*, Human Kinetics, Champaign, 1992.

MacAloon, John J. *This Great Symbol: Pierre de Coubertin and the Origins of the Modern Olympic Games*, University of Chicago Press, Chicago, 1981.

————, "Olympic Ceremonies as a Setting for Intercultural Exchange," in Moragas, Miquel de, MacAloon, John, and Llines, Montserrat, editors, *Olympic Ceremonies: Historical Continuity and Cultural Exchange*, IOC, Lausanne, 1996.

Mallon, Bill. *The 1906 Olympic Games: Results for All Competitors in All Events, with Commentary*, McFarland & Company, Jefferson, 1999.

Mallon, Bill, and Widlund, Ture. *The 1896 Olympic Games: Results for All Competitors in All Events, with Commentary*, McFarland & Company, Jefferson, 1998.

Manchester 1996—The British Olympic Bid, MOBC, Manchester, 1990.

Mandell, Richard. *The First Modern Olympics*, University of California Press, Berkeley, 1976.

———. *The Nazi Olympics*, University of Illinois Press, Urbana, 1987.

Maniatis, Gregory A. "Ringmaster: An Exclusive Interview With the CEO of Athens 2004," *Odyssey*, January-February 1999.

Manitakēs, Paulos N. *100 chronia neoellēnikou athlētismou 1830–1930* [*100 Years of Modern Greek Athletics, 1830–1930*], Athens, 1962.

Marden, Philip Sanford. *Greece and the Aegean Islands*, Houghton Mifflin, Boston, 1907.

Nikolaou, Lambēs. "Address and Opening," *Report of the Twenty-Eighth Session, 29 June-14 July 1988*, DOA, Athens, 1988.

Oikonomou, Alexandros A. *Treis anthropoi, tomos deuteros, Dēmētrios M. Vikelas (1835–1908)* [*Three Persons, Volume Two, Dēmētrios M. Vikelas (1835–1908)*], Ellēnikē Ekdotikē Etaireia, Athens, 1953.

Palaiologos, Kleanthēs. "O thesmos tōn Olympiakōn Agōnōn kai o rolos tou stēn pragmatopoiēsē tēs enotētas tou archaiou ellēnismou" ["The Institution of the Olympic Games and its Role in the Realization of the Unity of Ancient Hellenism"], *Leukōma tēs 21ēs Synodou tēs Diethnous Olympiakēs Akadēmias*, DOA, Athens, 1982.

Panousakē, Gianna. "To orama tou K. Karamanlē gia tēn anaviōsē tou Olympiakou Ideōdous" ["K. Karamanlēs's Vision for the Revival of the Olympic Ideal"], *Athlēsē kai Koinōnia*, Volume 22, 1996.

Patoulidou, Voula. *Ekrēxē Psychēs* [*Burst of Spirit*], Kastaniōtēs, Athens, 1977.

Politēs, Nikos. *Olympiakoi Agōnes tou 1896 opōs tous ezēsan tote oi ellēnes kai oi xenoi* [*The Olympic Games of 1896 as they were Experienced by Greeks and Foreigners*], Achaïkēs Ekdoseis, Patras, 1996.

Programma eortasmou Olympiakēs Ēmeras. VIIou Diethnous Klassikou Marathōniou Dromou, Athlētikōn Agōnōn kai Epideixeōn. Athēnai, 6 Apriliou 1967, Panathēnaikon Stadion [*Program of the Celebration of Olympics Day: VIIth International Classic Marathon Race, Athletic Contests, and Exercises, Athens, April 6, 1967, Panathenaic Stadium*], Athens, 1967.

Prooptikes gia tē monimē diexagōgē tōn Olympiakōn Agōnōn stēn Ellada [*Prospects for Permanently Holding the Olympic Games in Greece*], Ellēnikē Etaireia, Athens, 1980.

Rangavēs, Alexandros. *Apomnēmoneumata* [*Memoirs*], Volume 2, Athens, 1894.

Report of the Fifth Summer Session of the International Olympic Academy, HOC, Athens, 1965.

Report of the Second Summer Session of the International Olympic Academy, HOC, Athens, 1962.

Report of the Tenth Summer Session of the International Olympic Academy, HOC, Athens, 1970.

Report of the Third Summer Session of the International Olympic Academy, HOC, Athens, 1963.

Report of the 24th Summer Session of the International Olympic Academy, July 4–19, 1984,

IOA, Athens, 1984.

Richardson, Rufus. "The New Olympian Games," *Scribner's Magazine*, Volume 20, September 3, 1896.

Robertson, George S. "The Olympic Games by a Competitor and Prize Winner," *Fortnightly Review*, 354, June 1, 1896.

Roche, Maurice. *Mega Events and Modernity: Olympics and Expos in the Growth of Global Culture*, Routledge, New York, 2000.

Roessel, David. *In Byron's Shadow: Modern Greece in the English and American Imagination*, New York, Oxford University Press, 2002.

Santas, Alexandros S. *Olympia, Olympiakoi Agōnes, Olympionikai 776 px–393mx & 1896–1964* [*Olympia, Olympic Games, Olympic Winners, 776 BC–393AD & 1896–1964*], no publisher, Athens, 1966.

Samaras, Paraskeuas. *Ē anaviōsē tōn Olympiakōn Agōnōn stēn Ellada 1797–1859* [*The Revival of the Olympic Games in Greece, 1797–1859*], Vogiatzēs, Athens, 1992.

Schivelbusch, Wolfgang. *The Culture of Defeat: On National Trauma, Mourning and Recovery*, Henry Holt, New York, 2003.

Seferēs, Geōrgios. *Politiko ēmerologio A' 1935–1944* [*Political Diary, Volume 1, 1935–1944*], Ikaros, Athens, 1979.

Senn, Alfred E. *Power, Politics and the Olympic Games*, Human Kinetics, Champaign, 1999.

Skiadas, Eleutherios. *100 chronia neoterē ellēnikē istoria*, Ta Nea, Athens, 1996.

—————.*Gynaikeios athlētismos stē synchronē Ellada* [*Womens' Sports in Modern Greece*], Lavyrinthos, Athens, 1998.

Smyth, Ethel. *A Three-Legged Tour in Greece: March 24–May 4, 1925*, William Heinemann, London, 1927.

Spotts, Frederic. *Hitler and the Power of Aesthetics*, Overlook Press, New York, 2003.

St. Clair, William. *Lord Elgin and the Marbles*, Oxford University Press, Oxford, 1998.

Sullivan, James E. *The Olympic Games at Athens, 1906*, Spalding's Athletic Library, no. 272, American Sports Publishing Company, New York, 1906.

Svorōnos, Nikos G. *Episkopēsē tēs neoellēnikēs istorias*, Themelio, Athens, 1977.

Syrrakos, Kōnstantinos. *Olympiakoi Agōnes* [*Olympic Games*], Eurotyp, Athens, 1984.

The Ahepan. "Greeks Planning to Revive the Classic Olympic Games," November 1929.

The International Olympic Academy, IOC, Ancient Olympia, no date.

Tricha, Lydia. *Diplomatia kai politikē. Charilaos Trikoupēs-Iōannēs Gennadios Allēlografia 1863–1894* [*Diplomacy and Politics: Charilaos Trikoupis-Ioannis Gennadios Correspondence, 1863–1894*], ELIA, Athens, 1991.

Tsaousēs, D. G. editor. *Ellēnismos kai ellēnikotēta* [*Hellenism and Greekness*], Estia, Athens, 1983.

Tsigakou, Fani-Maria. *The Rediscovery of Greece: Travelers and Painters of the Romantic Era*, Caratzas Publishers, New Rochelle, 1981.

Tsiotos, Nick, and Dabilis, Andy. *Running With Pheidippides: Stylianos Kyriakides, the Miracle Marathoner*, Syracuse University Press, Syracuse, 2001.

Tsokopoulos, Vasias. "Ta stadia tēs topikēs syneidēsēs. O Peiraias, 1835–1935" ["The Stages of Local Identity: Piraeus, 1835–1935"], in *Neoellēnikē Polē* [*Modern Greek City*], EMNE, Athens, 1985.

Tsoukalas, Constantine. "Ideological Impact of the Civil War," in Iatrides, John O., editor, *Greece in the 1940s: A Nation in Crisis*, University Press of New England, Hanover, 1981.

Tzachrēsta, Vasilikē. *Mouseio Synchronōn Olympiakōn Agōnōn* [*Museum of the Modern Olympic Games*], HOC and IOA, Athens, 2000.

Tziovas, Dēmētrēs. "Dimitrios Vikelas in the Diaspora: Memory, Character Formation and Language," *Kambos*, No. 6, 1988.

Ueberroth, Peter, with Levin, Richard, and Quinn, Amy. *Made in America: His Own Story*, William Morrow, New York, 1985.

Vergopoulos, Kostas. *Ethnismos kai oikonomikē anaptyxē* [*Nationalism and Economic Development*], Athens, Exantas, 1978.

Whelpton, Eric, and Barbara. *Greece and the Islands*, Robert Hale, London, 1961.

Yarbrough, Richard C. *And They Call Them Games*, Mercer University Press, Macon, 2000.

Young, David C. *The Modern Olympics: A Struggle for Revival*, The Johns Hopkins University Press, Baltimore, 1996.

3. Newspapers, Websites, News Agencies, and Press Releases

Associated Press. "Race to Host 2004 Games Turns Sour," March 5, 1997.

_____. Orkin, Lisa, "Former 2004 Official says Government must Cooperate in Olympic Preparations," November 11, 2000.

_____. Wilson, Stephen, "Shape Up, IOC Warns Athens," April 21, 2000.

Athens News Agency. "Angelopoulou-Daskalakē Tapped as New 2004 President," May 11, 2000.

_____, with Agence France-Presse, "Athens' Candidacy File for 2004 Olympic Games Garners Widespread Praise," November 18, 1996.

_____. "Athens Formally Receives IOC Evaluation Commission," October 16, 1996.

_____. "Athens 2004 Organizing Committee Gets New Board," June 23, 2000.

_____. "ATHOC Responds to Washington Post's Criticism Over Games' Security," September 28, 2003.

_____. "Culture Minister and IOC President Discuss Olympic Games Preparations," October 3, 2003.

_____. "Discussion on Draft Bill Complete," February 13, 1998.

_____. "Gianna Angelopoulou-Daskalaki Interviewed on the Prospects of the Athens Olympics in 2004," September 30, 2000.

_____. "Government, Opposition Clash Over 2004 Bill," February 12, 1998.

_____. "Government Says Preparations for 2004 Olympics on Target," May 20, 1998.

_____. "Greece Back on Track, but Still Has to Beat the Clock for 2004, IOC Delegation Says," August 26, 2000.

_____. "IOC-Athens 2004-Rogge," January 27, 2000.

_____. "IOC Evaluation Committee Finds 3 Strong Advantages to Athens' Bid," October 29, 1996.

_____. "King Juan Carlos Backs 'Olympic Truce' Headquarters Proposal," May 28, 1998.

_____. "Protocol Signed for Establishment of 'Cultural Olympics' Institute," September 3, 1998.

_____. "Samaranch Satisfied with Progress Over 2004 Games," May 26, 1999.

_____. "Venizelos Satisfied with Progress, Transparency in Olympic Projects," February 13, 1999.

ATHOC. "Athens 2004 President presented in Prague the Medals for the 2004 Olympic Games," July 2, 2003.

_____. "Athens 2004 President presents the preparations for the 2004 Olympic Games to the 115th IOC session," July 3, 2003.

_____. "First ever global torch relay route approved by the IOC," February 21, 2003.

_____. "Statement of Athens 2004 President at the presentation of the Olympic Games' Security Program," October 16, 2003.

Eleutheron Vēma. "Apo tēn Archaian Olympia exekinēse chthes to ieron fōs" ["The sacred light Set Off Yesterday from Ancient Olympia"], July 21, 1936.

_____. "Ē iera flox ekinēsasa ex Olympias diēlthe chthes panēgyrikōs ek tou asteos tēs Pallados Athēnas" ["The Sacred Flame That Set Off from Olympia Passed Through the City of Pallas Athena in Celebration"], July 22, 1936.

_____. "Orthon kai praktikon ideōdes" ["A Correct and Practical Ideal"], August 17, 1936.

_____. "Semeiōmata" ["Notes"], July 25, 1936.

_____. "To Verolinon ypedechthei me synginēsē kai enthousiasmon to Apollōneion Fōs tēs Olympias" ["Berlin Welcomed the Apollonian Light of Olympia with Emotion and Enthusiasm"], August 2, 1936.

_____. Dēmaras, Kōnstantinos Th., "Olympiaka" ["Regarding the Olympics"], July 26, 1936.

_____. Geo, "Poioi kerdizoun eis tous Olympiakous Agōnes?" ["Who Wins in the Olympic Games?"], July 20, 1936.

_____. Geo, "Ti tha petychoun oi ellēnes athlētai?" ["What Will the Greek Athletes Achieve?"], July 12, 1936.

_____. Kavafakēs, Chrēstos A., "Ē nikē tēs Ellados eis to Verolino" ["Greece's Victory in Berlin"], July 22, 1936.

_____. Kavafakēs, Chrēstos A., "To Athlētikon Stadion tou Verolinou" ["The Athletic Stadium of Berlin"], August 4, 1936.

_____. Lanitēs, Nikolaos, "Ē Lampas eis to Verolinon" ["The Torch in Berlin"], August 7, 1936.

Eleutherotypia. August 3, 1976.

_____. "Aifnidiasmos me tēn Gianna" ["Surprise with Gianna"], May 11, 2000.

_____. Asēmakopoulos, Nikos, "Atlanta–*Coca-Cola*," September 19, 1990.

_____. Diakogiannēs, Giannēs, "Einai aplo, mas leipei ē sovarotēta" ["It's simple, we lack seriousness"], August 5, 1976.

_____. Drakos, Manōlēs, "Amoivaia Perifronēsē" ["Mutual Disrespect"], December 5, 2000.

_____. Drakos, Manōlēs, "Kitrinē karta stēn Olympiada" ["A Yellow Card for the Olympics"], April 21, 2000.

_____. Drakos, Manōlēs, "Ypainigmoi apo to klimakio" ["Insinuations from the Dele-
gation"], January 28, 2000.
International Olympic Committee. "IOC Praises Athens Organizers for Success of Sports
Events," August 19, 2003.
_____. "Progress Witnessed by IOC Delegation Visiting Athens," June 27, 2002.
_____. "Road and Venue Construction Remain Top Issues in Athens," September 28,
2001.
_____. "Statement of the IOC President Following his Visit to Athens," September 26,
2001.
http://www.dainst.org/index_548_en.html. "Olympia," Athens Section, German Archaeological Institute.
http://www.hoc.gr/en/info/history.asp. "History of the HOC."
http://www.karamanlis-foundation.gr. "Proposal for the permanent holding of the
Olympic Games in Greece."
http://www.olympic.org/uk/organisation/index_uk.asp. "Organisation."
http://www.olympictruce.org/html/news.html. "United Nations General Assembly
adopts Olympic Truce with unprecedented unanimity."
http://www.sport.gr/news/030224/2004.asp. "Apantēsē me epistolē" ["An Answer by Letter"].
Kathimerini. July 18, 1948.
_____. July 27, 1976.
_____. August 1, 1976.
_____. "Apo tēn Olympian" ["From Olympia"], July 18, 1948.
_____. "Aproetoimastoi kai aneuthynoi" ["Unprepared and Irresponsible"], September
19, 1990.
_____. "Ē ekdikēsē tōn Marathōnomachōn" ["The Revenge of the Marathon War-
riors"], August 8, 2003.
_____. Gavalas, Nikētas, "Kaname to kathēkon mas" ["We Did Our Duty"], September
19, 1990.
_____. Kōnstantopoulos, N. A., "Athēna: Meres tou 1896" ["Athens: Days of 1896"],
April 6, 1990.
_____. Sempos, Athanasios, "Ē panēgyrikē enarxis tēs ID Olympiados" ["The Gala
Opening of the XIVth Olympiad"], July 30, 1948.
New Democracy. "Dēlosē tēs ypeuthinou tou tomea Olympiakōn Agōnōn kas Pallē-
Petralia anaferomenē stēn episkepsē tou prōthypourgou sto kleisto gymnastērio tēs
Nikaias" ["Statement of the Head of the Olympic Games Section, Mrs. Pallē-Petralia,
in Reference to the Prime Minister's Visit to the Indoor Sports Arena in Nikaia"],
October 10, 2003.
_____. "Dēlosē tēs ypeuthinou tou tomea Olympiakōn Agōnōn kas Pallē-Petralia
schetika me tēn poreia tēs Olympiakēs proetoimasias" ["Statement of the Head of the
Olympic Games Section, Mrs. Pallē-Petralia, Regarding the Course of Olympic
Preparations"], September 3, 2003.
Paliggenesia. Editorials: October 21, 1888; January 1, March 25, and April 28, 1894.
Philadelphia Inquirer. Ford, Bob, "Olympics Video Merits A Gold in Sugarcoating,"

December 18, 1998.

Prōia. Androulidakēs, Geōrgios, "Ē teletē afixeōs tēs Ieras Flogos eis Dresdēn—exeretikai timai eis tēn Elladan" ["The Ceremony of the Arrival of the Sacred Flame in Dresden: Extraordinary Honors for Greece"], August 2, 1936.

Royal decree of January 25/ February 6, 1837, FEK 87/1836 [*Efēmerida tēs Kyvernēsēs*].

Ta Nea. June 30, 1988.

————. September 16, 1988.

————. Dontas, Dēmētrēs, "Analamvanei to thema prosōpika" ["He is Taking Over Personally"], April 26, 2000.

————. Dontas, Dēmētrēs, Anēsychia gia erga" ["Concern About Projects"], February 20, 1999.

————. Dontas, Dēmētrēs, "Apo to 2001" ["From 2001 Onward"], February 13, 2002.

————. Dontas, Dēmētrēs, "Olympiakoi Agōnes: Ē Athēna den echei xefygei apo to chronodiagramma gia ta erga" ["Olympic Games: Athens is Not Behind the Timetable for the Facilities"], September 3, 1998.

————. Kapsēs, Pantelēs. "Ē *Coca-Cola* Nikēse tēn Istoria" ["Coca-Cola Defeated History"], September 19, 1990.

————. Mavromatēs, Manōlēs, "Paraitēsē vomva gia to 2004" ["Resignation Bombshell for Athens 2004"], July 7, 1999.

————. Mavromatēs, Manōlēs, "Sēma kindynou" ["Danger Sign"], April 21, 2000.

————. Daleanē, Maria, "Echei Apantēseis" ["It Has Answers"], September 27, 2001.

————. Daleanē, Maria, "O Laliōtēs 'Ediōxe' ton Liaska" ["Laliotes 'Ousted' Liaskas"], October 19, 2000.

————. Rousakēs, Geōrgios. "Meltemi . . . aisiodoxias ["A *Meltemi* of Optimism"], August 8, 2003.

The Atlanta Journal-Constitution. Copeland, Larry, "Atlanta Team to Begin Marathon Bid to get Summer Games in '96," September 9, 1998.

————. Hinton, Ed, "Athens Gets Rolling in its Bid for '96: IOC Hears Greeks' Unity Cry, Vows to be 'Ready,' " August 30, 1989.

————. Hinton, Ed, "Atlanta Makes its Case in Seoul to Host '96 Olympics," September 13, 1988.

————. Hinton, Ed, "The Atlanta Olympic Watch," September 28, 1988.

————. Hinton, Ed, "The Battle for 1996," September 19, 1988.

————. Hinton, Ed, "Young Counters Athens' Dramatic Appeal to IOC: Olympic Speech Wins Points With Press," August 29, 1989.

————. Turner, Melissa, "Inside the '96 Olympics/Day 1, Billy Payne: Hero of the Hard Sell," August 6, 2000.

The Guardian. Williams, Richard, "Athenian's fast ascent defies Campbell charge," September 29, 2000.

The New York Times. July 22, 1948.

————. "A Greek Home for the Games," August 14, 1976.

————. "Greek Queen Dunks Son After his Yacht Wins," September 8, 1960.

————. "Torch Dispute is Ended," March 21, 1984.

————. "Tossing the Olympic Javelin," January 17, 1980.

_____. Anastasi, Paul, "Greeks' Plans for Olympiad are Imperiled," January 19, 1987.

_____. Bohlen, Celestine, "In 2004, Will the Glory Be Greece's, or Rome's?" March 7, 1997.

_____. Bradley, Bill, "Five Ways to Reform the Olympics," July 21, 1976.

_____. Danzig, Allison, "King George Opens Olympics for 6,000 from 59 Nations," July 30, 1948.

_____. Longman, Jere, "Athens Wins a Vote for Tradition, and the 2004 Olympics," September 6, 1997.

_____. Vlachos, Helen, "Return the Olympics to Greece Permanently. They Started There," August 12, 1979.

The Sun [Australia]. Skeggs, P, "Athens' Late Run," December 8, 1988.

The Sydney Morning Herald. Franklin, M., "Drowning in Olympic Spirit," September 17, 1990.

_____. Fray, Peter, "Athens lunges towards the finishing line," August 13, 2003.

The Times [of London]. Barnes, Simon, "Greece come trumps with sentimental card," September 11, 1990.

_____. Butcher, Pat, "Athens Ready for 1996 Games," October 6, 1987.

_____. Goodbody, John, "Athens triumphs in battle to host Olympics in 2004," September 6, 1997.

_____. Hughes, Rob, "Olympic Games come home as Athens flame burns again," September 6, 1997.

_____. Miller, David, "Alarm Over Support for Athens," August 11, 1990.

_____. Modiano, Mario, "Athens Claiming their Birthright," April 16, 1986.

_____. Modiano, Mario, "Greeks call off flame lighting ceremony," April 27, 1984.

The Toronto Star. April 16, 1986.

_____. Monsebraaten, Laurie, "Athens Beats Toronto Off Blocks With Bid to Host 1996 Olympics," October 16, 1986.

_____. Proudfoot, Jim, "Athens Widens its Lead in Footrace with Toronto," September 19, 1988.

_____. Sokol, Al, "General Carries Torch for Greece," March 10, 1987.

To Vēma. "Ē Panakrivē Olympiada" ["The Exorbitant Olympiad"], May 20, 2001.

_____. "Etoimoi gia to 2004," September 15, 1996.

_____. Lakopoulos, Geōrgios, "To 2004 Trōei ta paidia tou" ["2004 Devours its Children"], December 12, 2000.

_____. Margomenou, Marilē, "Ē Athēna mesa se enan fakelo" ["Athens in a Folder"], August 18, 1996.

_____. Margomenou, Marilē, "Pōs ē Athēna bēke stēn pentada" ["How Athens Made it Into the Five"], March 3, 1997.

_____. Sporidēs, Ēlias, "Ē exagora psēfōn gia tēn (chamenē) Chrysē Olympiada" ["The Bribed Votes for the (Lost) Golden Olympiad"], April 14, 1996.

USA Today. Fowler, Jonathan, "IOC Chief to Athens: Get Moving," February 22, 2003.

Washington Post. Vistica, Gregory L., "For Athens Olympics, A Security Gap: Tests Show Porous Defenses, Reports Cite Planning Breakdowns," September 27, 2003.

INDEX

Acropolis
  and IOA opening sessions, 131
  and 1936 torch relay, 110–111
  and program of Los Angeles 1932
    Olympiad, 89
  depicted on medals of Athens 1896
    Olympiad, 67
  IOC visit to, 91
  symbol of ancient Athens, 43, 44, 79
  tours of, during Athens 1906 interim
    games, 79
Aksoy, Yalcin, 189
Alimprantēs, Geōrgios, 70
Amis, Kingsley, 92
American Archaeological School in Athens,
  35
Amsterdam 1928 Olympiad, 88, 94, 107
Ancient Olympia
  ancient games at, 4, 10, 38, 82, 107, 111,
    196, 221
  as permanent Olympics venue, 142,
    148–149, 151–155, 159, 236
  IOA, 121, 123, 127–128, 238
  site of and excavations at, 91, 104–105,
    109, 123, 126–127, 129–130, 236, 238
  torch-lighting ceremonies at, 88, 101,
    106–108, 112, 157–158, 178, 236, 238
Andreadēs, Geōrgios, 173/fn 19
Andriakopoulos, Nikolaos, 48
Angelopoulos, Theodōros, 185
Angelopoulou, -Daskalakē Gianna
  and Athens's bid for 2004 games, 187–189
  and Athens's preparations for 2004
    games, 207–214, 217, 220, 225–226, 228,
    231–233
  and Athens's selection as 2004 host city,
    191–192
  appointment to ATHOC presidency,
    205–206
  appointment to bid committee, 185–186
  career, 185

Annan, Kofi, 233
Anninos, Geōrgios, 112
Antwerp 1920 Olympiad, 41, 80, 81, 84–85
Arledge, Roone, 230–231
Aslanidēs, Kōnstantinos, 138
Athanasiadēs, Theodosios, 138
Athanasiadēs, Tzōrtzēs, 149
Athens
  ancient city of, 50, 67, 221, 223
  ancient past, 43, 45, 79, 90, 99, 103, 227,
    233, 237–238
  and Coubertin, 30, 36, 52, 58, 90 235
  and 1996 games, 161–178, 182, 186
  as permanent Olympics venue, 26, 67, 74,
    149, 154
  Classical Games in, 77, 94
  descriptions and visits by travelers, 43–44,
    75, 78
  1896 games in, 1, 8, 25–27, 31, 33, 35, 37–52,
    69, 80, 96, 111, 147, 228, 235
  government in, 60, 102, 140, 204
  IOA, 129–131
  IOC's 31st session in, 90–91, 113
  IOC visits, 150, 187, 199, 201, 211, 217,
    219–220, 227, 229
  newspapers in, 22, 32, 73, 112, 114, 116, 124,
    148, 150–151, 171, 197
  1906 interim games in, 53–54, 57–58,
    62–66, 72–74, 94, 96, 111
  Olympic centenary celebrations, 178–179
  preparations for 2004 games, 213, 217,
    223–232
  security concerns for 2004 games, 209,
    218, 230–232
  sports clubs and activities in, 18–19,
    82–83, 87, 136–137
  sports facilities for 2004 games, 210–211,
    219, 226
  torch relay, 110–111, 137, 158, 223
  welcome of Greek medalists in, 133, 183
  Zappas Olympics in, 12–18, 22, 55

ATHOC (Athens Organizing Committee) or Athens 2004
and IOC, 217–218, 226–228, 230–231
appointments and resignations from, 200–201, 205–207, 212
August 2003 test events, 229
establishment of, 193
Greek character of 2004 games, 211–212, 227
New Democracy party's criticism of, 232–33
preparations for 2004 games, 209–211, 223–232
relations with government, 195, 197–198, 202, 204–207, 210–214, 217–218, 226
security issues, 230–232
Athens, Andrew, 196
Atlanta 1996 Olympiad, 179–183
Atlanta bid for 1996 games, 169–177
Australia
and Athens 1896 Olympiad, 25, 47
and Athens 1906 interim games, 72
and Athens 2004 games, 225–226, 230, 231
and Barcelona 1992 Olympiad, 180
and Moscow 1980 Olympiad, 153
Averōf, Geōrgios (philanthropist), 39–41
Averōf, Geōrgios (HOC member), 85, 87
Avramopoulos, Dēmētrēs, 178, 193, 199, 212

Bach, Thomas, 187
Baillet-Latour, Henri, Count de, 90, 98
Bakogiannē, Dora, 228
Bakogiannē, Nikē, 183
Bakourēs, Kōstas, 193, 197–198, 205–207
Balanos, Nikolaos, 79
Balkan Games, 83, 116–117, 134
Balkan Wars, 54, 76, 81, 93
Barcelona 1992 Olympiad, 180–182, 212
Bartels, Dr. H., 130
Belmont, August, 64
Belokas, Spyros, 50
Berlin 1936 Olympiad, 101–120, 236
Birēs, Nikolaos, 132
Blake, George, 72
Botasēs, Dēmētrios, 64–65
Boudourēs, Anastasios, 150
Bradley, Bill, 146–147, 153
Bréal, Michel, 49

Britain
and Athens 1906 interim games, 68
and Moscow 1980 Olympiad, 141
"Olympic credentials" of, 172
relations with Greece, 132
sport in, 20, 28, 42
Broneer, Oscar, 130
Brookes, William Penny, 8, 23, 29, 172
Brundage, Avery
and HOC, 136
and IOA, 127–128, 130, 159
and Munich 1972 Olympiad, 232
IOC president, 124
replaced by Killanin, 148
Buenos Aires bid for 2004 games, 188–191
Burke, Thomas, 47, 49
Butler, E. M., 104
Butler, Miss Maynard, 47

Calatrava, Santiago, 225
Canada, 72, 116, 136, 146, 153, 166, 175, 217
Cape Town bid for 2004 games, 188–191
Carter, Jimmy, 152
Chaidopoulou-Adams, Marina, 154
Chalkokondylēs, Alexandros, 49
Charēs, Petros, 134
Chatzēiōannidēs, Geōrgios, 150, 155
Chatzēiōannou, Iōanna, 216
Chatzēpaulēs, Ēlias, 139
Cholidēs, Charalambos, 180, 181, 216
Choremēs, Angelos, 154
Chrēstidēs, Dēmētrios, 17
Chrysafēs, Iōannēs
and Athens 1906 interim games, 63, 93
and Classical Games, 92–95
and Coubertin, 87–88, 94
career, 118
IOC, 91
Zappas Olympics, 8
Chytērēs, Tēlemachos, 224
Clark, Ellery, 44, 46, 49
Classical Games (1934), 92–97
Classicism, 57, 78, 86, 108, 237
Clinton, Chelsea, 178
Clinton, Hillary, 178
Coca-Cola, 161, 176–177, 223
Coe, Sebastian, 168
Connolly, James 47

Constantine I
  abdication of, 60, 84
  and Athens 1896 Olympiad as crown
    prince, 7, 26, 36–38, 46
  and Athens 1906 interim games as crown
    prince, 62–63, 67, 73
  and clash with Venizelos, 60, 75
  and Greece as a permanent venue, 52–53
  appointees of, 42, 57–58
  establishment of HOC, 60
Constantine II (until monarchy's abolition
    in 1974)
  and Greece's bid for 1996 games, 176
  becomes king, 136
  daughter Alexia's wedding, 200
  exiled, 138
  IOA, 131
  Olympic Games Day, 136
  Rome 1960 Olympiad, 133
Costa-Gavras, 135
Coubertin, Baron Pierre de
  and British sports culture, 28–30
  and Greece as the permanent site of the
    Olympics, 50–52, 55–56, 80, 87, 235
  and revival of Olympics, 1–2, 6–9, 23,
    31–36, 50–51
  Athens 1896 Olympiad, 26–27, 50–52
  Athens 1906 interim games, 53–54, 58,
    62–63, 68, 74
  career, 27–28
  Classical Games, 94, 97
  honored in Greece, 91–92, 99–100, 125,
    129, 131, 136
  intellectual formation, 29–31
  philhellenism, 30–31, 78, 86–90, 109, 125,
    238
  post-First World War return to classical
    tradition, 80–81, 84, 86–89, 99, 105,
    235
  visits to Greece, 36–38, 49, 87–89, 94, 121
Cultural Olympiad (2004), 195, 197, 239
Curtis, Thomas, 47
Curtius, Ernst, 104–105

Danzig, Allison, 124
Degalin, Igor, 154
Delēgiannes, Theodōros, 33, 35, 37
Dēmas, Pyrros, 182, 216

Dēmētriades, Kōstas, 86
Diakidēs, Themistoklēs, 71
Diakogiannēs, Giannēs, 141
Diathesopoulos, Dēmētrēs, 173/*fn* 19
Diem, Carl, 106–108, 120–122, 129–131
Dēmaras, Kōnstantinos Th., 103
Dōrizas, Michaēl, 71, 75
Dörpfeld, Wilhelm, 105
Dragoumē, Elenē, 109
Dragoumē, Liza, 109
Dragoumēs, Stefanos, 35–37
Drosinēs, Geōrgios, 22
Drosopoulos, Iōannēs, 96
Durrell, Lawrence, 127
Dyreson, Mark, 54, 61–62

Edward VII, 67–68
Eggleton, Art, 166
Ēliadēs, Nikos, 150
Eliot, T. S., 78
Erdem, Sinan, 189
Eskintzoglou, Odysseas, 133
Eutaxias, Athanasios, 60
Evert, Miltiadēs, 144, 145, 164, 174, 202
Ewry, Ray, 73

Farmakidēs, Iōannēs, 89
Felli, Gilbert, 199
Fermor, Patrick Leigh, 127
Ferrer, Carlos, 191
Filadelfeus, Alexandros, 106
Filaretos, Nikos
  and Athens's bid for 1996 games, 168, 176
  and Athens's bid for 2004 games, 189
  and ATHOC, 193
  and Karamanlēs proposal, 148
  and new generation of HOC, 142–143
Findling, John, 54
Floridēs, Giōrgos, 204
Fōkianos, Iōannēs
  and Chrysafēs, 93
  and fourth Zappas Olympiad, 22
  and Manos, 42
  and Sorbonne Congress, 34
  and third Zappas Olympiad, 20–21
  career, 19
Fouras, Andreas, 189, 194–195, 202, 204
France, 28–29, 63, 117, 231

Frangiadē, Annē, 109
Frangoudēs, Iōannēs, 49
Frank, William, 72
Fraser, Malcolm J., 153
French Archaeological School in Athens, 31
Freud, Sigmund, 44
Fürtwangler, Adolf, 105

Galaktopoulos, Petros, 139
Garret, Robert, 47
Gavrilēs, Anastasios, 154
Gennadios, Iōannēs, 23
Geo, 116–117
Geōrgakopoulos, Kōnstantinos, 95–96, 109,
    112, 129
Geōrgantas, Nikolaos, 69, 71
George I
    and Athens 1896 Olympiad, 50, 67
    and Brookes, 23
    and Greece as permanent venue, 26, 67
    and support for Olympic revival, 35
    arrival in Greece, 7, 15
    Zappas Olympics, 16, 21
George II, 57, 102, 111, 125
Geōrgiadēs, Iōannēs, 48, 70
German Archaeological Institute in Athens,
    105, 108, 129–130
Giannopoulos, Emmanouēl P., 10
Gosper, Kevin, 170, 172, 174, 225–226
Greek flag
    Athens 1896 Olympiad, 26, 48
    Berlin 1936 Olympiad, 115
    opening-day parade, 1, 236
    Paris 1928 Olympiad, 86
    Sydney 2000 Olympiad, 215
Greek identity
    ancient Greece, continuity with, 2–6,
        8–10, 12, 14–15, 17, 23, 31, 34, 39,
        41, 44, 52, 62, 77, 79, 82–83, 99,
        102–103, 112, 114, 122, 125, 129, 137,
        143, 147, 154–155, 168, 221, 224, 233,
        235
    ancient Greece, critiques of continuity
        theory, 149, 155, 163, 165–166
    European orientation of, 2, 4, 7, 12, 20,
        33, 34, 39, 41, 104, 145, 223, 225, 235,
        239

Greek team
    Amsterdam 1928 Olympiad, 88–89
    and HOC, 139
    Athens 1906 interim games, 69–70
    Barcelona 1992 Olympiad, 181
    Berlin 1936 Olympiad, 113
    London 1948 Olympiad, 132
    Los Angeles 1932 Olympiad, 89
    Munich 1972 Olympiad, 141
    national pride of, 115
    Paris 1928 Olympiad, 85
    Stockholm 1912 Olympiad, 76
    Tokyo 1964 Olympiad, 134
Greenspan, Bud, 231
Grēgoriou, Geōrgios, 50
Gould, George J., 64
Gouskos, Miltiadēs, 47
Guggenheim, S. R., 64
Guirandou-N'Diaye, Louis, 153, 154, 156
Guttmann, Allen, 54, 55

Halt, Karl Ritter von, 107
Hellenic Olympic Committee (HOC)
    ancient Greece, 87, 123
    ancient Olympia, 128–129
    and royal family, 138
    and the Second World War, 122
    Athens 1906 interim games, 63- 66,
        68–69, 75–76
    athletes, 85, 133–134, 150, 180, 194
    Berlin 1936 Olympiad, 99
    change of name, 60/fn 12
    Classical Games, 91–92, 95, 121
    Coubertin, 94–97, 100
    establishment of, 59–60
    Greece as a permanent venue, 141, 148,
        150, 163
    IOA, 121, 123, 125, 132
    Munich 1972 Olympiad, 140
    1996 games bid, 164, 173
    Olympic Games Day celebration, 135–136
    Olympics centenary celebration, 178–179
    relations with government, 138, 143–144
    torch relay, 108, 137, 157–158, 236
Helsinki 1952 Olympiad, 132–133
Hill, Christopher R., 162
Hinton, Ed, 170

Hitler, Adolf, 97, 101–103, 106, 108, 113–115
Hodler, Marc, 189, 197
Hoyt, Welles, 49

Iakōvou, Chrēstos, 139
Iōannou, Philippos, 17, 19–20
International Amateur Athletic Federation
[International Association of Athletics
Federation after 2001] (IAAF), 130, 190
International Olympic Academy (IOA),
121–132, 238, 240
International Olympic Committee (IOC)
ancient past of the games, 84, 86, 97–99,
124, 238
and Athens 1906 interim games, 54, 55, 57,
60, 63, 68
and Athens's bid for the 1996 games,
163–164, 166–169, 171–177
and Athens's bid for the 2004 games,
186–192
and Athens's preparations for the 2004
games, 192–194, 196–207, 209, 211, 213,
216–227, 229–232
and Berlin 1936 Olympiad, 102, 106–109,
113, 115, 236
and Classical Games, 92, 94–95, 97–98
and Cyprus's membership in, 143
and fortieth-anniversary
commemoration, 89–91
and Greece as a permanent venue, 55–56,
58, 74, 141, 147–148, 150–153, 156, 159,
236
and IOA, 121, 123, 127, 129, 131
and Los Angeles 1984 Olympiad, 157–158
and Montreal 1976 Olympiad, 146
and Olympic centenary celebrations, 178
and Olympic Games Day, 136
and recognition of People's Republic of
China, 146
and Salt Lake City 2002 Olympiad
bribery scandal, 153, 162, 173, 197, 199
and the *Olympic Hymn*, 46
Athens 1896 Olympiad, 42, 51
Coubertin's role in, 32, 56–7, 87
Samaranch's role in, 155–156, 239
Internationalism and nationalism, 29, 33, 39,
45–46, 51–53, 61, 145

Istanbul (Greek presence in), 69, 82
Istanbul's bid for 2004 games, 188–189

Jennings, Andrew, 162
Jobling, Ian, 162

Kachiasvili, Kachi, 182, 216
Kaklamanakē, Roula, 180
Kaklamanakēs, Nikos, 180, 183
Kakousēs, Periklēs, 69
Kandylēs, Geōrgios, 173/*fn* 19
Kapralos, Spyros, 205
Karaïskakēs, Geōrgios, 10
Karaïskakēs Stadium, 40, 210, 220, 227
Karamanlēs, Achilleas 148, 150
Karamanlēs, Kōnstantinos
and HOC, 148–150
and restoration of Greek democracy, 140
Greece's European identity, 145
PASOK's reactions to his proposal,
158–159
proposes Greece as permanent site,
141–142, 144, 146–148, 150
renews proposal, 152–156
Karamanlēs, Kōstas, 230
Karasevdas, Pantelēs, 48
Kardanōf, Amiran, 216
Karo, Georg 108
Karopothakis, Dimitrios 61
Karypidēs, Nikolaos 139
Kavafakēs, Chrēstos 114
Kazantzakēs, Nikos 127, 134
Kelesidou, Anastasia 215
Kenterēs, Kōnstantinos 215
Killalin, Lord 147–148, 150, 152–154, 156, 159
Kim, Un Yong, 217
Kissinger, Henry A., 153
Koimisē, Rena, 109
Kokkas, Leōnidas, 182
Kōlettēs, Iōannēs, 9
Kondylēs, Kōstas, 109
Koraēs, Adamantios, 2
Korbs, Werner, 130
Koumanoudēs, Stefanos, 22
Koutoulakēs, Anastasios, 72–73
Koutsēs, Iōannēs, 133
Kozanitas, Kōnstantinos, 70

Kyriakidēs, Stylianos, 116, 118, 120
Kyriakopoulos, Loukas, 173, 175

Lagoudakēs, Sōkratēs, 25
Laffan, Reverend Courcy, 56
Laliōtēs, Kōstas, 158–159, 194, 202, 206, 212–214, 219
Lambrakēs, Grēgorēs, 122, 135
Lambros, Spyridōn, 60, 64–65, 76
Lambrou, Maroula, 181
Lanitou, Domnitsa, 117–118, 132, 181
Lappas, Pyrros, 136
Leavitt, Robert, 72
Lenskyj, Helen Jefferson, 162
Liaskas, Kōstas, 173/fn 19, 190, 207, 212–213
Lightbody, James, 73
Linardos, Petros, 34–35
Lefousē, Thōmaē, 181
Lembesēs, Angelos, 149
London 1908 Olympiad, 53, 68, 72, 75, 94
London 1948 Olympiad, 124, 132, 133
Los Angeles 1932 Olympiad, 84, 89, 107, 116, 118
Los Angeles 1984 Olympiad, 141, 145, 151, 156–159, 166, 180, 194, 224, 237
Louēs, Spyros
    at Berlin 1936 Olympiad, 115
    marathon victory, 26–27
    national pride in, 49–50
    Pan-Hellenic trials, 43
    record, 116
Loundra, Dora, 109
Loundra, Liza, 109
Lucas, John, 61

MacAloon, John, 30–31, 113
Makropoulos, Iōannēs, 92
Malokinēs, Iōannēs, 49
Manchester bid for 1996 games, 169–170, 172–173
Mandela, Nelson, 188, 191
Mandell, Richard, 107, 119
Manianē-Tzelilē, Mirella, 216
Manitakēs, Paulos, 73, 86
Manos, Kōnstantinos, 42
Mantikas, Chrēstos, 116–117
Marathon (battle-site), 25–26, 42, 49–50, 72, 91, 122, 210, 229

Marathon (race)
    Athens 1896 Olympiad, 25–26, 48–50, 81
    Athens 1906 interim games, 71–73
    Atlanta 1996 Olympiad, 178
    Berlin 1936 Olympiad, 116, 118, 120
    Greek victories in Boston marathon, 85, 120
    Lambrakēs, 122
    popularity of, 42
    St. Louis 1904 Olympiad, 69
Marathon (tower of), 88, 107
Marden, Phillip Sandford, 43
Marinatos, Spyros, 128–129
Marinos Giannēs, 154
Mayor, Federico, 196
Mazarakē, Aleka, 109
Melbourne 1956 Olympiad, 111, 133
Melbourne's bid for 1996 Games, 170, 172–173
Melissanidēs, Iōannēs 183
Menem, Carlos, 190
Merkatēs, Alexandros, 56–57, 85
Merkourē, Melina, 164, 169, 176–177
Metaxas, Anastasios, 40, 75
Metaxas, Iōannēs, 102–103, 115
Metaxas, Spyros, 173, 175
Mexico City 1968 Olympiad, 139, 218, 230
Mygiakēs, Stelios, 154, 180
Miller, David, 174–175
Minōidēs, Mēnas, 13–14
Mētropoulos, Iōannēs, 48
Mētrou, Viktōr, 216
Mētsotakēs, Kōnstantinos, 175–176, 185
Moiropoulos, Euangelos, 138–140
Montreal 1976 Olympiad, 141, 145–148, 150, 157, 181
Morgan, Pierpont J., 64
Moschidēs, Othōn, 139
Moscow 1980 Olympiad, 141, 145, 154
Mouroutsos, Michaēl, 216
Mouskouri, Nana, 175
Munich 1972 Olympiad, 139–140, 145, 232
Mzali, Mohamed, 150

Nebiolo, Primo 190–191
Nemean Games, 10
Nēsiōtēs, Nikolaos, 153, 155, 158
Nikolaidēs, Alexandros, 216

Nikolaidēs, Apostolos, 85, 142–43, 149
Nikolaou, Lambēs
    appointed to HOC, 144
    ATHOC member, 193, 207
    2004 games bid, 167–168, 172, 176
Nixon, Richard, 146
November 17 (terrorist group), 171, 209, 219

Ocalan, Abdullah, 198–199, 204
Olympiakos, 82
Olympic Games Day, 1
Olympic movement
    and ancient Greek symbolism, 78–79, 84
        87, 95, 101, 109, 123–24, 126–128, 159,
        179, 237–240
    and Athens 1906 interim games, 54, 76
    and Greece, 1–3, 31, 51, 61, 76, 79, 87–88,
        95, 99, 119, 132, 136–37, 141, 144, 159,
        179, 188, 231, 233, 235–238, 240
    and IOA, 131–32, 143
    and IOC, 32
    commercialization of, 35, 143, 223
    difficulties of, 3, 53, 55, 57, 161
    emergence of, 2, 32, 58
    entry of communist countries into, 124
    in Greece, 4, 91, 142
    torch processions and relays, 106, 108, 113
Olympic Stadium in Athens (Spyros Louēs
        Stadium), 152, 156, 200
Olympic truce, 196–197, 220–222, 239
Orfanidēs, Geōrgios, 49, 71
Orfanos, Giōrgos, 201
Oswald, Denis, 217–220, 229
Othōn, 6–7, 9–11
Ouzlian, Tigran, 216

Palamas, Kōstēs, 46
Palaiologos, Kleanthēs, 142–143
Pallē-Petralia, Fanē, 195, 232
Panagiōtopoulou, Maria, 109
Panathenaic Games, 11, 82
Panathenaic Stadium
    Athens 1896 Olympiad, 25, 46, 48
    Athens 1906 interim games, 65–67, 71–72,
        75
    Athens 2004 medal design, 228
    Athens 2004 test events, 229
    Averōf donation, 39–40, 62

Berlin 1936 Olympiad, 106, 111, 148
Classical Games 77, 92, 96
Coubertin honored in, 88, 91
Olympics centenary celebrations, 178
Olympic Games Day, 1, 136, 148
welcome of 1996 medalists, 183
Zappas Olympics, 14–15, 20
Panathēnaikos, 82–83, 136, 142, 179, 183, 202,
    222
Pangalos, Theodōros, 204–205, 212–214
Pantazē, Elisavet, 181
Papadakē, Elenē, 91
Papadēmas, Angelos, 117
Papadiamantopoulos, Major Geōrgios, 25
Papageōrgiou, Nonē, 109
Papanikolaou, Chrēstos, 139
Papandreou, Andreas
    and Athens's bid for 1996 games, 163, 166,
        168–169, 171
    and Nikolaou, 144
    appointed a deputy minister for sport,
        206
    becomes prime minister in 1981, 144
    replaced by Sēmitēs, 185–186
Papandreou, George
    and IOC, 197
    appointed minister for foreign affairs, 199
    Athens bid for 1996 games, 169–171, 174,
        187
    Olympic truce, 196, 222
Papandreou, Vasō, 219
Papantōniou, Giannos, 217
Paparrēgopoulos, Kōnstantinos, 2
Papazōē, Elisavet, 199–200, 202
Papoutsēs, Chrēstos, 194
Paraskeuopoulos, Panagiōtēs, 47, 69
Paris 1900 Olympiad, 53, 54, 56, 66, 69, 72
Paris 1924 Olympiad, 80, 85–86
Patoulidou, Voula, 181–182
Paul I, 100, 108, 136
Payne, Billy, 169, 174
Pelle, Kimberly, 54
Persakēs, Iōannēs, 47
Pesmatzoglou, Loulou, 109
Petmezas, Geōrgios, 132
Petralias, Epameinōndas, 138, 148, 150
Philhellenism, 2, 30, 56, 77–78, 86–89, 91,
    104

Pietri, Dorando, 72
Pilgrim, Paul, 73
Poikilidēs, Geōrgios, 180
Poikilidēs, Panagiōtēs, 180
Pound, Ezra, 78
Pound, Richard
  Athens's bid for 1996 games, 175
  candidacy for IOC presidency, 217
  preparations for 2004 games, 203, 213,
    226
Pratsika, Koula, 101, 108–109
Pyrgiōtēs, Iōannēs, 213–214
Pyrgos, Leōnidas, 48
Pythian Games, 10, 131

Raïsēs, Iōannēs, 70
Rallēs, Geōrgios, 154
Rangavēs, Alexandros Rizos, 12–13, 15, 17, 35
Ranucci, Raffaele, 190
Renan, Ernest, 91
Repanakēs, Aristeidēs, 154
Reppas, Dēmētrēs, 204, 207
Richardson, Rufus, 44, 48
Riefenstahl, Leni, 111
Rinopoulos, Michaēl, 88
Robertson, G. S., 45, 48, 50
Roessel, David, 127
Rogge, Jacques
  and Sēmitēs, 211
  Athens and ancient history, 227, 238
  ATHOC-government relations, 201–202,
    212
  election to IOC presidency, 216–217
  2004 games preparations, as IOC
    member, 199, 201–205, 214
  2004 games preparations, as IOC
    president, 217–218, 222–223–226,
    231–232
Rome 1960 Olympiad, 133
Rome's bid for 2004 games, 188–191
Roosevelt, Theodore, 64
Roubanēs, Geōrgios, 133
Roubatis, Yiannis, 214
Rozan, Nikolaos, 110
Rudhard, Ignaz von, 9

Saint Hilaire, E. B., 74
Sakorafa, Sofia, 181

Salsopoulos, Nicholas, 64
Samaranch, Juan Antonio
  and Karamanlēs proposal, 155–156
  and Sēmitēs, 201
  and Stratēgēs, 195
  Athens's bid for the 1996 games, 166–169,
    172, 175–176
  Athens's bid for the 2004 games, 179, 185,
    190–191, 239
  commercialization of the games, 224
  Los Angeles 1984 Olympiad, 157–158
  Olympic centenary celebration in Athens,
    178–79
  preparations for 2004 games, 193,
    195–196, 200–204, 207, 211, 232
  Sydney 2000 Olympiad, 212
Samaras, Spyros, 46, 68
Sampanēs, Leōnidas, 182
Savramēs, Euangelos, 168
Schliemann, Heinrich 104
Schoeller, Philipp von, 153
Seferēs, Geōrgios, 57, 127, 134
Sēmitēs, Kōstas
  and Angelopoulou, 205
  and ATHOC, 225
  and Rogge, 211
  appointments and dismissals of ATHOC
    members, 193, 201, 212
  appointments and dismissals of
    government ministers, 198, 204, 219
  environmental concerns, 194
  Europeanization of Greece, 220, 223
  selection of Athens to host 2004 games,
    185–186
  preparations for 2004 games, 200, 205,
    218–219
Sempos, Athanasios, 124
Seoul 1988 Olympiad, 156, 171, 180–181,
  216
Sgouros, Petros, 193
Sheridan, Martin, 71
Sherring, William, 72–74
Sikelianos, Angelos, 79
Sikelianou-Palmer, Eva, 79
Simicek, Marton, 188, 207
Simicek, Otto, 188
Skarlatos Kōnstantinos, 71
Skouloudēs, Stefanos, 37

Sloane, William Milligan, 47
Smyth, Ethel, 91
Soutsos, Panagiōtēs, 9–11, 13
Spanoudakēs, Giannēs, 206
Speer, Albert, 106
Spender, Stephen, 127
Spetsiōtēs, Kōnstantinos, 71
Sporidēs, Ēlias, 177
St. Louis 1904 Olympiad, 53, 54, 57–58, 66,
    69, 71–72
Steinbach, Josef, 71
Stenhammar, Olof, 190
Stephanopoulos, Kōstēs, 178
Stockholm 1912 Olympiad, 76, 118
Stockholm's bid for 2004 games, 188,
    190–191
Stratēgēs, Stratēs, 193, 195, 197, 200, 205
Sullivan, James, 57, 64–66, 68, 74
Svanberg, Johan, 72
Svorōnos, Nikos, 149
Sydney 2000 Olympiad, 211–212, 215–216
Syllas, Nikolaos, 116–117, 133
Synadinos, Petros, 186, 189, 206, 214

Tampakos, Dēmosthenēs, 216
Thanos, Kōstas, 216
Thanopoulos, Dēmētrēs, 180
Thanou, Aikaterinē, 215
Thatcher, Margaret, 152
Theodōrakakos, Petros, 137
Theotokēs, Geōrgios, 59
Theodōrakēs, Mikēs, 174
Thōmopoulos, Panagiōtēs, 201, 206
Thompson, William Hale, 64
Tofalos, Dēmētrios, 71
Tokyo 1964 Olympiad, 134, 139, 146
Toronto bid for 1996 games, 162, 166–167,
    174
Triantafyllidēs, Iōannēs, 173/*fn*19
Trikoupēs, Charilaos, 21, 23, 32–33, 35–38,
    59
Tritsēs, Antōnēs, 177
Trivoulidas, Panagiōtēs, 85
Trudeau, Pierre, 146
Tsatsos, Kōnstantinos, 148
Tsigakou, Fani-Maria, 30
Tsiklētēras, Kōnstantinos, 75

Tsikouna, Stella, 216
Turner, Melissa, 162
Tyler, Albert, 49
Tzavela, Nikē, 201
Tziōrtzēs, Stauros, 139
Tziotēs, Daniēl, 18

Ueberroth, Peter, 157–158, 171
United States
    and Athens 1896 Olympiad, 47–48
    and Athens 1906 interim games, 57,
        62–64, 66
    and Athens 2004 games, 231, 240
    and Barcelona 1992 Olympiad, 181
    and Berlin 1936 Olympiad, 98, 102
    and Moscow 1980 Olympiad, 141
    and People's Republic of China, 146
    Greek immigrants in, 69, 85
    philhellenism in, 89
    relations with Greece, 123
University of Athens, 6, 17, 19, 22, 60, 93, 128,
    133, 154–155

Valyrakēs, Sēfēs, 168
Vasilakos, Charilaos, 43
Vasilikos, Vasilēs, 135
Vázquez, Pedro Ramírez, 153
Vellianitēs, Spyridon, 138
Veloulēs, Dēmētrios, 69, 72
Ven, Walter van der, 84
Venizelos, Eleutherios
    and Constantine in 1915, 60
    and HOC, 75–76
    and sport, 38, 54
    Liberal party demise, 102
Venizelos, Euangelos
    and Angelopoulou, 217
    and Cultural Olympiad, 195
    and diaspora Greeks, 196
    and HOC, 197
    and IOC, 197, 199, 224
    and preparations for 2004 games,
        195–199, 217, 219, 224
Vergē, Elsa, 109
Veroulē, Anna 180
Versēs, Sōtērios 47
Vialar, Paul 130

Vikelas Dēmētrios
  and Athens as the venue for the 1896
    games, 34–35
  and Coubertin, 55
  and Greece's attitude toward 1896 games,
    36
  career, 34
  Greece and Europe, 45
  honored by IOC, 91
  IOC presidency, 32, 56
Vlachos, Helen, 151

Waugh, Evelyn, 91–92
Weingartner, Herman, 48
Whitney, Casper, 64
Wils, Jan, 88
Winberg, Margareta, 228
Winkelmann, Johann, 104

Winter Olympic games, 134–135, 151, 193, 236
Woolf, Virginia, 78, 91
Worrall, James, 153

Xanthopoulos, Aftantil, 216

Yarbrough, C. Richard, 178
Young, Andrew J., 169–170, 174
Young, David C., 8, 23, 35

Zafeiropoulos, Nōndas, 185
Zaïmēs, Geōrgios, 133
Zalokōstas, Chrēstos, 125
Zappas, Kōnstantinos, 15
Zauli, Bruno, 130
Zerbinēs, Geōrgios, 89
Ziller, Ernst, 40
Zorba the Greek, 134, 224

A Note on Transliteration

In transliterating Greek, we have moved away from the reigning convention of pure phonetic transposition and returned to an earlier model, based on classical philology, which takes Greek orthography into account. As such, our intention has been to convey the actual orthographic form as opposed to simply the sound of the language, and to reproduce Greek spelling. In doing so, we have, as much as possible, directly mapped the Greek alphabet according to letters pronounced similarly in English. There were, however, a few instances in which we felt that a phonetic transcription rendered certain diphthongs in the Greek script more accurately: for example, μπ = b, γκ = ng, γχ = nch (aspirate "ch"), ντ = d. In addition, references to Greek authors published in English follow the Library of Congress catalogue; we have also respected reality in regard to Greek publications with English-language editions (*Kathimerini*, most obviously). In all cases, we have tried to avoid that foolish consistency that we believe to be the hobgoblin of current conventional phonetic transliteration.

greekworks.com